STRANDED ON EARTH

STRANDED ON EARTH

HOW NIGHT SKIES BECAME E.T. THE EXTRA-TERRESTRIAL

MAX EVRY

1984

STRANDED ON EARTH
HOW NIGHT SKIES BECAME E.T. THE EXTRA-TERRESTRIAL

This is a work of nonfiction. The events and experiences detailed herein have been faithfully rendered as remembered by the author and interviewees, to the best of their ability.

The 1982 film *E.T. the Extra-Terrestrial* was produced by Kathleen Kennedy, Steven Spielberg, and Amblin Entertainment, and distributed by Universal Pictures.

No generative artificial intelligence (AI) was used in the writing of this work.

COVER DESIGN / INTERIOR ILLUSTRATIONS: Ian Fried
EDITOR: Nick Rodriguez
LAYOUT: Arkadii Pankevich

Image credits appear in the back of the book.

LIBRARY OF CONGRESS CONTROL NUMBER: 2026944115

ISBNs: 9781948221450 (hardbound), 9781948221467 (ebook)

Printed and bound in USA.

1984 PUBLISHING
Cleveland, Ohio / USA
1984Publishing.com
info@1984publishing.com

FIRST EDITION / FIRST PRINTING

for Lily

a magical creature no longer confined by this planet...

CONTENTS

STRANDED ON EARTH
FEATURES NEW INTERVIEWS WITH

Henry Thomas
Dee Wallace
Rick Baker
John Sayles
Bob Gale
Joe Dante
Michael Finnell
Chris Walas
Michael Phillips
Matthew Robbins
Hal Barwood
Nick McLean
Geraldine Sutton Stith
Robin Love
William Stout
Mark Victor
David Robert Cellitti
Tom Hester
Craig Reardon
Mitch Suskin
Robert Short
Marci Liroff
Sean Daniel
Thom Mount
Frank Price
Caleb Deschanel
Mick Garris
William Dear
Joe Morton
Ernest Dickerson
Eric Luke
Greg Mottola
Sandy King
and
John Carpenter

THIS BOOK ALSO FEATURES NEW QUOTES FROM

Andy & Barbara Muschietti, Steven Soderbergh, Osgood Perkins, James Wan, Michael Chaves, Scott Derrickson, Renny Harlin, Alan Rudolph, and Kevin Feige.

ADDITIONAL COMMENTARY BY

Mark A. Altman, Steven Awalt, Jason Bailey, Julius Banzon, Andrew Barrer, Wesley Boutilier, Ryan Britt, Hoai-Tran Bui, Sam Chown Ahern, James L. Conway, Justin Decloux, Peter De Mooij, Daren Dochterman, Joseph Aguon Drake, Chris Evangelista, Andy Fosberry, Ian Fried, David Furtney, Adam Lance Garcia, Samanthuel Louise Gillson, Nick Gjoka, Dana Gould, Beverly Gray, Dan Harary, Devindra Hardawar, Derek Hayes, Paul Hynek, Kenneth Johnson, Jacob Johnston, Shellie McMurdo, Ashley Miller, Josh Miller, Adam Nayman, Phil Nobile Jr., David Nugent, Josh Olson, Kevin Otte, Harley Peyton, Amanda Reyes, Lindsey Romain, Mike Ryan, Aaron Sagers, Paul M. Sammon, Brian Saur, Stephen Scarlata, Jourdain Searles, Nat Segaloff, Drew Taylor, Eric Vespe, Danny Wagner, Harry Walton, Brandon Wright, and Matt Zoller Seitz.

"I would love to have seen *Night Skies* but to tell you the truth... Spielberg once told me something that's kind of profound. He said, 'You know, I have so many dark ideas. I mean, I've got some ideas that would make Cronenberg shudder, but I can't make them because of who I am right now.' A profound statement that also made me incredibly sad. If you're Steven Spielberg and you feel that you have these limits put on you by the society around you and you're capable of this other end of the art spectrum—of the happiness spectrum—that's kinda sad."

—**MICK GARRIS**, Director (*The Stand, Amazing Stories*)

"I'd love to see those dark ideas Spielberg has..."

—**KEVIN FEIGE**, President of Marvel Studios

"If he'd done a gritty horror movie it wouldn't have been as successful as *E.T.* The reason *Gremlins* was successful was not because of the gremlins but because of Gizmo, which is the heart part of the movie. It's always the heart part of Steven's movies that sells them. *E.T.* had the heart and *Night Skies* wouldn't have had it. The industry would not be the same but it wouldn't have been as good."

—**JOE DANTE**, Director (*Gremlins, Small Soldiers*)

In 1978 Columbia Pictures asked filmmaker Steven Spielberg to develop a sequel to *Close Encounters of the Third Kind*, at the time Columbia's highest-grossing movie ever. Reluctant to rehash his film, Spielberg recalled a documented alien incident from his research known as the Kelly-Hopkinsville encounter. The filmmaker decided a fictionalized version of this story—wherein a family's rural farmstead is terrorized by malevolent alien visitors—would make for a compelling follow-up to *Close Encounters*.

Spielberg assembled a dream team to make *Night Skies*, all in their career infancy: director Ron Cobb, producer Kathleen Kennedy, screenwriter John Sayles, and creature effects wizard Rick Baker. After an intense period of development and on the verge of production, Spielberg made a bold choice: He scrapped the film. Not entirely, though...

Piggybacking off Sayles' written ending—where the one sympathetic alien who made an emotional connection with a young boy is stranded on earth by his brethren—the filmmaker made that the starting point for a new script. Written by Melissa Mathison, this revised project was initially known as *A Boy's Life*, then *E.T. and Me*, and finally *E.T. the Extra-Terrestrial*. While initially thought to be a small Disney-esque kids movie, it captured the hearts and minds of the world as it went on to become the most successful movie of all time.

This will be the story of that journey...

AUTHOR'S NOTE

To be clear, even though my book *Stranded on Earth* goes to great pains trying to pinpoint where certain ideas may have emerged from, in some cases ported over from unmade projects, it is in no way trying to infer anything was "stolen" from anybody.

In most cases the major focus projects were done in direct collaboration with Steven Spielberg as producer, co-writer, and/or director, so without a case-by-case assessment from Mr. Spielberg about which ideas came from him or the other writers/artists it is difficult to trace every notion. In all cases where projects were made under the auspices of Spielberg, it can be assumed he had every right to mine ideas, lines, or visuals... and in almost every case he put a new twist on them.

The fun of this book is to see how certain stories evolved into others. Later on, when we look into movies not necessarily with Spielberg's involvement, we leave it up to the reader to decide if the filmmakers were influenced by made/unmade projects. Draw your own conclusions, since at no point does this book intend to point fingers or say *"J'Accuse...!"*

For the record, this author has the utmost respect for the visionary storytelling of Mr. Spielberg and all the subjects of this book, which was written in the spirit of celebrating the creative process and the enduring power of ideas. Enjoy!

"...all the sprocket holes engage, the leader snakes through the guts of the machine and fastens to the take-up reel. Shine brings down the lights and the audience grows quiet. The title appears blurred at first, as if seen through a film of tears, and Shine is a technician for a moment longer, adjusting till it is sharp. There is an applause of recognition. Shine turns out all but the pilot light in the booth and waits as the clatter of the machine fades from his mind, taking the rainstorm with it. He flows onto the shaft of dancing light and is carried forward to safety, to the bright, warm colors, into the pulse and flicker of life."

—**JOHN SAYLES**, *Children of the Silver Screen*

PART I
BLUE SKY

CHAPTER 1

Alien Origins: Steven Spielberg's Firelight

"My interest in the phenomenon stems from my growing up in the '50s and '60s. I was born the same year Kenneth Arnold coined the term 'flying saucers'... it was something to speculate about."

—**Steven Spielberg**, *The Christian Science Monitor*, October 1977

The filmmakers of the '70s and '80s who birthed a new era in silver screen science fiction—George Lucas, John Carpenter, Ridley Scott, Robert Zemeckis, James Cameron—also happened to be of the inaugural generation to grow up with space travel as a reality. Méliès' quaint turn-of-the-century visions of men in sailor's outfits being shot in a giant bullet to the moon were replaced by NASA-influenced industrial hardware, while Ray Harryhausen's pie-plate flying saucers made way for hovering light shows much to Pink Floyd's envy. One filmmaker could arguably be called the chief architect of revisionist sci-fi among the New Hollywood, still carrying that torch into 2026 and beyond.

Born in Ohio on December 18, 1946, Steven Allan Spielberg was the oldest of four children raised in a Jewish household by Leah (a concert pianist) and Arnold Spielberg (an electrical engineer). The family made several moves across Steven's childhood, first from Cincinnati to Haddon Township, then from New Jersey to the sunnier climes of Phoenix for a decade, until finally making the leap with his freshly divorced dad from Arizona to Saratoga, California... a mere 5-hour drive away from Hollywood.

Throughout this somewhat transient time Steven was making short films with family and friends. Having first picked up the camera in 7th grade, his early sojourns into moviemaking spanned a variety of genres, including westerns (*The Last Gunfight*), comedic parodies of westerns (*Gun Smog*), and war films (*Fighter Squad, Escape to Nowhere*). The latter was partly inspired by his dad's WWII exploits as part of the Signal Corps in India, while his 8mm Kodak camera—originally a Father's Day gift—was permanently borrowed from Arnold as well.

He said in 1975, "My father just couldn't seem to shoot good family films, so I took the camera away from him. That's how it all began..."

For *Fighter Squad*, Spielberg purchased 8mm reels of stock from Castle Films and wrote stories he could film around footage of exploding planes and trains. Edited in-camera to earn a photography merit badge, the 3-minute-long *Last Gunfight* shot over eight hours on a budget of $8.50. It featured good guys in white hats saving the day, a sentiment that recurs in multiples over his six-decade career as an eternal cinematic optimist.

"I never ever got in with the real insiders from school, sports jocks, that kind of thing," he told *20/20* in 1982. "I was always the wimp. I was always the wimp. Movies gave me a chance to be the leader of my own group."

He told *Cosmopolitan* in 1980 that making movies not only gave him "a sense of power bossing around a few kids who otherwise would be slapping me around," it was a chance to gain acknowledgement from strict parents who only let him watch Disney movies and frequently kept a blanket prohibitively over the TV. Filmmaking allowed for more primal creative impulses: "My parents were rigid about not letting me see horror films, so I staged my own, faking the chopping off of arms and legs and using buckets of blood."

Spielberg was enamored with Forest J. Ackerman's seminal movie magazine *Famous Monsters of Filmland*, telling *Starlog* in October 1978, "I used to imitate the makeups in them. I was somewhat of a shrewd makeup artist, so I would practice on my three younger sisters. They'd line up: one, two, three. If I failed on the older sister, I'd start on the middle sister. If the makeup ran on her face, I'd go to the younger sister."

Young Spielberg's deep abiding interest in UFOs was sparked by a dazzling meteor shower his father abruptly drove him to, which he later described as "phantasmagoric." The experience of being dragged out of bed by his dad in the wee hours and driving to a field with 100 stargazers to watch the night skies was later recreated with Richard Dreyfuss in *Close Encounters of the Third Kind.*

He told the audience at CinemaCon in 2026, "I've been curious ever since I was a little kid about what's happening in the night sky."

During his 1963 junior year at Phoenix's Arcadia High School (where the circular library was nicknamed "the spaceship") a 16-year-old Spielberg wrote and directed what could be called his first feature, an 8mm amateur sci-fi epic titled *Firelight*. In 1976 Spielberg described it to the AP's Bob Thomas as "a hardcore sci-fi, full of the creeping unknown." He told *Starlog*, "I remember being seized by what I have not felt since... divine inspiration. I've had spurts of it since, but nothing like when I made a film called *Firelight*." After staying up for 24 straight hours, he had banged out the 140-page screenplay in stream-of-consciousness fashion, then made 5 or 6 copies before starting production.

With a cast of nearly 100 and listed runtime varying from 90 to 150-minutes, the film's story centered on a group of scientists investigating how strange lights appearing in the night sky may be related to disappearances in a small (fictional) Arizona town called Freeport. Those "strange nocturnal lights" eventually cut the town off, preventing escape. Stock characters included "the scientist, his lovely female assistant, and the cynical Army major who'd rather fight." Good or bad, earthlings are seen by outer space denizens from planet Altaris as a threat who could potentially bring concepts like hate, war, and prejudice to their world. The Altarians' solution is to transport whole cities in miniature form to be exhibited as a human zoo on their own planet. The filmmaker claimed it was heavily indebted to the B-movies of Bert I. Gordon and William Castle.

Remembers Leah Spielberg to *People* magazine, "Once he got a hospital to close off a wing for one of his location shots. Another time he got the airport to close a runway. No one ever said no to him, and it's a good thing. Steven doesn't understand no."

Firelight earned Spielberg some of his first major press coverage, including a two-page spread in a December 1963 *Arizona Republic* titled "Teenage Cecil B." He told journalist Esther Clark of his impulse to make films: "It grows on you. You can't shake it."

Said Leah at the time, "We're all for Steve's hobby... we know and the parents of his teenage friends know where they are; they're not cruising up and down Central Avenue."

Beginning with a *Firelight* "pilot" film made for $60 and featuring a cast of 15 teens, Spielberg transformed his family home into a virtual studio, complete with flashing red light on the garage door signaling "Quiet on the Set" to neighbors.

Said his mother Leah in 1982, "I lived in a beautiful house, and I got as far as the carpeting and the drapes and the Steinway and then he took over. My house from the time I can remember was a studio."

A clarinetist in the school orchestra, Spielberg noodled the score on the instrument, which his mother transformed into sheet music and the Arcadia High band performed. *Firelight* was a contemporary story, so the clothing budget was low. Arcadia classmates (including Andrew Owen and Carol Stromme) along with older actors from the Arizona State University drama department made up the cast, with all sound dubbed in post.

As he told Barbara Lewis in May 1969, "I got the actors together in the living room of my parents' home and flashed the picture on the wall, and the actors spoke their lines, synchronizing with the lip movements."

Due to an incident years later where Spielberg loaned two reels of his one *Firelight* print to a Hollywood production company that went out of business (taking the print into the black hole of bankruptcy), very little of his debut opus still exists... at least to the general public. A short 3-minute 45-second excerpt is all that is available, although longer cuts were reportedly shown in (now-retired) Dr. Drew Casper's Spielberg class at USC.

Prominent in extant clips is a blood red orb in the sky resembling one his Boy Scout troop observed, as well as the plucky red alien light in *Close Encounters*. Other shades of that 1977 movie include a small girl (his sister Nancy) taken by said red dot, filmed by simply placing a red gel on a white light.

These clunky celestial phenomena were funded by Spielberg white-washing trees at 75 cents a head (20-25 trees per day, $15/day, $75/week), plus some dough chipped in by his "angel investor" dad Arnold to the tune of a whopping $500 budget (over $5,000 in today's dollars). He still had to get creative to make that money match his ambition, such as revolving a clothing line with Christmas lights to create the illusion of a couple inside a moving vehicle (a.k.a. "poor man's process"). One visceral moment of violence was achieved by splashing the female actress with cherries jubilee.

The original plan was to preview the film for Arcadia High drama classes, then a public debut in January of '64 to benefit the Perry Institute for mentally handicapped children. At 8pm on March 24, a now-17-year-old Spielberg held the premiere of his regional blockbuster *Firelight* at historic Phoenix Little Theatre on North Central Ave. The precocious showman booked a limo to ferry local dignitaries to his big event.

"There was just one public screening, for 500 people at a dollar a head," Spielberg told *Jefferson Parish Times* in 1977. "The next day, my parents moved us to San Francisco and the film got packed away and forgotten, but it had made back its cost."

A Phoenix Theatre entryway now boasts a wall with a large photo of the director and a dedication from him: "I am proud to be one of the many individuals who have been touched by the magic of this beautiful venue... Congratulations to you all, and break a leg in the years, decades, and centuries still to come."

J.J. Abrams at the *Star Wars: The Rise of Skywalker* premiere.

Flash forward 17-years, as if Spielberg himself had been reincarnated from that *Firelight* premiere. At the time of *Poltergeist*'s production, a group of budding teen filmmakers came together for a program at L.A.'s Nuart Theatre boasting "The Best Teen Super 8 Films of 1981." Put on by public access host Gerald Ravel, the program had shorts by at least three teens who would later become major Hollywood players:

—Larry Fong (DP, *300*), whose *Toast Encounters of the Burnt Kind* spoofed *CE3K* with animation and a miniature neighborhood model. "Right now, I just want to go back to UCLA and get my degree in film studies," said the linguistics major.

—Matt Reeves (director, *The Batman*), whose *Stiletto* was a gory film noir murder mystery which made the filmmaker proclaim, "I'm never going to do another horror film again," preferring to make a movie like *Ordinary People*.

—Jeffrey Abrams (director, *Star Wars: The Force Awakens*), whose *High Voltage* was a comedy-horror hybrid with a "tongue-in-cheek look at high school stereotypes." This was the Nuart audience favorite by popular ballot.

The fest was kicked off when Abrams contacted cable host Ravel about showing his shorts on TV, which got a huge response. Ravel was "amazed at how professional it was," then decided to organize the showcase, which got written up twice in the *L.A. Times*.

"I see stuff by Steven Spielberg and John Carpenter and I want to do it too," Abrams told the paper. "I've always wanted to be a director. I did a clay animation thing on my parents' home movie camera when I was 7 and I've been making films ever since."

This piece caught the eye of Spielberg himself, who recruited J.J. Abrams and Matt Reeves to clean and repair splices in his old 8mm childhood films, which would later be transferred to tape with excerpts shown on Japanese TV in 1982.

As Abrams wrote on *Quora* in November of 2011, "Matt Reeves and I were asked to help repair two films Steven made when he was a teenager. One was called *Firelight* and the other was *Escape to Nowhere*. Matt and I were 16 years old and had just been in a super 8 film festival. The *L.A. Times* wrote an article about it, Steven saw it and had his assistant (Kathleen Kennedy at the time!) contact us and ask if we'd be interested in repairing them. We thought it was a prank phone call. We did the repairs and made $300, but we never met Mr. Spielberg himself."

"It was insane," added Abrams on *Jimmy Kimmel Live*. "It was like giving us the Mona Lisa and saying, 'Will you clean this?' Dogs are walking past it and siblings as it's on the floor of our bedroom. I wanted to steal a frame, because it said 'written and directed by Steve Spielberg.' I was like, 'Come on, we have to,' and Matt's like, 'No!' So, we didn't."

To this day Spielberg remains very guarded about these early films, remarking of *Firelight* in 1978, "I'm not anxious to resurrect it." As Spielberg scholar

Steven Awalt remarks about Abrams and Reeves, "They've seen sights none of us have seen."

Abrams added on Howard Stern in 2011, "There aren't copies to be made when you're making 8mm films. The truth is he was entrusting 15-year-old strangers. It makes no sense whatsoever! To this day I'm like, 'Something fucked up...'"

Spielberg explained to Abrams in an *Entertainment Weekly* interview, "When I saw the picture I said, 'Those are the two most trustworthy faces I've seen in months!'"

In the 2020s an *Arizona Republic* columnist named Phil Boas recruited a small group of Phoenix movers and shakers to form Project Firelight, which envisioned several ways for the area to honor Spielberg's childhood there. One was a storytelling space for schoolchildren called Firelight Center. Another was a Firelight Festival similar to SXSW, as well as fundraisers based on Spielberg's past projecting Disney movies like *Davy Crockett* to neighbors on a backyard bedsheet, then donating the money to Perry Institute. Project Firelight was pitched at Amblin, though the company demurred due to "complications arising from ownership rights to his story."

"Steve has this background of a middle-class kid growing up, and it infests everything he's done," says Hal Barwood. "It culminated in *The Fabelmans*, an outright biography. It's also there in *Catch Me if You Can*. Those of us who know Steve know *Catch Me if You Can* is about Steve. 'Hey, I passed the test.' He did. He wormed his way into Universal."

As the story goes, at age 18, Spielberg snuck onto the Universal Studios lot via a tour, eventually making his way to an open sound stage. He spotted Alfred Hitchcock directing the opera house sequence in *Torn Curtain*... before being tossed out by an assistant director. Years later Spielberg would be astounded hearing Hitch in radio commercials for the Universal Studios Tour encouraging visitors to come see the shark from *Jaws*. Teen Spielberg began sneaking into Universal by dressing in a suit, carrying a briefcase, waving at the guard, and setting up an office for himself in true con artist fashion.

"It started with my taking a tour and I walked into a random doorway," Spielberg told Mark Kermode in 2006. "I asked this gentleman, the head librarian for Universal Studios, if I could use his telephone. When I used the phone and asked for a ride and told my story to my cousin, he overheard and said,

'Did you really get off the bus and just wander around? What do you want to do with yourself?' I said, 'I want to be a director, and this was the best idea I had to be able to watch other directors working.' He took an interest in me and gave me a pass to come back the next day. I came back on the lot the fourth day and just took a chance... instead of showing Scotty the guard my pink pass, I waved to him and he just waved me onto the lot without checking my papers."

"It's a 'print the legend' more than anything," says Steven Awalt. "No shade on Steven. When you're a young artist, you gotta build up legends. He had a patron his father knew at Universal, Chuck Silvers in the editing department. Chuck got Steven in on a pass numerous times so he could watch him work, and he liked him a lot. I don't think he jumped the gate and went by Scotty. 'Hey, Scotty.' He always likes to say 'Scotty' specifically. He may have prolonged things or went where he wasn't supposed to, but he had entry into Universal because of Chuck Silvers. It's not a story he needs now, but when *Catch Me If You Can* came around, he started re-perpetuating it."

Even without this mythmaking, his origin story is no less Horatio Alger in nature, bootstraps fully pulled up. While studying Film and Electronic Arts at Cal State Long Beach, Spielberg filled notebooks with ideas, took acting lessons with Jeff Corey, and began a short about bicycle racing starring Tony Bill entitled *Slipstream* (never finished due to financing and weather issues). Eager to create a calling card, he cobbled together $15,000 for a lyrical, dialogue-free 26-minute short, titled *Amblin'*. The simple story of a young guy and girl who meet, fall in love, and ultimately part while hitchhiking across the Mojave was lensed in 35mm by Allen Daviau. Once screened by Universal Television exec Sid Sheinberg, he signed the 22-year-old director to a 7-year contract.

"I didn't know who he was," Spielberg told *New York Post* in

Night Gallery creator Rod Serling (1971).

1975 of Sheinberg. "He tells me he's the head of television for Universal Pictures and says, 'I love your short and I want you to come to work for me.' I said, 'You're putting me on.'"

Spielberg's first at bat for this contract? *Night Gallery*. This two-hour (with commercials) TV movie pilot was based on Rod Serling's supernatural triptych book *The Season to Be Wary*. The *Twilight Zone* impresario was scripting and hosting in front of an array of eerie paintings. Touted as Serling's return to the fantastic, the anthology series came during a low ebb in the celebrated writer's career when he was a commercial pitchman for everything from 6-12 Plus Mosquito Repellent to Ziebart's Rustproofing: "I spend 11 weeks on a screenplay but get about the same money for a one-minute commercial." When the subject of 21-year-old "wunderkind" Spielberg (actually 22) helming one of the pilot's segments titled "Eyes" was brought up by Cecil Smith in February 1969, 44-year-old Serling lamented, "Maybe I'm too old for television."

Then vice president of Universal TV Frank Price told this author, "Sid Sheinberg asked me to view *Amblin'* by a young guy he was thinking of putting under contract. He wanted my opinion since I was the star young producer there. We screened it and it was clear Steven had great visual skills. It was without dialogue, but the film was good. He was signed, and I think Sid put him on the wrong picture initially, a *Night Gallery* directing Joan Crawford. She saw this kid come on set... so the picture had a lot of problems. When NBC saw it, they said, 'Never let Steven Spielberg direct another picture for us.'"

Spielberg admitted to Barbara Lewis in 1969, "Sid gave me the script. It didn't blow me out, but it was a script. Two weeks later, Sid called and told me that Joan Crawford would be the star. All I could say was '*Oy Vey!*'"

"This particular segment was produced by Bill Sackheim," recalled Sheinberg to Archive of American Television. "I convinced Bill to use Steven because he used to take pride in starting young directors, as I do, and all of a sudden it's like the world is going to end. Word gets around that it's terrible... There's one story that Lou Wasserman got a call complaining about Steven from Joan Crawford. I don't believe there's a scintilla of truth to it. I got a call or a note saying could I stop by and see her next time I was in New York, and I did stop by her apartment. I was afraid to go in there... she says, 'I just want to tell you how incredible this young director is, you really have an incredible find there.' Coming from Joan Crawford, that's better than chopped liver."

As Spielberg told *In Cinema* in 1981, "When they gave me *Night Gallery*, my entire budget for the 9 days of shooting, including Joan Crawford's salary, was under $500,000, and even that was considered a very big risk to take on a new director."

Although the youthful acne-faced director ingratiated himself with notoriously difficult Crawford, his troubles with the crew and network were, in his words, "traumatic." His voice was cracking. The crew laughed at him. When he went a day behind, execs showed up to prevent more overages. It would not be the last time he went over schedule.

As he told Awalt, "They used to call me 'Sheinberg's Folly,' 'cause I was the young kid that he had hired... this abstract young person that only loved lenses and dolly shots and didn't know anything about acting. At least that's the reputation I had then."

Serling's material was not his best either, telling the story of a rich blind woman (Crawford) who pays for the eyes of a poor man (Tom Bosley) in an ethically dubious operation that will give her sight for only one day. As ordained by the gods of irony, as soon as the bandages come off there is a blackout across all of New York City. With her apartment elevator broken, she spends her one night of sight in darkness before witnessing the sunrise through her window... which she falls out of to her death.

It's a sweaty premise, reminiscent of Serling's far more effective "O. Henry ending" to 1959's *Twilight Zone* classic "Time Enough at Last" where Burgess Meredith's last man on Earth is overjoyed upon finding a library where he can read all he desires, only for his glasses to break. Frustratingly, Sackheim made it clear that Serling would not allow anyone to change a preposition of his dialogue.

An admirer of Serling and *Night Gallery*, Dana Gould is a renowned comedian as well as a two-time Emmy-winning writer of *The Simpsons*. He officially adapted Serling's 1965 screenplay for *Planet of the Apes* as a graphic novel for Boom! Studios and performs as a parody version of ape character Dr. Zaius for a panel talk show on YouTube.

Gould says, "'Eyes' was a perfect metaphor for what this guy was going to become. Spielberg was 22 at the height of the Easy Riders, Raging Bulls revolution in Hollywood. It was the death of the old studio system. Young people were taking over while old studio bosses were proven to not know what they were doing. Here comes this wunderkind firmly mired in the old school. He's working at a studio on a conventional television series with fucking Joan Crawford. His approach could not have been more traditional, so in that regard he was a Trojan horse. I believe the first time he ever called action as a DGA sanctioned director was on Rod Serling's intro. The first time you called action as director was on a writer pretending to be an actor? Serling represented that mid-century old school Roosevelt liberal, and those values are still in Steven's work."

Says Steven Awalt, "'Eyes' is an interesting short film. It's got visual experimentation, shots through chandeliers, upside down, stuff he would not do later. If you look at his film 'Make Me Laugh' from *Night Gallery*—probably the worst thing he's ever directed, and got taken out of his hands—there is more Spielbergian framing in that one. The three-shot with two people in the foreground/one behind them."

Providing further insight is Amanda Reyes of the book *Are You in the House Alone?* and podcast *Made for TV Mayhem*: "'Eyes' is overly flourished, but you can see signature Spielberg. Wide-angle shots were uncommon in TV because screens weren't big and everything was tight so people could see what was happening. *Duel* has beautiful wide-angle shots where he lets the audience decide what to look at instead of telling them. That's pretty brave. Sometimes when you bring in people new to the TV format, they're making what they think is cinematic. They don't know the boundaries, so they don't mind pushing them."

"It's certainly well directed," adds Gould of the *Night Gallery* segment. "It's lit like a game show, but you had network restrictions, couldn't get too creative with lighting. You look at those *Columbo*'s they're all light-blasted. The camera movement in 'Eyes,' the focus shifts, the way he fills a frame... this guy knows how to tell a story."

Several pieces of imagery from "Eyes" were later incorporated into Spielberg's 2002 sci-fi hit *Minority Report*, including an eye operation where Tom Cruise wears a similar mask to Crawford's, as well as a children's merry-go-round echoing a scene with Bosley.

"He took a year off after 'Eyes' in 1970" Awalt explains. "He begged Sheinberg to let him try to get stuff out there for feature films. *Ace Eli and Rodger of the Skies* was sold in 1970. He didn't plan on staying in TV for long, even though he had the seven-year contract. One year got pushed back to the end of it because of that 1970 sabbatical."

With a story by Spielberg, *Ace Eli* was announced in early 1970 for producer Joe Wizan to deliver Spielberg's feature debut (under the Amblin' Productions banner), but the newbie was replaced by John Erman. Released in late 1973, the film starring Cliff Robertson as a barnstorming stunt pilot was a critical and commercial flop.

Convinced he could "produce quality TV in sausage-factory time," Spielberg returned to Universal's episodic mill cranking out entries for *Marcus Welby M.D.*, *Owen Marshall Counselor at Law*, and a lauded episode of *The Psychiatrist* starring Clu Gulager. A one-off January 1971 sci-fi dream episode of *The Name of the Game* titled "L.A. 2017" (runtime 76-minutes) may technically qualify as Spielberg's first Hollywood feature. The traditional qualifier, *Duel* (74 minutes), would come that November. He also helmed the first series episode for *Columbo*, starring Peter Falk as the title detective with variations on his signature catch phrase, "Oh, just one more thing..."

Says *Inverse* entertainment editor Hoai-Tran Bui, "Watching that *Columbo* episode, his style is already so defined, his particular finesse. Like, 'Wow, this is really well-directed. Who directed it?' Spielberg's name pops up. It feels like someone with something to prove, doing this incredible dolly zoom through a window for the opening shot."

According to Frank Price, "We put him on various television shows and that work played a strong role in what happened to his career."

Sci-fi and suspense writer Richard Matheson (*The Incredible Shrinking Man*, *The Twilight Zone*) wrote his short story "Duel," about a man in an automobile pursued by a nefarious truck, for the April 1971 issue of *Playboy* thinking it would never work for film or television. Spielberg's secretary Nona Tyson highlighted the story for her boss, which by then was already in Universal's pipeline for *Name of the Game* producer George Eckstein.

A major player in turning Universal into the world's largest television programming supplier, Price said, "I was handling all our sales to ABC television, and had sold them *Movie of the Week*. We were getting that ready when I was approached by Dick Irving, one of our vice presidents and a former mentor of mine… and Amy Irving's uncle. He had this short story *Duel* and I liked it. He proposed it for *Movie of the Week* and we thought this would be a good one for Spielberg. You had to have somebody who knew what he was doing visually; but when I submitted it to ABC they rejected it. They said, 'No audience will sit for 90 minutes with no dialogue. That won't work.'"

To Spielberg's chagrin, the network forced Matheson to add more internal VO monologues for driver protagonist David Mann (Dennis Weaver) in his teleplay.

"Fortunately, in the contract I was able to do three puts out of the 14 pictures we delivered to them in case there was a disagreement," Price says of his arrangement with ABC, whose vice president in charge of movies for television was Barry Diller. "I had the right to do three of them that they rejected, so that was one we did. I knew they would try to punish us because they don't like puts, so I played a very low profile, stayed away from dailies. I wanted ABC to take ownership. A woman there named Lillian Gallo did take ownership. Finally, ABC liked what they were seeing, so it became quite an event."

Shooting lasted 13 days in high desert environs north of Los Angeles from September 13 to October 4, 1971. It went three days over schedule with only ten sleepless days for editing. Spielberg's canny use of camera, extensive mapped-out planning of the shoot, and Weaver's tightly-wound performance all ratcheted up the suspense for a propulsive experience still considered a pinnacle of the TV movie genre… even if it was not the instant smash one imagines. *Duel* initially aired as an *ABC Movie of the Week* on November 13, 1971, earning a Nielsen rating of 20.9 and an audience share of 33%.

Says Reyes, "It's an interesting case study, because it is an undeniably great film, yet when it originally aired it was middling in the ratings, #47 for the season. It wasn't a huge hit, but got a lot of great reviews. It's clearly transcended because Steven Spielberg made it, but at the time there were other filmmakers who were going to become famous making great TV movies that never got a home video release, including Peter Hyams' *Goodnight, My Love* and John Badham's *Isn't it Shocking? Duel* got its longevity because the network liked it, gave it that theatrical release and home video, tons of reruns."

Concurs Awalt, author of *Steven Spielberg and Duel: The Making of a Film Career*, "*Duel* wasn't a crushing ratings success, it was a modest success. People within the industry saw this extraordinary talent working in television…

the frame contained him, something bigger was ready to break out. The night *Duel* aired he kept getting offers."

Spielberg began making his first promising steps toward a theatrical feature. One potential project was an original sci-fi movie going by many titles including *Star Dancing* and *Hansen's Planet* before eventually settling on *Home Free*. A melding of story and visual ideas which eventually found purchase in *Alien*, *Star Wars* and other films, it concerned two astronauts tasked with traveling outside Earth's solar system to a planet where they eventually discover a race of intelligent humanoid aliens. While the senior astronaut is brought to safety, the lower man on the totem pole is left to deal with the lifeforms. It was written by a pair of exciting young USC grads named Hal Barwood and Matthew Robbins, who became key Spielberg collaborators.

As Robbins describes the story, once the secondary astronaut in *Home Free* is stranded he is "roaming its featureless grassy hills in a tracked vehicle. He discovers an abandoned, spooky world under its surface and, in the end, is joined by dozens of willowy, benign aliens who communicate via bioluminescent markings on their bodies. Several of these elements found their way into *CE3K* and, later, somehow, *Avatar*."

"That's when we met Steve," explained Barwood. "We were struggling screenwriters back in 1970 and Larry Tucker, a producer who did *Bob and Carol and Ted and Alice*, wanted to do a science fiction movie. He said, 'Look, I just want it to be weird.' We wrote *Home Free*, and in those days science fiction was what died on Saturday night. You got one weekend of decent box office, and that's it. Very different now, because science fiction has become what westerns were as I was growing up, the dominant form. Larry wanted to attach a director who would give the concept substance. He heard of this young guy doing TV, Steven Spielberg, so he brought Steve over to his house in Bel Air and we met him. We thought he was a really neat guy."

By this point the reputation of *Duel* had grown significantly through repeat airings and a Best Movie Made for TV Golden Globe nomination.

"I got a lot of calls," Spielberg told Awalt in his book. "Postcards and letters came to me over the next couple of weeks. A lot of calls the next day from friends who I know had seen it, and my parents had seen it and loved it. It scared them, which was fun, 'cause it was fun to scare your own parents."

Interest in releasing *Duel* overseas was driven by British film and TV critic Dilys Powell, who wrote a glowing review of both the film and the young talent who made it.

Explains Awalt, "That's what made Universal through CIC [Cinema International Corporation], their partnership with Paramount at the time in international territories, decide to expand the film and release it theatrically in Britain, Europe, Australia, and parts of Asia. That helped build Spielberg's international reputation."

The European version of *Duel* is estimated to have grossed $6M. Barwood and Robbins were present during three days Spielberg spent reuniting with Dennis Weaver to add scenes, including a school bus full of children as well as a new opening.

"He was doing inserts for *Duel*," says Barwood. "It was going to become a feature in Europe. He needed to complete the cinematic package; like when the car is starting up, you wanted rubber burning on a wheel. We watched them do it. That was really fun."

Unfortunately, *Home Free* was not a beneficiary of Spielberg's newfound momentum, as Robbins confirms: "We tried, unsuccessfully, to get the film set up at Universal with executive Ned Tanen. The closest we came was with Robert Aldrich directing. I think he had to drop the project because of heart trouble."

Concept illustrations to sell the film were done by Ralph McQuarrie, an artist whose only work to hit screens were illustrations of the Apollo missions for news broadcasts. His *Home Free* drawings—depicting a space-suited astronaut exploring an austere grassy environment and encountering tall beings with grids of light emanating from their bodies—caught the eye of Barwood and Robbins' Bay Area pal George Lucas, who recruited McQuarrie to be chief visual architect of *Star Wars*. The artist would also design spaceships for *E.T.* and *Close Encounters*.

"Ralph's illustrations certainly impressed George Lucas, who snatched him up and allowed him to make history," adds Robbins

"We became pals, then things drifted away," Barwood said of Spielberg. "The big problem with *Home Free* was Doug Trumbull made a movie called *Silent Running* that was a complete failure. It put the idea of science fiction in the freezer."

While it may be hard to understand Spielberg's drive to leave his successful career in television, he was not the only young prodigy Sheinberg cultivated during the 1970s. Don Coscarelli (*Phantasm*, *Beastmaster*, *Bubba Ho-Tep*) was 19-years-old when he sold his first (parents-financed) feature, 1976's *Jim the World's Greatest*, to Universal Pictures. He was the youngest director to have a film distributed by a major studio. Sheinberg offered the teen a similar style of studio contract Spielberg signed to direct episodics. The independent-minded Coscarelli rebuffed the offer, as he told this author...

"Back then it didn't appeal to me because TV was a different animal completely," Coscarelli said (for Coming Soon). "Nowadays, television is a magnificent art, but the '70s was a period where television was really bad. They used to call it the placebo or narcotic of the masses, a pejorative description. A lot of crummy stuff, and Universal was right there. They were making eight hours of primetime shows a week, cop shows and *The Bionic Woman*. I just didn't see anything there for me, but hey, it worked out okay for Steven Spielberg! Maybe I should've tried it."

Spielberg himself was frustrated with his television apprenticeship, finding it creatively and financially stifling due to his claim that "my take-home pay was just a little over $100 a week" as he lived in a shared apartment. By all accounts, he shot his final two post-*Duel* made-for-TV movies (*Something Evil* and *Savage*) with little enthusiasm.

The director was loaned out to CBS to helm a family-in-peril haunted house script penned by Robert Clouse. The 1972 horror entry *Something Evil* starred Sandy Dennis and Darren McGavin as a city couple who move to an idyllic Pennsylvania farmhouse with their two kids. They run afoul of supernatural shenanigans fueled by satanic forces.

Says Reyes, "*Something Evil* came out around the time of *Crowhaven Farm* and *The House That Would Not Die*, and has that feel. They have flying toys, circles on the floor, and it's about family like *Poltergeist*."

Then came 1973's *Savage*, a backdoor pilot for a potential series starring Martin Landau as a reporter investigating a Supreme Court nominee's (Barry Sullivan) involvement in a murder/cover-up. *Columbo* creators William Link and Richard Levinson were brought in to turn it into a show called *The Savage Report*. The team asked Sheinberg to talk Spielberg into directing it, but the filmmaker said (according to Link in Joesph McBride's bio), "he wasn't in the Universal business, he was in the Steven Spielberg business." An angry Sheinberg threatened Spielberg with suspension if he did not make the film, purportedly bringing the director close to tears.

"Spielberg doesn't look back on those with any great regard," explains Reyes of these last two TV movies. "With *Savage* he felt strong-armed into it, but it's very good. The opening shots in the control room of the studio where Savage is doing his news report becomes a television movie about the technical making of television and how there isn't a lot of artistry. Yet, he makes a very artistic TV movie to buck the system. Like, 'You're telling me I have to do things a certain way, but this is how I'm going to do it.' There's this great scene where Barry Sullivan's being interviewed where Barbara Bain goes one way and Martin Landau another way, then they meet in the middle in this one beautiful shot. He's getting confident yet not embellishing like 'Eyes.' It's subtly strong."

Spielberg was anxious to break out of TV jail. He spent several months developing *Cruising* alongside *The French Connection* producer Philip D'Antoni, who put Spielberg up in a New York hotel for a month as he shadowed NYPD detective Randy Jurgensen. The cop took the bespectacled director to real-life murder locations where gay men were slain by someone impersonating police. The film sputtered during the writing stage, eventually made by William Friedkin to no small controversy in 1980.

Another no-go was a gambling comedy called *Slide*, with a script by actor/writer Joseph Walsh. Set up at MGM with Steve McQueen, a regime change led to Spielberg and Walsh taking the project to Universal where it was eventually made by Robert Altman as *California Split*. These are the more main-

Director Steven Spielberg with Goldie Hawn on the set of *The Sugarland Express* (1974).

stream projects Spielberg developed while dodging offers to helm the kind of exploitation pictures Coppola (*Dementia 13*) and Scorsese (*Boxcar Bertha*) had to churn out for Roger Corman during their own "waiting to get your pilot's license" period.

Crucially, a new post-*Firelight* alien project emerged from Spielberg's pen as a short story/treatment titled *Experiences*. The tale centered on a "lovers' lane in a small midwestern town and a light show in the sky overhead that these kids see from inside their cars." A car couple witnessing a UFO would later show up in *Night Skies*.

"Steve went off to do whatever he did," continues Barwood. "He was a young guy, running a house somewhere with roommates. We were off doing other stuff, then he came back to us. He had this newspaper clipping about Ila Fae Dent and Bobby Dent and how they kidnapped Kenneth Crone."

Spielberg first came across the Dents' story after it occurred in May 1969, when the couple's abduction of the aforementioned highway patrolman and the multi-car chase that followed came to a tragic end. With permission from police to stop at Ila's parents' house to see their three children, Bobby entered and was shot by the sheriff of Robertson County, who had never before killed a man in his 25-year-career. That sheriff's name? E.T. "Sonny" Elliott.

The young filmmaker had tried to pitch a fictionalized version of the story to Universal shortly after his *Night Gallery* segment, but was nixed as being too downbeat. Now with the heat from *Duel* he wanted to pursue it again, opening the film with fictional Lou Jean breaking husband Clovis out of jail (the real couple had already been out of prison two weeks prior to the event) and reducing the number of children from three to one.

As Barwoord continues: "He said, 'I want to make a movie about this.' We sat down and he outlined what he'd like to see, then Matthew and I wrote it."

Said former Universal executive Thom Mount, "Steven started out directing television for Universal, and the guy who was his champion during that period was Jennings Lang. Jennings kept touting 'this kid Spielberg, who was doing some great television,' getting people to look at things. Finally, Jennings managed to convince everyone we should let him make a feature, *The Sugarland Express*."

"Jennings was key to launching and overseeing it," confirms Robbins. "He was the Universal executive who heard our pitch and immediately sent us to

Houston, Texas for research. Steve, Hal, and I rode with the highway patrol down there for a week, absorbing the cop culture and hearing the lingo."

Creating a realistic spectrum of Texas life required a "good imagination" for the writers, with New England native Barwood having only explored the south on family trips.

"It's a wonderful experience to hang around with cops," Barwood said. "They're a bit like you see in that movie. They love their work. It's adventurous, better than sitting in an office. There is a kind of zaniness. Part of it is an armor against the downside of life as a cop. You see a lot of terrible stuff. You don't see people at their best."

Adds Robbins, "I had an immediate fascination with the Texans, their outsize personalities and colorful talk. Bringing them to life and writing their dialogue was my greatest pleasure on that film. The highway patrol guys must have been similarly fascinated by us young Hollywood city slickers. I remember their amazement that I had never eaten a 'nacho' and didn't know what it was."

Originally titled *Carte Blanche*, *Sugarland* followed an unstable woman named Lou Jean (Goldie Hawn) who breaks her husband Clovis (William Atherton) out of pre-release prison so they can go to Sugarland, Texas to retrieve their young son from a foster home. Along the way they kidnap a police officer named Slide (Michael Sacks) who comes down with a severe case of Stockholm syndrome. What ensues is a bonkers travelling media circus as the trio are pursued across the state by police and news people.

This film's southern milieu, copious car chases, and antagonistic relationship between law and scofflaw are very much in line with *White Lightning*, a Burt Reynolds vehicle about a moonshine runner who works undercover to take down a corrupt sheriff (Ned Beatty). Spielberg earmarked that film (initially titled *McKlusky*) to be his big debut.

"I spent two-and-a-half months on the film," Spielberg told a 1978 *Film Comment* about *White Lightning*. "Met Burt once, found most of the locations and began to cast the movie, until I realized it wasn't something I wanted to do for a first film. I didn't want to start my career as a hard-hat, journeyman director. I wanted to do something that was a little more personal."

According to Barwood, "Steve has a warm, fuzzy human interior and the fact that there was a lot of wonderful humanity to be found in *Sugarland* beat *White Lightning*."

Lang was instrumental in getting things going, but power producers David Brown and Richard Zanuck got the reluctant greenlight from Lou Wasserman, then snagged Academy Award-winner Goldie Hawn (*Cactus Flower*) to be the anchor star.

Said Spielberg at a 50th anniversary screening of *Sugarland* in 2024, "Universal, at the time under Jennings Lang, said, 'We love the script but you can't make the film without a movie star...' Richard Zanuck and David Brown had just come over from Fox to Universal, they had an independent deal... they were the ones who sent Goldie the script... I went up to Goldie's house, met her, and that was the beginning. The movie wouldn't have gotten made without her."

"Jennings was in charge as we wrote the screenplay, but things changed when Zanuck brought Goldie Hawn onboard," recalls Robbins. "He and David Brown basically took the film away from Jennings, who bore a grudge long thereafter. Zanuck also wouldn't let us come to the set, thought we would take up Steve's time... yes, he was 'Steve' back then. We stayed in L.A., consulting with Steven by phone, which happened often."

"This is one of those huge trade-offs in life," mused Barwood. "In order to get the movie made, we needed Goldie, but her reputation of being this terrific comedian subverted the movie. She's perfectly aware of it. There's a wonderful quote of hers: 'Me on the poster with a big smile, and they thought it was a comedy, but it was a tragedy.' Goldie knows, and it's a shame because she's wonderful... but it ruined our chances. People came to the theater with the wrong expectation, then they went away and said, 'Don't go.'"

Sugarland was deliberately lensed in widescreen to distinguish it from Spielberg's TV work, heavily storyboarded and shot over a 50-day schedule five times what he had on *Duel*. The natural light cinematography by Vilmos Zsigmond consciously echoes what the Hungarian DP was doing at the time with director Robert Altman (*McCabe & Mrs. Miller*, *The Long Goodbye*), combining dolly moves with zooms. When interviewed by paper *Grand Illusions* in 1977, Spielberg said Vilmos was "especially helpful when you are wet behind the ears and just starting a movie making career."

First assistant cameraman Nick McLean told this author, "We had what was called the 'bullet car,' very dangerous but kind of fun. We had two cameras on the front of it and one in the middle, and the bullet car could zoom in and out of cars on the freeway. That's how we got a lot of those good shots with the police chase. Steven was pretty young, 26, but he was great, even the way he cast real people to be extras and little bit parts. Zanuck and Brown could tell he knew what he was doing, so they kind of stayed away. That's also where I taught Steven how to ride a motorcycle. We had a great time, and I really enjoyed the Lone Star beer."

"*Sugarland Express* is just my shit," enthuses contemporary critic Jourdain Searles. "It's country, realistic about the world. It's about regular people that I understand, that I'm rooting for. It's fun, even with the downer... as is *Thelma and Louise*."

Far more in line with Terrence Malick's poetic road movie *Badlands* than other "car films" of that era, *Sugarland* takes deliberate cues from *Ace in the Hole* and *Bonnie and Clyde*, both downbeat stories about the intersection of folk anti-heroes and the media. It sticks out like a sore thumb in Spielberg's filmography for falling into the bummer ethos part and parcel of '70s filmmaking. The movie ends with Lou Jean pressuring Clovis to go into the foster home to retrieve their son, even though both he and Slide know it is a trap. Clovis is gunned down by Texas Rangers and Lou Jean goes back to prison.

Peter Biskind's *Easy Riders, Raging Bulls* states that Spielberg's instinct midway through production was to switch this out for a more upbeat ending in defiance of real-life Bobby Dent getting shot down by police... the kind of Pollyanna-ism foundational to the director's commercial instincts throughout his career. Writes Biskind, "He thought *Sugarland* might do better if the couple survived. He had to be restrained by Zanuck, who urged him to stick to the original concept."

Robbins disputes this claim: "To my knowledge this never happened, and had it become a real issue, we would have been involved."

Spielberg has his own version, which more-or-less confirms it with varied details: "I discussed with Hal and Matthew about reshooting the ending, and they said, 'What are you crazy?' They talked me immediately out of it, but when the studio saw the film... they were upset with the ending. They said, 'We need to put a legend at the end that said she got her baby back,' and I said, 'No, you can't do that, the ending is what it is.' They said, 'We won't get anybody to see the movie unless we tell them that the baby's okay and the mom got the baby back.' I protested this as far as I possibly could. I couldn't go very far with that and the studio said, 'No, you're going to put that legend on the end of the picture,' and they did. It didn't work, as people still didn't come out to see the movie!"

The $3M budgeted *Sugarland Express* skidded when it hit theaters in early 1974, earning only $6.5M total. It was still an auspicious enterprise that first paired Spielberg with longtime composer John Williams, *Jaws* producers Zanuck & Brown, and *Close Encounters* cinematographer Zsigmond. The director bought a police car from the movie covered in bullet holes for $700, driving it around Hollywood to and from meetings.

Barwood, Robbins, and Spielberg won Best Screenplay at the 1974 Cannes Film Festival, with the picture itself nominated for the Palm d'Or. Grand dame of critics Pauline Kael wrote in *The New Yorker*, "In terms of the pleasure that technical assurance gives an audience, this is one of the most phenomenal début films in the history of movies." For an interview profile, *Newsweek*'s Paul D. Zimmerman said Spielberg was "an unguided missile, loaded with talent but not yet pointed in any firm direction."

"*Sugarland* was not a hit by any means, but it also broke even, which was a small miracle," reveals Mount. "Didn't cost much to make. Sheinberg pushed Jennings out of the way and took over the Steven relationship because he thought he had a horse that could win. Remember that life inside studios is always, shall we say, really competitive. Even though these guys aren't filming, these studio executives want to be associated with greatness and success. They push and shove each other around to make sure they are the ones credited in somehow making things happen."

The next year of Spielberg's life would be occupied turning Peter Benchley's trashy beach read *Jaws* into one of the most successful and beloved motion pictures ever made. It was a harrowing near-disaster of inflated budgets and countless filming day overages related to the mechanical shark and ocean filming. Spielberg never left the Martha's Vineyard location during the epic 159-day shoot for fear he would be replaced.

Still considered a pinnacle of the thriller genre five decades later, most would agree the true power of the film lies in its incredibly effective characterizations

Spielberg shooting *Jaws* (1975).

of small-town Americans going through a crisis (i.e. shark attacks scaring away beachgoers). While the novel reveled in the ever-boiling tensions between Police Chief Brody (Roy Scheider), oceanographer Hooper (Richard Dreyfuss), and salty fisherman Quint (Robert Shaw), Spielberg threw such dross overboard—including an unnecessary affair between Brody's wife and Hooper—in order to humanize the characters at every turn.

One modern day genre filmmaker who took Spielberg's sympathetic view of humanity to heart is Osgood Perkins, who has delivered such gory hits as *Longlegs* and *The Monkey*. The son of *Psycho* star Anthony Perkins, he homed in on the secret sauce that makes every great Spielberg film work: Their beating heart.

Perkins told this author, "More than anything, the thing about Spielberg is, and you hear people talk about it all the time, the fact that *Jaws*… not so much even the lore around, 'Oh, the shark broke and they didn't have a shark.' That's all interesting, but the scene of Scheider and the kid at the table… J.J. Abrams talks about that scene a lot, where he's got his head in his hands and his kid mimics it. There are things like that in *Close Encounters* too, where the human element is the best effect. Human interaction... the heart and soul of things... the small moment becomes the movie in microcosm. That's the most exciting part of those movies for me. Everything Spielberg did is astonishing, what he was able to generate. He's the greatest of all time, probably, but I think one can't overlook those little beats that really flower and make the whole thing so much fatter."

Spielberg truly believed that characters were the soul of his pictures, "otherwise people would have rooted for the shark," he said in 1981. "It's hard to see a caress in a mural. Sometimes people miss the gentleness in my films."

Most of Howard Sackler and Carl Gottlieb's screenplay alterations to Benchley's text made the islanders more sympathetic, yet one seemingly minor/obvious change from the book proved to be a rare instance of Spielberg making material darker. In the novel the character of Mayor Vaughn (Murray Hamilton) keeps the beaches open due to sizeable debts he has to the mob. With that unnecessary complication excised, the story of *Jaws* actually becomes a sharper indictment of simple American greed and how the town's selfish business interests trump public safety at every turn.

Says screenwriter Josh Olson (*A History of Violence*), "I went to the IMAX version of *Jaws*, and one thing I hadn't noticed before was actually additive. When they're on the ferry the car has a sign on it that says 'Vaughn Realty,' and you realize the mayor is also the local real estate baron."

Another gifted filmmaker who felt a seismic impact from *Jaws* is Renny Harlin, whose "super-smart sharks run amok" movie *Deep Blue Sea* is often considered the second-best film to feature the toothsome fish after Spielberg's masterpiece.

"Definitely it had a huge impact on me," says Harlin of *Jaws*. "I've studied that film a lot. There's a lot of stories about the making of it and the challenges they went through, and every filmmaker can relate to that. How Spielberg reshot the head coming out of the boat in his editor's swimming pool. As a director you've got to be relentless and go after what you believe to get the maximum impact. Spielberg did a lot of things that people don't even notice. Already his staging of actors and blocking of scenes was on its own level. He took a lot of his cues from movies of the 1940s when you would have long takes where you move the camera. You move the characters in space and create this really dynamic storytelling without any cuts. *Jaws* is known for so many things, but your average audience member doesn't realize all the artistry that went into that movie."

As Joe Jackson sang, "I had a giant rubber shark and it really made a mark. Didja looka looka lookit alla blood?" Often credited with singlehandedly creating what we think of as the modern summer blockbuster, *Jaws* grossed $123.1M in its initial run, the fastest film to cross $100M at the box office (one of the first to gross that much after *The Sound of Music*), as well as the most successful film ever until *Star Wars* two years later. This gave Spielberg the clout to, quite literally, reach for the stars.

CHAPTER 2

Are You An Artist?: The Close Encounters Phenomenon

"There'll be no little green men packing ray guns. The attitude of the film, in keeping with those sightings that have been reported, is that they're not monsters."

—**Steven Spielberg**, February 1977

In November of 1977, journalist George Anderson asked Steven Spielberg how his new movie compared to his $500 debut *Firelight*.

"It's a sequel," joked the filmmaker. "I made that movie under the influence of the 1950s science fiction films where people were consumed and di-

gested by beings from outer space. I don't want to use the word 'benign' about *Close Encounters*, but in 1977 we're ready for an encounter of this magnitude."

"This goes back to his teen years," says Michael Phillips, who produced *Close Encounters of the Third Kind*. "The roots of it are so old for him, so personal. I think it's an exception among his other films. This one goes way back. It's important."

Spielberg's first legitimate extraterrestrial opus premiered at New York City's legendary Ziegfeld Theatre on November 16, 1977. With an estimated budget of $19.4M, the Columbia Pictures production had roughly 38,800 times the financial resources the director had to work with on *Firelight*.

Close Encounters tells two parallel stories, the first involving scientist Claude Lacombe (French New Wave filmmaker François Truffaut) leading a government-affiliated group tracking a string of unexplained incidents, including UFO sightings and re-appearances of long-lost Navy planes. Meanwhile, an electric utility lineman in Indiana named Roy Neary (Richard Dreyfuss, reuniting with Spielberg after *Jaws*) experiences a close encounter with a UFO while driving in his truck. The incident jars something within him, and he becomes obsessed with what he saw. Driven by strange recurring visions, this obsession costs him his job and alienates him from his wife Ronnie (Teri Garr) and three children. Increasingly drawn to the small community who believes in such things, he joins up with a woman named Jillian (Melinda Dillon) whose son Barry (Cary Guffey) was abducted by aliens. They eventually cross paths with Lacombe's group en route to Devils Tower in Wyoming, where a giant mothership shows up to engage in first contact. Barry and dozens of other abductees are returned. The aliens single out Neary to be whisked away on their ship as our ambassador... leaving Earth seemingly forever.

Spielberg's attempt to do *Firelight* writ large began in earnest around the time he was editing *The Sugarland Express* in '73. A young producer named Michael Phillips, just kicking off his own career with *The Sting*, would run into Spielberg in the Universal commissary as they worked on their respective pictures. They bonded over a mutual love of science fiction, particularly *The Day the Earth Stood Still*.

Phillips was already enamored with *Duel*. He and wife/producing partner Julia Phillips had an unassuming house on Nicholas Beach Road in Malibu where many movers and shakers would congregate. The list was long and luminous: Goldie Hawn, Robert Redford, Joan Didion, Brian de Palma, John Milius, Paul Schrader, et al. Spielberg became a frequently entertained guest and made friends with many of his contemporaries there.

"One day he said, 'I want to come out to the beach and talk to you and Julia about a movie idea I have about UFOs and Watergate,' which had nothing to do with what it finally ended up as," remembers Phillips. "We said, 'Great, come out!' Later I asked why he even came to us, and he said he felt he needed 'a little tailwind' at that moment in his career since we had *The Sting*, even though it hadn't been released. People were watching it, because it's two big stars and a big director. He came out to the beach and pitched this idea about a UFO debunker for Project Blue Book who has his own experience and converts. We listened to it, we wanted to be in business, we said yes, it was great. This was the summer of '73, and we immediately set it up for development at Columbia."

At the time the floundering studio had just been taken over by David Begelman, a former MCA talent agent who founded Creative Management Associates (CMA) in 1960 with Freddie Fields. Spielberg had been one of their clients, and his *Watch the Skies* would be among the first projects Begelman put into the development pipeline, alongside *Taxi Driver*. The UFO film was pitched as costing $2.8M, a figure Spielberg shrewdly pulled out of the air because he thought it sounded reasonable.

Steven Spielberg (*left*) and Michael Phillips (*right*).

A major source of Spielberg's research—and one of the figures the initial main character had a basis in—was astronomer/professor J. Allen Hynek, who earned a PhD in astrophysics from the University of Chicago. Hynek was a central authority on UFOs while serving as a government debunker from the late-‘40s to late-‘60s under Project Sign, Project Grudge, and the infamous Project Blue Book. This period is in many ways defined by the ridicule he endured in 1966 for explaining away a mass UFO flap in Dexter, Michigan as the result of "swamp gas," also known as "will-o'-the-wisp."

While Hynek was content to moonlight as a debunker when not acting as an astronomer for the Smithsonian or professor at Northwestern University, the April 1964 case of New Mexico patrolman Lonnie Zamora—who reported two small bipedal beings disappearing near a floating craft which flew off into the desert—marked a turning point.

"The incident was very interesting, to say the least," Hynek addressed in the 1974 film *UFOs: Past, Present, and Future*. "It seems to differ from practically all the earlier cases we investigated from one standpoint: The vehicle had left pod marks. There was an insignia observed by Lonnie Zamora on the side of the craft. The insignia was unidentifiable, not American nor Russian. Last of all, the observation of these two people in some sort of suit."

Says the scientist's son Paul Hynek, "I went to Socorro with Jacques Vallée, who told me it was that case that made my father feel comfortable talking about entities and not just crafts. It was a particularly compelling case in terms of the witness, but also the timing. By then he'd seen enough. The accumulated weight of the data pointed to that being something that could be talked about now. The time had come."

J. Allen eventually flipped his position, criticizing government efforts as "totally inadequate." He went on to found his own investigative group Center for UFO Studies (CUFOS) in Evanston, Illinois to take the study more seriously in 1973, the same year development on *CE3K* began. Part of his motivation for attaching his name to Spielberg's film was to raise awareness of CUFOS, so people would "know there is a place they can go to report."

"For my father, I think there was an accumulated frustration at his role tamping down hysteria as a PR exercise," said Paul Hynek. "In 1952 they started the Air Intelligence Service Squadrons. They would have been the ones dispatched to crash retrieval sites, that was their charter. It wasn't originally for UFOs but for any kind of crash landing. They had Russian speakers and all that, probably got the pick of the litter for cases, and Project Blue Book got the ones they thought they could explain easily enough."

"Hynek is immensely important," says paranormal expert Aaron Sagers. "He was a scientist and started out on Blue Book with an open mind, then realized that's not what the government wanted out of him. They wanted someone to rubber stamp dismissals and label everything as 'swamp gas,' which led to his disenchantment and cynicism about the whole project. He leaves and becomes this figure that is not only open minded but an advocate for discussing ufology and the potential of what's out there."

Hynek's 1972 book *The UFO Experience* serves as a Dante-esque settling of scores with those in charge of Project Blue Book, which he paints from first-hand experience as a bad faith endeavor. The nonfiction tome provided Spielberg with numerous case studies of UFO incidents, along with the actual *Close Encounters of the Third Kind* title. Hynek has a cameo as a pipe-smoking scientist in the film's finale.

Explains Paul Hynek, "The original title of *Close Encounters* was 'Watch the Skies.' Spielberg came across *The UFO Experience* then reached out to my father. He sold the rights to the title for 1000 bucks, then got in hot water with Henry Regnery, the publishing company, because it wasn't his to sell. They worked that out. He had a lot of calls with Spielberg, met several times, and my father gave him accounts of real reports. A lot of things in the movie came from reports, like that toll booth on the border of Ohio and Pennsylvania, or the sunburned face."

The director told Mick Garris in 1980, "A lot of the research I did really came from sightings that were not altogether well-founded. I researched a few myself, debunked a few myself, and a few I couldn't explain. Then Dr. Hynek came on board after the script had been written and he was very beneficial in reading a scene and saying, 'Well, that is absolutely into science fiction, but this is more like what I have been researching.'"

Hynek confirmed to Jim Shetzer in 1978 that he received $1,000 for the title and $1,500 for serving as the movie's technical advisor, telling the columnist, "I have already lost more in legal fees than I ever got from Columbia."

Reading the book after seeing the movie, one can almost see it as "source material" even though the film is ostensibly an original story.

"He was a consultant, that was his field, but it was not an adaptation," Phillips says of Hynek's contribution. "What Steven wanted was to try to get the most commonly reported features of craft and aliens, and Hynek's book reiterated a lot of this. The appearance of the creatures was based on sifting through many reports and coming up with something right there in the middle."

Says Sagers, "There's a lot of throwaway moments in *Close Encounters* referencing things like Flight 19, a real case from 1945: five aircrafts went missing off of Fort Lauderdale, Florida. They referenced the ship SS Cotopaxi which was a big part of Bermuda Triangle lore, even though that has since been explained. This vessel did go missing, but was ultimately discovered off the coast of Saint Augustine. They're throwing around case files like Easter eggs. Neary's car blinking out, everything going dead, then the experience of him seeing craft lights, the radiation burn... all taken from case files. The chasing around of law enforcement... we have multiple cases where law enforcement was pursuing things they couldn't explain, then later told to just forget it. The second scene in the movie at air traffic control could have been pulled from the 2017 *New York Times* article which launched this new era of exploring UAPs."

That particular *CE3K* air traffic control scene in Indianapolis tracking two commercial flights—both witnessing a brilliant light in the sky alternating between red and white—is very similar to a real-life report in *The UFO Experience.* A Lear jet pilot and a National Airlines pilot had a mid-air encounter with an accelerating red light over Winslow, Arizona, relayed to an Albuquerque control tower tracking them on radar:

> ***ALBUQUERQUE:*** *Do you want to report a UFO?*
> ***NATIONAL PILOT:*** *No.*
> ***ALBUQUERQUE:*** *Do you want to report a UFO?*
> ***LEAR PILOT:*** *We don't want to report.*

As with *Jaws*, *Close Encounters* was a case of the director being perfectly in tune with the zeitgeist. A 1977 Gallup poll showed 54% of the United States believed in the existence of UFOs, while 11% claimed sightings or actual contact with alien beings. The newly elected President Jimmy Carter was one of those 11%, having seen a bright object in the sky that appeared "luminous, not solid," changed colors (blue, red, white), then vanished into the horizon. This incident occurred at a Lions Club event in 1969, two years before Carter became Governor of Georgia, witnessed by a dozen others.

"I'll never make fun of people who say they've seen unidentified objects in the sky," said Carter during his '76 campaign. "If I become President, I'll make every piece of information this country has about UFO sightings available to the public."

Once elected, Carter ultimately reneged on this promise of disclosure due to supposed national security reasons, but always maintained he did not think the object he saw was extraterrestrial in nature. Spielberg was also a healthy skeptic but appeared to operate under Fox Mulder's axiom of "I want to believe."

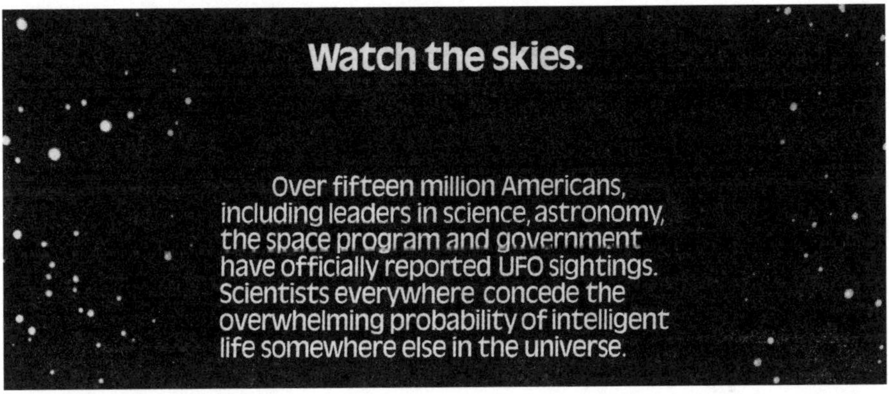

He told the AP's Bob Thomas in 1976, "I am an agnostic. I always have to see something to believe it. But I consider myself a rational, logical person, and I believe that enough evidence has been amassed to confirm the reality of UFOs. Men have been hanged for murder on much less evidence."

Two decades later Spielberg would tell a student directly during an *Inside the Actors Studio* interview, "I do believe in aliens."

At one point during production on *CE3K*, Spielberg halted filming so that the entire cast and crew could observe what he believed might be an actual UFO in the sky. "Everyone was lying there on their backs with binoculars," said Melinda Dillon about their observance... which turned out to be an Echo satellite.

"I don't think Steve could have the deep impulse to do that movie if he didn't semi-believe it," opines Hal Barwood. "I felt the same way, and probably Matthew did too, and the cast. You tell yourself, 'We're onto something.' For a while I thought we were gonna find out, you know, *they're here*, but it didn't get revealed."

As Spielberg told *The Post Standard* in 1977, "I'm trying to be open-minded toward the possibility that we have been and are being surveyed by very foreign intelligences. The government seems to have systematically pooh-poohed the possibility of such a phenomenon occurring, while the evidence on hand is too hot to ignore. There is something going on up there and we have every right to be informed."

Phillips, however, insists that Spielberg's belief in aliens was actually "zero."

"Is there life elsewhere in the universe? I am certain there is," Phillips elaborated. "I think Steven probably believes that too, but after looking at all the evidence about the UFO sightings... to claim there are actually aliens visiting and scouting us? No, he did not. He was asked this point blank by David Begelman, the head of the studio... 'Do you believe in aliens?' His answer was, 'No.' Yes, we believe there are aliens out there, but do we believe these UFO sightings are alien visits? He did not believe. I did not believe."

Huge swaths of the public believed, though, and Spielberg had faith that would translate to butts in seats if he could concoct a compelling enough story. He came up with a plot about a government debunker who turns believer after a close encounter of the second kind, then gets involved in a government project to send him to the stars. The ensuing process took a litany of writers to shape the director's sketchy ideas into a cohesive film.

The first writer hired (for $35,000 dollars after delivery of one draft plus revisions) was Paul Schrader, a movie critic turned screenwriter whose violent magnum opus *Taxi Driver* was simultaneously being produced by Michael and Julia Phillips. That psychotic vigilante movie was offered to Brian De Palma before Martin Scorsese made it his own. Even with Robert De Niro attached as Travis Bickle, *Taxi Driver* nearly did not get made.

"Keeping that package together was very difficult," says Phillips of *Taxi Driver*. "Columbia loved *Close Encounters* and hated *Taxi Driver*. We didn't have a go picture. Steven volunteered to be there if needed, and was open to directing when we thought we were losing Marty. As a friend he offered to be around. There was a community. At that time everybody was so eager to break in and generous in helping each other, read each other's scripts, editing suggestions."

Spielberg's presence was ultimately not required on *Taxi Driver* and Scorsese transformed Schrader's script into a dark classic. When Schrader turned in his draft for Spielberg's UFO film—initially titled *Kingdom Come* in late '73 then registered with the WGA as *Close Encounters of the Third Kind* in January '74—the director took advantage of that film community by getting Hal Barwood and Matthew Robbins' two cents.

Said Barwood, "The reason we got involved with *Close Encounters* is because Paul had written a screenplay. Steve gave it to us and said, 'What do you think, guys?' Turns out he didn't like it at all. Like Schrader's stuff it was really good but a very cold/serious version of something like *Men in Black*. Really grim, a bit like *French Connection*."

"It wasn't what I like, my personal tastes," said Phillips. "We started with Schrader, which turned out to be not a good idea. Paul and Steven are oil and water in terms of what they love about movies. Paul wrote a very serious script, which he referred to as 'Saul on the road to Damascus.' It didn't have the joy that is pleasantly Steven."

Spielberg was even more blunt, telling *Future*, "I sat down with Paul and fed him my story infinitus. Paul simply sat down at a typewriter and, within weeks, returned my story to me in the form of many convoluted pages consisting mostly of 1,000-word monologues. I remember reading that script and wanting to close the account of my interest in UFOs. The Air Force debunker angle had to go and so did Paul Schrader."

Schrader's 134-page first draft of *Close Encounters* deals with a character not dissimilar to J. Allen Hynek. In fact, the hero's name is J. Paul VanOwen, and opens—cheerily enough—with him having a sensor graphically surgery-ed into his chest. Like Saul's conversion to Paul the Apostle, he goes from debunker to believer and abandons his family early on by faking his death. Those longer-than-long monologues of experiencer stories Spielberg complained about are a problem. While there is a world where they could have given the movie a documentary-like verisimilitude, this kind of writing was not compatible with a show-don't-tell blockbuster.

Says author/journalist Matt Zoller Seitz, "I am intrigued by the idea of Spielberg initially having Paul Schrader involved, because if there's anything that Schrader's work has told us is there's not a hell of a lot of practical difference between piety and obsession. So many of his characters are tormented religious pilgrims, even if they're fallen people like Travis Bickle or the drug dealer in *Light Sleeper*. It seems perfect to have had him involved, even if he didn't end up going the distance."

Producer Julia Phillips specifically asked Columbia Pictures head David Begelman not to read the draft Schrader wrote, fearing it would kill all momentum on the movie. She wrote in her memoir, "Certainly it was not a screenplay Spielberg wanted to direct, although it very much created the Roy Neary character, a man obsessed by something way beyond his intellectual but within his visceral comprehension."

The original writer confirmed in *Schrader on Schrader* that he and Spielberg fell out "along strictly ideological lines," and that "I said, 'I refuse to send off to another world, as the first example of Earth's intelligence, a man who wants to go and set up a McDonald's franchise,' and Steven said, 'That's exactly the guy I want to send.' Steven's Capra-like infatuation with the common man was diametrically opposed to my religious infatuation with the redeeming hero—I wanted a biblical character to carry the message to the outer spheres, I wanted to form missions again."

He went on to say, "The only thing I deserve a credit for is changing Steve's mind about doing the film as a UFO Watergate. I thought it ought to be about a spiritual encounter. That idea stayed and germinated."

Explains Barwood of the Schrader draft, "You had that tough feel and Steve didn't want to do that, so he decided to write it... and he did."

Other writers including John Hill, David Giler, and Jerry Belson made passes at the script. Michael Phillips brought a hot young talent named John Landis to the *Jaws* set as a possible *CE3K* writer. While he did not get the gig, Landis stuck around the set and made friends with the shark movie's director. Spielberg ultimately took it upon himself to collate his own draft taking the story in a new direction following an everyman instead of a government official. He typed up his version in the evenings after coming home from the editing suite on *Jaws*, writing from 11pm to 8am.

"I'm a night person, basically," Spielberg told *Rolling Stone* in 1978. "I always stay up late, I sleep late in the mornings. I love the night."

"At some point, Steven realized he had to write it himself because it was really hard," remembers Phillips. "It was something he wanted to do his whole life, and nobody was going to get it exactly right. He was talking about these cuboids at the end... it was hard to understand what he had in his head."

Those "cuboids," floating bright white blocks intended to feature in the finale, were designed and even partially shot for the Devil's Tower sequence and teased with the inclusion of *Sesame Street*'s "The Square Song" during Barry's intro. They ultimately had to be scrapped after two days filming. The effect and interactivity with the scientists were untenable given the VFX limitations of the time. They are also a good example of Spielberg's excesses. Yes, cuboids are unquestionably "neat," but what purpose did yet another light show serve?

Commented Barwood, "Steve is not really a fluent screenwriter, and over the years always collaborated with others. When he was done, he showed it to us. It was on the way, pretty much there, but we had suggestions. He put us up in some addition to his Beverly Hills mansion for a week or so, working. Rick Dreyfuss was in on it too."

Although Spielberg often says he wrote the part of Neary with Jack Nicholson in mind, Dreyfuss told *The Miami News* that he read the first draft and stated "'I just wish I were 10 years older.' I didn't talk him into anything, though after putting my two cents in I did sort of hang around the office a lot." He later related to *Rolling Stone*'s Cameron Crowe in 1978 that he wrote, "One speech. They cut it out."

Of Dreyfuss' contributions, Robbins says, "I believe he came up with 'I want to lodge a complaint,' when we were writing his exchange with Truffaut."

Said Phillips of Robbins and Barwood, "He trusted and relied on them. They were there and contributed continuously."

Without question Barwood and Robbins' biggest addition was the character of Jillian's 3-year-old son Barry, whose abduction from and ultimate reunion with his mother at the end provides an emotional thrust that went beyond the intellectual impact of humanity "elevated out of our ordinariness to become part of the celestial population." All of the mothership's *son et lumière* was not enough to invest audiences, and Barry was the key.

"When he's delivered back to Melinda Dillon at the end, you have a human denouement which is positive, that beats out spectacle," opines Barwood. "We invented Barry and the sequences he's involved with, which enriched Melinda's part."

As lensed by Vilmos Zsigmond, the red-light-tinged sequence of Jillian trying to frantically escape the alien presence as it attempts to enter her home gives us our first taste of Spielberg depicting aliens as less "benign" and perhaps terrifying. The isolated country house foreshadows the rural horror he would attempt after.

"The scene where Barry is abducted from his home offers a glimpse of what *Night Skies* might have felt like," says musician Andy Fosberry, who created a *Night Skies* tribute album in 2022. "The exterior of Jillian's house looks beautiful but also remote and ready to be haunted. I let those feelings run wild when I was composing the album."

Barry's abduction is the closest to a true horror scene in *Close Encounters*, although Barwood—who conceived it—doesn't agree.

"He wanted to make sure they were a force to be reckoned with," says Barwood of the aliens. "Give them some personality that showed they weren't human. There's something about them that is awe-inspiring and a little bit blood curdling. I don't see it as a horror thing because little Barry seems very interested in what's going on out there. It's not like he's cowering in the corner and they're going to grab him. He wants to go."

"We added this high-stakes, personal element for basic dramatic reasons," Robbins adds. "It was Steven's staging and lighting that created the eerie atmosphere."

"It's a horror sequence," adds journalist Eric Vespe, host of *The Spiel* podcast. "So much of the DNA that would become *Poltergeist* is in that scene, with toys coming to life. He's so good at scaring you, man. He will focus on details like the screws coming out of the grates in the floor. You need a showstopper sequence that makes you think, 'What's coming next?' You get this horror set piece where the mother is terrified, and—even if you know they're not there to hurt anybody—at that moment you understand why she's upset. Stephen Colbert challenged Spielberg to pick a single frame from his movies that most represents him, and he said Barry opening the door in that sequence. That incredible shot of him silhouetted by the bright lights outside. Out of everything he's done, the single frame of his career is a simple shot of a threat outside, a lonely little boy in front of an open door where anything beyond your imagination could be out there, then the parental figure coming in and slamming that door. The core of who Steven Spielberg is shows through in that moment. It's extremely telling."

In his book on the film for the academic series *Constellations*, Jon Towlson writes, "Alien abductions taking place at a remote farmhouse would become a staple of UFO movies post-*Close Encounters–Communion* (1989), *Lifted* (2006), *The Fourth Kind* (2009) to name just a few; in particular, M. Night Shyamalan would take inspiration from the scene for *Signs* (2002) which draws also on the August 1955 Kelly-Hopkinsville true case in which a family were menaced in their farmhouse by humanoids from a UFO."

Columbia Pictures' vice president of worldwide production Stanley R. Jaffe took great umbrage with Spielberg adding this sequence, which he felt was not in keeping with the tone of the script he greenlit prior to Barwood and Robbins' contributions. Jaffe threatened to axe the whole production, but Julia Phillips managed to soothe the studio exec by getting Spielberg to shoot an alternate take where Jillian saves Barry from being abducted at the last second.

"Stanley Jaffe almost cancelled the show after he read our draft," Robbins confirms. "Days prior to commencement of photography he came to Wyoming, insisting that our additions be thrown out. Worried about mounting costs, he threatened to pull the plug, but Julia called his bluff and won the day."

Adds Barwood, "Jaffe was certainly very upset that Steve was doing these big revisions that didn't go through him, which included a new character. Luckily, they didn't shut it down. I think if *Jaws* hadn't already been in Steve's background they might have, but Jaffe was smart enough to realize, 'Hey, this guy knows what he's doing.'"

"Columbia was on the brink of bankruptcy," Phillips says of the studio's position at the time. "This was after *Jaws*, and they really bet the farm on this movie. The director of *Jaws* plus UFOs sounded like a—cross your fingers—worthy bet. But there was tremendous pressure from the studio, from bankers, and it was a high budget movie. The budget was $17M and ultimately came in at $19M, something like that."

While the studio was floundering, the producers were also in a fractured state, with Michael Phillips having officially vacated the Malibu beach house in 1974. In order to continue to function as business partners, Michael ran point on *Taxi Driver* while Julia spearheaded the massive *CE3K*.

"During the period of production Julia and I were divorcing," he says. "It was not a good environment for us both to be in the same place at the same time. I had been the on-set producer on *The Sting*, and felt that *Taxi Driver* was better for me. She was tremendously capable and very bright, so she stepped in and took on the battles which were continuous... to fight for the money that production needed."

Production designer Joe Alves is often credited for pinpointing Devil's Tower as the lynchpin totemic image Neary has a vision of. Hal Barwood claims it was he who remembered the monument amid the Black Hills of Wyoming from a trip he took with his wife in 1964.

Recalls Barwood, "I had some photographs, and I showed them to Steve. I said, 'Look, you need something that magically, sculpturally gives significance to this moment. They don't just land in the middle of the plain somewhere.' He sent Joe up there to see what it was like, but I had been there. Devil's Tower gives you tremendous stuff: the mashed potato scene; Rick crazily building this huge clay thing, ruining his house; that a poison gas leak is why we have to get everybody out of there and that's happening on TV and he finally looks at the television and sees, 'Oh my God, that's what's going on'; that whole sequence when the group escaped confinement, running up the slopes of Devil's Tower."

Barwood and Robbins weren't the only ones contributing to this fluid blockbuster-in-the-making. Bob Gale and Robert Zemeckis had been summoned to the set of *Close Encounters* so that Spielberg could brainstorm *1941* with them once he was done shooting on any given day. Both young men were in awe of the massive production.

"It was staggering to think he set this thing up, built this set in a big, abandoned airplane hangar in Mobile, Alabama," recalls Gale. "We'd hang out with Richard Dreyfuss and we met François Truffaut. That was pretty damn great."

At one point the two Bobs were asked to rewrite the Barwood/Robbins-conceived government summit scene where officials debunk UFO sightings to a room full of experiencers, including Neary. Because actor George DiCenzo distinguished himself in this scene, he was later cast as Lorraine's father in *Back to the Future*.

"That's the one scene where Steven said, 'You know, this should be better,'" said Gale. "We came up with the idea where he has this projection: 'This is a UFO that I took a photograph of... it's made of pewter and was shot in my backyard.' We wrote that."

At one point in the scene, a military man says...

"Now, there are all kinds of ideas that would be fun to believe in: mental telepathy, time travel, immortality, even Santa Claus."

What's fascinating about this line is that Zemeckis would go on to direct the *Back to the Future* trilogy and *A Christmas Carol* (dealing with time travel), *Death Becomes Her* (two women take an immortality potion), *The Polar*

Express (a child meets Santa Claus), and *What Lies Beneath* (a woman shares a telepathic connection to a murder victim). In retrospect, it's almost as if the writer was drafting a shopping list for his career.

Zemeckis in particular was singled out in Julia Phillips' infamous 1991 tell-all memoir *You'll Never Eat Lunch in This Town Again* as "an incredible pest on the set of *Close Encounters*." That general resentment extended to Spielberg himself along with the staggering commitment *Close Encounters* asked of her.

She wrote, "My life on hold, my dreams on hold... 'All great movies are the product of one person's obsession,' [Spielberg] keeps telling me. My obsession, his film. Not a very good deal." The producer blamed the director for stalling her own directing ambitions and exacerbating her cocaine habit. "Cocaine had never been a problem before. It was only after I started working with Steven. He was such a perfectionist." Spielberg supposedly found her so wired that he referred to her as the "Madwoman of Beverly Hills."

Nick McLean, who claims he lived with Phillips for a time during the shoot, says he has many stories about her "but I can't tell you them." He does confirm that the relationship between she and the director did sour.

Of the Steven/Julia feud, Matthew Robbins (who also directed second unit of Dreyfuss creating Devil's Tower and some electrical blackouts) says, "I never witnessed any clash. As far as I knew, Julia was an energetic-if-occasionally-manic fighter, whose determination helped keep doubtful studio execs at bay."

According to Michael Phillips, her greatest strength was that "she could fight for the film. She was really very, very bright and creative, but, as is known, she started getting substance problems and it became a big problem."

According to a 1982 *NY Times* article by Robert Lindsey, "Some people have attested to the large quantity of drugs on the location of the critically acclaimed *Close Encounters of the Third Kind*. The movie's producer, Julia Phillips, who has said she started snorting cocaine on *Close Encounters*, has estimated she spent more than $1 million on her cocaine habit. Steven Spielberg, the director of *Close Encounters*, has never been implicated as a cocaine user."

Phillips' issues went embarrassingly public. Columbia CEO Alan Hirschfield called her up personally in September of '76 to read her what co-star François Truffaut told *NY Times*: "The picture started with a budget of $11 million and now I think it is up to $15 million, but that is not Spielberg's fault. It is the fault of the producer, Julia Phillips. She is incompetent. Unprofessional. You can write that. She knows I feel this way. Sometimes it was so disorganized they had me show up and then do nothing for five days."

"It didn't do much for personal relationships, and a lot of this business is personal relationships," Phillips told *Time* in 1981 of using during 18-hour days on *Close Encounters*. "I could stay up all night thinking up ideas, but I wasn't likely to present them in the nicest fashion possible. Tact goes out the window."

Spielberg wrote a response letter to *The Times* defending Phillips for spearheading a "difficult undertaking" while praising her "constructive and consistent support," but before long the axe fell. After repeated disputes between her and the director during post-production, Begelman booted Julia off the project, forcing Michael Phillips to take over. Columbia eventually cancelled an adaptation of Erica Jong's *Fear of Flying* which Julia planned to direct. Despite several hits and an Oscar, her career never recovered.

There was also tension between cinematographer Vilmos Zsigmond and his director. The two of them were on more equal footing during *Sugarland Express*, but by *Close Encounters* there was no question who the 400-pound gorilla was.

"Later, when we did *Close Encounters*, they didn't get along so well," said Nick McLean, Zsigmond's camera operator. "We had a problem getting some of the shots. We didn't have enough light. One of the shots took us three nights to get. We were supposed to be flying a saucer over Richard Dreyfuss' truck, and finally, finally, finally got it right. Took us three tries, but we got it. They got along very good after that."

"I'm not the easiest person to work with in terms of my crew," Spielberg told *NY Times* in May of 1977. "When I say I think something should take two hours, and they say four and then it takes six, I get angry. I lost my temper and walked off *Close Encounters* five times. I walked off and cooled off. Everybody walked off that set."

More conflict arose around shooting at Building 17 of the Brookley Field Industrial Complex in Mobile, Alabama. The first contact landing area under Devil's Tower was constructed in hangars 5 and 6, coming in at 600 feet long, 400 feet wide, and 100 feet high... the largest indoor set ever built for a film at the time. Members of the crew posted a big sign on one of the rock formations reading "NOT SINCE C.B. DE MILLE," bringing to mind that 1963 edition of *The Arizona Republic* touting Spielberg as "Teenage Cecil B."

Zsigmond told *Rolling Stone* in 1980, "We had come from Wyoming and they wanted to shoot the next day. I said, 'Wait a minute. I have to light this.' Steven thought he could get the look he wanted with available light. He didn't realize that reality and reality on film are different. We had to bring in all the lights in Hollywood, and Columbia made me the bad guy, saying I was using too many lights."

Despite Julia Phillips' attempts to find a replacement, Spielberg allowed Zsigmond the leeway to continue his fine work. One innovation Zsigmond and McLean brought to the table was the incorporation of lens flares, something they did in tandem with Douglas Trumbull's VFX team. These flares required intensely powerful bulbs. The look not only became synonymous with Spielberg but influenced other filmmakers including Peter Hyams, John McTiernan, and especially J.J. Abrams.

"In the olden days, a lens flare could get you fired," McLean explains. "Now, if you got a lot of lens flares you might get another $1,000 a week. Everybody loved them, a new thing we incorporated into the system. Sometimes we even put star filters on the lenses to make those flares even more precise. Giant flares. When we couldn't get it right Vilmos got lights off an aircraft carrier. That's how we got the big scene."

Then there were the aliens, a makeup issue for which Spielberg used the Egyptian method, i.e. throwing more people at it. Once it came time to shoot the

Tom Burman alien mask.

beings created by Tom Burman, which were essentially oversized head pieces placed on 6-year-old ballerinas, the results were so inadequate that Zsigmond deliberately overexposed the film to obscure them. He also tried experimenting with film speed and POV shots.

Bob Baker's separate marionette of an alien with extended limbs/translucent skin nicknamed "Daddy Long-Legs" was considered too frightening, including one shot of it interacting with J. Allen Hynek. It was part of a sequence where several aliens begin feeling humans that was jettisoned for being too bizarre and dreamlike. Spielberg said fifty ETs fondling and stroking technicians "looked like a violation of the Morals Act."

Says Paul Hynek, "There was a scene where everyone else runs away, and that long spindly alien is interacting with my dad, playing with his pipe. It just didn't play well."

This design—which Spielberg compared to the sculptures of Alberto Giacometti—was mostly excised from the movie except a brief shot that has an eerie effect. Stanley Kubrick encountered the same problem on *2001*, where he employed multiple artists (including his sculptor wife Christiane) to come up with strange not-of-this-earth beings before junking them all in favor of a more amorphous alien intelligence. Spielberg now related to this, but ultimately felt he had to give his audience some space men with their ticket, to "confront the audience's imagination with my own imagination."

Just as he practiced makeup on his three sisters growing up, Spielberg gave himself three tries to get aliens right for *CE3K*. Months after principal photography wrapped, a more friendly/functional ET nicknamed "Puck"—incorporating characteristics based on witness accounts of a traditional grey as well as star Cary Guffey—emerged from the ship thanks to animatronics maestro Carlo Rambaldi.

Having cut his teeth on horror films for the likes of Mario Bava (*Planet of the Vampires*) and Dario Argento (*Deep Red*), the Italian had just earned a visual effects Oscar for the remake of *King Kong*... for which, controversially, 99% of the onscreen creature work was actually done by 26-year-old Rick Baker in a suit of his own making. Baker and Rambaldi reportedly argued over the suit throughout production, with the latter sometimes overriding Baker about the mask's mechanics. Instead of honoring Baker's contribution, he was backgrounded in favor of Rambaldi's 40-foot non-functional mechanical monstrosity which could neither—as promised—jump rope nor do nearly anything the script required of Kong. It basically stood immobile.

"All the publicity was about a 40-foot robot that is in six shots in the movie," Baker told Kevin Smith in 2019. "They did build the robot. It was only done at the very end of production. They wanted to keep me a secret. I understand... it sounds a lot more impressive if there's a 40-foot robot instead of some joker in a gorilla suit. The reason I got any publicity at all is... I put the suit on in the morning, put my hard contact lenses on, wore the suit all damn day. Director John Guillerman comes up and goes, 'Today *Time* magazine's coming to do an article about *King Kong* but we don't want him to know that you're playing King Kong, so if the guy talks to you don't say anything.' They made the mistake of showing him like 20-minutes of footage—all me—and they go, 'Now we're going to show you the big King Kong,' which wasn't finished. He goes, 'Well where's the finished one? I want to see the finished one that's in the movie I just saw.' They went, 'Uh...' then they said, 'Well, actually, it's just this guy.' I got some publicity."

"I heard all the horror stories from the *King Kong* group," Spielberg told *Future*. "I met with Carlo personally and saw his portfolio of all the films he's done in Rome... the man is a remarkable physical makeup artist and miniature manipulator."

Rambaldi made the move to Hollywood. He reportedly completed the diminutive Puck in three months on budget for $30,000. With insides constructed of aluminum, a head of fiberglass, and skin made of quarter-inch thick polyurethane, Puck was operated by seven people via fifteen thin cables, with the director himself using the controls to make the alien smile. It took 5 days to get the 4 shots of him in the film.

Puck is stiff, about as lifelike as Lincoln in Disneyland's Hall of Presidents, but the movement and back-lighting effectively make an otherworldly impression... enough to sustain a minute of screentime, at least. A proper student of human psychology, Spielberg understood implicitly the effectiveness of mirror neurons, i.e. if he included shots of hundreds of people looking at a half-baked puppet in awe, then most of the audience would experience a similar awe. Not to compare the two, but this is the foundational principal of how all pornography works: The people you are looking at are aroused, therefore you are aroused.

Carlo Rambaldi and Puck.

The director claims that during May 1977 pickup filming in Burbank he "kept wondering what would happen if Puck had stayed and become friends with the Neary family and moved right in," essentially an interstellar season of *Wife Swap*. This idea would eventually germinate into the kernel of *E.T. the Extra-Terrestrial*.

Due to the political divide between Zsigmond and Julia Phillips/Columbia, the Hungarian was not asked back for additional pickup shoots. Instead, an array of DPs lensed certain sequences, including a new opening in the Sonora desert by William Fraker (who later shot *1941*) and the India section by Douglas Slocombe (who later photographed the Indiana Jones trilogy). Along with John A. Alonzo and László Kovács, these men were given prominent credit to the detriment of Zsigmond. This had less to do with Spielberg, who asked Zsigmond to get inoculated for the India shoot before the hatchet came down.

Says McLean, "Julia invited me to go to India but I couldn't go. I regret not going now."

The cast of *Close Encounters* were not exempt from trouble, either. During the Alabama shooting of "Muncie" exteriors at Dillon's rural homestead, Dreyfuss set off a firestorm.

Revealed Douglas Trumbull during a TIFF masterclass in 2012, "We had problems on this set because the week we were shooting in Mobile the Ku Klux Klan was doing a March in town and Richard Dreyfuss made derogatory remarks about the Ku Klux Klan."

The KKK were given a license to parade in Mobile on July 4. Dreyfuss told *Florida Today*, "I wrote a letter to the newspaper which was published saying I thought it would have been nice to have had some blacks represented in some way on that day."

Part of this statement included Dreyfuss' claim that, "The Klan is evil. The Klan is death… the enemy of everything I believe in. The Ku Klux Klan has, under the Bill of Rights, the unobstructed freedom of assembly and speech… and so do I," speaking only for himself and not Columbia Pictures. Then a news director at WALA-TV in Mobile named Carlton Cordell said a telephone call from a male voice referred to Dreyfuss as "a dead man" for his screed against the Klan. The tape was turned over to the FBI. According to a 1977 piece for *Time*, Dreyfuss had to be "whisked away for two weeks" due to the incident.

"I was under police guard for a while," Dreyfuss added. "It wasn't just a bluff. It was a bit scary. Those people really exist and they're there."

Trumbull said members of the Klan "started driving by our set all day with guns. Very frightening. We had to have a lot of security while we were shooting this sequence."

Besides publicly roasting the film's producer, François Truffaut was reportedly having a difficult time with many of his English lines, needing to have them printed on pieces of paper and pinned to other actors. It is often said his character of scientist Claude Lacombe was inspired by Hynek's own protégé Jacques Vallée, who was part of an informal series of scientific UFO discussions nicknamed "The Invisible College."

As Vallée explained to *Conspire* in 1997, "When I met Steven Spielberg, I argued with him that the subject was even more interesting if it wasn't extraterrestrials. If it was real, physical, but not ET. He said, 'You're probably right, but that's not what the public is expecting... this is Hollywood and I want to give people something that's close to what they expect.' Which is fair."

Paul Hynek says the character was equally influenced by Claude Poher, a French astrophysicist who was introduced to the UFO world and Invisible College by the senior Hynek in 1969. In 1977, Poher founded Group for the Study of Unidentified Aerospace Phenomena (GEPAN), a French counterpart to CUFOS.

The ending of *Close Encounters*, where Roy Neary abandons his life on Earth to join the aliens onboard the mothership, was witnessed by François Truffaut but inspired by another art house auteur... Ingmar Bergman.

"*Seventh Seal* was a big influence on me when I was a kid," remembers Barwood. "When I saw that movie I realized, 'Oh, my God, these are works of art that are done by people with an idea.' It really hit me. I understood what movies were."

When Spielberg and his agent Guy McElwaine urged Barwood and Robbins to create a package of stories to be sold to Columbia, one was "a pirate adventure in which a bunch of mutineers establish their own country ruled by the emerging political ideas of the Enlightenment." Another was an untitled UFO story unrelated to *Home Free* or *Close Encounters*, but with shades of the latter as well as the rural setting of *Night Skies*. Taking their cues from *The Seventh Seal*, where a character named Jof (Nils Poppe) has a vision of Mary leading the infant Jesus, Barwood and Robbins concocted a narrative.

"Someone has a vision, but you don't see the Virgin Mary... in the modern world, you see a flying saucer," remembers Barwood. "The story took place somewhere in Tennessee where a cop gets called out to a ranch because panicked people out there are reporting a flying saucer. They're in their barn and they're doing all this crazy stuff. He's kind of a rookie cop—'You're the rookie, get out there!' 'Oh my God, this is stupid.'—and he goes out there and sees the flying saucer."

Adds Robbins of the police officer character not unlike Lonnie Zamora, "He was a small town, rural policeman who is sent to investigate a UFO that supposedly snatched a cow from a local farm. His snide disbelief vanishes as his investigation proceeds and the evidence becomes compelling and scary."

"It goes away, but he has seen it," continues Barwood. "What we were interested in exploring psychologically is that divorces him/cuts him off from humanity."

Says Robbins, "As his skepticism turns to obsession, his marriage falls apart and he's fired. He suffers from alcoholism and homelessness but in the end is rescued by the arrival of the UFO he glimpsed at the beginning. As you can see, lots of this turned up in *CE3K* a few years later."

"Everyone else is skeptical, but he knows the truth, and at the end of the story he eventually goes off in a flying saucer," adds Barwood. "He is so divorced from humanity, he goes away. We told Steve about this, and we said, 'Yeah, for *Close Encounters* just don't let him get on the saucer and go away.' Eventually we realized we're not going to get our movie made, especially after *Close Encounters*. Whether we said, 'Hey, go with God' or not Steve was going to do it. So we said, 'Hey, Steve, he gets on the flying saucer and goes away. That's great.' We forgave him. We actually kind of said, 'Tip of the hat.'"

While Barwood and Robbins did not get credit for their myriad contributions, they did receive a few lucrative points in the movie as well as a cameo playing Flight 19 pilots. As Barwood told Ray Morton, "We each had a small net percentage. I put my kids through college on it, so I'm happy." With the exception of Schrader, the other writers who worked on the film (John Hill, David Giler, Jerry Belson) all begged off credit during arbitration, reportedly at the insistence of Julia Phillips on behalf of Spielberg. Hill stated some scenes were similar to what he wrote but, "they were told to me by Steven. They were his ideas." Spielberg received sole credit for the screenplay. Giler appeared to show little ill will, based on his cameo appearance in *Poltergeist* and penning *The Money Pit* for Amblin, while Belson wrote Spielberg's next Richard Dreyfuss starrer *Always*.

Schrader did arbitrate for credit, but ultimately had very little sway since Spielberg contributed the story for Schrader's draft plus five drafts on his own afterwards. In a letter to WGA West's Marge White dated November 15, 1976, Schrader wrote:

> Steve, Michael and Julia Phillips (the producers) and I remain close friends and I don't wish to become involved in what might be an acrimonious arbitration... Although I was in constant discussion with Michal, Julia and Steve, I think they will agree that the

> material I subsequently wrote was 100% my own... Although Michael and Julia assure me that Steve rewrote the script entirely (and I have no reason to doubt them) I feel I must pro forma arbitrate because I have net profit points... I am enclosing the names of three arbiters from your list who I would prefer not be asked to decide this case.

For the curious, the "names of three arbiters" Schrader did not want were Alexander Jacobs, Terrence Malick, and Jeffrey Fiskin, the latter of whom wrote Spielberg's aborted pirate movie. In *Schrader on Schrader* he claimed, "At Steven's request I withdrew from the credit arbitration, which is something I've come to regret in later years, because I had points tied to credit. I gave up maybe a couple million dollars." Contract specifications were 2.5% of net plus $25,000 should he have received screen credit. Also right of first refusal should a sequel be produced, along with 50% of his fee upon commencement of photography on that sequel plus another 1.25 net points.

Once the final bells and whistles were put on the movie, there came the most frightening time of all: how it would be received by the public.

"Columbia Studios was very nervous about the picture and about Steven Spielberg," wrote Jerry Ziesmer in his autobiography. Ziesmer was brought in as an assistant director for the aforementioned additional scenes, including the Sonora opening. After previewing assembly footage from principal photography, newly instated production head Daniel Melnick approved $4M in reshoot money.

When the ten most senior Columbia execs gathered at the Todd-AO building to see the very first rough cut of *Close Encounters*, there were nerves aplenty. His embezzlement scandal already in full swing, David Begelman was invited by Melnick to watch the movie from the projection room. Alan Hirschfield, Joseph Fischer, and Robert Cort were among those from the studio biting their nails as Spielberg and Trumbull awaited their response after months in the editing room. Spielberg had called the VFX "spectacular," but told the *L.A. Times* he was "sweating blood, it all takes so long," with Trumbull's budget going up a quarter-million every few months. Opticals and added photography were a big reason the picture had been delayed, from Easter to Summer to Christmas.

During an early production meeting on the film, Julia Phillips boldly predicted to studio heads that *Close Encounters* would earn upwards of $100M.

This proclamation frightened Spielberg, always anxious there was a disconnect between what he thought would please the audience or make them hiss. But the studio heads reacted jubilantly, cheering, ready to seek public approval. The jubilance would not last long.

Remembers Barwood, "Some journalist snuck into the preview, and word got out in the media that this was not a success, and it scared the hell out of Columbia."

"The very first test screening was in Dallas, Texas," adds Phillips. "There was supposed to be no press, but a reporter for *New York* magazine snuck in and wrote a bad review."

Journalist William Flanagan not only snuck into the October '77 *CE3K* preview at Dallas' Medallion Theater, he detailed the shady way he went about it by scouring the line for someone who looked like him, then paying the man $25 dollars to swap drivers licenses and scram for two hours. Flanagan got past three armed guards at the door. His big takeaway? "I can understand Columbia's anxiety about *Close Encounters*. In my humble opinion, the picture will be a colossal flop."

Flanagan gave a rundown of the whole story from top to bottom, adding cracks like, "The creature in charge has a neck right out of a Modigliani print, eyes like a fawn, head like a muskmelon, skin like a prune." He stayed for a questionnaire which included reactions to the film and queries asking viewers if they had ever seen a UFO. Even though most of the audience rated the film "very good" or "excellent," the journalist jabbed, "When you give people free tickets to a movie, most of them are nice enough not to bitch."

Remembers Phillips, who had the article framed, "Flanagan writes this scathing review, and Columbia stock tanked. Millions of dollars lost from the value of the company because of this premature prediction, but that's the craziness of that time. There was so much riding on this, beyond normal. A studio was at stake, which meant a lot of people were running against it. That's Hollywood. They loved the idea it's going to be a flop. 'Steven had too much success, he deserves a flop... the Phillips' had too much success.'"

Flanagan's piece appeared in the Rupert Murdoch-owned *New York* magazine on October 31, causing Columbia stock to go from $18.375 per share to $15.50. A positive review by Frank Rich calling the movie "dazzling" raised the stock price to $16. As *The Lowell Sun* remarked on November 17, "Wall Street brokers were shaking their heads—and more than one insider wondered if Rupert Murdoch had black-balled the movie expressly to snatch up Columbia stock at a bargain."

For whatever reason, the bad actor-esque piece focused on a negative personal reaction rather than the wider response, which was evidently ecstatic.

"We had not seen it in front of an audience... the screen goes up, it opens with a crescendo and a bang, and the audience gasped and applauded," recalls Phillips. "It was such a great feeling to know they were invested. They already loved the movie before they saw anything, and the response to the film... it was loved. It had a sense of wonder. You've seen something surprising. You haven't seen it before. You're dazzled, you're moved. You're always thinking about, 'Wow, what would it be like if I were in his shoes? I wonder where they're going?' A great feeling, a great reward."

Says former Universal executive Thom Mount, "I went to an early screening at the old MGM theater of *Close Encounters*. It was not finished. Steven was there, I was there, maybe 10 other people besides me. I thought the movie was great. Afterwards Steven said, 'I'm going to drive up to the high desert near Palmdale. We shot part of this up there, and there's a huge rock outcropping, and I'm going to lie down on that rock tonight and tell them they can come and take me.' I thought, 'Well, that's an interesting take on how committed you are to this movie, to the idea that there are aliens out there that might show up if you ask them to.' I have no idea if he did that."

If true, this would have bookended Spielberg's description of driving to Pearblossom (24 minutes from Palmdale) towards the start of development on *CE3K* right after *Jaws*: "There's nothing around for miles, and if you want to watch the cosmos that's the place to do it. You feel like a grain of salt and the stars are so vast. It's almost like looking down at the sky because the sky surrounds you. It's an amazing planetarium show. I went out there, parked my car, turned the lights out, sat on the roof and looked up at the sky and said to myself, 'If something comes down here right now and lands on the road and an opening appears would I get on and take a ride?' I thought about it and looked up at the sky and got very very nervous because I realized that I wouldn't get on and take a ride. As a matter of fact, I was getting so nervous by embracing and romancing that thought that I got back in my car I drove back to Los Angeles. I was terrified."

By late '77 soft rock group The Carpenters was climbing the charts with their cover of Klaatu's "Calling Occupants of Interplanetary Craft," while Electric Light Orchestra's Out of the Blue tour built a six-ton spaceship to hover 25-feet in the air during shows. The band's production manager Andy Trueman told *Wisconsin State Journal*, "We will be giving people in Madison a close encounter." The tremendous cultural impact of *Star Wars* only whetted the public's appetite for science fiction.

In the doc *UFOs Are Here*, Spielberg claimed, "There is a rumor in *U.S. News and World Report* that Jimmy Carter might make some unsettling disclosures about the UFO phenomena sometime in December. My movie opens in December, so it's perfect timing."

Says author Paul Sammon, "The marketing campaign… the secrecy… the way drums were slowly beating in the background for *Close Encounters* was masterful. Ordinary moviegoers were aware this movie was coming and was going to be a major event. After that first trailer—a stylized, almost Lynchian POV shot going down the road with lane dividers coming at you—there was such a buzz."

Part of making Columbia's big bet palatable to the general public was using the trailer to define what a "close encounter of the third kind" even was.

In *The UFO Experience*, J. Allen Hynek popularized the term "high strangeness" for any report with "a number of separate very strange items, each of which outrages common sense." Of equal importance in the field was The Hynek Scale for classifying UFO sightings, which encompassed six different levels for measuring the veracity of any given report:

1. Nocturnal lights
2. Daylight discs
3. Radar-visual
4. Close encounters of the first kind (CE1)
5. Close encounters of the second kind (CE2)
6. Close encounters of the third kind (CE3)

On the junket circuit for 2008's *Cloverfield*, director Matt Reeves told this author how *Close Encounters*' promotional campaign influenced the "Mystery Box"-style trailer for his found footage monster movie. Said teaser featured shaky handheld footage of a party interrupted by massive explosions in Manhattan, capped by the decapitated Statue of Liberty and a mysterious roaring sound. There was no movie title in the ad. J.J. Abrams and Reeves set out to make that trailer "in the spirit" of *Close Encounters*.

"When Bryan Burk and J.J. Abrams and I were kids—I've literally known them since childhood—we made 8mm films together," said Reeves. "It's kind of an amazing thing to make a movie with your best friends. When we were kids we'd go to movies, and there was one particular teaser we all remembered for *Close Encounters*. All this weird documentary footage and this eerie narrator who sounds like the scary guy from *Frontline*. He said 'Close Encounters of the First Kind' and you're seeing these weird images of something in the sky, and he said 'Sightings.' Then 'Close Encounters of the Second Kind' and you saw footage of a footprint and they said 'Evidence.' Then 'Close Encounters of the Third Kind' and you wouldn't see anything, the music was just building and it said 'Contact' and it cut to black. We were like, 'What the hell was that? I gotta see that!' Didn't know who was in it. Before that trailer you didn't even know what 'Close Encounters' meant. That was an exciting thing... you had a sense of discovery."

Columbia's gambit worked a charm. *Close Encounters of the Third Kind* opened nationwide on December 14, 1977 into 270 theaters where it grossed \$10.1M in one week, averaging over \$37K per theater while breaking house records at NYC's Ziegfeld (\$121K in 5 days) and LA's Cinerama Dome (\$61K in 3 days) by selling out every show. Spielberg turned 31 three days later.

CHAPTER 3

...of the Fourth Kind: Making a Reluctant Sequel

"Sequels are not done for the audience or cinema or the filmmakers. It's for the distributor. The film becomes a brand."

—Francis Ford Coppola

Shortly after the tidal wave of *Jaws'* success, Steven Spielberg echoed the above statement by Coppola, telling a San Francisco Film Festival audience, "making a sequel to anything is just a cheap carny trick... like operating a slot machine knowing you're going to get three cherries every time. It reduces moviemaking as an art to just a science."

Austin Pendleton, Kevin J. Stephens, and John Francis Daley (*left to right*) in *5/25/77*.

While he toyed with the idea of a *Jaws* prequel about a young Quint aboard USS *Indianapolis*, Universal went ahead without him once his heart was set on *Close Encounters of the Third Kind.* First they hired up and coming director John D. Hancock (*Let's Scare Jessica to Death*, *Bang the Drum Slowly*) to wrangle the *Jaws* follow-up, but his vision of a mobbed-up, economically devastated, fog enshrouded Amity Island was too downbeat. Hancock was fired after a few weeks of filming, then replaced with Jeannot Szwarc, another TV movie/*Night Gallery* helmer in the Spielberg mold.

In summer 1978 *Jaws 2* earned a bit over $100M domestically and the same overseas. A carbon copy of the first movie's plot with another big shark attacking beachgoers (Murray Hamilton back as the same shitty mayor!) combined with a reluctant return by Roy Scheider made it a pale imitation. Despite the success of films like *Rocky II* and *The Godfather Part II*, the word "sequel" still carried an air of the gauche. During this sequel-glutted period audiences were barraged with lackluster product: *The French Connection II*, *Exorcist II: The Heretic*, *More American Graffiti*... all unworthy asterisks to their predecessors. Lightning in a bottle could not be manufactured on demand.

It would be harder for Spielberg to turn down a sequel to *Close Encounters*, since it was a film he originated—not from a novel or a news story—that made over $160M domestically and $300M+ globally, the biggest grosser in Columbia's history. It was equally beloved by the public, who reacted rhapsodically to its optimistic power.

"This I'll do a sequel to," he told Tom Snyder in January 1978. "This movie is designed for sequels, as opposed to *Jaws* which was a once in a lifetime event."

Close Encounters was riding a wave of interest in all things occult during the 1970s, exemplified by the popularity of pseudo-science documentary house Sunn Classic Pictures, whose theatrical "nonfiction" features covered a range of phenomena including Bigfoot, the Bermuda Triangle, monsters, near-death experiences, JFK conspiracies... and UFOs. The whole "ancient aliens" media industry was kicked off when Sunn released the German doc *Chariots of the Gods* in the US to $25M in box office and a Best Documentary Oscar nod. James L. Conway, who developed several pictures for Sunn including 1976's *In Search of Noah's Ark* ($55M gross), has a unique understanding of why these subjects were popular in both fiction and nonfiction form.

Says Conway, "It was people questioning what the norm was: 'What is real? What isn't real?' One thing would feed into another, with very few outlets back then to experience these things, few TV channels. Through a theatrical window we were able to make movies about these subjects. They were incredibly popular, because there was no other place for people to get knowledge about this... no YouTube, no Wikipedia, no social media. If you wanted to see something on the unusual side, it was a theatrical motion picture."

Another such "documentary" was 1974's TV special *UFOs: Past, Present, and Future*, wherein two major figures from Spielberg's early cinematic world collide: Rod Serling (host) and J. Allen Hynek (on-camera subject). This feature was reportedly made with the cooperation of NASA as well as the Department of Defense by ad man-turned-screenwriter Robert Emenegger and Allan Sandler, a producer previously known for *Lancelot Link: Secret Chimp*. Incidents depicted mirror *Close Encounters*, such as the November 1957 (mistakenly cited as 1967) sighting in Levelland, Texas where Pedro Saucedo and Joe Salaz claimed a brightly-lit craft hovering above their truck stalled the engine/headlights, then took off with a great deal of heat. This flap affected 10 vehicles in the area, chalked up to "ball lightning" by the Air Force. The dramatization clearly influenced the scene of Roy Neary's first encounter, down to the Ford F-250 pickup truck.

One curious aspect of *UFOs: Past, Present, and Future* is the decades-long insistence of Emenegger that in 1973 he was introduced to Paul Shartle, head of the Air Force Film Depository at Norton Air Force Base, who insisted there was footage shot from three vantage points of an alien craft landing at Holloman Air Force Base. Supposedly three extraterrestrial beings emerged from the craft and were face-to-face with Air Force personnel à la the finale of *CE3K*. During 1988's *UFO Cover-Up?: Live!*, Emenegger told host Mike Farrell, "Although the pentagon had been very cooperative all the way, at the last minute the film was confiscated, and we lost the whole finale of our show." In 1994 he confirmed, "We had to recreate the Holloman ending with drawings." However, ufologist Grant Cameron claims there are eight-seconds of the actual landing in the Golden Globe-nominated special, re-released post-*Close Encounters* as *UFOs: It Has Begun*.

Says Paul Hynek, "In the 1970s you had the *National Enquirer* offering money for cases. There were big cases like Pascagoula and Travis Walton. That's when Roswell became known; it wasn't really in the zeitgeist before that. There seemed to be something in the air in the '70s. Still a lot of stigma but talked about more than before. *Close Encounters* helped legitimize it. Here's this everyman schlub dude from Indiana who wants nothing to do with this stuff making mashed potato mountains and going up in a saucer."

The film's December bow prompted President Jimmy Carter's science advisor Dr. Frank Press to request NASA reopen investigations into UFOs as originally conducted by the Air Force under Blue Book. The space administration's Robert Frosch rejected the request, calling it "wasteful and probably unproductive," adding that NASA was ready to analyze "bona fide physical evidence from credible sources," should such evidence be found.

Close Encounters had a profound effect on many young filmmakers, none more than Illinois High Schooler Patrick Read Johnson, who—on a fateful trip to Hollywood where he saw an early rough cut of *Star Wars*—actually met Spielberg on the stages of Doug Trumbull's Future General Corporation as visual effects for *CE3K* were being shot. During a reset on the cloud tank, the most successful filmmaker in the world took Johnson (accompanied by *American Cinematographer* editor Herb Lightman) on a production tour, showing off storyboards and mothership designs. The experience is captured in Johnson's autobiographical film *5-25-77*, where the *Jaws* director is portrayed by Kevin J. Stephens, a non-actor barista at Caribou Coffee who happened to be a dead ringer for Spielberg.

As Johnson explained in 2013, "A friend of mine said, 'My brother looks just like him.' I thought, 'Sure.' She brings me this prom picture and I went, 'He

Spaced Invaders (1990).

looks so much like Steven, but I'm pretty sure Steven didn't go to prom.' It was amazing how much he looked like him. Doug Trumbull, a good friend of mine, saw the footage and goes 'Time machine. Seriously, how did... That's exactly what he looked like and acted like!'"

Spielberg would play a critical role in landing Disney as distributor of Johnson's directorial debut *Spaced Invaders*, a comedy about five mischievous aliens who cause havoc in a small rural town... almost the comedy version of *Night Skies*. It made over $15M. Johnson graduated to writing and/or directing major studio movies like *Baby's Day Out*, *Angus*, and *Dragonheart*, although *5-25-77* is his magnum opus, an entirely independent/deeply personal exercise which consumed two decades of his life. Ostensibly focused on Johnson (played by future writer/director John Francis Daley) and his *Star Wars* obsession, the Spielberg scene is a resonant part of that tapestry.

The *5-25-77* version of Spielberg says, "I used to watch planes take off from the local airport. Of course, to me they weren't airplanes, they were spaceships. Growing up on all those '50s films with flying saucers full of aliens coming down to Earth to destroy mankind... Which may explain why my first real film was a little epic called *Firelight*, which was essentially about aliens coming down in my backyard and destroying my sisters."

"Steven, I owe him a lot," said Johnson. "He got my first movie *Spaced Invaders* released, so... it's his fault. *Close Encounters* is Spielberg's most complete emotional thought. He's done more mature or technically proficient films, but he poured everything he had into it. He was compressed, did not have free reign, had people sitting on him. The studio was punishing him, not supporting him, and he had to somehow carry this thing through. When it came out, I saw that 34-times in the theater. I still see it a couple times a year."

Another filmmaker it had an impact on is Steven Soderbergh, the Oscar-winner behind *Traffic*, *Erin Brockovich*, *Magic Mike*, and the popular Ocean's Trilogy.

"*Jaws* was the movie that activated me in terms of thinking about films as something other than just entertainment," Soderbergh told this author. "That was a 'before and after' moment. The person I was when I walked in was not the person I was when I walked out. It immediately began a process of, 'What does Directed By mean and who is Steven Spielberg?' By the time *Close Encounters* rolled up two-and-a-half years later I was very primed and also living in a neighborhood identical to the one where Roy Neary lived. You could have shot that on our street. This feeling he had—and that the film conjures so well—of the stultifying nature of a certain kind of suburbia was very intense and beautifully drawn. The sheer technical virtuosity of it... His pure movie storytelling sense... His gift for transitions... It was a continuation of what he built in his first few theatrical features and *Duel*. He kept delivering on the promise he was showing with each film."

Although known for taking a more experimental approach to his movies (which he shoots and edits himself), Soderbergh has of late worked with Spielberg's blockbuster screenwriter du jour David Koepp on a trio of genre movies (*Kimi*, *Presence*, and *Black Bag*) that vacillate between artful and mainstream. Spielberg's singular visions have also had a direct impact on Soderbergh's approach to filmic language. Even the main titles for his haunted house movie *Presence* were in outlined Helvetica font à la *Poltergeist*.

"What I'm trying to accomplish and what I like to feel in a movie is a sort of discovered precision," Soderbergh says. "I prepare and think about it and know what the general approach is. I know what the rules are and what my tool kit is, but generally I don't know what the shots are until I'm on the set with the actors blocking. I like to see something in which I feel the decisions were more intuitive than they were thought out beforehand. Sometimes that's an illusion. Spielberg likes to storyboard things, but his movies never feel storyboarded. They have that energy and sensation that he saw it in front of him and got very excited and is just very very good at thinking up shots."

The '70s era of films make frequent appearances on Soderbergh's annual log of all the media (books, TV, films) he consumes during the calendar year. Those who enjoy these lists on his Soderblog have clocked *CE3K* at least once every year or two.

He explains, "*Close Encounters* is something I return to a lot to plug into those early days of being overwhelmed with excitement about movies, you know what I mean? What happens, though, is it's like a kid that eats candy and then there's a real crash after. I'm super excited while I'm watching it, then by the time the credits start this melancholy sets in because movies don't occupy the same cultural real estate they did when that movie came out. It's hard not to get pulled into a sense of, 'Wow, that's when movies mattered in a way they'll never matter again.' It isn't because we don't make good movies anymore, it's just the world has changed and the business has changed. I have to be careful when I dip into stuff from that period because the comedown can be pretty intense."

Filmmakers Andy and Barbara Muschietti of the horror hit *Mama*, DC Comics movie *The Flash*, and twin adaptations of Stephen King's *IT*, were particularly enraptured by *Close Encounters*. According to Barbara, Spielberg as a filmmaker meant "everything" to them.

"It's the first experience in a movie theater for us, where we basically imprinted on Steven Spielberg," Andy Muschietti remembers. "Our first powerful experience was *Close Encounters*. I was four, Barbie was six, and our parents would take us to the drive-in a lot. That was the first movie that blew our minds. Spielberg forever left a big dent in us because we were kids when he was doing those amazing movies filled with magic. When you're that age, you take things very, very, very deeply emotionally. We were imprinted, a whole generation of people, with *E.T.* later. For me *E.T.* was important, but not as powerful. I lean more towards the tone of *Close Encounters*. *E.T.* is a little cuter in terms of 'everything will be fine.' *Close Encounters* is about a family in total fracture. By the end of the movie they don't even come together. Dreyfuss goes on his own crazy adventure into space. He doesn't see his family again, which is weird. It's a dark idea, but it was the '70s."

It is also important to keep in mind the political impact of a movie like *Close Encounters*, whose plot involving government cover-ups to deceive the public (a remnant of the "UFOs and Watergate" version) became another nail in the coffin of institutional trust during this turbulent era. In his 1981 nonfiction treatise on all things fantastical titled *Danse Macabre*, *IT* author Stephen King made the following observation:

"The children of World War II produced *The Thing*; twenty-six years later a child of Vietnam and the self-proclaimed Love Generation, Steven Spielberg, gives us a fitting balance weight to *The Thing* in a film called *Close Encounters of the Third Kind*. In 1951, the soldier standing sentry duty empties an automatic into the alien when he hears it coming; in 1977, the old guy holds up a sign reading STOP AND BE FRIENDLY. Somewhere between the two, John Foster Dulles evolved into Henry Kissinger, and the pugnacious politics of confrontation became détente... Events determine point of view and point of view determines politics, and *CE3K* seems to me every bit as preordained as *The Thing*."

Spielberg's working title for both *Close Encounters* and *Night Skies* was *Watch the Skies*, a line taken from the very end of Howard Hawks' *The Thing*. In 2025, King revealed via social media his 10 favorite movies of all time, which included *CE3K*.

"They're so sweet and innocent, they're just being mischievous. Experimenting. They're certainly not hostile," Melinda Dillon told *Starlog* #12 of

CE3K's aliens. "Dr. Hynek went to a UFO convention where a story was told about two farmers who saw little people get out of a spaceship. They shot at them. The bullets dematerialized before they could hurt them but... my god, we shoot at things. We're afraid of the unknown. We're even afraid of the known... Maybe Steven's young enough to think differently. He's part of another generation that doesn't find hostility necessary."

Michael Phillips claims it was he who steered the story towards a benign meeting of the minds at the end, but it was Spielberg who brought the razzle dazzle that set audiences aflutter. Or, as the director put it to Roger Ebert, "A total visual orgasm. An orgy."

"We were debating a lot about what the movie would be, and one of the points was how to end it," Phillips said. "My favorite movie was *The Day the Earth Stood Still.* If these guys are smart enough to get here, they're not going to come to eat us or kill us. I really felt they should be benevolent, but Steven was a little concerned the meeting of these two species wasn't enough because it's not a conventional film. You don't have traditional conflict. The reason he gave us this cornucopia of visuals was he didn't quite trust that the meeting would satisfy. I'm so glad he did, because every time I watch the last 40 minutes of the film I sit back and smile. It's a great gift. Ray Bradbury said the movie is about 'galactic brotherhood.' I can't think of a comparable feeling in another movie where you get the joy of this connection and its possibilities."

The reverential tone of the finale incited a religious fervor in many, with the director telling *Cosmo*, "A lot of people claim it represented the Second Coming. I still receive letters from Sunday School teachers saying they use the movie to show kids what angels of the 1980s look like. Well, I never talk about my intention in making a movie, but that ain't it. My creatures were based largely on what people reported seeing around the world: spindly arms, bulbous head, large eyes, little or no mouth."

There were naysayers too. On the 1978 set of his breakthrough *Halloween*, a 30-year-old John Carpenter chastised *Close Encounters.*

"I didn't care for it," Carpenter remarked. "It was pretentious and I think it got out of control. I think he lost control of it. There were parts of it that were not well done. I just didn't care for it as much. Didn't have a single purpose in it, it went off in several directions. One of the things I admire about a great work is that—even if it's flawed—the director is completely in control of it and he directs the film or tells the story with a great deal of authority. I felt that wasn't there in *Close Encounters.*"

Noted sci-fi novelist Ursula K. Le Guin (*The Left Hand of Darkness*) went ham on both Spielberg and Lucas' 1977 films in her essay "Close Encounters, Star Wars, and the Tertium Quid," that Latin phrase referring to an undefined "third thing" which derives from two other things. In the essay she takes *CE3K* to task for using chaos and noise to jar emotion from the audience in place of genuine storytelling, then makes the case it is not science fiction but some other less coherent thing. Spielberg did not prefer the sci-fi label either, classifying *CE3K* as "science speculation."

Le Guin writes that *Close Encounters* is "essentially an occultist movie... definitely on the side of the angels, but the arrival of benevolent aliens in saucers is a theme science fiction hasn't dealt with, except facetiously, for at least a generation. Fiction writers got out long ago, leaving the field to believers, faddists, amateur photographers, psychologists, and the Air Force. Saucerism has a lot to do with religion, as Jung pointed out, but nothing at all to do with either science or science fiction. Indeed, the movie seemed almost entirely irrational... How does the U.S. government know when to expect the aliens? Why do they have a troop of—well, exchange students, I guess—all dressed up in red pantsuits (one woman, or was it two, in the whole troop) ready to go aboard the saucer? How do they know they'll be wanted? What the dickens is François Truffaut doing there? And if he's there, amidst all the security officers and dead sheep, why aren't there any Mexicans or Chinese or Russians or Canadians or Peruvians or Samoans or Swahili or Thai? Why does the United States get to hog the cosmic show? I was brought up to believe that science fiction, whatever its shortcomings in the way of character, catharsis, and grammar, was supposed to try to be intellectually coherent: to have an idea and to follow it through."

The work of Swiss psychologist Carl Jung that Le Guin refers to is his 1959 book *Flying Saucers: A Modern Myth of Things Seen in the Skies*. In his intro, Jung's definition of the nature of UFOs, if taken out of context, could almost be levied as a critical review of the film Spielberg would make over two decades later: "Something is seen, but one doesn't know what. It is difficult, if not impossible, to form any correct idea of these objects, because they behave not like bodies but like weightless thoughts."

A fan of both Le Guin and Spielberg, contemporary author/journalist Ryan Britt says, "Le Guin is very savage. She feels that this is the end of culture. If you're a science fiction writer in the 1970s and Spielberg and Lucas ride in, you're like, 'It's over. People will never read serious science fiction again, because this is what its become.' I'm a big science fiction person, it defines who I am. I think that Spielberg is a strange populist. He'll gravitate towards something—a novel like *Jaws*, or a great novella from Philip K. Dick, or a popular blockbuster novel by Ernest Cline—and he'll be like, 'I want to do that too.' I say this with all love, but sometimes I feel like Spielberg doesn't have any taste of his own... yet it feels as though that's also his greatest strength, right? He doesn't hate anything. His complete lack of cynicism makes him somewhat irritating... 'Wait, you like everything?' But that's probably what makes him such a great filmmaker."

"When Spielberg first emerges, he's so much the commercial director," says movie journalist Hoai-Tran Bui. "Le Guin was criticizing blockbuster directors like Spielberg for appealing to the lowest common denominator of audiences. That's not something she wants to do as a writer. She wants to pull them up. She wants to challenge them. A lot of cinephiles these days would bristle at that because he's Papa Spielberg, this prestigious director, but at that time in the '70s he was kind of a sellout."

Important Cinema Club host Justin Decloux takes the criticism to its apex, stating that not only is the movie flawed but the aliens themselves are demonstratively not benign, contrary to the pulsing light, swelling music, and smiles: "I have a controversial opinion about *Close Encounters*... I can't connect with it, because the whole movie is people that have mind-implanted things they

can't control. 'Follow your mind-implanted dreams.' It would make a difference if Neary's obsession was genuinely rooted in something that grew organically and they can't control it, but the movie's text is it was not their choice."

CE3K's idea of an implanted vision came during early *Kingdom Come*-era development from Brian De Palma, who suggested it as a plot solve for how government agents would know where to meet the aliens, before the everyman aspect was grafted on by Spielberg. Decloux's alternate slant on the film calls into question Neary's decision to leave his family behind when he gets on the ship as possibly being the result of alien brainwashing.

"There's at least some degree of mind control and wholesale abductions," adds Paul Hynek. "The people that come back are in World War II fighter clothes, so little time has elapsed for them. Not showing them being abducted, only befuddled but nonetheless no worse for the wear, takes the sharp edge off the fact they were kidnapped."

The creatures kidnapped quite a few people unwillingly and then returned them, in some cases decades after the fact as with those Flight 19 pilots. What of their families left in distress and grief all those years? As Le Guin would likely point out, these loop-holes represent storytelling as a shell game, or three-card monte of the heartstrings.

For Hal Barwood, whose alternate UFO script was the source of the "man leaves on the ship" idea, Spielberg is often guilty of making story decisions more out of enthusiasm than rational thought, using 2005's *War of the Worlds* as an example: "That whole story felt to me like a brainstorming session. 'Oh no, the aliens don't arrive in ships, they've been here underground for 10,000 years!' It's this insane idea that probably caught on because of the enthusiasm of the moment, but it was completely wrong."

Critic Jourdain Searles has a more positive spin: "I love *Close Encounters* specifically because it doesn't try to make you feel good about what's happening. This obsession has completely driven this dad crazy and it's fractured this whole family... and I love it."

Spielberg later regretted having Dreyfuss' character abandon his family at the end of *CE3K*... even though it is ambiguous if he's leaving forever or simply going on a joy ride.

He told *Cinema Confidential*'s Thomas Chau in 2005, "*Close Encounters*, because I wrote the script, was about a man whose insatiable curiosity and a developing obsession and a kind of psychic implantation drew him away from his family and with only looking back once, walked onto the mothership. That was before I had kids... I wrote that blithely. Today, I would never have the guy leaving his family and going on the mothership. I would have the guy doing everything he could to protect his children, so in a sense, *War of the Worlds* does reflect my own maturity, now having seven children."

"That's a maturity thing... he was a guy in his 20s, no kids, with a main character with a dream and he wants the character to pursue it," the film's producer Michael Phillips (who did have a child at the time of filming) told this author. "I didn't deal with it, actually. There was a little bit of concern, but not enough to stop the creative direction. It's a choice that Roy Neary makes, that he has to make. He's compelled. The feeling at the end of the movie is that he's supposed to be doing what he did. He's making the right choice for himself. He was specially chosen."

"I thought it was really good, the proper fate for Roy Neary," concludes Barwood. "It's interesting, though... There's an idea in *Close Encounters* that certainly runs through Carl Sagan's attitudes which is that aliens are benign. They will be the better angels of our nature. They will inform us and bring us out of our war-like craziness and we'll eventually become civilized, won't blow ourselves up and so on. This is Cold War fears taking shape, but the truth is if somebody came across the light years to get here, you're not coming just to say hi, right? That's not what would be going on."

None of these harsh takes on *CE3K* were taken seriously at the time. As former Universal exec Sean Daniel states, "For people in the industry, *Close Encounters* was the most compelling science fiction movie anyone had ever seen. Others may take issue with that, but when you saw it, you didn't forget it. You couldn't. You wanted to immediately see it again. It touched something higher than just a science fiction movie."

"This great great great film, *Close Encounters*... this film still holds up," said Spike Lee on Instagram in 2025. "I showed this film to my class. I'm a tenured graduate film professor at NYU. We showed them the film, the lights come on, and Steve Spielberg and I appeared in front of the class! Look at this film. You might have seen it a long time ago, but if you haven't seen it, watch it. Steven, once again, you were light years ahead of everybody else! And God bless humankind, 'cause we don't know what this motherfucker is up there."

By January of 1978 Spielberg was already holding story conferences with George Lucas and screenwriter Lawrence Kasdan for *Raiders of the Lost Ark*. On April 7, 1978 it was announced that the director had purchased cargo space aboard one of the first 16 flights of NASA's then-new shuttle program. NASA referred to these $3000-to-$10,000-a-piece deals as a "Getaway Special," cargo space meant to hold non-explosive packages weighing less than 60 pounds that are "related to a scientific or technological objective."

It has become part of lore that Spielberg bought the space for a film camera to shoot the Earth from orbit for the opening scenes of *Night Skies*. However, no such shot is in the script. Michael Phillips has a different explanation for this mysterious space purchase...

"I gave it to him as a gift of, whatever it was, six cubic feet of cargo space on the NASA mission," reveals Phillips. "There was an offer by NASA to sell cargo space on one of its missions. It was General Electric and Ford, all these big companies, plus my purchase. I may have bought some for myself, but I bought it for him as a gag gift. We had 3 years to provide NASA with the specifics for our planned usage. He never figured out what to do with that space, nor did I, so it expired. The mission went up and paid for, but not used. I never expected to be awarded space because this was not intended for individuals. It was for large corporations who had serious purpose to send experiments up and gather information. I got a lot of communications from NASA, 'What experiments exactly do you want to do?' I put them off as best I could. He did say, 'We should send up Julia!'"

After a $61,000 embezzlement scandal, Spielberg's Columbia ally David Begelman was ousted as president of the motion picture and TV divisions in February 1978, replaced by producer Daniel Melnick (*Straw Dogs*), who in turn promoted 48-year-old Universal Television head Frank Price to president of production in June. Price's second-in-command was John Veitch, who had been at the studio for 15 years. Because Hollywood is a forgive and forget town, by late 1979 Begelman would be heading MGM.

"A certain amount of musical chairs has taken place," Price told the AP in 1980, after replacing acting president Melnick six months into his tenure, as planned.

Melnick had specifically chosen Price for his rep as a levelheaded exec who could deal with volatile situations diplomatically, plus strong intuition for material. As for their new slate of 65 movies in development within the walls of The Burbank Studios, Veitch said, "We have a lot of young filmmakers and we want this to be their home... we're interested in who's going to inherit the business."

Considering what an enormous success *Close Encounters* had been, helping to make 1978 a record fiscal year for Columbia with $68M net income, no one seemed more poised to inherit the business than Spielberg. At a west coast press conference for *CE3K* in late '77, he teased a sequel, then at an AFI Q&A in 1978 he told students, "The things I didn't do in *Close Encounters* I'll do in the sequel." By October of '78, he had lined up a full dance card, with *After School*, *1941*, and *Raiders of the Lost Ark* as his next directing commitments.

"I expect to produce several films over the next few years for other directors, some of whom I'm helping to get started," he told *Penthouse* in 1978. "I am also being more courageous in finding new ideas for films. I am losing the fear of failure... In a few years, perhaps I'll change my whole philosophy, be anxious to do a personal movie and not give a shit about what the majority thinks of it."

As for *CE4K* (working title), according to *Starlog* he was "definitely committed to writing and producing it, but whether his schedule will permit him to direct it as well is still an open question."

Sometime in the midst of this he became reluctant to deliver a proper *Close Encounters Part II*, still one among those 65 projects on the board at Columbia. Instead, he proposed a smaller-scale film based on the Kelly-Hopkinsville incident (tentatively titled *Watch the Skies*) that would confirm not all encounters were of the friendly variety. This one would be more "ahhh!" than awe, could be delivered on a smaller budget with one central location and, more importantly, no big payouts to returning stars... or producers.

Plans were clearly underway for *Watch the Skies* by December of 1978, since Richard Dreyfuss confirmed to *Rolling Stone*, "Roy Nearly is not in the sequel. I guess Spielberg's taken it out of my hands... I would have gotten on board." He did admit that playing Roy Neary was a challenge, adding, "I'd like to try the character again."

Ever cost-conscious, Spielberg later put the final nail in before *E.T.*'s release in June 1982: "I've pretty much decided not to pursue or continue *Close Encounters*. It would be sacrilegious. I also don't want to pay Richard Dreyfuss $3 million."

As political support for her *Close Encounters* Best Picture nod, Spielberg escorted Julia Phillips to the Academy Awards in April of '78. His girlfriend Amy Irving had been unable to attend the ceremony, where Spielberg was nominated for Best Director, so when cameras panned to him he romantically mouthed "I love you, Amy." He lost the award to Woody Allen for *Annie Hall*. Vilmos Zsigmond won Best Cinematography for his boundary-breaking work, handed the award by actors who previously graced his camera, Goldie Hawn (*Sugarland Express*) and Jon Voight (*Deliverance*). During a short acceptance speech, he thanked neither Phillips nor Spielberg.

Frank Price speculated to this author, "I don't think Spielberg liked working with Julia Phillips, and that was part of the reason he didn't want to do a sequel to *Close Encounters*, because her and Michael Phillips were tied to the property."

Michael Phillips disagrees, stating, "No. Julia might financially have participated, but that's not true. Julia was already fired and out of the picture."

In April '79, Veitch claimed (via Marilyn Beck) a *Close Encounters* sequel was gearing for production by May 1980, with Spielberg in the producer's chair. The Phillips' were totally out of the loop, with Michael stating, "Julia and I haven't been told a word about any sequel. We are, frankly, absolutely in the dark about the entire project. All I know is that Columbia is under contractual obligation to have us produce any follow-up to the film."

"I think *E.T.* is the sequel, his way of continuing the untold story" Phillips told this author. "But no, he never wanted to do for Columbia another version of *Close Encounters*."

Spielberg was hesitant about a direct *Close Encounters* sequel, but also paranoid over misappropriation of footage. This was piqued in April 1978 by the 9th episode of CBS' *The Incredible Hulk* Season 1 titled "Never Give a Trucker an Even Break," where approximately 218 cuts from Spielberg's 1971 *Duel* were integrated into a new plot with inserts of Bill Bixby in the same car from the ABC TV movie.

"This was something we did all the time at Universal," admits *Incredible Hulk* producer Kenneth Johnson. "*Duel* had been on three or four years before—I remember being really impressed with it—and thought, 'Maybe we can use some footage from that?' I had done it before with *Sometimes a Great Notion* and *Airport '77*, where we grabbed a lot of footage or outtakes from the film to enhance production values of our one-hour series. I looked at *Duel* and it wasn't going to cost us anything. We designed the show to incorporate that."

Johnson says he did not ask for Spielberg's blessing, but it was less a legal matter (both *Duel* and *Hulk* were Universal properties) as a diminishing of the 1971 film. Spielberg told *The New York Times* three weeks after the show aired that he had rewritten his studio contracts so "no one can cannibalize my films and regurgitate them into some other show. I'd hate to see the mothership from *Close Encounters* land on *Laverne and Shirley*."

Johnson got beef from *Duel*'s original producer, saying, "I never heard from Steven about it personally, but George Eckstein got really infuriated."

Spielberg had already been secretive about *Close Encounters* before release to prevent a rash of rip-offs and TV movies: "I didn't want to see *Close Encounters* on ABC, CBS, or NBC before it opened in theaters." That instinct proved correct, with a flurry of UFO-related content by 1978, including the Season 3 opener of Alan Lansburg's *In Search of...* titled "UFO Captives," Jack Webb's Blue Book-inspired series *Project U.F.O.*, and the TV sitcom *Mork & Mindy* parodied what a friendly space visitor would be (spoiler: Robin Williams). There were low-budget UFO movies like *Laserblast* or *The Visitor*, even Disney's *The Cat from Outer Space*. Sunn Classic's James L. Conway got in on the action with fiction film *Hangar 18*, about the government cover-up of a UFO sighting by NASA astronauts.

Says Conway, "Once Hollywood realized how popular these subjects were, they were suddenly everywhere. There were movies of the week, there were episodes, there were some television series."

By 1980 UFO projects percolated at the studio level including Columbia's *Midnight Encounters*, a bizarre-sounding parody of both *Close Encounters* and *Midnight Express* to be directed by Sidney Poitier. It would have followed an alien who lands in Turkey. At Universal was an adaptation of author Raymond Fowler's *The Andreasson Affair*, a nonfiction book (introed by Hynek) about Betty Andreasson's claim of being visited by aliens who abducted and probed her before introducing a messianic entity called Quazgaa. Lewis John Carlino (*The Great Santini*) would write and direct. Neither film was made.

After $120M in worldwide rentals, the last bits of *CE3K* business were done. It was time for the studio to allow Spielberg "the luxury of retouching the painting." This new "Special Edition" of *Close Encounters* was announced to the public in late '78. Columbia insisted the ending be extended to show what the interior of the mothership looked like once Neary stepped aboard. That element was needed to justify the extra $1.5M in expenses for new scenes and editing, with at least a quarter of that going towards more VFX magic.

"It gives the re-release a little marketing hook," Columbia's marketing VP Bob Cort told *NY Times*. "'Come see what you couldn't see before.'"

In that same article Doug Trumbull explained the new ending would help audiences "learn more about the inside and outside of the saucers" and also "excite people's curiosity as to a possible sequel."

Says model maker Mitch Suskin, "I worked with Greg Jein on all the stuff with the interior of the mothership. I did the wall of ETs. Also a lot of weird things like a little insert where Tinker Bell—the little red spaceship—comes down the highway and goes around the billboard. For the billboard I bought a Big Mac and shot it at my desk."

"I worked with Mitch on that," says effects generalist Robert Short. "We were down in Marina Del Rey in the Doug Trumbull facility. Greg was the genius behind all this. I was helping Greg in a general capacity as well as a model builder. I helped find and refurbish the freighter for the *Cotopaxi*. I did new masks for the alien kids, as well as miniatures of the heads of the aliens in VacuForm to do force perspective stuff going on in the background of shots. There's a sequence where a huge shadow comes across the landscape as Neary is driving his truck. Myself and Mike Fink built a 20x20-foot miniature. The shadow itself is a circular piece of corrugated plastic on monofilament runners. We built a tiny truck with self-contained headlights that would illuminate the highway. The highway was made out of neoprene wetsuit material, the truck held in place by a motion control system to drive down the street at exactly the pace we wanted. There was a slice down the neoprene allowing the arm underneath the truck to travel through it so it would open and then seal behind the truck. Did that without opticals."

Cartoonist-turned-concept illustrator Ron Cobb fell into Spielberg's orbit by designing new scenes for the Special Edition: the foreground miniature shot of the real-life lost vessel S.S. Cotopaxi mysteriously dropped into the Gobi Desert, as well as the look of the mothership interior with Richard Dreyfuss inside.

"I met Ron Cobb in Marina Del Rey when he came down to show us the drawings," says Suskin. "He and I and [Cobb's wife] Robin hit it off. I gave them a ride in my old beat-up car and we became friends."

The Art of Ron Cobb author Jacob Johnston says of The Cobbs' gregariousness, "Ron and his wife had this house with a loft above. When she was first starting out, Kathleen Kennedy lived in this loft. It was wild the friends the Cobbs had: Ray Bradbury, Michael Crichton, Douglas Adams. Massive dinner parties where they'd invite these people over and have philosophical debates over spaghetti, pontificating about space."

"His enthusiasm and his vision... he was a lot of fun," Suskin says of Cobb. "He had the drawings for *Close Encounters* all figured out, what the interior of the mothership and these mechanical things did. Greg had other things going, so I wound up being more of a lead on that."

This was another evolution in Cobb's cinematic exploration of extraterrestrials after designing several cantina creatures for *Star Wars* and his extensive work on *Alien*. Incidentally, the large obelisk inside the mothership that resembles the universe's most elaborate chandelier was later flipped/converted into the iconic police station in *Blade Runner*, a building which graces much of the promo art and posters for that 1982 film.

"Ron Cobb designed the interiors that lift up above Roy Neary," Suskin reveals. "He didn't really give us a lot of details about what the top was. I got some plasticine and sculpted a little piece of it. The mold was laying around the shop when they came to do *Blade Runner*. They said, 'Hey, can we use this?' I go, 'I guess.' It was gonna get thrown away. I never expected to see it on the poster!"

Spielberg never wanted to show what Neary finds inside that ship because anything after he walks onboard is incidental. It is merely a metaphor for the great reward awaiting anyone willing to sacrifice everything in pursuit of a dream. Columbia Pictures did not run on wishes on a star, though.

"I compromised and had Richard Dreyfuss walking inside the mothership, which I never should have done because that should have always been kept a mystery," Spielberg said in the 1997 documentary *The Making of Close Encounters of the Third Kind*.

"A very bad idea," says Michael Phillips. "Everybody's saying, 'Gee, I would like to know what the interior of the ship looked like.' He shot it, and they looked to me like The Muppets. Then he realized people did not like seeing the inside."

Neither Phillips was involved to dissuade Columbia from forcing the director's hand on this blunder, which robs the movie of mystique by making the ethereal more concrete.

"Steven and Julia were over," remembers Phillips. "That was a broken relationship during post-production, so he didn't want to have anything to do with her. I had an ongoing good relationship with him through the editing and mix, but somehow I felt he wanted this to be his baby. He didn't need or want to get involved with debating what to do. He feels something is missing and he could just do it because the studio is going along with him. That's the nature of how he worked at the time."

It is quite possible that—beyond Julia's drug abuse—Spielberg watching his producers drift apart and divorce in the middle of his film was an unpleasant rehash of his own parents' split. There's no argument Arnold and Leah Spielberg's divorce is central to many of his films, including *CE3K*, so the broken union of the Phillips' may have been a business deal breaker as well. The filmmaker has long gravitated towards devoted husband-wife pairs to be the stewards of his moviemaking empire, with Kathleen Kennedy and Frank Marshall during the Amblin era, then Laurie MacDonald and Walter Parkes during the DreamWorks Pictures period. According to Nicole LaPorte's book *The Men Who Would Be King*, Kennedy/Marshall were often referred to at Amblin as the "parents."

"Steven basically casting his mom and dad every single time... that's not insane," Ashley Miller, a screenwriter who worked under Parkes at DreamWorks, says of the parental analysis. "That is not insane because Walter and Laurie fit that bill. She's the one who takes the edge off of him and grounds a lot of things. That's fascinating to me."

Shortly after cutting ties with the Phillipses, Spielberg took on arguably the most important creative and business partner in his career: Kathleen Kennedy. She was born in 1953 (alongside twin Connie) to lawyer Donald R. Kennedy and local California theater actress Dione Marie "Dede" Dousseau (stage name Dede Kennedy). Donald (later a judge) enjoyed taking 8mm movies of his family, and he wound up being the cameraman on Kathy's first amateur high school film, a Vietnam-themed story for which she borrowed a neighbor's baby. During WWII Donald was a radioman who received the distress call from the ill-fated USS *Indianapolis*, as referenced in *Jaws*.

According to an interview in *Elle*, Kennedy "didn't actually see a lot of movies" growing up in Redding, California, although she admitted catching David Lean's *Doctor Zhivago* 25 times at the Skyview drive-in. In college her tastes veered serious (Truffaut, Antonioni, Fellini, Bergman, Coppola, etc.) while she gravitated towards a focus on "the image" via black-and-white still photography. According to a 1982 *NY Times*, Kennedy had initially aspired to be a ski instructor, but in order to have "a career to fall back on" she studied nursing... until her first cadaver drove her towards public television.

Her classmate Gary David Goldberg (*Family Ties*, *Spin City*) wrote in his autobiography: "Even back in college, we all knew there was going to be no stopping Kathy."

After graduating from San Diego State with a communications degree, she spent four years working at local TV station KCST where she covered sports, operated floor cameras, and produced the call-in show *You're On*. Then a 1977 showing of *Close Encounters* wound up being a bellwether for Kennedy. She went to Hollywood, where her college roommate Mary Ellen Trainor (later an actress and Robert Zemeckis' wife) helped get her a gig as an assistant to John Milius during the production of *1941*, mainly as a PA/gofer.

"I got the job," Kennedy told *American Cinematographer* in 2025. "The company was A-Team, and it was in an L-shaped building on Hollywood Way. One part of the L was Milius, and at the other end of it were Steven Spielberg, Bob Zemeckis, and Bob Gale, who had just written *1941* for Steven to direct. John was producing. I was in the middle of this L, working with John and occasionally for Steven when he needed it. Eventually, Steven asked me to come work for him as his assistant, and I said yes."

She made it her mission to be part of "everything Steven was doing. I was always enthusiastic. I wanted to know everything. If Steven took a meeting, I went into the meeting, I didn't wait to be asked... the worst that could happen is I'd be thrown out."

According to Kennedy in the 2002 book *E.T. the Extra-Terrestrial: From Concept to Classic,* when she was first poached by Spielberg "one of the things we discussed was the research he had done with a scientist and astronomer named J. Allen Hynek during the making of *Close Encounters*. Steven asked me to investigate a particular case."

Spielberg elaborated in 1996 about the Kelly-Hopkinsville incident of 1955, stating it was when "a farm family was terrorized one evening by gremlin-like extraterrestrials."

Says Aaron Sagers, "The story goes that because of his consulting on *Close Encounters*, Spielberg had a lot of sincere respect for Hynek. In their conversations, Hynek did bring up the Kelly-Hopkinsville case, which happened over 70-years ago. It was these adults and kids telling a story about gremlin-like creatures later called 'little green men' that were terrorizing their farmhouse. Two of the guys go outside and start trying to shoot at these things. They feel like they have enough safe cover to usher everybody into their vehicle and drive down to the police station and report it. The police try to investigate and they don't find anything, just some bullet holes."

"This farm family basically huddled together for survival, and then once the little grays went away, they made a mad dash to the sheriff's office and brought the sheriff back to the house," Spielberg told *EW* in 2011. "The sheriff looked around, didn't see any physical evidence, and left. After the sheriff left, they all came back and started to harass the family again. It's a story that's well-known in the world of ufology, and we based our script on that story, and Rick Baker actually started developing some of the grays."

Adds Sagers, "Hynek said, 'You have to look at cases with a skeptical mindset.' For cases where they didn't have an explanation... that interests me more. When an operation like Blue Book, setting out to debunk and discredit, couldn't find something solid enough to use to debunk, that makes me perk up. With Kelly-Hopkinsville, Spielberg learned about it through Hynek's work. If Spielberg and Hynek were having a chat and Hynek brings up Kelly-Hopkinsville, in my mind that means Hynek may have believed in what took place. Why bring it up? Unless he was joking... 'Yeah, man, those local yokels...' I think he was bringing it up to say, 'There's some weird shit out there.'"

The cost-conscious $10M budget for *Watch the Skies* was presented during a time of austerity at the studio after their close encounters with bankruptcy on *CE3K* and *1941*.

"I don't think we'll be doing $30M-$40M movies," Veitch said in March 1980. "Ancillary rights (sales to networks, cable TV) help bring down the risks, but we're still very concerned about soaring costs, and when you get involved in films with special effects, it becomes impossible to predict ultimate spending."

To his credit, Price never thought *Watch the Skies* would materialize as initially presented. It was anathema to the positive spin on extra-terrestrials *CE3K* just popularized, as if Alan J. Pakula turned around after *All the President's Men* and made a positive biopic of Richard Nixon. It was reverting to *Invasion of the Saucer Men* clichés.

"There had to be some unique twist that made it worth going to that well again, or else you don't do it," Price stated bluntly. "I had, basically, a one-page summary of it. I never saw the script. Steven was working on it. I was not having any contact with him. *Night Skies* was there, just way down on my priorities. It was something that would come up, but I probably was working harder on *Out of Africa* or *Ghostbusters*. I had things that were uppermost. That didn't rise until the outline on *E.T.* came in... then it got interesting."

Columbia head Frank Price (*right*) and Richard Pryor (*left*).

CHAPTER 4

UFO Straw Dogs: The Kelly-Hopkinsville Incident

"There are so many close encounter stories left on Earth."

—**Steven Spielberg**, *Starburst*, December 1978

"Many people have had these experiences," says *Night Skies* screenwriter John Sayles of human/UFO encounters. "That they believe it and it's part of our culture to me is fascinating. What that does to you, if you've seen something that you think, 'Oh, my God, there's a whole 'nother thing going on that we're not dealing with but seems to keep its distance and not interfere.' That stuff is out there."

J. Allen Hynek's definition of "close encounters of the third kind"—involving an "entity" either present or piloting said UFO (i.e. "contact")—are considered the most tangible on his scale. Counter to this, "light in the night sky" reports are actually the least credible since they can be—and often are—something mundane/explainable such as landing lights, a meteor, or even advertising. It's interesting that *Night Skies* became the title for Spielberg's follow-up to *Close Encounters* since the term denotes an inherent lack of credibility... the opposite of a close encounter of the third kind.

During Hynek's years with Project Blue Book, any report in the nocturnal lights category had to have at least two or more observers (the average was 3.5) before seriously being considered by investigators. For 1955's infamous Kelly–Hopkinsville incident, nearly a dozen people were eyewitnesses to not only nocturnal activity, but an actual encounter with entities whose intentions did not seem benign at all.

Geraldine Sutton Stith was born in 1961, but it was not until a Sunday afternoon in 1969 that she first became aware of her family's legacy. Eight-year-old Geraldine answered the door to find a man and woman who wanted to speak to her father about "the green men." Already obsessed with horror and sci-fi, little Geraldine lit up, so Elmer "Lucky" Sutton sat his child down and told her what happened on Sunday, August 21, 1955.

Elmer's mother/Geraldine's grandmother Glennie Brasher Lankford (née Sutton) owned a small farm off Old Madisonville Road in the rural Kentucky hamlet called Kelly, roughly 8-miles outside of a town called Hopkinsville (or "Hoptown") off US-41 on the western side of the state. The three-acre farm grew tobacco as well as vegetables for the family's personal use, along with pigs used as livestock, one dog, and several cats. 500 feet behind the house, in a field owned by Gaither McGehee, was a 40-foot-deep gully. This area was the likely landing spot for a "circular object 40 to 50 feet in diameter."

On the August night in question, family matriarch "Miss Glennie" had, including herself, 11 people (eight adults) inside her home: her grown sons Elmer (age 24) and John Charley "J.C." Sutton (age 21), their wives Vera (age 29) and Alene (age 27), Alene's brother O.P. Baker (age 30), friends Billy Ray (age 21) and June Taylor (age 18), as well as Glennie's three young children from her second husband named Lonnie (12), Charlton (10), and Mary (7). Elmer, Vera, Billy Ray, and June were all traveling carnival workers stationed in Evansville at that time, paying Glennie a visit.

According to Stith, "They get there on a Friday, and here comes Sunday evening when all this occurs. My grandmother went to church, had gotten back. They had eaten supper. Everything was quiet like it should be in the little community of Kelly, with a population of around 100 back then, sparse little farms. They were playing cards, and Billy Ray decided to go out to the well to get water. They didn't have plumbing. He's out there and hears something. Looks toward the sky and, lo and behold, going across the sky was something silver with the colors of the rainbow flowing behind it. It was about 40-feet in the air from him. It goes by, stops, comes down in the gully behind the house."

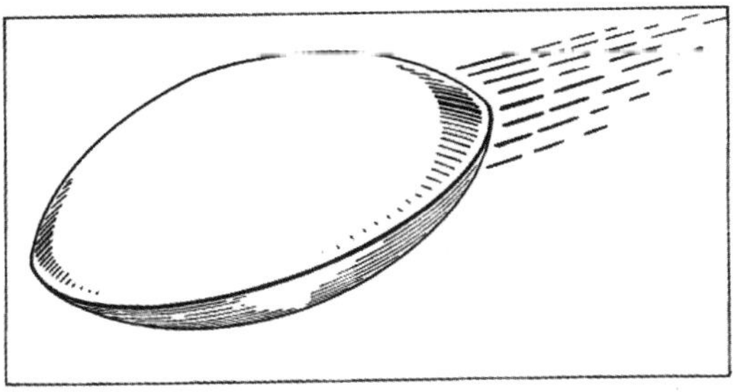

Figure 14. THE "SPACESHIP" AS DRAWN BY LEDWITH FROM TAYLOR'S DESCRIPTION

Rainbow trails are not unheard of in UFO reports, as Kentucky's chief investigator for MUFON Kevin Otte confirms: "I've read about cases where they have trails of different colors behind them, so I can't say that it's atypical. Some have been reported with them, some have been reported without. It's within the realm of possibility."

Recounts *Monsters Among Us* podcaster Derek Hayes of the incident which began around 7pm, "Billy Ray ran into the house and told everybody about this UFO/flying saucer that crashed. He'd mentioned the trail coming off of this craft was rainbow color or iridescent, all sorts of different colors mixed into it. Everybody was playing cards, then all of the sudden... 'I just saw a flying saucer crash into the woods.' This family were pranksters, so everybody assumed he was telling some joke. It took time to get them convinced something actually was going on out there."

Continues Stith, "My grandmother tells him, 'Maybe it was just a shooting star?' He was telling her, 'No, Miss Glennie, I know what a shooting star looks like.' 'Well, maybe it was a meteor shower?' We were having August meteor showers that we still have today. 'No, Miss Glennie, I know what meteor shower looks like.' He kept on trying to tell them there's something out here, and his wife could tell something was wrong because he's not normally like this. My dad says, 'Listen, let's go back out there.'"

The two men headed to the well, where Billy Ray pointed out to Elmer where he saw the UFO... but nothing was there now. Elmer suggested they go back inside since they had to return to work the next day, when suddenly, as Stith describes it, "the old hound dog comes running by, tail tucked, ears down, and runs straight under the house."

"The dog started going nuts," tells Hayes. "Once that happened, they see a glowing light emerging from the woods. What was making the glowing light was this being floating off the ground. Some reports say a few inches, some five feet, but either way it wasn't touching the ground as it came toward them."

In a vintage news report, a now-grown Lonnie Lankford confirmed what he saw when he was 12: "Bare feet, webbed hands, pointed ears, and big round eyes. It was about three-foot-tall, and they had silver uniforms on."

"Well, the men don't know what this is," says Stith. "They both run in the house, slam the door behind them. Everybody stops what they're doing: 'What's wrong with you two?' They're thinking, 'Alright, Billy Ray got Lucky out there to go along with this story to scare the girls.' Billy Ray's wife was only 18. They kept on, and my grandmother says, 'You two have got to settle down. I've got to get these three to bed.' She does that, and when she comes back, Dad's at the front door with a shotgun, Billy Ray at the back with the rifle, and she's thinking, 'Okay, there is something going on here.'"

Details Hayes, "Mrs. Lankford was adamant about getting the kids out of the way. She sent them off into the back room, closed the door. Her older boys and some of their friends took up arms. There was a 20-gauge shotgun, a 22 rifle... some say a 22 pistol."

According to Stith, Glennie decided to "go to the backyard where Billy Ray is, and she squats down there beside him and asks, 'Billy Ray, what did you see?' He told her, 'Miss Glennie, I hope it's something you never have to see.' They hear all the banter going on in the house, when all of a sudden around the corner there it is, pretty as you please, three-and-a-half-foot tall, big glowing eyes, ears, round head, arms to the ground. She screams. Everybody comes running—it must have been a bloodcurdling scream—and she tells them, 'There is something out here. I just saw it.'

"They hear a shot ring out the front. Poor Uncle J.C. shoots one through the window. Well, Billy Ray decides to run out because he's thinking there's a body out there. 'Now we've got the evidence.' He runs out... no body to be found. As he's standing there under the little stoop, a clawed hand comes down to grab his hair. Well, Aunt Alene yanks him back in the house. Then dad goes out, turns toward the roof where the hand came down, and there it sat staring at him. He shoots it. He hits it. He hears a hit. These are country boys, could probably shoot by the time they could walk, but it floats away."

"They defended the house as these creatures started coming toward them, taking shots at them," says Hayes, with initial reports indicating four boxes of .22 shells were fired during the conflict. "When they hit these creatures, they didn't react the way normal living creatures react when hit with a bullet. It had a pinging sound, like when you shot a bucket or gas can. They would float or flip backwards each time they were hit—kind of like resetting—then they would come back at them. It was as if they had some sort of force field around them. Their movement was very erratic, had everybody freaked out."

In his 1975 book with Hynek titled *The Edge of Reality*, Jacques Vallée compared this organized hostile non-terrestrial engagement with a 1954 case told to him by Brazilian researcher Olavo Fontes: "A man drew a knife and hit the 'occupant,' and the knife rebounded as if it had hit a metallic surface. Then he picked up the 'occupant,' who was very light, maybe fifteen pounds, but the thing just hit him, and he [the man] went rolling away as if he had been hit by

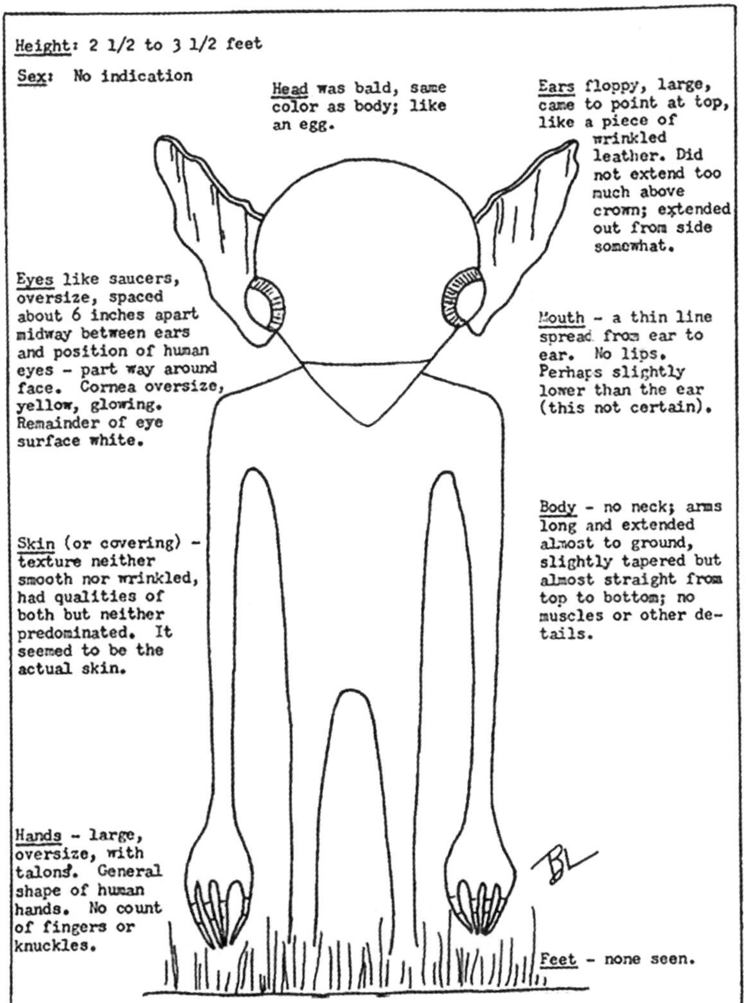

a truck, so mass and inertia somehow were out of range. There have been cases in this country where 'occupants' have been fired at, and in one case, the Hopkinsville incident, the 'occupants' seemed to absorb the energy from the bullets and start glowing brighter."

As Stith tells the story, "Somebody screams, 'There's one in the tree!' He turns around; there it is in the big tree in the front yard. Shoots it, floats to the ground, rolls off. They're not dying. They're hitting them and they're just scurrying off and coming back. They seem to be, to their mind, trying to get in the house. The mindset was, 'Shoot now, ask questions later,' and that's what they did. June is huddled in a corner covering her eyes because she does not want to see these things. As far as I know, she's the only one in the house that did not see them, but everybody else did. The kids are crying, the women are crying, 'What are these things?!' My dad said, 'Listen, we'll go to Hopkinsville and get help.' They're sitting there all quiet when they hear little nails going across the tin roof. This really sends everybody into hysterics. He tries to settle them down again, tells Billy Ray, 'Let's go out back here and check it out real quick.'

"They go out the back door, looking around, can't see anything. It's just quiet. No sounds of frogs, no bugs that you hear in August. Something's wrong. As they're standing there, they hear something, turn around and see one going up the side of the house to the roof. Well, my dad shoots it. It floats down, and this really gives me pause, because it gets up, floats to the fence post across the yard, which is about 40 feet away. They're thinking, 'Oh, man, this is real.' He shoots it again. This time he may have hurt it, because instead of floating off the fence post it actually falls and leaves a glowing substance. They're thinking, 'Okay, so they can be hurt.' They go back in the house and Billy Ray says, 'Don't worry. It's okay. It's okay. We've got this under control.' They sit there a little while longer until it does get quiet again."

"It dies down. Everyone in the house decides this is their opportunity to get out," recounts Hayes of the exodus near 11 o'clock in the evening. "They load up in two different vehicles and head off into town straight to the Hopkinsville police station. They report to the police what's going on and convince them to go out to the farmhouse." Newspaper accounts described the family's appearance as "highly excited."

As Stith sets the scene, "You've got 11 people from the age of 50 to 7 running into the police office in the middle of the night, which is obviously unusual. One little officer on duty, that's it, all trying to tell him something's going on. He's not understanding. He's hearing 'little men being shot at.' That's what he's hearing. He's like, 'You're shooting at little men on your farm?' He tells them to settle down and calls Chief Russell Greenwell. The Chief says, 'Call Fort Campbell Army Base. Get ahold of some of the state troopers and officers, we're going to Kelly.' By the time it's all said and done, you got about 25 people heading back out to Kelly in the middle of the night."

Hayes continues, "The police head out there with the family and look around. They could see something was going on. There are holes in the screen. There's buckshot in the door and window frames, shells everywhere. The family's very upset, very distraught, very concerned about everything that's going on. The police are poking around, and eventually the military police show up to do a bit of an investigation there as well."

According to reports, those investigators included more than a dozen Hopkinsville city police (Greenwell, T.C. Gross, Dorris Francis, Gray Salter), Christian County police (Deputy Sheriff George Batts), state police (R.N. Ferguson Jr. and G.W. Riley), four military police from Fort Campbell, and a newspaper photographer from the *Kentucky New Era*. The Air Force reportedly had the strongest presence, although a document from Wright-Patterson Air Force Base in Ohio two years later suggested that those at Fort Campbell responsible for "resolving incidents of this nature under the provisions of AFR 200-2" had "no knowledge of such reports."

In addition were two Hopkins County deputy sheriffs and three state troopers from Madisonville, all remaining on the Sutton premises until 2am. The 11 family members were not allowed back until the official group had a chance to survey the scene. Hackles raised at one point when a cat's tail was accidentally stepped on by an MP.

"Obviously something has happened here," Stith describes. "It feels wrong, an eerie feeling. They searched the grounds, used their little lights, couldn't find anything. The only thing they saw was the glowing substance on the ground, but when you go up on it, the glow would stop. When you walk away from it, you could see the glow again. Chief Greenwell looked at it. Sure enough, you could tell a big difference from the grass around it where the spot was. Something had been there or was there. What was it? Finally, they're just like, 'There's nothing we can do here.' The Chief goes to my grandmother and says, 'Miss Glennie, I'm so sorry but there's nothing here. Something happened, I'm not discrediting that, but no bodies, no body parts, no blood, no guts, nothing to show.' They left the family there to fend for themselves."

Figure 10. "Little Man" as described by Elmer Sutton, J.C. Sutton and O.P. Baker drawn by Andrew (Bud) Ledwith

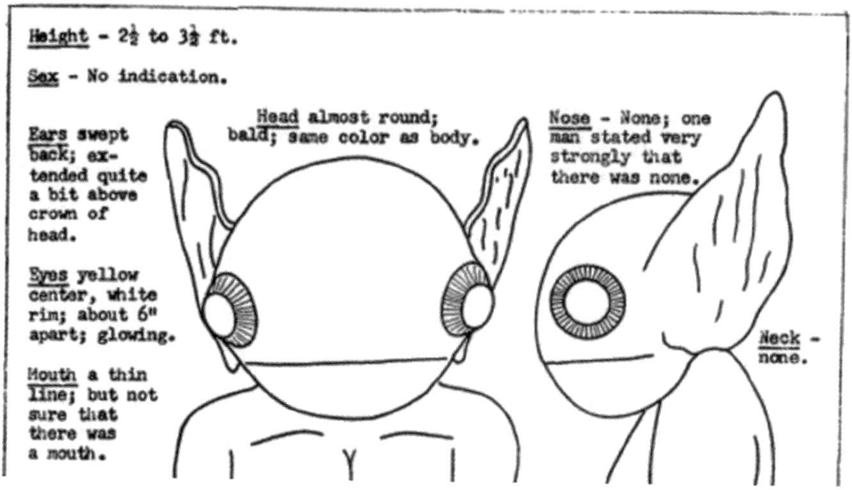

"Things die down, all those people leave, and the family's back at the house," continues Hayes. "Now's the time to get some shut eye, 11 people sleeping on couches, floors, and chairs. Then... something starts scratching on the window again."

As Miss Lankford told Major John E. Albert, an Army reservist who was the only military official to interview the family, "About 3:30am I was in my bedroom and looked out the north window and saw a small silver shining object about two-and-a-half feet tall that had its hands on the screen looking in. I called for my sons and they shot at it and it left. I was about 60-feet from it this time. I did not see it anymore."

"You got to realize these people have been through total heck that night... they're physically and mentally exhausted," emphasizes Stith, describing what began to happen around 3:30am. "She's lying down. My dad's in the rocking chair beside her, shotgun in lap. She's trying to go to sleep, opens her eyes and sees one at the window. She screams out for my dad and he jumps up and they start to battle again. This continues until the sun comes up and they're gone. Where did they go? We don't know. My dad sits the family down and says, 'Listen, no good can come of this story. They were laughing at us last night. I heard them. Just let it go. Do not talk about it. Don't talk about it to anyone.'"

"The next day police come back again, but there's also reports of plainclothes government officials that show up to investigate and interview," says Hayes.

"This story stands out because of the multiple witnesses and the fact that police and military showed up," adds UFO researcher Brandon Wright. "Project Blue Book looked into it. Why did they put so much time and effort and energy with men out sweeping around, looking for things?"

Complicating matters was 27-year-old "J.C." Sutton's decision to go along with plans he made to go hunting with the farmer who lived next door. According to Stith, this farmer confirmed he had also seen lights in the woods the night before, but when he heard commotion and gunshots decided not to leave his home for fear of catching a bullet. Elmer—who along with Billy Ray had gone back to Evansville—had instructed everyone not to talk about what had happened, but J.C. decided to confide in the man.

"He went ahead and told him," explains Stith. "J.C. went back home. Guess what? We had an invasion of the people. They were in the yard, setting up tables, selling stuff. They were taking souvenirs out of the yard, walking through the house. 'What is going on here?' They were camping out. People were wanting to see the little men that came to Kelly. They were coming from California and Texas to talk to the family."

By August 23, the *Evansville Press* was reporting Sheriff Batt "chased about 20 spectators away from the Sutton home about 9 last night so the Suttons could get some rest," only for more to gather the following morning "to look for traces of the saucer or little men."

Adds Hayes, "Police come out all the time to break up crowds wanting to buy souvenirs off the family, curtains and fence posts. They passed up opportunities to make money."

Swarming of the house by locals and non-locals was driven by the *Kentucky New Era* cover story on August 22, 1955. Billy Ray and a gun-toting Elmer (mistakenly referred to as "Cecil") appeared in front of the house for a photo taken during the nighttime investigation. The unfortunately-worded headline read, "Story of Space-Ship, 12 Little Men Probed Today." It listed the estimated number of beings as between 12 and 15, and even more crucially printed that "All officials agree that there was no drinking involved."

"A lot of people who went out to investigate assumed everybody was drinking and things got out of hand," says Hayes. "But the family was adamant there was no alcohol on the scene. Glennie Lankford was very religious and she would not even allow it in her house, let alone on the farm. Surviving members of the family to this day swear up and down there was no alcohol, but that was mentioned in a lot of reports. Bad information was delivered immediately, then in the weeks and years after that."

Adds Wright, "A lot of people said, 'Well, they were just drunk.' I don't know people that get drunk then automatically start seeing the same hallucinations and they're all shooting at things. I can't see her grandmother participating in all of this."

"Our grandmother was Pentecostal," confirms Stith. "You do not drink, do not cuss, do not do all these vices people do today... and back then. Not around the kids."

Glennie Lankford later said bitterly to interviewer Isabel Davis, "The lies they told about us. Said we were drinking..."

Soon more reporters swooped in, often with photographers in tow, from wire services as well as regional newspapers in Kentucky, Indiana, and Tennessee. Perhaps the most crucial interviews of the family were conducted by a non-journalist.

Explains Stith, "Bud Ledwith, an engineer for one of the radio stations in Hopkinsville, came and talked to the family, took them one by one in a room and asked them to tell him what happened. They all told them their side, described the little drawings that you see today, and he was totally amazed. They all told the same story, the little drawings looked almost alike. He went away with a whole different attitude towards life."

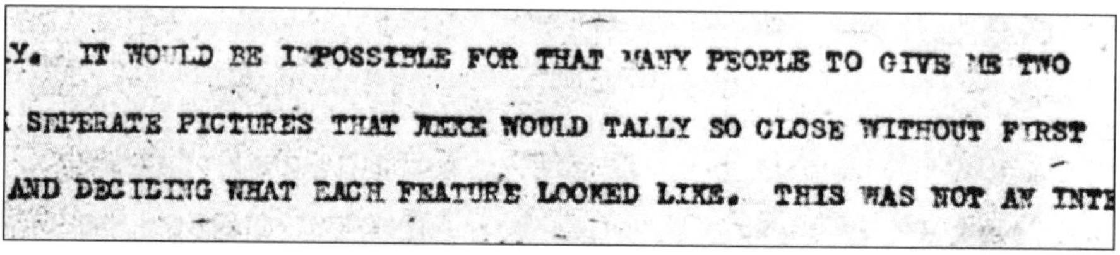
Y. IT WOULD BE IMPOSSIBLE FOR THAT MANY PEOPLE TO GIVE ME TWO
SEPERATE PICTURES THAT XXXX WOULD TALLY SO CLOSE WITHOUT FIRST
AND DECIDING WHAT EACH FEATURE LOOKED LIKE. THIS WAS NOT AN INT

Says Hayes, "A lot of confusion came with that game of telephone where people are trying to describe these creatures: Some say it had a nose, some say it didn't have a nose. The women at the house claimed it was much stockier, more muscular. The men thought it was skinnier, had kind of a scrawny look to it. At the end of the day, they all seem to describe the same thing: three-and-a-half or four-feet tall, silver or gray, big ears, big yellow eyes, claws on its hands which dragged on the ground."

Ledworth did sketches of the creature based on these seven testimonies, which matched. Still the insanity went on, with Stith explaining, "Grandmother went and tried to get help because people were taking stuff. She asked one of the officers, 'Can you help us?' Once officers ran people off they'd always come back. What were they supposed to do?"

"Eventually everything dies down," concludes Hayes. "Two weeks later, they actually sell the house and move away, they're that concerned about what happened. Within two weeks the whole place is empty and it's all a memory at that point."

"She sold the farm and moved to a Hopkinsville apartment complex," confirms Stith. "'Safety in numbers, get out of the barn, we don't know if they're going to come back.' The community of Kelly was scared. My mom and her first husband with their seven kids lived in Kelly at the time, and she said, 'Yes, people who lived in Kelly were terrified because they did not know what these were, if they would come back.'"

According to Craig Campobasso's book *The UFO Hotspot Compendium,* today there is a large silver UFO built at Kelly Station Park—a quarter mile from the farm on Old Madisonville Road—commemorating the Hopkinsville incident.

"In UFO lore, this story is a pinnacle," explains Derek Hayes. "One of the most outrageous UFO alien encounters on record. It's not often one or several of these things come out of a ship and attack a house. Anytime somebody sees a creature or several of this description, this case is immediately brought up. Not only for the wild claims, but the amount of people that witnessed and the research done afterward. A ton of police presence, military, reporters showed up. Then the population of Kentucky showed up."

"The stories from these people remain compelling," says Aaron Sagers, an expert in paranormal pop culture seen on Travel Channel. "They were consistent, and it didn't seem like they wanted attention. The Kelly-Hopkinsville goblins are not as well known in the mainstream, yet this story remains one of the more compelling experiencer stories because there was a malevolence involved. These things were terrorizing them."

"The problem was there was a lot of sensationalism going on with media coverage," explains Hayes. "For starters, they labeled them 'little green men'... these things weren't green. They were described as being 'gray' or 'having silver suits on,' and may have glowed in the dark through their skin or outfit. Newspapers went wild with it, and that's where the 'hillbilly meets alien' story came from. Reporters get out there and it's this house full of carnival workers, rural Kentuckians. I don't want to put labels on anybody, but these were country folk. They weren't used to seeing UFOs nor were they the kind of people the press talked to about flying saucers. A lot of it was misconstrued."

"What did they gain from it?" asks Brandon Wright. "They never made profit. They destroyed their house. For a big joke, it seemed a little extreme. This was back in 1955, they didn't have TV shows where you become talking heads."

"Can't explain it, just don't make me feel right, you know, because I don't think they believe us," Lonnie Lankford told a newsman.

Skeptics have posited different theories or alternate explanations for what was happening, such as painted monkeys. There was a circus in town that August weekend which did have monkeys, but no reports of them being painted or an escape.

In 1957, Major John E. Albert, on the scene on August 22, 1955, blamed the family's trip to a "Holy Roller Church" as working them "into a frenzy, becoming emotionally unbalanced," followed by the hypothetical sighting of a monkey that "might have escaped, giving the appearance of a small man... The window that was pointed out to be the one that she saw the small silver shining object was about two-and-a-half feet tall, that had its hands on the screen looking in, was a very low window and a small monkey could put his hands on the top of it while standing on the ground."

Opines Hayes, "Monkeys are loud, monkeys are hairy, monkeys act differently than this. When you shoot a monkey, they usually die... they don't go flying backwards."

"There was something there that had them spooked, that they were shooting at," says Otte. "Some people thought it might have been owls…"

Hayes said of these skeptics, who include the late Joe Nickell of the International Committee for Skeptical Inquiry, "They claim a couple of breeding great horned owls were in the area, defending a nest. These guys grew up in Kentucky, where everybody knows what a horned owl looks like. When you shoot an owl they also die, usually."

Adds Otte, "If you shot at an owl with a .22 and a shotgun you're probably going to hit something with as many shots as they fired. Little country boys in Kentucky can shoot."

"I don't think they were owls either, because you would know what an owl is," confirms Wright. "Unless you're getting swarmed, owls don't come around and start attacking."

Captain Gregory September 10, 1958

J. A. Hynek

Hopkinsville Case

Russell Greenwell

The Chief of Police in Hopkinsville is [redacted] It was he who stated that the affair was investigated by Air Force officers from Fort Campbell. I understand that MP's and a Pfc from Fort Campbell investigated at the farmhouse on late Monday afternoon. The Pfc was a Mr. Hodson and his account and pictures were published in the Clarksville Tennessee Leaf Chronicle.

Greenwell

Chief [redacted] also stated that the affair had been investigated by two men from an unidentified agency at Standiford Field in Louisville, a commercial field. The Kentucky State Police investigated the case and their report and available sketches are on file with Trooper Riley's case report at Frankfort, Kentucky. Attached is a list of

After 10 months of the family refusing to say peep about the incident to anyone, an intrepid ufologist named Isabel Davis flew to Kentucky in order to conduct her own investigation. In 1954 she and Ted Bloecher co-founded one of the earliest American UFO groups, Civilian Saucer Intelligence (CSI), based in her home city of New York. Their quarterly newsletter was considered a respected periodical in the field, and they served as a primary source of UFO reports for J. Allen Hynek during the Blue Book years.

Davis was able to speak to the witnesses and found their stories stayed consistent from Ledwith's interrogations, as when Glennie Lankford again described her famous image of seeing the creature at her window screen: "I turned my head three different times, because I thought maybe my eyes were fooling me, but every time I turned my head back, there he was.... close enough to put his little clawy hands up on it."

Davis and Bloecher's eventual book, *Close Encounter at Kelly and Others of 1955*, came out in 1978, the year development on *Night Skies* began. When provided with an early copy of her manuscript, Hynek wrote that Davis's work "fully supports the earlier investigations of Ledwith. Considered together, these accounts give us a picture of a truly bizarre and, in ordinary terms, completely unexplainable event."

Since the Kelly encounter occurred, some drew a shaky connection to another incident that happened an hour-and-a-half north of Hopkinsville in Evansville, Indiana. On August 14, 1955 Mrs. Naomi Johnson, her three children, and a friend went swimming in the Ohio river near Dogtown along the Indiana/Kentucky border. While enjoying the water 15 feet from shore, Johnson felt something grab her left leg and pull her under. She described the hand that yanked her as having "large claws and a furry palm." After kicking at it, the thing pulled her under again. Johnson's friend, Mrs. Louise Lamble, was in an innertube and tried to scare the unseen thing away. Once Johnson was able to swim to Lamble's tube, the thing loosened its grip. She made it to shore where alcohol was applied to scratches on her leg before being treated at the hospital.

Johnson later read the Sutton's description of their aliens having "exceptionally large hands with webbing between six-inch long fingers and clawlike fingernails." Crude illustrations in the papers (not unlike *Creature from the Black Lagoon*) accompanied the account. This triggered her memory, stating "that's the little devil that had a hold of me." Lamble also recalled seeing "a shiny object in the sky" that was "not an airplane." The incident referred to as the "Green Clawed Beast of the Ohio River" was picked up across the country, but connection between both stories is tenuous. Although the carnival Elmer and Billy Ray came from was in Evansville (specious at best), the Kelly aliens themselves were never described as furry. The link seems to have formed entirely in the mind of Johnson's sister Wilma Tooke, who pointed out the "little green men" story to her. From there it simply carried forth in folk tale fashion.

According to Otte, "In Project Blue Book case #3737 there is a report from Fort Campbell air base from a guy named Charles Kirk, who was the first lieutenant USAF."

In said Blue Book files, a US Air Force Captain named Robert J. Hertell did bring a reported sighting to Kirk's attention, one that happened a few months prior to Kelly Goblins in the South Christian area not far from Hopkinsville. The incident involved a local attorney as well as "a negro handy man" witnessing a UFO "streak across the sky, perform several abrupt changes of course, and finally disappear in the direction of Bowling Green." The source being a respected community member, Fort Campbell reported the incident "in accordance with AFR 200-2, by confidential message."

"You haven't really heard much more about that part of Kentucky after that incident," Otte confirms. "Kelly is a remote area, or at least very remote back then."

No other significant extra-terrestrial encounters occurred in the Kelly-Hopkinsville region, but an hour's drive away in the city of Franklin a major UFO flap occurred on January 7, 1948... one that cost 25-year-old Air National Guard pilot Thomas F. Mantell his life. It was initially reported by the Kentucky highway patrol as a westbound circular object 250 to 300 feet in diameter. Sgt. Quinton Blackwell, a tower operator at Fort Knox, described it as "an ice cream cone topped with red" around 1:20pm.

RONNIE

Roy, what did it look like?

ROY

It was like an ice cream cone.

RONNIE

What flavor?

Four F-51 fighter jets approached the area at 1:45pm, with Blackwell requesting mission leader Mantell get close to the object in question. Mantell spotted something bright, "a metallic object or possibly reflection of sun from a metallic object, and it is of tremendous size." Around 3:15pm his wingmen (1st LT. Clements and 2nd LT. Hammond) broke off while Mantell continued to pursue the object above 25,000 feet. At some point he likely passed out due to lack of oxygen, which caused him to crash. Franklin resident William

C. Mayes then witnessed Mantell's jet circle, then dive, then explode "halfway between where it started to dive and the ground." The local Louisville Courier headline was "F-51 and Capt. Mantell Destroyed Chasing Flying Saucer."

In the aftermath, Air Force advisor J. Allen Hynek initially speculated the brightness Mantell and other witnesses observed was from Venus, remaining the official explanation until 1952 when Hynek retracted this, saying Venus would not have been visible from Earth. Eventually it was decided the Mantell UFO was actually a Skyhook observation balloon, the same type the United States Navy Office of Naval Research (ONR) began launching in secret around late 1947.

In an interesting footnote, at one point the Department of Physics at the United States Air Force Academy integrated the Kelly Goblins story for a 1968 training manual titled *Introductory Space Science Volume II* until it was dropped in 1970, with the info later folded into a 1972 book titled *Environmental Space Sciences*, both edited by Lt. Colonel Donald G. Carpenter. The specific section is on "Human Fear and Hostility" towards supposed alien visitors, using examples such as airships spotted in Ireland around 1,000 AD being treated as demonic, or the UFOs fired upon by Russians on the Kuril Islands in 1957. It then details the Sutton incident in 1955:

Geraldine Sutton Stith at GoblinCon in Hopkinsville, Kentucky.

"This reported incident does bear out the contention, though, that humans are dangerous. At no time in the story did the supposed aliens shoot back, although one is left with the impression that the described creatures were having fun scaring humans."

Whatever side of the fence you fall under when hearing the Kelly tale, there is no doubt it remains true to the word Sagers coined: "Compelling." This book, *Stranded on Earth,* seeks to neither prove nor disprove the story... not that it would likely move anyone one way or the other.

"People don't choose their beliefs," says Paul Hynek. "You don't say, 'My life doesn't have a lot of meaning. I'm going to believe in that God.' You just do. We don't need to dig deeper, in terms of free will and all that. You don't choose your beliefs, and you don't often question your beliefs. It's hard for an adult—me, you, anybody—to change a fundamental belief about reality, and it's not often facts will do that. Very few people like to have their answers questioned."

"I do 100% believe that they were shooting at something," Wright offered. "Were they aliens from a spaceship? I don't know. Will we ever really know? I do believe that something did happen. I don't think it was a hoax."

The Kelly-Hopkinsville incident acts as a counterpoint to another famous supernatural case, that of the purported haunting in Amityville, New York following the real Ronald DeFeo murders in his family home. This poltergeist tale—which later homeowner George Lutz purportedly collaborated with author Jay Anson to fabricate—eventually formed the basis of Anson's popular *Amityville Horror* book as well as the film series.

"In my opinion, this is the exact opposite of Amityville," says Hayes. "At Amityville, the Lutz family knew what they were getting into when they moved in. A lot of reports say they came up with a plan once they got into the house and developed a hoax around everything that supposedly happened. With the Kelly-Hopkinsville Goblin case, this family had nothing to do with any of this. They didn't make a dime or try to write books. The family is very reactionary to the attack that took place. They wanted nothing to do with it. It upset them greatly. Nobody believed them. Some of the witnesses said they wished they avoided all the speculation and ridicule they received for years."

Geraldine agrees: "I used to be friends with Christopher on Facebook, one of the Amityville kids. He hated the whole thing, said a lot of it was made up to make money. My dad wouldn't have wanted this to happen to him. He didn't want any attention. He was a quiet man, and my grandmother didn't want any of this messing up her three kids. They didn't want it to happen, unlike Amityville where I think the Lutzes did make things up."

While Lucky Sutton and family shunning the spotlight does not prove their claims as "real," their story had an incredible ripple effect on the culture regardless of substantiation. It not only inspired many important films and shows, as we will see, but gave America a homegrown "little green men" myth while opening up discourse about how we disseminate and interpret experiencer stories.

As Paul Hynek tells, "There's the joke about how Niels Bohr had a horseshoe above the doorway to his office at the university. Someone said, 'Professor Bohr, why surely you don't believe in horseshoes?' And he says, 'You don't have to believe in it for it to work.'"

As someone whose job it is to listen to people's paranormal experiences, podcaster Derek Hayes concludes, "I don't know that I believe in any of it, but I want every bit of it to be real, to prove it's actually out there. It's hard to invest that much time into something like this and not hope it's real. It's easy to not believe because a lot of these claims are wild, frankly, but you at least want it to be real to spend all this time researching and reading and listening to people tell their stories. It's a lot of work. It's draining because you never get

answers. Imagine doing something your whole life and never reaching a conclusion. It takes a certain kind of person... hopeful."

The Sutton family's fateful encounter certainly put the rural Kelly-Hopkinsville area on the map. Starting in the early 2000s, the Hopkinsville-Christian County Convention and Visitors Bureau put on Kelly Green Men festivals beginning on the 50th anniversary in August 2005. The first featured an expert UFO symposium, parade, costume ball, poster contest for kids, and a golf scramble. It became an annual tradition until attendance died off.

Cut to 2025, the Bureau's newly installed exec Amy Rogers decided to pull out all the stops for the 70th anniversary with the first of what she hoped would be many official conventions built around the legend. The two-day GoblinCon event on October 17 and 18 of 2025 was held inside the Bruce Convention Center in Hopkinsville.

Rogers told this author at the event, "I made the first phone call to Geraldine to say, 'Hey, how do you feel about this?' She was in, we had a meeting, and it just went from there."

At one booth was local Curtis Cansler, whose business Secret Base typically sells comics and toys, but for this event he and his wife created special aliens in a jar, crocheted items, even a painting depicting the Kelly aliens invading a church. When asked about growing up around the legend, Cansler

said, "I remember being a kid in the '70s and '80s and it was very eye roll. Since the internet came around, it's gotten popular as a story. People are more accepting of it. It does bring people to come visit."

Another guest was Tyler Strand, one of the forces behind the Planet Weird doc series *Hellier*, which attempts to connect mysterious reports of small cave-dwelling pale creatures in a Kentucky mining town with the Kelly aliens of 1955... suggesting these "goblins" may have been terrestrial after all.

"These things are from here," speculates Strand. "They're part of the environment. People have probably been communing with them since the dawn of time. Those who have been tried for witchcraft had interactions with these beings. They tend to develop abilities: the gift of second sight, prophecy, the ability to heal, things associated with the witch's familiar, which some could call a goblin."

Contemporary lore sometimes refers to these cryptids as "pale crawlers," as spotted frequently with the same descriptors in areas geographically aligned with Hopkinsville.

Derek Hayes receives frequent calls about these creatures for his show *Monsters Among Us*: "My guess is they live underground because they're seen in places with a lot of cave systems. Almost exclusively seen at night, very pale, very skinny. They don't quite look like Kelly Goblins—don't have the ears or the eyes—but everything else matches up. It's difficult not to make that connection when calls come from Kentucky or Southern Ohio or Tennessee or Indiana."

Continues Strand, "In the *Hellier* case, it began with these strange emails from a man named David Christie in Hellier, Kentucky who talked about encountering these creatures he said had round bird-like eyes and thin lipless mouths like grey aliens. He believed they were coming from an abandoned mine shaft at the edge of his property. Because this happened in Eastern Kentucky, it was logical to think about Hopkinsville, how this family also had a strange occurrence with little creatures."

The paranormal podcast *Tinfoil Tales* is hosted by Brandon Wright, who had a table at GoblinCon. He said of Saturday attendance, "Today's been a lot busier, but for the first one they've had a lot of turnout. Hopefully it's something that can continue to grow. They don't always start off as huge bangers. It takes time."

According to Amy Rogers, the inaugural GoblinCon pulled in "easily 800" attendees, and as of this writing is set for a second event in August of 2026.

Rogers said excitedly, "Being such a huge hit and a success, everybody's like, 'We can't wait until next year!' This is definitely going to be something I will continue to do over and over and over until I can't do it anymore. I'm hoping the longer I put these on I can get Spielberg to give me a 30-second video. I did reach out to his publicist, and they're like, 'No, he doesn't have the time.' I'm like, 'Okay, yeah, sure, yeah, sure.'"

PART II
DARK SKY

CHAPTER 5

Solar Sayles: Crafting the Script

"Terror, horror, death. Film at eleven."

*—**Piranha*** (1978)

After Lawrence Kasdan turned down the gig due to his *The Empire Strikes Back* commitment, Kathleen Kennedy recommended up-and-coming scribe John Sayles to write *Night Skies*. Having penned some Roger Corman exploitation films (*Piranha, Battle Beyond the Stars*), Sayles had just made his directorial debut *Return of the Secaucus 7.*

"You know, I really hadn't been working as a screenwriter for that long," Sayles admits to this author. "I'd written three movies for Roger Corman. That was the money I used to make my first feature, and I'd written another couple things at that time. I don't think *The Howling* had come out when I got hired, but Steven Spielberg had seen *Piranha* and liked it, so he knew me from that as well. Kathy wasn't exactly a producer, she was Steven's assistant. She certainly was doing a lot, had her antenna out. Frances Dole, who was Corman's assistant, had a very similar position, and that's how I got to Roger's attention. She'd read some short stories I'd had in *Atlantic* magazine."

By the late '70s when Sayles got his first Roger Corman gigs, the B-movie king had been responsible for directing a string of influential low-budget films in the '50s and '60s, including *Little Shop of Horrors*, *The Wild Angels*, and several lush Edgar Allan Poe adaptations starring Vincent Price. As a producer he helped launch the careers of filmmakers like Francis Coppola, Martin Scorsese, Ron Howard, and star Jack Nicholson. These films proved popular with the emergent counterculture, as Corman tended to throw elements of art house style and lefty politics into the movies he produced... no matter how shoddy those productions might be.

The late Corman explained to this author in 2017, "I was working as a craftsman, like somebody making a fine piece of furniture. He knows the table he's making isn't going to be a work of art. It's somebody doing his best to make the best table he can possibly make. I was making low budget exploitation films as well as I could, and in a number of them there were thoughts that do resonate." He added, smiling in his typically effusive manner, "Having a thought is inexpensive, it doesn't affect your budget."

Once he struck out in the '70s with New World Pictures, his own production and distribution company, Corman was in the position of having to crank out 10-12 pictures per year in order to "feed the dinosaur" (i.e. the distribution side). Still, he knew the difference between filmmakers who would begrudgingly accept a cheapie picture as a mere "take the money and move on" assignment versus guys like Jonathan Demme, who would land a job à la *Caged Heat* then set out to make the best women in prison picture ever made. New World had a knack for nurturing (and exploiting) hungry creatives.

As Corman explained, "The guys who said, 'I'll just knock this thing off,' they had no careers. The ones like Jonathan who—no matter what the project was—said, 'I will do the best job I can, no matter what the circumstances,' went on to have success."

"That was the attitude you had to have in order to survive at that place," confirms director Joe Dante, who cut his teeth editing at the New World trailer department before helming his own first two pictures there. "If you were condescending to the material, it wasn't gonna turn out well. If you said, 'Okay, I'm gonna buy into this, and do what Roger thinks the audience will want,' then the movie usually turned out pretty well. Roger used to say, 'If you make two good movies for me, you'll never have to work for me again.'"

Born in Schenectady, New York on September 28, 1950 to an Irish-Catholic family, John Thomas Sayles attended Williams College in Massachusetts, earning a degree in psychology in 1972. It was there he met longtime life/production partner Maggie Renzi as well as frequent on-camera collaborator David Strathairn. After college he began writing short fiction for *The Atlantic*, such as the trucker story "I-80 Nebraska M.490-M.205." In 1975 Little & Brown published his first novel *Pride of the Bimbos*, revolving around a baseball player who dresses in drag. *The New York Times* called it "an oddly unsettling satire of American machismo."

Sayles was, in fact, a pinch hitter brought on to 1978's *Piranha* after director Dante did not like the original script penned by *Kingdom of the Spiders* scribe Richard Robinson.

"I remember being asked to do the movie, read the script and said, 'You can't make this script. It's terrible," Dante recalls. "That's when Frances Dole, Roger's factotum in charge of the writers, remembered that John had written this book called *Pride of the Bimbos*, which she liked. She got Roger to read it, and they decided to go with John."

Corman knew writing talent when he saw it, having made the early exploitation screenplays of *Chinatown* scribe Robert Towne a decade earlier (*Last Woman on Earth*, *The Tomb of Ligeia*). Other writers the producer championed included Oscar nominee Peter Bogdanovich and Oscar winner Curtis Hanson. A newbie to the medium, Sayles took to it quickly with a collaborative spirit that infused the B-movie about a swarm of genetically modified piranhas set free to unleash carnage on a small lake town.

"We talked about what we were going to do," says Dante of the process. "I wanted to add science fiction to it and make sure it had some political content, which is something John excels at. Plus, there had to be a piranha attack every reel, the main requirement for Roger. When it came in, we didn't really do much to it. It was pretty good the way it was."

Said Sayles, "I was working for Roger Corman, and yes, if Roger paid you $10,000 to write a screenplay, he was going to make that screenplay. There was no hiring other people. If the director and actors wanted to change it that was their business."

A trained stage performer, *Piranha* also became Sayles' onscreen debut. "As I often do, I had him come to set while we were shooting," Dante explains. "I like to have the writer around, if possible, so we made up a scene for him where he plays a soldier and it allowed him to be on set. A lot of times actors have questions or ideas or whatever. It's always better to have the writer there to deal with it."

One change came with the casting of Bradford Dillman (*The Way We Were, The Enforcer*) as backwoods guide Paul Grogan, who leads whip-smart skiptracer Maggie (Heather Menzies) on the trail of two missing hikers. Since this was a Corman film, Sayles was expecting an inexperienced actor as Paul, writing spartan dialogue for that character. However, Dillman was a 20-year movie veteran trained at the Actors Studio, having performed Eugene O'Neill on Broadway. When Dillman requested the character be filled out a little, Sayles was happy to accommodate.

Piranha not only featured environmental and political commentary, it made bold choices like having the piranha attacks on the summer camp and the resort (which the military officer owns a piece of) be bloody and brutal. Scenes of sheathed dead bodies in the aftermath call to mind Vietnam.

"*Piranha* is a pretty hilarious movie, especially the stuff with Dick Miller and Paul Bartel where the guests are getting eaten," says *Pure Cinema Podcast*'s Brian Saur. "When people do genre they get a little too self-serious, and Sayles does not take that attitude at all. That applies to his dramatic work as well. One of the keys to his filmmaking is to make heavy stuff more humanistic through those lighter moments."

"It's not coincidental that Dante and Sayles are so close," says critic Adam Nayman. "They rebutted Spielberg collectively with *Piranha*, a great joke about *Jaws* that you can't afford one big shark, so here's a bunch of little fish to eat it... the B movie riposte to *Jaws*."

On hand were two budding makeup effects men who would impact both Spielberg's *E.T.* (Robert Short) and Dante's *Gremlins* (Chris Walas).

Remembers Short, "Joe Dante and Jon Davison came in to ask Don Post to do castings of piranhas for *Piranha*, and Don turned down the assignment. That opened the door for me and Chris Walas, who was working there at the time, to say, 'Let's partner up and go do *Piranha*.' I quit Don Post Studios and segued to doing on-set effects. Chris and I handled underwater mayhem, piranhas eating people's arms off. I was able to massage that job into existence because I had a background as a scuba diver."

"I'd gotten to know Bob Short really well," adds Walas. "He got a job on the *Piranha* effects crew because he was a certified diver, and I was terrified of water. They were filming at USC's Olympic-sized pool, which was huge. I'm not getting in the water, I'm the guy who's refilling all the blood tanks and pumping this and that on the edge of the pool. They were filming at the deep end, and I was doing everything at the shallow end because that's the way logistics worked out. They were getting worn out going back and forth underwater, so they said, 'Okay, you just have to get in the pool and meet us halfway.' 'Okay, but I'm not getting in the water.' It just kept going, until finally the scuba pro got me suited up, but he says, 'Okay, quick lesson: Don't rise faster than your bubbles or you'll die.' My introduction to scuba diving. That was a wild show."

Ever the workhorse, Sayles churned out scripts for *Piranha*, period gangster epic *The Lady in Red*, and sci-fi oddity *Battle Beyond the Stars* in quick succession. He developed a reputation as the best writer who ever worked at New World Pictures.

"John Sayles was incredibly fast," confirms producer Michael Finnell, who started as a PA on Corman pictures. "I mean, he could turn out a script in a week or two, right?"

Adds Dante, "He writes a lot on the plane. A lot of his scripts are written on the plane from New Jersey to California."

"I got spoiled," Sayles says wistfully of his time at New World. "The first three screenplays I wrote for pay got made, and I had no idea how rare that was."

As Corman himself told this author in 2019, "These pictures generally cost about $100,000 to $150,000, and the first picture we made that moved up to a bigger budget was a science fiction picture called *Battle Beyond the Stars*."

Sayles' script for the $2M *Star Wars* knockoff *Battle Beyond the Stars* echoed George Lucas' hit—loosely based on Akira Kurosawa's *The Hidden Fortress*—by taking its cues from another of the Japanese master's films, *The Seven Samurai*. It revolved around naïve farm boy Shad (Richard Thomas) flying through space in a big-bosomed ship rounding up mercenaries to defend his home planet of Akira against the evil Sador's forces. The spirited intergalactic adventure was directed by Jimmy T. Murakami, and featured designs and VFX (including the "spaceship with breasts") by a future Oscar winner.

As Corman told this author (for Coming Soon), "The picture was a big success, but we were falling behind in our special effects, so I sent my assistant Gale Anne Hurd to find out why. She told me the special effects man I'd hired slightly exaggerated his experience, but she said 'There was a young guy building spaceship models who really knows more than anybody else.' It was Jim Cameron, his first job in Hollywood. I did something with him... the only time I've ever done it in the midst of a picture... I said, 'Jim, I'm going to give you a raise and you're going to be promoted to co-head of special effects.' That was the beginning of Cameron's career."

Cameron went on to make his directorial debut on a sequel to Dante and Sayles' *Piranha*, subtitled *The Spawning*. While an inauspicious launch, the rest—as they say—is history.

Throughout these early B-pictures, Sayles never talked down to the audience, always attempting to "bring some kind of awareness to them."

"Even hack work is about something," he told *Film Comment* in 1981. "*Battle Beyond the Stars* began with just Corman's idea of doing *The Seven Samurai* in space, but is about death, different life forms' attitudes toward death. It's no big heavy thing, it's just something to base the characters around. In *Piranha* the horror is caused by the military, and I hope that there's awareness, from the characters themselves, that we've been down this road before... The tension that is interesting to me is taking something totally fantastic and sticking it in a very realistic setting. 'Okay, what would really happen if you walked outside and there's this giant alligator there?'"

Says Ernest Dickerson, who got his start as a DP on Sayles' *Brother from Another Planet*, "John definitely had genre chops as a writer in the films he did for Corman. His scripts always showed a reverence for the material. That's one of the things that attracted me to *Brother*: the fact that he was treating an alien being trapped here with reverence, but also making the historical connection to slavery."

With three exploitation pictures under his belt and some money in his pocket, Sayles self-financed his own $60,000 debut feature as writer/director, 1980's *Return of the Secaucus 7*. Corman offered to help Sayles find financing, but the project was so small adding another producer proved unnecessary.

The story was dictated by the resources the fledgling filmmaker had, i.e. actors he worked with previously in summer stock theater. Because they were all in their late '20s/early '30s, the story focused on former college friends reuniting for a weekend of fun, reliving memories of their politically idealistic days as students during the '60s. Like many of Sayles' future films, the script is constructed around vignettes which build on each other to reveal character, in this case various groupings of friends playing music, getting high, coupling, and reflecting on where they are against where they hoped they would be. It is a charming and funny hangout movie that feels personal even though Sayles himself admitted it is not autobiographical.

As Richard Corliss wrote in his review for *Time* magazine (which later was transferred wholesale as an official poster for the film), "He creates more than a dozen complex, contradictory characters through their speech rhythms, the way they walk and sit and prepare food, and the diminishing space between the heads of two people trying to decide whether to spend the night with each other. The characters are like the film: funny, rueful, modest, utterly engaging—alive."

Corliss ended his review telling of his excitement for "the Sayles to come," which by that point included the scripts for two semi-studio genre films from Corman alum: Lewis Teague (*Alligator*) and Joe Dante (*The Howling*).

It was around this time that Kathleen Kennedy, who was doing her research into the Kelly-Hopkinsville encounter, happened to catch Sayles' directorial debut.

"I'd seen this movie called *Return of the Secaucus 7*," she said in 1996's *Making of E.T.* "Now why in the world this had anything to do with *E.T.*? This is the kind of thing I sort of feel I've lost about myself and wish I could get back... but for some reason I was intrigued with John Sayles and no one knew who John Sayles was at the time. I went running downstairs after the screening to meet him. I said, 'I love the writing in your movie and I think you might be perfect for this project that I'm working on with Steven Spielberg. Could you come meet with us?'"

Even though he parodied *Jaws*, Sayles was a genuine admirer of Spielberg at the time, including the movie he would be following up on: "*Close Encounters*, the acting is terrific. The family drama between Richard Dreyfuss and Teri Garr is compelling, then the hardware comes in and the wonder and the space people... but the first-half or two-thirds of that movie is really, really good."

Kennedy stated in *E.T.: The Extra-terrestrial: The Ultimate Visual History*, "I came back to Steven and I said, 'I think this is the guy that should write this.' Steven actually agreed with me."

To his credit, Spielberg also admired *Secaucus 7*, astutely telling *The New York Times* in 1983, "John's actors aren't acting for you, they're acting like you."

At the time, early 1980, Spielberg had set up shop at Lucasfilm's pre-Skywalker Ranch headquarters at 3855 Lankershim Blvd in Universal City, a renovated former egg warehouse known as the Egg Company. The office's spacious kitchen was used to audition actors for *Raiders of the Lost Ark*.

"I remember one meeting when Spielberg's office was at something called the Egg Company," said Sayles. "I didn't have that many meetings because Spielberg was busy cooking up other movies. He's usually got two or three things cooking at the same time, so you kind of got fit into the schedule."

"He came over to the Egg Company," continues Kennedy. "He sat down and he met with us. We gave him the research on *Night Skies* and he wrote the first draft of *Night Skies*."

Once Sayles was hired to write the script, initially titled *Watch the Skies*, he was given several key pieces of source material which, based on the writer's descriptions, appear to have included *Close Encounter at Kelly*, *The UFO Experience*, and possibly *Passport to Magonia* or *The Andreasson Affair*.

"Spielberg gave me three or four books he had read when he was doing *Close Encounters*," recalls Sayles. "The main one he wanted me to base the script on, which was this account by a farm family having these aliens attack them at night. It was a siege like *Straw Dogs*, had that feel to it. They're figuring out, 'how are we going to fight these things? They're all over the place.' They're like awful killer squirrels or something. He talked to me a little bit about what he wanted, and the tone then was a thriller. One of the other ones was a general UFO sighting book, and there might have been one where people were taken up into the ship."

Says Mitch Suskin, who worked on the practical ETs, "*Night Skies* was about five aliens who land on Earth in a remote area, and they're not sure whether the intelligent life is the cattle or the humans. One character wants to dissect them, another wants to befriend them. It was intended as a follow up to *Close Encounters of the Third Kind*. It was a little bit more hard hitting than *E.T.* was."

Despite the inherently benevolent creatures of *CE3K*, Sayles stated there was "no reason why the aliens had to be wonderful creatures... these were totally different creatures compared with *CE3K*. We didn't even know if we were going to show a spaceship or not."

In '81 Sayles described it to Will Jones as, "Low-key science fiction. A very small encounter, not a lot of hardware... *Drums Along the Mohawk* with extra-terrestrials."

Drums Along the Mohawk (1939) was the first color feature by Spielberg's directorial idol John Ford, later portrayed in *The Fabelmans* by David Lynch. It stars Claudette Colbert and Henry Fonda as a young couple aspiring to build a home and family amid the Revolutionary War happening in their frontier backyard of Mohawk Valley, NY. It features actress Sarah McKlennar in a standout role as a well-to-do widow remarkably outspoken for her time, a perfect model for Sayles' strong female characters.

Ford's film has several attacks on the settlers by Seneca raiding parties, joined with British Loyalists, where the Natives are portrayed as crazed drunken wild men. They set homes ablaze and chase after settlers with a manic energy that certainly could have inspired the nasties of *Night Skies* and later *Gremlins*. Critics have pointed to *Drums Along the Mohawk* as a prelude to Ford's Eastmancolor marvel *The Searchers* (1956), whose Chief Scar (Harry Brandon) gave *Night Skies*' principal baddie Skar his nickname.

"Sayles and Spielberg are both interested in the values of the Western," says Nayman. "Sayles is interested in characters who hold on to American values and practice them. Spielberg is more interested in how those values become imbued early on, but they're both interested in principle and integrity. Sayles is community minded. Spielberg has communities all looking up in a stunned/religious way. If you compare Sayles to Spielberg, by principle he occupies a different rung within the industry. You define the Spielbergs by the Sayleses. In the '80s, that division is the story of the American decade... if Sayles had been working in the '70s, would he have been Hal Ashby? Would he have been Michael Ritchie? Slightly more mainstream? There was a more mainstream appetite for that stuff that disappears fast, as the middle class disappears."

Beyond a few pages of notes, the original *Watch the Skies* draft did not appear to be part of Sayles' extant files. Instead, the widely circulated second—and ultimately final—draft where the title switched to *Night Skies* is the one we will focus on in this chapter.

The title *Watch the Skies* is inspired by the famous final line "keep watching the skies" in Howard Hawks' *The Thing from Another World*, and it was also the original working title for *Close Encounters* (supposedly suggested by Martin Scorsese's 9-year-old daughter Cathy, according to Peter Biskind). As he says in *Sayles on Sayles*, "It eventually got called *Night Skies* because somebody had the rights to the words 'Watch the Skies.'"

Spielberg likes the first shot of his movies to be a defining metaphor for the entire movie, and Sayles' script does just that. It opens with a field mouse darting through grass until it is suddenly picked up by a hawk who swoops in from the sky and takes it in its claws, then lands by a barbed wire fence to pick at it.

Nearby driving a fence post into the ground is Tess Bishop, a girl in her late teens, alongside Jaybird, her non-verbal autistic brother (age 10) who is arranging Tess's tools in neat rows. When she tells Jaybird they have to go he begins stimming (flapping his hands) before she gently guides him to a pickup truck.

They drive over to Spradlin's Package and General Store where Jaybird immediately climbs onto a bucking coin-operated rocket ship outside, which he is too big for. This underscores his mental handicap while foreshadowing what's to come. After Tess buys some baking supplies, she has a conversation with a Native American named Mr. Bullbear about grazing stock at Jim Turley's farm being mutilated the night before.

We transition to Tess pulling up to the Turley ranch where a group of men (including her father Ed, Sheriff Love and his son Von) are circled around the deceased body of a Hereford cow in the grass. All the skin from its neck is gone, as are its genitals, with a perfect circle the size of a grapefruit hollowed out of its head. Turley speculates it's "one of those hoodoo outfits," meaning Satanists.

To tie this back to "real" incidents, in the 1979 book *The Terror* author Michael D. Albers details an exchange he had with an actual long-haired, pentagram-wearing member of the Sons of Satan, who denied Satanists were to blame for cattle mutilations. The cult member blamed the dead animals on Martians, saying, "They're taking the animal parts for study. Lots of people out there have seen their flying saucers. Maybe they're going to clone the cattle and only need small pieces?"

Says Sayles, "I came up with this idea these were the same creatures who were mutilating cattle and horses, which was a strange phenomenon. I've talked to various people who had that happen on their ranches. Right about that time there was a lot of literature about it."

That literature included 1976's *Mystery Stalks the Prairie* by Roberta Donovan and Keith Wolverton and 1979's pamphlet *The Night Mutilators* by Gene Duplantier, as well as the seminal 1980 documentary *A Strange Harvest* by Peabody award-winning journalist Linda Moulton Howe. In the Donovan/Wolverton book, descriptions very much match what is in Sayles' script: "The cow's bag, teats, rectal area and reproductive organs were removed, thus making it possible to look completely through the bag area and out the rectal opening... the cut, obviously made with a very sharp instrument, had serrated edges similar to those created with pinking shears."

CUFOS' J. Allen Hynek seemed dismissive of a relationship between cattle mutilations and UFOs. He told an audience at Southern Illinois University in '78, "At first, we thought it was a satanic cult," though he admitted to not knowing what the cause was since there never seemed to be tracks near the bodies. "People don't want to talk about it. I hope it's got nothing to do with UFOs, but if it does it's something we'll have to deal with."

There is even an allusion to the work Sayles was doing on *Night Skies* in Joe Dante's *The Howling*, which he wrote around this same period. After some cattle are found mutilated near a barbed wire fence, members of the colony set out in the daylight to hunt for what killed the animals. One of them, old codger Erle (John Carradine), states, "I still think it was UFOs. Them cattle mutilations!" To which Noble Willingham's Charlie replies, "Good, Erle, good. You watch the skies for us now!"

Dante was not surprised, saying, "John was also writing *Alligator* at the same time. I've long been of the opinion that one of my dream sequences ended up in *Alligator* and their dream sequence ended up in mine. They would bring him to town and he would hole up in a motel on Sunset Boulevard. You'd make an appointment to see him, hear him typing at the door. You knock on the door and he says, 'Who is it?' 'It's the guys from *The Howling*.' 'Okay, just a minute...' He'd pull out the paper that he was typing *Alligator* on."

Back to the scene on Turley's farm, in an important character beat Ed asks his daughter Tess why Jaybird is there and she says, "he likes to get out of the house," to which Ed replies, "He doesn't know the difference."

Then a mysterious helicopter arrives next to two more cow carcasses on the property, bringing officials contacted by the sheriff who has "a special number for this kind of stuff." A pair of Air Force investigators named Jerry and

Sam hop out of the copter to question Turley. The Air Force Office of Special Investigations (AFOSI) are often referred to as "the real Men in Black." Turley tells them that the night before he saw red and white lights which were gone by the time he got to the animal bodies. Sam tells the sheriff these mutilations have been moving in a steady progression northward from the south.

Tess and Von tentatively make a date for that night, a clear history between them. The third carcass' entire head has had the skin removed, revealing the skull, while the udder has been scooped out and repacked with sand. Jerry takes photos. Jaybird kneels by the second body, tracing his finger around the circle cut in its head. Sam says get away.

Comments autistic film director Sam Chown Ahern (*The Stimming Pool*), "This carcass skull probably isn't like anything any of them have ever seen. There's an alien element in that, and he's clearly quite fascinated by the circular, symmetrical motion, the shape that makes. If he's very structured in terms of ordering up all the tools, then I can imagine that would be very pleasing for him to see it as a perfect sphere, so to speak, in the head of a cow. That's lovely, even though it's quite dark at the same time."

We transition from the mutilated cow bodies to a plucked chicken being gutted and cleaned by Tess's mother Ruth in their modern kitchen, while Gram (Ed's mother/Tess's grandma) chops stuffing. Gram asks Ruth to fetch eggs from the chicken house in the backyard. While heading out Ruth gets a migraine, which she thanks the lord for.

In his script document, Sayles included a helpful floor plan for the house, showing placement of all the bedrooms, kitchen, living room, pantry, Watt's workshop—even the cat door into Jaybird's room. A similar schematic was included in Raymond Fowler's book *The Andreasson Affair*. There is also an overhead layout of the farm, including cattle pens, tractor shed, stable, silage, and chicken house.

Inside the chicken house we are introduced to the third kid in the family, Watt (age 16), Tess and Jaybird's teenage brother sitting on feed stacks reading *Heavy Metal* magazine while listening to music. We cut to an old piano in the chicken house which Tess plays, having intended to join a music conservatory on scholarship but deferred so she could stay home and take care of Jaybird. As it turns out, this story element bears a striking similarity to the life of Kelly-Hopkinsville historian/family member Geraldine Sutton Stith, who was exactly the character of Tess's age at this point in 1980, having just graduated from high school. That's not the only similarity, though...

"He's passed away now, but I had a younger brother that was mentally handicapped, and I helped take care of him," Sutton says of younger brother Daniel. "When he started school back then they didn't have classes for the mentally handicapped, so I made sure he was in his room every day, I took care of him at recess, made sure he got home. I took care of him until the day came they realized it wasn't doing him any good to go to school and took him out. When I was reading *Night Skies*, I thought, 'Wow, it sounds like this kid's autistic.' Daniel was severely mentally handicapped, but to look at him you couldn't tell it... he looked like a normal kid. The funny thing is, later on when things finally started coming into order with people like him, we were able to get him tested and they found out that he was partially autistic also."

Sutton states that when she first read Sayles' script she found the echoes of herself and Daniel compared to Tess and Jaybird to be "kind of eerie." After her father Elmer married her stepmother they had five children in a row, so it made sense that much of the care of Daniel went to Geraldine, the oldest. As she said of her late brother, "he was mine."

After Ruth tells Watt not to blast his Top 40 music around the livestock, he and his black and white border collie Kelso are met by Tess, who rushes to tell Watt about the mutilations. Already fascinated by the subject, Watt begins speculating the aliens who did it might be from the Dog Star (i.e. Sirius, brightest star in the night sky), as in an article he read about an abductee.

Ed comes home and tries to get Jaybird out of Tess's truck, making it obvious to the audience that he has very little to do with the boy normally. As Sayles told this author, "I started thinking about, 'What are the family dynamics?'"

When Jaybird is brought inside Watt says "Hiya, Einstein" to his little brother, with Tess chastising: "Don't call him that. He's probably smarter than all of us."

"I knew people who had autistic kids in their family," Sayles explained. "Growing up with a brother or sister who has some kind of disability changes the siblings."

The family spitballs what might have caused the mutilations: Religious cult, Indians, ETs doing field research, the government working for agribusiness to scare them off their land, etc. Ed then sends Watt to fix the fence out by the transformers.

In Tess's room she contemplates an empty suitcase as we see framed reviews of her piano concerts. She goes through the connecting door into Jaybird's eerily neat room, where he studies a checkerboard silently. She tries to initiate a game, but he keeps moving her red pieces back to starting position. Then their cat Fritz (an R. Crumb allusion) comes through the cat-door and jumps on the board, sending pieces flying. Jaybird freaks out at the sudden disorder, flapping his hands and shaking his head. Tess grabs his head and yells at him to stop, then she begins crying, "Oh honey. What am I gonna do with you?"

Sayles said, "I remember one woman whose brother was autistic, pretty far on the spectrum, and she thought he would like chess because he had this mathematical mind. She tried to teach him chess and he would get so upset when she showed him the rules. She realized it was because he loved having them in their place, and moving them messed up the symmetry of it. He really loved it. 'Oh, this is where the rooks go, this is where the knights go, and it makes such a beautiful picture.' It ended up being a great present that he always kept on his dresser, but you didn't move a piece."

We cut to Watt exerting himself with a post-hole digger by power lines in a vast range, radio blaring from the pickup truck. Suddenly both the sound of the radio and the buzz of the transformer spikes. Watt turns off the radio, goes back to digging, then a vast shadow drifts toward him as the electric buzz ceases. The teen looks up to see a scary, red-tinged cloud directly overhead in the clear sunny sky. Kelso growls at it, hides under the truck. Watt tries to run to the shadow's edge but the cloud moves with him.

Then a beam of light shoots down from this cloud, causing him to run back to the truck. At first the vehicle will not start, then the field becomes sunny again and the cloud is gone. Kelso hops in the front seat and the ignition works, with the radio jolting on à la *Close Encounters*. He heads for home.

Meanwhile the rest of the family is having lunch in the kitchen. Ed admonishes Jaybird for spinning a honey lid on the table instead of eating. He makes Tess take it away from him, causing him to stim. "He'll eat if he's hungry," Tess tells her dad. Ed then discusses putting Jaybird in a state home, telling Tess she's throwing her life away looking after him. She insists Jaybird does not belong in an institution.

Watt comes in to tell everyone about his extraterrestrial encounter, with Ed replying skeptically, "You didn't invite him to lunch?" Tess has a flicker of belief in what Watt is telling them, but Ed thinks he's stoned and Gram compares him to his great-grandfather who went crazy "digging in the garden like a gopher."

There's a cut to a few of Sayles' signature vignettes around the farm. Jaybird's in the chicken house arranging eggs methodically into cartons when both the chickens and Jaybird become still and alert at something we cannot see. Suddenly the chickens and Jaybird go crazy, which Sayles' script notes confirm is Jaybird having "mental contact" with the aliens, something 1982's *E.T.* would approach more extensively/positively.

Meanwhile Ed and Watt ride on horseback to examine a calf with an infection in its eye. Still glancing up at the sky, stirred from his encounter, Watt tells his dad he wants to join the Air Force, which Ed will not abide. This has echoes later in 2005's *War of the Worlds*, where Tom Cruise's son (played by Justin Chatwin) wants to join in the Army's fight against the invading nasties, to his father's chagrin.

We see Tess playing a beautiful Chopin piece in the chicken house as Jaybird watches the piano's innards of strings and hammers move, fascinated. Then Von arrives in his TransAm to pick up Tess for their date and she goes to the stable, explaining to him, "That's where I hide my diaphragm these days."

Jaybird and Fritz the cat run into the house, the boy beginning to open and shut the refrigerator door to see the light blink on and off. He moves over to the blender, turning it on, dropping bits of food into the blades. Gram swoops in, grabbing Jaybird and the cat, saying "You'll be tossing Fritz into the blender," possibly inspiring the scene of the mom blending one of the *Gremlins* in that 1984 film.

Jaybird then unemotionally observes his mother using a sewing machine on a pair of pants. When the needle stops, he just stares, waiting for it to turn on again. Ruth hugs him, saying she wishes he could talk to her, and that she talks to the Lord about him.

Sayles illuminates, "I thought that was an interesting thing, that just as the aliens are a mystery to the farm people and the farm people and their livestock are a mystery to the aliens, here's a kid in their own family and he's a bit of a mystery to them."

Transition to one of the aliens' POV as it scuttles from the road through riverside growth to hear Tess and Von as they canoodle, Von talking about how much he had been thinking of her and Tess saying, "right there." The writer stresses in the script that there will have to be a discussion of what an ET's POV looks like (infrared, black and white, segmented, etc.). He then time jumps post-coitus as the two of them, half-undressed, stare into the woods by the riverside. Tess says she saw something move in the trees, but Von brushes it off as they make love again.

Back at the farmhouse Ruth tells Watt to tie up Kelso since the neighbor's dog is in heat. After Watt finds the dog and tells him "No nookie for you tonight, buddy," he takes him toward the chicken house and tells him to "watch the skies for me."

We cut to a scene at the local dive bar, which crosses the conversation between Tess and Von about Jaybird's delayed development with ranch kids Les and Joel playing pool while debating cattle mutilations. At one point they echo the Satanist's line from *The Terror* about aliens bringing cattle pieces back so they can clone them (to make hamburgers). The conversation with Tess makes a point of saying Jaybird will sometimes listen to Watt's broken transistor radio for hours, "picking up different stations than we are." Von tells Tess she's throwing her talent away by staying put.

The two lovebirds transition to sitting in Von's TransAm overlooking a dark bluff at night, chatting about a boy Tess has been seeing in Von's absence. Suddenly they notice a kind of eerie glowing God light emanating from between the rows of trees near Rinker's orchard in the distance. A frightened coyote darts past the car away from the light. Von drives the car down the hill until the lights switch off and it rolls to a stop. Then the light begins revolving, jolting up over the trees and disappearing. Whatever made the light left a phosphorescent glow on the trees.

Tess and Von move further into the clearing to investigate, spotting a crazy old man wearing only denim overalls sitting on a stump. When Tess touches his shoulder he leaps up and starts talking crazy about "angels," then Von's father Sheriff Love arrives. Examining the crazy man with a flashlight, the Sheriff and his partner Curtis spot strange marks on his arms and shoulders.

At the farmhouse Watt is getting a Turkish station on his ham radio as Jaybird traces the circuits with his fingers when Tess returns, telling her family about the UFO and crazy man she just encountered. As she speaks excitedly, nobody notices Jaybird walk out the door she left open. He walks through the cultivated field with Fritz when a beam of light appears behind him, heading towards him. Revolving red and white lights indicate the ship above about to land. Jaybird imitates their spinning, then when they disappear he simply walks away as if nothing happened.

The boy comes back in the house acting wired, spinning the TV dial rapidly until someone leads him away. Without warning the lights begin dimming like a brown-out as Kelso barks outside. Watt calls to the dog, whose barking stops suddenly. Ed checks the fuse box on the back porch when an arc jolts him back. The lights go out completely. Ed meets Watt in the yard, where they find Kelso's rope cut. They head to the cattle pens where lead alien Skar skitters past their flashlight as they discover one of their cows mutilated, its facial skin and eyeballs removed.

Inside the house, Ruth is beginning to go into a religious state, chanting to the Lord. Although Geraldine Sutton Stith's family was very religious, especially her grandmother Glennie Lankford (who attended church on the night of the Kelly encounter), she found Ruth's religiosity in the script to be "a cliché"... as did Spielberg in his script notes.

"My grandmother was really religious, and the mother in this script is really religious, praying and all this stuff," says Stith. "It's funny how they throw religion in when it comes to extraterrestrials. It makes you wonder why they do that. My grandmother went to church like a good little woman should and believed she should raise her children to be right, to be just, to be godly. It's how she lived, but she wasn't a fanatic."

Film journalist Lindsey Romain agrees: "That is a city person's perspective of rural people, where there's the one steadfast Christian person. Usually, a whole family is like that. Families are all different, but I would say in my experience it's a little inauthentic to be like, 'All of us have these different personalities!' The Margaret White in *Carrie* thing is an apt comparison as a stereotype fanatic mother. The name 'Ruth' is an interesting evocation, because Ruth in the Bible is, like, family... loyal... mother... steadfast... hopeful... obviously there's some correlation there."

The kitchen microwave begins to literally melt. Jaybird arranges marbles in his room by moonlight when the cat door's flap moves. Jaybird's cat then walks into frame from inside the room, so whatever is at the cat door is not the cat. The arm of the benevolent alien Buddee reaches in and grabs one of the marbles, similar to the way E.T. is introduced grabbing Reese's Pieces. In exchange, the alien leaves a small silver ring, which spins on its own, making a buzzing sound which fascinates Jaybird. Tess enters the room with a lit candle, sets up a white sheet of paper and some fingerpaints for her brother. She leaves, then Buddee re-enters through the open window.

Meanwhile, outside on the range Ed and Watt swing their flashlights along the yard, noticing the cattle are spooked. Suddenly, they hear galloping and see briefly in the beam of Watt's light a cow running past them with the alien Squirt riding its back. Then they hear a chattering nearby and see Skar's gleaming eyes staring at them. Ed blasts it with his shotgun, but misses, thinking it might be a coyote. As Hicks said in 1986's *Aliens*, "I like to keep this handy... [cocks shotgun]... for close encounters."

Hearing the shot ring out, Tess begins locking all the windows and doors as her zealot mother Ruth begins speaking apocalyptically of "the time has come." Then Ruth turns around to see the alien Klud looking through the window from the outside. She screams and Klud bolts away. "They're here! They're here!" she says, echoing a line heard in both *E.T.* and *Poltergeist*, the latter using it as a tagline. She thinks the thing is a demon.

Inside Jaybird's room, the boy is fingerpainting intricate patterns that resemble circuits while Buddee sits across from him looking on. The boy paints on the cute alien's face, then Buddee starts painting on another sheet of paper.

Watt and Ed run inside. The lights glow then shut off again as the candles go out. The camera pans from person to person as scratching is heard on the wall outside. Gram repeatedly askes "What's happening?" (another pull for *Poltergeist*). Ed spots Klud in the window and blasts it. Hearing Kelso barking, Watt opens the door only to see the ET Hoodoo standing there, Ed immediately firing on it as it ducks. They lock the door.

Tess runs to grab Jaybird. When she walks in on he and Buddee sitting together like best pals, she screams her lungs out. Startled, the alien hops out the window, leaving behind a celestial map it painted on a sheet of paper. In the living room, Ed covers the door with a shotgun as Ruth prays and Tess clutches a squirming Jaybird. Then a blue light peers through the window as a voice calls for "Ed Bishop"... it's Sheriff Love and his deputy Curtis, asking Ed to lower his gun. Von is there too. The crazy man in the orchard is in the police car to be taken to the Air Force guys, the marks on his arms now gone.

The Sheriff and Ed survey the damage around the property, discovering a dead chicken drained of all its blood as well as Ed's own shotgun damage. This mirrors the police intervention mid-way through the Kelly-Hopkinsville ordeal. Ed talks about how he shot them and could not have missed, just like Kentucky. Also mirroring real-life, Tess sits at the kitchen table sketching what the being Buddee looked like, as the Sutton family did for Bud Ledwith. It would not be surprising if Buddee's name was inspired by Bud Ledwith, just as Sheriff Love's name was likely a nod to *Night Skies* director Ron Cobb's wife Robin Love. (Says Love, "Perhaps John found me a bit overbearing!")

When Tess finishes her drawing with input from the others, the crazy man sees it and screams "Angel of Death!" Love takes the orchard man in handcuffs along with the sketch, saying he's going to show it to the Air Force people. Von gives Tess a worried look from the police car as it drives off. Kelso is still missing. Jaybird is put to bed by Tess. After telling everyone not to say a word of what they saw, Ed takes Watt to go check on the livestock, leaving Ruth alone as Tess goes to take a bath. Gram mutters to herself about how nutty her whole family is while wrapping leftovers from dinner.

Things start to settle. Ed examines the stable. Watt checks the chicken house, where he starts relaxing with a copy of *Hustler*. Tess undresses for her bath. Ruth watches a televangelist on TV as the picture starts to flux just as Buddee's weird ring, resting on the coffee table, begins to spin on its own. The hand of Hoodoo presses against the TV screen, causing the picture to return. As the ring spins hypnotically, Ruth stares at Hoodoo as she goes into a trance, saying "yes" over and over. The script notes refer to Ruth thinking of Hoodoo like a "Shaman" (his initial script nickname), while the sinister TV manipulation is something carried over/elaborated on in *Poltergeist*.

In the kitchen Gram is putting Saran Wrap away when she opens the pantry and screams as the small alien Squirt stands inside the cabinet with uncooked spaghetti poking out of its mouth. The sticks drop as it starts chattering. Gram tells it to shoo, swinging a broom at it, but the creature merely holds onto the end of the broom delighted at the ride as he is swung around the room.

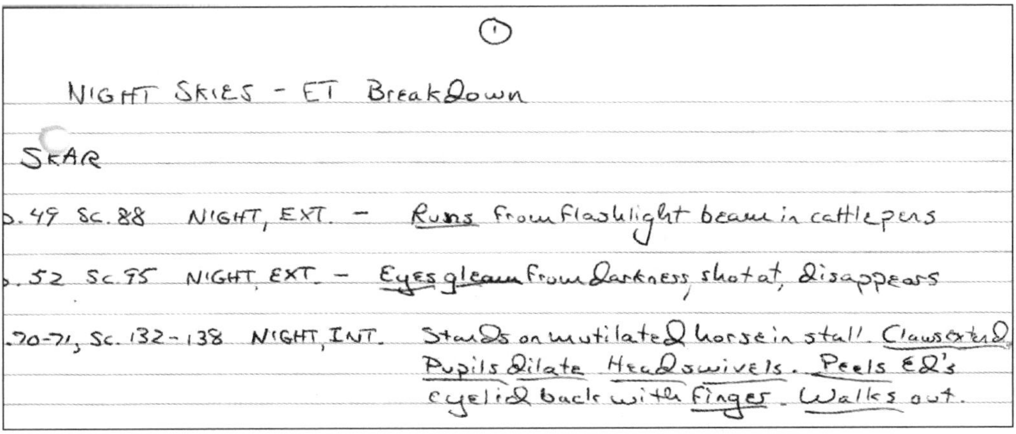
1

NIGHT SKIES - ET BreakDown

SKAR

p. 49 Sc. 88 NIGHT, EXT. - Runs from flashlight beam in cattlepens

p. 52 Sc. 95 NIGHT, EXT. - Eyes gleam from darkness, shot at, disappears

p. 70-71, Sc. 132-138 NIGHT, INT. Stands on mutilated horse in stall. Claws extend. Pupils dilate. Head swivels. Peels Ed's eyelid back with finger. Walks out.

Inside the stable Ed finds the lead alien Skar standing over an eviscerated horse, the ET's bloody claws extending not unlike the aliens in 1957's *Invasion of the Saucer Men*. Demonstrating his psychic ability, Skar's pupils go so wide his eyes are entirely black, making a standing horse kick its hind legs into Ed's face, the farmer falling to the ground. Skar lifts the man's eyelid to make sure he's unconscious, then flees.

Back to Watt in the chicken house, his porno mag gets poultry shit on it as he notices the chickens are now loose around the structure. He spots the alien Klud in the rafters, the being floating down next to the teen boy. It takes a gander at the *Hustler*, then grabs the blaring transistor radio before getting chased out by Watt.

Cut to Skar outside Jaybird's window, extending glowing red fingers to melt the glass and reach in. In the bathtub, Tess begins to notice finger paint marks near the clothes hamper. The lid rises with Buddee's eyes peering out at her, making her gasp. She tries to cover herself as Buddee watches, climbing across the wall over to the toilet to get a better view of her. It accidentally flushes the toilet which scares a screeching Buddee, who jumps into the tub with Tess. She promptly leaps out and runs out of the bathroom.

In Jaybird's room the boy tries touching Skar's face the way he did Buddee, but Skar screeches and runs in circles. Jaybird mimics this. Tess comes into the room gasping at what she sees, snatching Jaybird into her adjacent bedroom, slamming the door.

Explains Sayles, "There was a range of behavior with the aliens. Some of them were just curious and others were a bit more, 'Well, we're gonna kill these things and stuff them and bring them home.' That helped to have some shades on both sides of the battle."

In the kitchen Gram continues battling Squirt as he turns the stove on and throws random food into the flames. The older woman tries to beat him with the broom, which catches fire. Squirt hops on a table and begins poking her face until her false teeth fly out, which freaks the screeching alien. Gram pops her teeth back in and swats the alien good with her broom, saying she means business. It is a silly scene which very much brings to mind the kitchen battle in *Gremlins*.

In the living room Ruth is praying before Hoodoo, who leaves when Skar beckons his squad with a clacking sound from outside. Klud, trying to communicate with a chicken he's holding, scoots out to join the alien gang in the yard. Inside the family regroups and attempts to call Sheriff Love, but the phone is disconnected. They barricade themselves in the kitchen, pushing tables and chairs to block off the living room passageway, and nailing scraps of wood to the windows à la *Night of the Living Dead*. Ruth tells Ed that Hoodoo sent her a psychic thought warning the family to "act better." Something unseen begins reinforcing the barricade from the other side, as if it wants them there.

Buddee watches as Klud and Hoodoo take a trunk from Tess's room, then makes his way to Watt's workshop. The ET turns the short-wave radio around and—just as fascinated by the inner workings as Jaybird—the thing begins rapidly rewiring it at "three times normal speed," after which Buddee turns the dial so a red light starts blinking, as if sending a signal. This has obvious linkage to the Speak & Spell communication array E.T. makes (designed by Henry Feinberg) in the 1982 film.

On the kitchen floor the entire family is huddled together in the dark as they hear piano-playing in the chicken house. The blender revs to life, startling everybody. The fridge leaks as if rapidly defrosting. Ruth opens the freezer door and their cat Fritz leaps out growling. Windows crack as the boards over them bend and break. An intense white light streams through the cracked windows as long tubular tentacles with beams of illumination at the end make their way through the windows into the house, light flowing through them in strobes. Ed tries to shoot one, but he is zapped by several shocks emanating from it like a taser, doing the same to Tess so she lets go of Jaybird. Three tentacles in all herd the family against a far wall as the door bursts open and Jaybird runs into the yard.

Watt goes out there to try to start the truck but it's dead, so he gets on one of the horses to—according to Ed's instructions—call the fire department to say "the house is burning," Ed's instinct to deny that night's events. Meanwhile, on a grassy knoll, the four sinister aliens (Skar, Hoodoo, Klud, Squirt) encircle Jaybird as he lays down with his arms outstretched in a kind of ritualistic scene. Hoodoo extends his long fingernail and traces a precise circle on the child's forehead, then another on his chest over the heart.

"I got the idea that one of their sons was autistic, and the alien creatures were fascinated with him," Sayles says of this scene. "You're worried because you've seen them killing livestock and emptying them out... is that what they're going to do to him?"

As Ed walks the range looking for Jaybird, Gram helps Tess push her piano out of the chicken house and into the yard. Back at the knoll, Skar has his palm on Jaybrid's forehead about to mutilate him like they did to the animals... when his hand gets knocked away with a "WHAP!" by Buddee. The friendly alien begins to fight the nasty alien as the two slash at each other with their claws, tumbling down the knoll with the other three following, leaving the autistic boy alone. Suddenly Jaybird hears stormy piano music blaring from the distant yard as Tess plays hard. The bloody brawl between Skar and Buddee is intercut with Jaybird searching out the music as Ruth and Gram shine flashlights looking for him, Ed also looking among the cattle. Buddee runs away from the other aliens as Ed finally finds Jaybird.

The scene of piano playing in a field during a skirmish with a hostile threat was directly inspired by John Huston's 1960 western *The Unforgiven*, which features a scene of Lillian Gish playing a piano in a field to drown out the drums and flute playing of a Native American war party. Her sons (Burt Lancaster and Doug McClure) stand by with rifles as she plays, which spooks their enemies. Multiple Native Americans then cross a lake on horseback to destroy the piano, picked off one by one by the men.

Cut to the unlit main road into town as Watt gallops on his horse. Out of the distance a light appears, heading towards him. Picking up the horse's pace, he gallops towards the vehicle until it swiftly lifts up in the air. Realizing it's a spacecraft, Watt turns his animal towards the opposite direction with the ship in pursuit. He returns to the homestead to warn everyone "They're coming!" as the spaceship hovers over the illuminated livestock.

As Klud and Hoodoo advance, the family is led by Ed to shelter in the tractor shed as the ship's spotlight searches for them. The two aliens scatter toward the barn. Once locked inside, Watt lights a bug candle as they hear the piano destroyed, Tess declaring, "What'd they have to do that for?" Ruth is praying to the lord when beams of the large cultivator go on behind them as the engine starts. The large vehicle smashes into the back wall, with Ed quickly stabbing a tire iron through the ventilator, stopping the engine.

Skar reaches in through the new hole in the wall as a ray of laser light burns a square hole in the roof for the bright alien tentacles to get in. Ed tries to fight them off, but the family huddles together to meet their fate... when suddenly the approaching aliens stop. There is a rumbling, a changing of the light. At Skar's barking command, the ETs grab the tentacles and are whisked out of the barn.

A concussive boom leads Jaybird to unbar the door, letting in a new kind of ET we haven't seen yet, a tall Cypress-shaped creature. Its giant metallic ship hovers in the air behind it as Jaybird approaches, with Tess yelling his name. The family comes to the front of the shed where Jaybird has turned to face them with a focus we have never seen in the boy. Cypress has placed its hand on the back of the boy's neck, allowing him to speak through the non-verbal child. The dialogue opens with "I am come. There has been a hurting... a sorrow." It proceeds to essentially tell them in broken speech that what happened to them was not meant to happen, that their species' normal behavior is just to observe, as they have done throughout time. It says they will be left alone, ending with a cryptic line: "Across time you will know."

"At the end of the script, these higher aliens—kind of the adult aliens—show up, and they can communicate with this kid," Sayles said. "Very simple things, nothing too complicated, but somehow they can help the kid communicate to his own family."

Cypress lets go of Jaybird, but then the boy tugs on the alien's arm, pleading to let him speak just once to his family. The alien complies, replacing the hand, upon which—in a very emotional beat—Jaybird looks at each member of his family saying, "He loves you." Jaybird then shudders and drops to his knees as Cypress floats away into a light beam that flashes him onto the ship.

The craft blasts away in an instant, gone. Watt makes a comment about their dog being missing, probably on its way to the Dog Star.

Cut to the next morning as we survey all the damage done to the homestead (the tractor shed demolished by the cultivator, the piano smashed, torn out windows, etc.). Ed puts a patch of screen on one of the windows, beginning the healing process as it were. Gram and Ruth clean the kitchen as Watt examines the short-wave in his workshop, which shocks him. Jaybird is fingerpainting in his room (Buddee's celestial map nearby) as Tess enters to say goodbye, telling him he will do well at the special school he's going to. Jaybird begins drawing circuit diagrams over the celestial map.

Tess packs her suitcase, then puts it down to look at her brother one more time. She asks, "You aren't gonna forget who I am, are you Jaybird?" Uncharacteristically, Jaybird looks back at her and seems to know she is leaving. He goes to the orderly checkerboard at his desk, moving pieces out of their rows, staining them with fingerpaint, then sits on his bed staring toward the wall. "I'll miss you so much," Tess says.

Ed comes in, saying he's going to see Sheriff Love to tell him the story, hoping it can stay out of the papers, echoing Elmer Sutton's standpoint of not wanting people invading their lives. He suggests that with a potential insurance payout they can buy her a new piano. Tess smiles, telling her dad to give Von a message that she'll be in for lunch after she packs. Ed then turns to Jaybird, asking if he'd like to come to town for the rocket ride he likes. No response. Showing warmth toward the boy for the first time, Ed takes Jaybird's hand and says, "Come on, son."

As they cross the yard, Jaybird looks up at the sky and spies a hawk soaring above, on the hunt. The camera stays on the hawk's shadow as it flies over the vast, unpopulated prairie. Eventually we see Buddee, who has been left stranded on earth by his fellow ETs. Covered with cuts from his fight with Skar, there are still traces of Jaybird's blue paint on him. We pull back into an aerial shot of Buddee as "*a solitary stranger in a strange land*."

Comments Josh Miller, "This movie is almost like a weird prequel to *E.T.* given the fact that it ends with Buddee left stranded on Earth, kind of tragically.

I'm not sure what we're really supposed to feel. His friends all suck, so maybe it's also a little happy. You hope that Buddee and Jaybird will reunite."

The most popular current podcast revolving specifically around unmade scripts is the show *Best Movies Never Made*, hosted by screenwriter Josh Miller (*Sonic the Hedgehog* franchise) and film producer Stephen Scarlata (*Jodorowsky's Dune*). In fact, the very first episode of the show was dedicated to *Night Skies*, with Rick Baker's sculpt of the alien Buddee serving as their social media avatar.

Says Miller. "I don't know how necessarily super famous *Night Skies* is to the average person, but it's more the idea that it became *E.T.* and *Poltergeist* and a billion other things. That's what makes it so fascinating, because everybody saw *E.T.*, and one of the most heartwarming movies of all time spawned from this mean spirited, creepy cattle mutilation alien movie."

"It's probably one of the first unproduced movies you hear about," adds Scarlata. "There was this rumor you heard for years, 'Spielberg almost made this evil alien movie, and it didn't get made but it inspired *Gremlins* and *Poltergeist*, then turned into *E.T.*' That was just a rumor for years and years and years. This project was mentioned in *Cinefantastique* and *Starburst* and all these magazines, always came up in conversations."

Screenwriter Ian Fried (*Spectral*), who also did the illustrations for this book, admits the motivation of the impish ETs in this script is murky at best: "There are a lot of things in *Night Skies* where you're like, 'What?' They're here to do experiments and then they run out of time for some reason? Because the Cypress alien shows up, the one with no mouth. For a first or second draft, are the bones solid here? Does this work as a movie? Yeah, but there's stuff we can work on and refine and develop further."

Even though her family did a great deal to keep the Kelly incident out of the limelight for decades, Elmer Sutton's daughter Geraldine Sutton Stith now embraces the legend. She also embraces the *Night Skies* script, which she read for the first time specifically for this book, telling the author, "It's not a bad little story at all. There are similarities like the little things coming up to the doors and windows… of course, these were coming in the house. They weren't that active in Kelly, they weren't doing all the things they were doing in this story, but it's okay. That makes it a little more exciting. You've got something mutilating cattle, that puts an eerie element into it."

The script's biggest surprise is the realistic depiction of Jaybird's autism, at that time neither widely understood nor a household word. The film which brought autism into public consciousness was director Barry Levinson's 1988 Best Picture winner *Rain Man*, starring Dustin Hoffman as a deeply dysfunctional autistic-savant who goes on an emotional road trip with his estranged brother, played by Tom Cruise.

"*Rain Man* was the best thing that ever happened to autism," psychiatrist Dr. Darold Treffert told *The Guardian* in 2018. "No gigantic public education or PR effort could have produced the sensational awareness that *Rain Man* brought to the national and international radar screen."

Spielberg was at one time prior to Levinson the director on that film, developing it for many months with screenwriter Ron Bass. In the same *Guardian* article, the first screenwriter Barry Morrow claimed, "The word 'autism' never appeared in my original screenplay." Morrow's main character took inspiration from a real individual with intellectual disabilities named Bill Sakter, whom Morrow previously wrote a TV movie about. It was not until Spielberg was onboard that Hoffman suggested changing Raymond from a mentally handicapped man to someone far down the autism spectrum, combined with the savant abilities of another real individual named Kim Peek.

To quote Spielberg from his 1987 script conference with Bass, "We met several savant autistics... talking to them briefly, I saw Dustin was right. It was very hard for them to accept affection of any kind, but they had a kind of social behavior I found very interesting that Dustin imitates and will eventually perform very well."

As Bass recalled Spielberg saying for a *New Yorker* profile, "'This is a love story between two brothers. What's the most important thing in any love story? It's the obstacle—what is it that keeps these two people who are supposed to be in love from being in love until the end? If the guy is retarded and runs around holding somebody's hand, what's the obstacle? Just that Tom Cruise is a hard case? You know Tom's going to soften, and you can see the end of the movie coming at you down Fifth Avenue. But if the guy's an autistic, an incredible pain in the ass, he hates people—you've got a difficult love story.'"

Those words resonate with the emotional core of *Night Skies*, namely the brother/sister relationship between Jaybird and Tess. As in *Rain Man*, the change in Jaybird from beginning to end is minute in the subtle acknowledgment of love for his sibling... but the realm of autism is not about overnight cures or big changes in emotional makeup. Sayles' script feels sensitive in a way other writers in the early '80s would have been ill-equipped to pull off, especially in a genre context.

In the realm of neurodivergence, filmmaker Sam Chown Ahern identifies as autistic and dyspraxic, while also showing signs of dyscalculia. Part of a group called Stims Collective, Ahern hosted a neurodiverse-friendly relaxed screening of *E.T.* at the BFI in 2025, one of her favorite films. She stumbled upon the *Night Skies* history as part of her research.

"It's fascinating," says Ahern of the portrayal of Jaybird in Sayles' script. "This non-verbal kid who's stimming is very knowledgeable, although from the outside wouldn't show it. He's clearly observing things, an interest in life and nature. From the outside people just see a child who's quiet and a bit weird, and as it says in the script, can't even write his own name. Yet, he's probably one of the cleverest people in the room."

Adds Romain, "Sometimes the sensitive autistic child is a not great trope, but this one didn't come off as insensitive to me."

Says Sayles, "Everybody perceives the world in their own way. Then there are people who perceive it in such a different way they have a hard time fitting in, whether it's Asperger's syndrome or not reading faces. A friend of mine has a kid on the spectrum, and now that they have eye gaze computers, they showed him and some other autistic kids some movies. The minute a new shot came on screen, some of the kids would look for the electrical outlet, and that's where their eyes would stay. Everything else was way too busy for them. That's a different way of perceiving the world. A lot of my work deals with that. I've had movies where half the movie is in Tagalog and half in English, and there's only about three words they understand communally. We as the audience reading the subtitles get to see into their heads... but they don't understand each other."

Spielberg nearly directed another Ron Bass script about a real-life married couple with Asperger Syndrome named Jerry Newport and Mary Meinel. Bass' pitch, tentatively titled *Newport*, was purchased by the newly-minted DreamWorks SKG for $2M in 1996, with Spielberg circling to direct Robin Williams in the title part. The screenwriter told Marilyn Beck that Spielberg has long been interested in the "set of issues and problems" that face people with autism. It was eventually directed by Bass as *Mozart and the Whale* in 2005.

The *Night Skies* script has circulated for years online through fan communities, but there is very little info on Sayles' first draft, or Spielberg's initial

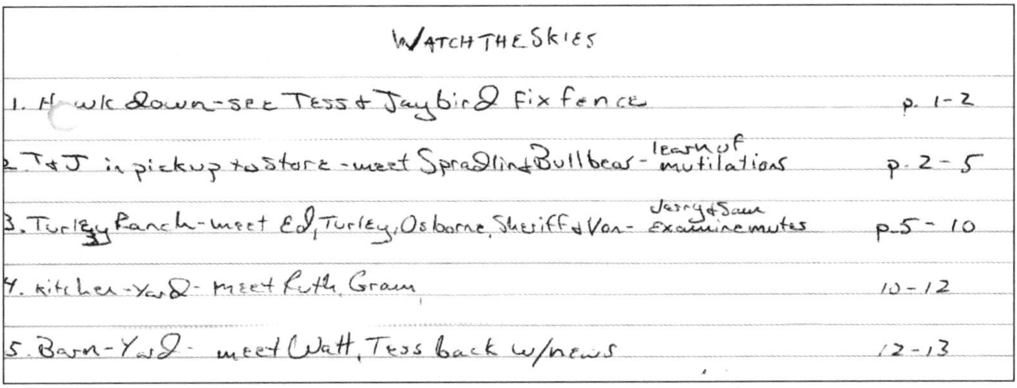
WATCH THE SKIES

1. Hawk down - see Tess & Jaybird fix fence p. 1-2
2. T&J in pickup to store - meet Spradlin & Bullbear - learn of mutilations p. 2-5
3. Turkey Ranch - meet Ed, Turley, Osborne, Sheriff & Von - Jerry & Sam examine mutes p. 5-10
4. kitchen-Yard - meet Ruth, Gram 10-12
5. Barn-Yard - meet Watt, Tess back w/news 12-13

treatment which allegedly featured 11 ETs instead of the 5 in the screenplay. The beat-for-beat in Sayles' hand-written notes for the first draft (titled *Watch the Skies*) is similar to the second except for minor differences. For one, instead of making love by the creek, Tess and Von smoke dope—echoed later with the parents in *Poltergeist*—as Tess tells her beau she has no plans to leave town. The aliens' mind control is discussed more directly by the family.

The "ritual" scene in the "Watch the Skies" notes where aliens encircle Jaybird features six ETs, not four. Assuming Buddee is still missing from the circle, this lines up with a statement by David Robert Cellitti, who claims, "Spielberg was obsessed with Disney, and there were going to be seven aliens, like the seven dwarfs... you know, wink wink."

A lack of nicknames or distinctions for each alien in initial notes became important in the later *Night Skies* draft when Sayles had to break down every shot with an ET along with their actions, presumably to aid Rick Baker and Ed Verreaux in storyboarding.

The family calls to Jaybird with a tape recording they make of the ETs themselves, not Tess's piano playing (no mention of pianos in draft 1 notes). There is a bit about how Jaybird "leads a skirmish line of ETs," with Tess talking him down from blasting his own family with a laser. That scene comes just before the cultivator section, and from there the ending is the same.

In *Watch the Skies* notes there is also a significant (crossed out) addition of Ed fixing the cultivator when Air Force investigators Jerry and Sam return to question the dad. They show him Tess's drawing of the alien, but Ed does not comment. There is a hand-written line: "don't think you see things." The Air Force/Men in Black characters are a dead end in the second draft considering they do not come back at any other point, although Sayles was able to weave two similar characters into *The Brother from Another Planet*.

Overall, John Sayles was able to execute the assignment with aplomb, while planting many seeds for what eventually became Spielberg's Amblin formula (funny, scary, emotional). This was accomplished over a few scant months in 1980 as producer Spielberg was busy making *Raiders of the Lost Ark* while assigned director Ron Cobb was preoccupied designing *Conan the Barbarian*.

Explains the writer, "I did a draft. I met Ron Cobb. I hadn't heard of any other director. This is way before Zoom, so they actually flew me to Paris. That was the one sit down meeting where we were all there at the same time. It was the first time I got to leave the country, except to drive up to Toronto and meet a friend. Ron was coming from Spain because he was doing the production design for *Conan*. Steven and his party had been scouting in Tunisia for *Raiders*. The only place we could meet was not in Hoboken, where I was, but Paris. Playing right near the hotel they put me up in was *1941*, which I hadn't seen and quite liked, but it had been Spielberg's big failure."

Sayles' duties were to develop the material with the principles. He interacted mainly with Spielberg, Cobb, and Rick Baker.

"I didn't meet the executive guys," the writer admits. "I didn't have that many meetings. I think I met John Dykstra for it, maybe... was he involved?"

John Dykstra clarified for this author, "As to *Night Skies*, I may have spoken with John Sayles, but I don't have any real memory of the exchange. We did a test for Steven for *1941*, but he defaulted to the newly minted ILM in Marin. I'm pretty sure Doug Trumbull was already doing tests for him even before it became *E.T.*"

However, it's possible both men crossed wires about this project, with Mitch Suskin clarifying, "I don't remember Dykstra or Trumbull working on it. I went to work on *Star Trek* before that with Trumbull and Dykstra. I don't remember either being on that show, but my real sphere was Rick Baker's studio in North Hollywood and don't know everything that went on outside that."

Under Sayles' tenure the *Night Skies* project never got as far as seriously looking for actors, with casting director Mike Fenton's assistant Marci Liroff saying, "I vaguely remember this script but I don't recall being involved at that point." In the realm of what ifs, when suggested that a *Foxes*-era Jodie Foster would have been ideal casting for the part of Tess, Sayles agreed.

"Yeah, she always had that kind of strength under whatever she was doing, and was a person taking risky things," says the writer of Foster. "But every once in a while there's actors you realize, 'Oh, I wish they'd been in more.'"

When this author brought up actresses contemporaneous to the 1980-81 period within the viable age range (Foster, Kristy McNichol, Tatum O'Neil, Diane Lane, Elizabeth McGovern), journalist Lindsey Romain of *Vulture* had a different view of a fan cast.

"I would ex Jodie Foster out of there, even though I think she'd be good at it," opines Romain. "She was so Jodie Foster, and my instinct for Tess goes right to Diane Lane. Kristy McNichol is interesting, though. Jodie would probably be the best at it, but I associate her with that kind of character already... spunky, rural. Clarice Starling fits into that. She would nail it. Each of those actresses would change the tone of the movie, have different presences. Whoever the person was would probably affect how I feel about that character. On the page the structure of a good female character is there, but I didn't necessarily find myself super compelled by her, if I'm being honest."

While Valerie Bertinelli was certainly the exact age of the Tess character while the script was being written, her personal relationship with Spielberg was over by the time this second draft was turned in, making her casting less likely.

The most tangible window into the development process is a letter from Spielberg to Sayles detailing his thoughts on the second draft we explored here. Dated August 5 of 1980, the 2-page typed letter is an astute assessment. The biggest takeaway is that Spielberg's instinct was to make *Night Skies* as stark in contrast with *Close Encounters* as possible, hoping for bigger scares and an even darker tone in the drafts to come, which ultimately never came...

August 5, 1980

John Sayles
210 13th St.
Hoboken New Jersey
97030

Dear John,

I spent last night reading the second draft to NIGHT SKIES and I like it very much. I feel we're certainly moving in the right direction. My initial reactions include some of the following.

Even though it was my idea, I don't like the ET's playing the piano. It's a direct steal from the movie, The Unforgiven, as is Tess playing the piano to the ET's.

What happened to the examination of Tess? What happened to the ET reading Hustler magazine and to the ET watching Johnny Carson and switching channels?

Generally I feel the incidents of the ET human contact have increased and Tess's character has greatly improved. There is, however, still a basic lack of fear of the unknown, suspense and spine tingles. I think one of the reasons for this is the first impression we get of the ET's (BUDDEE), one of trust and benevolence. It takes longer for SKAR to show how scary they can be than it does BUDDEE to show how ultimately kind they are. I know this to be in direct antithesis to my own Close Encounters of the Third Kind philosophy and my rather Disneyesque point of view regarding ET contact but we don't want to give the audience in NIGHT SKIES what they have come to expect from the Close Encounters experience. This should be an altogether different approach. After all it's a totally different movie.

I think the structure is terrific and I think all the characters work very well but what this movie thus far lacks are the two or three scenes in the contact section that our audience will never forget as long as they live. Something that just jumps off the screen, whether it's at their throats or at their hearts. Having read both drafts, I don't think we've gone far enough shaking out our imaginations.

Here are some scattered criticisms:

Prior to the Cypress involvement, there never seems to be a rapid progression to any one single climax. You think the climax will come when the family barricades themselves into a room of the house and before you know it they are again barricaded in the chicken coup but the normal rules leading to a climax don't apply and I never felt these people were in any real jeopardy.

I think Ruth's religious obsession was a little much–she somewhat reminds me of Carrie White's Bible beating mother, (Piper Laurie), in the movie CARRIE.

I still like GRAM the best and understand ED even more than I did in the first draft. He changes the most. TESS is sexier and more talented and her struggle to leave or not leave JAYBIRD; to live or not to live for herself, is tremendously emotional. I like the "touched" man from the woods and involving him further into our story is a great addition. He's a signal of what might happen with our family should the "encounter" go all the way.

Once again as I'm sure you've been told many times, you have a very free and natural association with rural behavior, dialogue and attitudes. You have accomplished something very miraculous in a story like this. You've managed to create a reality of setting and mood that would make a five-legged dog an extraordinary occurrence in these people's lives.

I'd like to propose the following: To meet with you and Ron as soon as possible in London to discuss the movie. Kathy will be in touch with you to see if this is feasible from the stand point of your busy schedule.

Regards,
STEVEN SPIELBERG

Cc: Ron Cobb
Shel Schrager
Kathy Kennedy

CHAPTER 6

Cobb Salad: Finding a Director

"It was inevitable that my interests in architecture, engineering, science, fantasy, adventure, and art would lead to the movies—the technological re-creation of dreams."

—**Ron Cobb**, *Colorvision*, 1981

From the outset Steven Spielberg had little ambition to tackle the extra-terrestrial world again as a director, channeling his darker interests through an intermediary helmer. Although at some point later he spoke to Tobe Hooper about directing *Night Skies*, the plumb Columbia Pictures assignment was initially handed over to a man who had never directed so much as a TV spot: the renowned artist Ron Cobb.

Born in Los Angeles in 1937 and raised in Burbank, Cobb was the oldest of three children. As he stated in Universal's press release for *The Last Starfighter*, "I continually confounded my family's ideas of normal childhood by extending my preoccupations with fantasy and fantastic drawings throughout most of my adolescence."

Coming out of Burbank High School in 1955 where he was a C student, his first artistic gig was an "inbetweener" at his hometown's Disney Studios on 1959's *Sleeping Beauty*, the last of their animated features with hand-inked cels. Laid off upon its completion, he held several odd jobs (mailman, sign painter) until he was drafted into the U.S. Army in 1960. During his stint he delivered classified documents and worked as a Signal Corps draftsman in Vietnam.

Said Cobb of his Army years, "It was a drastic way of expanding my horizons, of confronting a larger world and breaking out of the circular boredom of suburbia."

Upon leaving the service, Cobb set out to put his incredible drawing skills to use, despite no formal training in the field. He first submitted cartoons to *Playboy*, including one of a deranged-looking man selling salted peanuts, saltine crackers, and potato chips in an empty sun-bleached desert. They rejected his submissions, but he used the same samples to earn a place as the editorial cartoonist for the *Los Angeles Free Press*, a radical paper popular with the burgeoning counterculture for whom Cobb became a hero... even though Cobb himself never felt comfortable with the Love Generation.

"He was not a hippie," says his wife Robin Love. "He was, in many ways, contradictory. This is someone who'd allowed himself to be drafted into the US Army and then enlisted for an additional year because it meant he would go to Vietnam. It was before the war so he was there as a draftsman. He wasn't particularly a peacenik. He did take sides in a lot of political issues, but most

of his cartoons were statements about democracy or justice or the future of technology... from a leftist perspective."

His cartoons were syndicated in around 90 other lefty publications like the *East Village Other* or the *Berkeley Bard* and he made money off of them "but never enough to live on." To make ends meet he sold his art to private collectors and painted gorgeous covers of iconic monsters (including the *Invasion of the Saucer Men* alien) for *Famous Monsters of Filmland*, whose editor Forest J. Ackerman served as Ron's agent at the time.

During the '60s he made two more indelible contributions to pop culture, the first being the cover art of a biplane for Jefferson Airplane's 1967 album *After Bathing at Baxter's*. Then in 1969 he designed the copyright-free image of the official ecology symbol, a melding of E for "environment" and O for "organism," ultimately resembling the Greek letter Theta. *Look* magazine editor Jack Shepherd incorporated the symbol into the ecology flag for their April 1970 issue.

Towards the end of the '60s Cobb entered a "decline," where he admitted he could neither paint nor draw, was dependent on amphetamines, and could not "snap out of it." Then in 1972 he got thrown a lifeline when the cultural Aquarius Foundation invited him and his folk singer pal Phil Ochs to tour a few university campuses in Australia. The foundation was run by a woman named Robin Love, who later became his wife. They stayed in Australia for a year before moving back to the US together in 1973, where Love would support her husband over the next five years. Even as his film design career began to take shape, she said she "never expected Ron to make any money."

"When we first arrived in L.A., I realized he had absolutely no way of supporting himself," Love told this author. "He had these plans of going to work with this outfit called Ecology Action, to go into schools and run seminars. He never made very much from the cartoons because the fellow who was syndicating them took most of the money."

It was around this time that a USC film student named Dan O'Bannon asked Cobb to contribute a spaceship design to a short comedic sci-fi thesis film *Electric Dutchman*, which the artist sketched on the back of a napkin at an all-night diner. Later expanded into an irreverent feature titled *Dark Star*, the movie made a name for O'Bannon as well as its co-writer/director John Carpenter.

Said Jacob Johnston, who wrote *The Art of Ron Cobb*, "Nick Castle, who was one of Ron's best friends, worked with him on *Dark Star*, and talked about his ability to draw in three dimensions on a flat surface. Drafting is not as important in the film business as it used to be, because of everything the computer can do. Nick talked about how you could get Ron a napkin and he could give you an orthographic view of a ship to understand what it looks like... There is a tangibility to that, and I think it's what makes his work stand the test of time. James Cameron said the same thing, that the reason Ron's work continues to be so influential in the science fiction world, even the aviation world, is it's all real. So many concept artists will be like, 'Oh, I added this engine here because it makes the ship look cooler,' but everything Ron did was for a reason."

O'Bannon would later help Cobb get some work designing ornithopters on Alejandro Jodorowsky's aborted adaptation of *Dune*, then pulled him into a fateful sci-fi project by another USC alum.

As Cobb told Paul M. Sammon for the *L.A. Times* in 1982, "Dan O'Bannon again came out of the blue, telling me he was working for a fellow named George Lucas on something called *Star Wars*. He then asked if I might contribute some aliens for what was then a very secretive bar scene. I spent about a week-and-a-half knocking out six little paintings."

The designs included "Aquatic Air Breather" (aka "Hammerhead") as well as blue aliens with elliptical eyes which would strongly influence his *Night Skies* extraterrestrial sketches. The eventual alien supplier for that project, makeup artist Rick Baker, contributed some of those cantina scene aliens, winning a Saturn Award for his trouble.

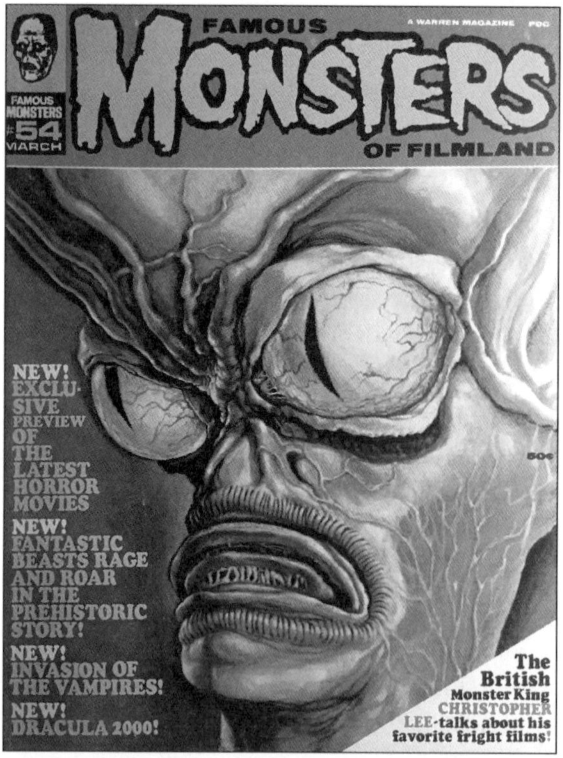

Love expanded on the story, saying, "I'd sold my restaurant, and said to Ron, 'We're never, ever going to have this amount of money again. Let's go travel in Southeast Asia until the money runs out.' Ron said, 'Great,' and we packed up our apartment. Then Dan O'Bannon came over and said George was really worried about the cantina scene in *Star Wars*, felt there wasn't enough going on in it. Ron gave them the designs and we went off and traveled for the best part of six months—maybe nine months—and we came back in May when *Star Wars* was coming out. We'd missed any cast and crew screenings, but Ron and I went down to the second show of the day in Westwood Village. People were coming out of the theater hysterical, trembling with joy saying, 'It's the greatest science fiction movie ever made!' I was rolling my eyes thinking, 'Oh, really?' We went in knowing nothing about it, having just come back from our last port of call in the Philippines, and suddenly, this phenomenon of *Star Wars* erupted into Westwood Village. That was Ron's big launch."

As it happens, even before he was hired for the cantina, Cobb had already inadvertently supplied some concept art for *Star Wars* without any foreknowledge. While preparing his Cantina aliens he came across a production still of a stormtrooper on the back of a big lizard. It looked like a painting he had done for John Milius. As Cobb told *Starburst* magazine in 1979, "Many months later I was talking to Milius and he knew, 'Your lizard painting's in *Star Wars*. Lucas was up here one night and he saw it and said he wanted to try to put it in *Star Wars*.' They ended up with camel-like legs, whereas mine had great big iguana-like legs. It was an image I thought John Milius would like."

Cobb fell in love with working on movies because it allowed him a venue for his myriad interests: myth making, architecture, technology, etc. Not on that list? Making money.

Cobb said of *Star Wars*, "I designed all these aliens and I think I got $100 a piece for them and that was about it. They made them into toys."

Love eventually had to step in to help her husband get better deals, stating, "Ron arranged *Star Wars* without me. We didn't have a contract protecting anything, but we didn't know it was going to be *Star Wars*. I ended up being his business manager because most people in the film industry were represented by managers and lawyers who take a huge chunk of their income for doing very little. It was more protective that I got involved in negotiating contracts and making sure he got paid properly."

Fittingly, Cobb first encountered Lucas and Milius' buddy Steven Spielberg during the early design days on another film about a hostile alien... 1979's *Alien*. Cobb had been "the first person to draw money" on that film during early planning by co-writer O'Bannon. Over a grueling 2+ year stint earning $400 dollars a week he made hundreds of drawings, including a failed stab at the title creature before H.R. Giger locked it down. Cobb had a profound impact on the look of the Ridley Scott movie's industrial space shuttles and hardware, even crafting a semiotic visual language for ship signage.

"At one point Spielberg was considered as a possible director for the original *Alien*," confirmed Cobb in his 1981 book *Colorvision*. "It was just a brief thing, he could never work out his schedule to do it, but he was interested."

Cobb's next big assignment was tackling the Iron Age sword and sorcery of John Milius' big budget adaptation of *Conan the Barbarian* starring Arnold Schwarzenegger, a project which trudged along slowly over several years. Brought on by producer Edward Pressman for initial designs in 1978, Cobb then returned to his pal Milius' western *Half the Sky*. When that unmade movie got stalled in the script phase, Milius became interested in *Conan* and took Cobb back with him. The former cartoonist made a major leap from concept artist to full production designer on this action epic. Cobb's commitment lasted through the end of the Spanish shoot in mid-1981.

The screenplay, originally penned by Oliver Stone before massive rewrites by Milius, follows Conan from a traumatic enslaved childhood through to maturity as he becomes a formidable warrior and thief. Although the movie feels akin to both the Robert E. Howard stories and the Marvel Comics adaptations which revived their popularity, Milius went his own way with a story concerning an evil snake cult. He de-emphasized the mystical aspects, focusing on an adventure drawn equally from Icelandic sagas and Japanese films like *The Seven Samurai* and *Kwaidan*.

Says famed commercial/comics artist William Stout, who became Cobb's right-hand production artist on *Conan*, "After I got hired, there was a local Valley theater showing 50 Years of Japanese Cinema. I grabbed the list of all the films and brought them back to Milius. He circled two dozen, said, 'This is your homework. See all these movies.' I got a crash course, saw every Kurosawa film... Tatsuya Nakadai and Toshiro Mifune."

Stout was an avowed Conan fan. In 1974 he rendered his own Frank Frazetta-style painting of the character since he "couldn't afford to buy a Frazetta Conan!" A few years later he happened to run into Cobb at an American Booksellers Association show in L.A. "I don't know how Ron knew me or my work, but he said I was the person he wanted to work with the most on *Conan*." Milius had approval over every artist on the picture but, upon seeing Stout's portfolio, he recognized an adaptation of Harlan Ellison's "Shattered Like a Glass Goblin" from Heavy Metal, then bellowed, "Hire 'im!" The two-week assignment turned into "two years in a room with Ron Cobb."

"The design sense that Ron came up with was we wanted this to be a real world, Conan's world," explains Stout. "Ron said, 'Okay, this is what Egyptian architecture looked like 1,000 years ago. This is what it looked like 2,000 years ago. This is what it looked like 3,000 years ago. Now, imagine what it looked like 6,000 years ago.' We would start from realism, from actual history, and use that as a basis for our designs."

Ron Cobb (*left*) and William Stout (*right*).

That look which Cobb and Stout manufactured for *Conan* combined disparate elements from sword and sandal as well as Viking and samurai movies to create "a whole new genre." For example, at the prop shop in Madrid they would often mash together parts of different weapons to get the unique look of a fantasy world that feels torn from the pages of history which never happened.

Milius' A-Team offices, located near Warner Bros. in Burbank, reflected his "zen anarchist" sensibility. Cobb drew a shackled man on the wall which Milius encouraged staff to throw Ka-Bar knives at. Stout says, "We almost skewered several people coming to visit the offices. We were told, 'Hey, next time you throw the knife, yell THROWING!' as a warning to anyone who was about to 'round the corner."

The two Bobs were also frequent flyers at A-Team while developing *Used Cars*. As Stout remembers, "John had these slings. We would go in the parking lot and John would say, 'Okay, up there, see that office there, that's Zemeckis and Gale's office.' He had a big bag full of plums, and we would use the slings and try to hit their window with the plums."

"Bob Zemeckis and I met Ron when he was working for Milius designing *Conan the Barbarian*," said Bob Gale. "I was a huge Conan fan, read all the Robert E. Howard reprints when I was in high school, and knew John was the perfect guy to direct a Conan movie. This was the first time I'd met Ron and discovered there was more to him than the great editorial cartoons he used to do for the *L.A. Free Press*, which I read when I was in college. Ron was a cartoonist I admired, then I saw 'Oh, my God, he's a production designer! He's designing these swords, these sets!' He was a very affable, guy."

As he explained to the *Los Angeles Times* in 1988, Cobb and Spielberg later crossed paths again in 1979-1980 at A-Team, where Kathleen Kennedy was starting as a receptionist and eventually transitioned to Milius' assistant before becoming Spielberg's. Cobb was doing *Conan* and Spielberg was finishing *1941* while planning to direct *Raiders of the Lost Ark.* A ride-or-die pal of Milius, Spielberg got Cobb and Stout to drop their *Conan* pencils at 6pm almost every day to come across the hall and work out/storyboard ideas for the first Indiana Jones adventure, including the giant Nazi flying wing and an early sketch of Christopher Lee as SS officer Toht (later played by Ronald Lacey).

"Ron Cobb had conceived in a number of drawings the fact that Toht has a right arm which he never uses," Spielberg told *Prevue*. "Apparently, it's dead, a wooden arm. When the gunfight at the Raven began, Toht aimed his finger and fired through it. He took a banana clip and inserted it into his wrist. Suddenly the sleeve fell away and you saw a gun built into where his right hand used to be. He lost it in some kind of weird, Hitlerian experiment. Ron and I had designed a machine gun that shot right through his finger."

"Steven and John were best friends, but they were also like big kids... whatever one had the other wanted, and vice versa," recalls Stout. "Milius had me and Cobb, but we were doing little stuff on the side for Steven, who thought, 'Man, I want Cobb and Stout.' He kept trying to get us to jump ship and leave *Conan* to work on *Raiders*. He really, really wanted Cobb. I came in to work one day and I said, 'Ron, you look shell shocked. What happened?' He says, 'It's Steven. He said, if I would leave *Conan the Barbarian* and be the production designer for *Raiders the Lost Ark*, he would let me direct the sequel to *Close Encounters*.' I said, 'Oh my God. What did you say?' He said, 'I can't do that to Milius, he gave me a tremendous break making me production designer on this film.' I said, 'So what was Steven's reaction?' He said, 'Well, he got angry and said well, then you can't direct the sequel to *Close Encounters*.' Later Spielberg contacted Ron and said, 'Look, I apologize for the way I acted. I'd still love to have you direct the sequel to *Close Encounters*. Consider that a greenlight and get to work.'"

Although there is plenty of evidence to suggest Spielberg enjoyed absorbing Milius' talent pool (Kathy Kennedy, the two Bobs, Cobb), Robin Love refutes the idea that Spielberg tried to get Cobb to beg off of *Conan*.

Says Love, "Ron worked out of A-Team with John Milius in one office and Steven Spielberg down the hall in the other office, and Ron was sitting there doing art. Ron got to know Steven very well in the five or six months before *Conan* moved to Europe. You know the big ball rolling down at the beginning of *Raiders*? He did sketches on that. He also designed the flying wing, but there was never an offer of a job."

He was more than just another pencil-and-paper man, though. Spielberg would often take Cobb's advice on *Raiders'* intricately planned storyboards in ways that mimicked directing the picture, such as shooting over a character's shoulder followed by a close-up of his shadow. It was not long before Spielberg told Cobb he thought the man could direct... and wanted to back his debut. The powerhouse instructed his new protégé to "get yourself an agent." Cobb explained to Spielberg that he didn't "know how to direct," to which Spielberg replied, "Yes you can, you just need to get up earlier in the morning... and never have a lawyer on retainer."

"It was actually Spielberg's idea for Ron to direct," says Johnston. "It wasn't something that Ron was gunning to do. He liked the storytelling process, but while he was on *Raiders* pitching storyboard ideas and helping to construct sequences, Spielberg was like, 'Wow, you want to direct a movie?'"

Explains Stout, "Ron said, 'Steven, I don't know how to direct.' Steven's response was, 'Well, I'm directing today. Come to the set and I'll show you how.' Like you could learn in one day. That was the sort of naivete of Steven, the innocence of the guy, to think that."

"I wanted to do a scarier version of alien visitation," Cobb told *ABC Radio National*'s Robyn Williams in April 2005. "I suggested the cattle mutilation rumors and all this nonsense that was going on and a few other instances wherein people were terrorized by little glowing people. There was an incident that occurred in Kentucky. He said, 'Go ahead, do your research, get yourself a writer and put it together.'"

"Kathy was instrumental in coming up with the project, helping to facilitate this for Ron," Love confirms. "At that point they started talking about the Kelly-Hopkinsville incident and seeing if they could come up with a writer. Sayles was Kathy's suggestion. She may have come up with another suggestion as well. Ron and I had seen *Secaucus 7* and loved it. Kathy threw that into the mix and we all said yes."

"I originated the story," Cobb wrote on his official website. "My choice for screenplay writer was John Sayles."

"They wrote a script called *Night Skies*," says Stout. "They wrote it together."

After all the extraterrestrials he ideated over his career, it's no wonder Cobb was keen to develop Spielberg's alien siege movie, but there was a catch: According to Cobb himself, the Kentucky family involved in the Kelly encounter—including Elmer Sutton—had no desire for a movie of their story due to the notoriety it would inevitably generate.

As Sayles told *Starburst* in 1983, "The people concerned didn't really want to talk about it as they knew everybody would think they're crazy."

"By the '70s it was finally quiet in their life," says Geraldine Sutton Stith of her family. "People would contact my dad wanting to talk about it, but he never would. He didn't want it brought back up, didn't want the spotlight again. He probably didn't realize what Spielberg was. My dad didn't know anything about that kind of thing, he was a country boy farmer. I just can't see him knowing Spielberg, I'll be honest. If someone got hold of him to do a movie, he probably would have laughed them down and gave them a few choice words. That was his big thing: 'Let it go. We're not going to talk about this. No good can come of this story.' If the movie people went out to the actual farm and talked to the distant relatives that live in the house now, they would threaten you to an inch of your life. They didn't want no more to do with it. My dad didn't choose to be there that night and have that happen to him. He would have gave his right arm for it to not have happened. Of course they didn't want the attention."

Aaron Sagers explains, "Interviewing a lot of people who've had paranormal experiences, I don't think most of them are looking for their 15 minutes of fame. A lot of them are reluctant to share their story. There is still stigma attached to having those experiences. I can't speak to the finances of that family when Spielberg approached them, but I could imagine having Hollywood knock on your door and offering to give you some cash... that's very tempting. For you to say no, there has to be a good reason. This family was already ridiculed, held to a lot of scrutiny. That they didn't want to do it makes their story a little more compelling."

The family purportedly threatened to sue, but Cobb was a clever man and proposed avoiding a lawsuit by changing the story's venue from Kentucky to Montana, grafting elements of the cattle mutilation phenomenon onto the tale, as well as reducing the number of aliens at the farmhouse. Instead of being a rundown of the Kelly-Hopkinsville encounter, it would merely use that as a jumping off point. Cobb bringing in the cattle mutilation aspect makes sense, considering he was something of a UFO buff.

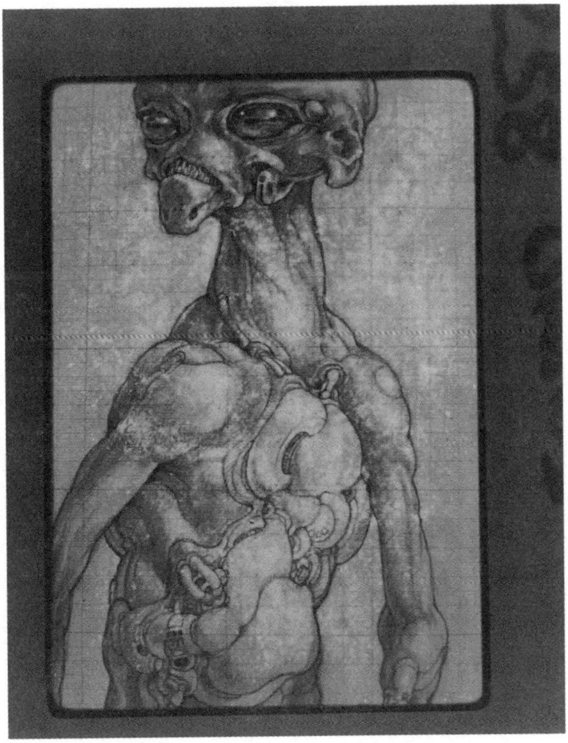

"Yes, he was always interested," confirms Love. "He was not a believer, always convinced there was a rational explanation for most of the sightings, but he also believed there was definitely some intelligent life out there and we would be arrogant to assume we were alone. He'd pay attention every time there were sightings. He saw the rich dramatic potential, shall we say."

After Sayles met Spielberg at the Egg Company to iron out the deal and collect research material, there was an impromptu story meeting with Sayles and Cobb at Spielberg's home on a Saturday morning, which was the only time everyone was available.

"There was a lot going on that morning," Love remembers. "Steven had a house full of people. He had Karen Allen there trying out dyes with the hairdresser. I ended up playing snooker with Harrison Ford on Steven's billiards table. He got a wine delivery, and said, 'You're Australian, you know about wine. Tell me what wine I should order from this batch.' Then he disappeared, because his new Porsche was being delivered. He left everybody, went outside, then came back and said, 'Well, I didn't learn to drive my Porsche but I did learn to use the windshield wipers because it was raining.' Then he and John and Ron had a pretty full-on meeting about *Night Skies*."

"Ron really was interested in pushing it into the gothic," Paul M. Sammon told this author. "I always thought of Ron as being a more hard science fiction guy, but the emphasis was a flat-out horror film."

Sayles went off to work on his draft in Hoboken as Cobb flew to Yugoslavia to location scout for *Conan*. That Dino De Laurentiis production was already shaping up to be a disaster, with Yugoslavia lacking the proper amount of Styrofoam to build massive sets and the art department having an electric cord run up from another floor to light one single lamp. "One of those hanging bulbs you see in poverty-stricken places," adds Stout.

"Ron then contacted me in Australia and said, 'It doesn't look like I'm coming back in a hurry, but I've got to go to Paris and meet Steven and John Sayles,'" Love recalls. "We went to the Hôtel Plaza Athénée. I flew in from Australia, Ron was coming in from Yugoslavia, and Steven was coming up from Tunisia. Mike Fenton heard me checking in at the foyer and introduced himself and said, 'Do you think Ron will have a tie? We're eating in the hotel tonight, and I brought ties for Ron and Steven and John.' The Plaza actually has one of the really good restaurants in Paris. Sayles didn't come. He didn't want to turn up for dinner. He disappeared off into Paris by himself, and I don't blame him. If that was the first time I'd been in Paris, I wouldn't want to sit in the hotel."

This was likely around the start of production on *Raiders*, which began shooting the Nazi submarine scenes on June 23, 1980 in La Rochelle. During a 1988 interview with *The Philadelphia Inquirer*, Sayles mentioned this meeting as having taken place in "the fanciest hotel I've ever stayed in," and that "Spielberg flew me over to Paris for a day-and-a-half. I'd never been there. It was great, but I didn't have much time..." Sayles did get to visit one small museum while in the City of Lights.

As Sayles told this author, "Ron Cobb was an interesting guy. He had done all these great cartoons. He told me a story about working on *Conan*. He was designing James Earl Jones' palace, and it just didn't look right to him. He showed his drawings to a friend who was an architect, and the guy said, 'Well, one thing is, the roof will fall in. Doesn't have enough support.' He put some pillars in there, and all of a sudden it looked right. He said, 'Oh, then I can put all kinds of cool stuff on the pillars, right?' Because his cartoons were very two dimensional, he was making that transition to think, 'The camera's going to move through this thing, so I'm going to start thinking in three dimensions.'"

"Ron was getting used to being a production designer for the first time, so he was very preoccupied," adds Love. "Also, that weekend in Paris he wasn't feeling great and the next day I took him to the American Hospital in Paris where he was diagnosed with shingles. He was not in great physical health at that time, so the excitement was not there. He got treated for shingles, then got on a plane back to Yugoslavia."

After four weeks in Yugoslavia, Ron and his *Conan* production department were given instructions by De Laurentiis to pack everything as they moved the company to more accommodating locations in Spain. According to Love, this action was "done very suddenly, and I suspect leaving behind unpaid bills."

Says Stout, "I wish we stayed in Yugoslavia, because there were unique locations that have never been shown on film there, whereas all the places we shot in Spain I've seen in other movies. It was our accountant's fault, he had a house in Spain, didn't want to be away from his family, so he started making up terrible rumors about the Yugoslavians in order to get production moved to Spain. That was a nasty thing to do the Yugoslavians. They were incredibly helpful, enthusiastic, and would bend over backwards for us."

Says Sammon, who was imbedded on the *Conan* set in Madrid as both journalist and Universal marketing exec, "Ron was burly, soft spoken, and friendly on the set of *Conan*. He was ubiquitous, which is interesting because a lot of production designers usually are back in the art department. They'll show up on a particular day, but Ron was always everywhere. He'd be in the wardrobe department. He'd be with Emilio Ruiz del Rio, the guy doing all the hanging miniatures... he'd be there."

Once he was ensconced in Spain, Cobb was never party to any discussions with studio executives or even producers vis a vis *Night Skies*. He was surprised at how Sayles was able to produce a fairly tight, workable script in short order.

"Ron probably thought he'd be spending more time with the script," claims Love. "But John Sayles was incredibly fast and efficient and BANG, the script just appeared."

Cobb being Cobb, the artist-cum-director did contribute some initial sketches of what the creatures might look like...

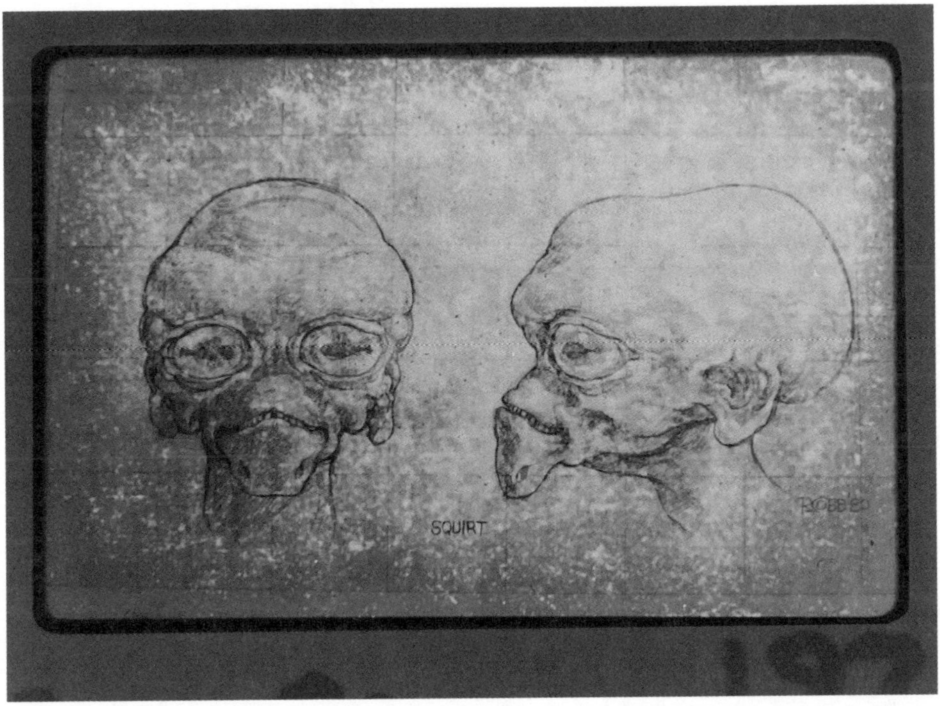

"They're not warm and welcoming," says Love of Ron's alien designs. "They would never have been. Elliott would not have wanted to make friends with them."

While the eyes and physiology are mostly distinct, the maw and jawline of Cobb's aliens do resemble 1984's title *Gremlins*. After all, the long-eared Kelly-Hopkinsville creatures have been oft-referred to as "gremlins"... including by Spielberg himself.

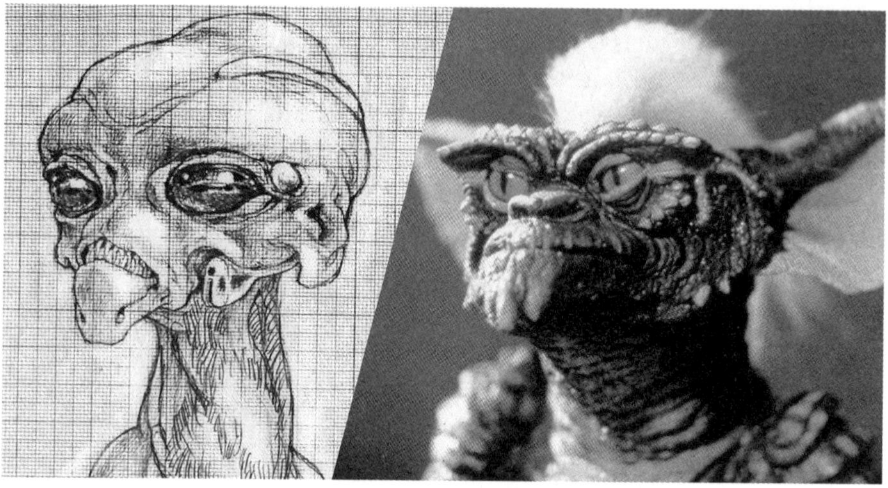

Having a consummate interest in physiology, Cobb also designed a uniquely elongated inner skull. This prefigures the similar noggin of the aliens in Spielberg's 2008 film *Indiana Jones and the Kingdom of the Crystal Skull*, though the final skin-bearing ETs look more like traditional Greys. As Indy himself says, "This is not the Mitchell-Hedges skull."

"I think Ron was more interested in the aliens," remembers Sayles. "He talked with Rick Baker a little when they were just figuring out what the creatures were going to look like. Steven had a couple ideas, that one might walk

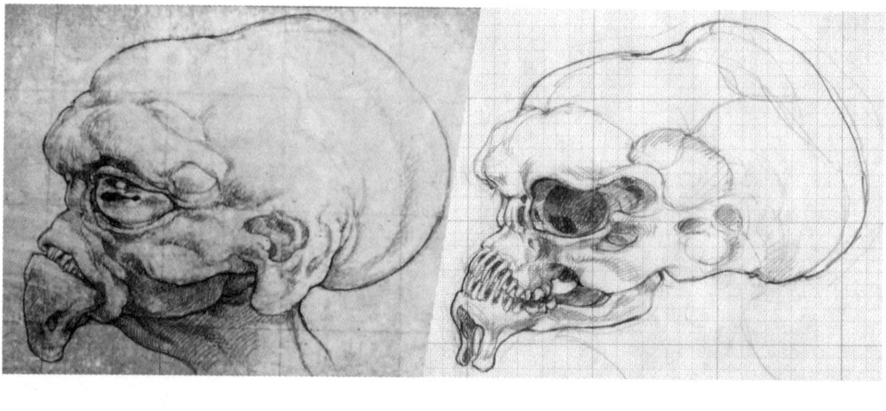

with their arms above their head, and maybe their bodies were more like fingernails than skin. If you hit him with a shotgun, you would hear a rattle on a window or something like that. They were still playing around with that, which is an important discussion. A nice thing for a writer/director is when you're just a writer on a project you get this window on how that director thinks about things, how they see the world, how they prep a project."

Says Mitch Suskin, who worked with Baker on the animatronics, "Ron had an amazing ability to visualize things, to communicate and to infect you with what he was visualizing. I started out as an engineer, wanting to be an architect and then also a filmmaker. That's part of why we connected, we could communicate on that level. He was very knowledgeable about real design and engineering. He could connect the dots and see into the future. It wasn't just that he was doing cool stuff… he knew how everything was going to work. That was the fun thing about working with Ron."

"At that point he was hungry to direct," Sammon says of Cobb. "Ron was older than a lot of people he was working with, more mature. He also had a laissez-faire attitude towards the whole process. I think he was bemused by a lot of it, obviously drawn to it for the art, but at the same time well aware of the fickleness of everything."

"Ron was enjoying the process of working with John Sayles," Stout adds. "John's brilliant, really brilliant. I think Ron was always wary of Steven because of Steven's power and influence. Eventually, that awareness proved to pay out because of Steven's involvement in starting to change everything that Ron was doing with *Night Skies*."

CHAPTER 7

Rick Baker, Nightmare Maker: Constructing Five Creatures

"When he was ready to begin carving, he had before him a new concept: he turned Christ's head and knees in opposite directions, establishing through his contrapuntal design a graphic tension, the intense physical and spiritual inner conflict of a man who is being pulled two ways."

—**Irving Stone**, *The Agony and the Ecstasy* (1961)

For *Night Skies*, Steven Spielberg set out to up the ante for onscreen aliens, having set the bar mightily with *Close Encounters*. At the recommendation of his friend John Landis, he hired 30-year-old up-and-coming makeup talent Rick Baker to create the five nefarious ETs at the center of the film.

"I have never met anybody more talented than Rick Baker," says former business partner David Robert Cellitti. "They were having a show at the Museum of Art in Los Angeles called 'The Romantics to Rodin.' It was largely representational sculpture from the early 1900s. Jaw-dropping pieces. I was working out of Rick's home at the time where he had this office and a studio at the back. I walked in and there was this sculpture of the god Pan on this beautifully sculpted pedestal from the breast up, head slightly turned holding the pipes, with little horns and curly hair. Absolutely gorgeous. I turned to Rick and said, 'Where did that come from?' He said, 'Oh, I was so inspired by the show I just did that last night.' I'm looking at this thing thinking, 'I should become a shoe salesman.' I could work a month and couldn't have done what he did in an evening."

Born December 8, 1950, Richard Alan Baker inherited much of his talent from father Ralph Baker, a professional artist. Both his parents were fans of fantasy and science fiction, allowing their only child to scour the TV schedule for horror movies. A showing of Universal's *Frankenstein* on weekend late night TV convinced an 8-year-old Baker he wanted to make monsters for a living, solidified later that year when he picked up issue #3 of Forrest Ackerman's *Famous Monsters of Filmland* with an article about how to turn a boy into a creature using makeup.

Ralph encouraged his son with his first tubes of Max Factor greasepaint. As Rick's autodidact home makeup skills improved, his dad taught him about drawing, sculpting, and making molds with Plasticine and plaster of Paris. An employee of Don Post Studios named Bob Burns, also a famous movie memorabilia collector, became a mentor to both father and son. Burns helped the younger Baker hone makeup technique while also instilling a lifelong fascination with ape suits.

Baker told the CBC in 1977, "At about 13-years-old I said, 'Hey, a gorilla is the closest thing to a real live monster I could find.' I thought it was possible to do a man in a gorilla suit that was convincing, so I started studying gorillas and became very fascinated with the animal because it's not at all what people think. Hollywood has given gorillas this savage, rape women kind of image and it's not true. They're very passive vegetarians. They don't fight, they just kick back and relax and take it easy and have babies."

In the spirit of Don Post monster masks, Baker began manufacturing his own classic creatures like Mr. Hyde or The Wolf Man, typically taking two weeks per mask. These were displayed in his "secret lab," i.e. his childhood bedroom lined with monster photos and Aurora model kits. On paper he also designed inner-mechanics for a "Martian Hand + Arm" not far from the ones he made for *Night Skies* 15 years later.

At age 15, Baker was introduced by Burns to a union rep, who tried to get the budding artist to swallow a bitter pill about the industry: "I brought up a box full of some head masks I made, photos of makeups. The business rep looked at my stuff and said, 'First of all, this shit you like to do, those jobs are few and far between. Most of the time you're just going to be mopping sweat off some bitchy actress. The other thing is you can't even serve an apprenticeship until you're 21, and the apprenticeships are going to a Westmore or one of the people related to somebody in the industry. Give up, you're never going to get in.' It was hard to hear, but I felt that if I'm really good somebody's going to hire me."

While a freshman at Northview High School, he discovered a brand-new special issue of *Famous Monsters* called the "Do-It-Yourself Monster Make-Up Handbook," featuring photographically illustrated how-tos for acquiring materials, creating skin textures, artificial eyes, and so forth. The booklet was created by Dick Smith, a New York City-based prosthetic makeup pioneer whose work had been featured on the show *Way Out* (including a memorable episode where Hunchback of Notre Dame makeup becomes permanently affixed to an actor), and later on gothic soap opera *Dark Shadows*.

"Rick and I and everybody else my age all have the same story," says Cellitti. "We all read *Famous Monsters*. We all wanted to work in special effects, but there were basically only three people: John Chambers, Dick Smith, and the Burmans... and the Burmans are who you went to when everybody else said no."

Baker gravitated to Smith, whose work was also featured in Vincent Kehoe's cornerstone book *The Technique of Film and Television Makeup*. As he told *Archive of American Television*, "The work that really stood out in that book was by this Dick Smith guy. I said, 'Wait, Dick Smith, that's the same guy that made these monster things I liked.' They didn't have very much of Dick's monster type work in there, but it was more of these really great old age makeups. I was fascinated, because Dick's makeups looked real and I liked fooling people with makeup."

The teen eventually worked up the nerve to contact Smith, penning a letter which kicked off a mentorship that profoundly impacted both Baker and the industry. Across his career Smith was known as a generous disseminator of makeup wisdom to budding filmmakers, including Guillermo del Toro and J.J. Abrams. Smith's bond with Baker was similar to one he struck up in 1968 with a young Craig Reardon.

As Reardon told this author, "Rick Baker found a way to contact Dick in 1969, the following year. He sent Dick some Polaroids of his early masks. Dick was suitably impressed and shared one with me. He suggested I get in contact.

I first visited Rick at his home in West Covina, his bedroom taken over with a workbench his dad most likely constructed that wrapped around half the room. He'd cranked out many latex rubber overhead masks that either recreated popular monsters or were original ideas. Rick's efforts far exceeded anything I'd tried to do. This guy had something and I would have to up my game to compete with him, even in a friendly way. I was the first guy of my generation to contact Dick Smith and show admiration for his unique talent. Rick was the second. I was also the first fellow makeup enthusiast Rick knew, and vice versa."

"The famous quote was Dick Smith turned to Rick and said, 'You were born to do this stuff,'" adds Cellitti.

As a high schooler Baker landed his first job at Clokey Productions, founded in 1955 by Art Clokey for his stop-motion kids shows *Gumby* and *Davey and Goliath*. By Baker's tenure, Art had taken LSD, run for office, and divorced his wife Ruth who now controlled the company. Another young man there named Doug Beswick bonded with Baker.

"Before that I had a friend in my neighborhood that was my monster buddy that got *Famous Monsters* too, but he grew out of it," Baker told this author. "I met Doug at Clokey's and we both loved the same stuff, Ray Harryhausen films, stop motion, all those things, so we instantly clicked."

They teamed up on a short about cavemen fighting a prehistoric bird. Also in the Clokey art department were Sneaky Pete Kleinow of Flying Burrito Brothers and a miniature prop maker named Harry Walton.

"When Ruth and the animation director would go into Hollywood to meet with clients, we would cut up and do crazy things like have water fights back in the stage and spitball fights," says Walton. Sometimes even Gumbys and Pokeys would be flung.

Eventually, Baker and Beswick booked their first movie gig, creating the suit for Harry Essex's no frills 1971 B monster flick *Octaman*, with the title tentacled creature's circular mouth making him look like a veiny green sex doll.

"We had no time, no money, and I was a full-time student," Baker says of his first experience as movie monster maker. "We had six weeks of evenings and weekends, a couple thousand bucks. It was pretty good for what we got paid in the time we had."

Walton told this author, "From 1968 to 1970, Doug and I rented a 1000-square-foot shop in Azusa where I was making my first armatures and Doug got one of his first jobs, *Octaman*. I assisted Doug and Rick Baker on this Octaman suit, mixing up foam rubber, cutting little foam pieces and scales and sewing them on, and they used me for trying on the suit. Doug and Rick did 85% of the work. When this suit was completed, a bunch of the guys just starting in the business came by to see it: Jim Danforth, Dennis Muren, David Allen, Phil Tippet."

Said Baker of the group, "We were all monster kids. We all loved the same shit."

Sadly, the *Octaman* shoot would act as an introduction to the indignities of a Hollywood makeup artist. Baker and Beswick arrived on the empty Bronson Canyon set only to find production had been pushed a day and no one told them. Playing off their youthful long hair, the salty older crew referred to them as "the girls." Production only wanted to pay one $50/day fee, so they had to alternate days on set to get their full rate. Finally, there was a disastrous instance where Essex did not rehearse a scene where Octaman is attacked with a (real) tree limb, then picks up the leading lady.

As Baker recounts in a Blu-ray featurette, "The first guy he knocks down is laying on the ground pretending to be unconscious. When he knocks the tree limb, the tree limb landed on his hand and broke his hand. The tree limb ripped the suit. He picked up Pier Angeli, he's walking around and can't see what he's doing. The guy is laying spread-eagle on the ground, he steps right on his nuts, falls over backwards and throws Pier Angeli up against the Winnebago. Pier Angeli is crying for her mother, this guy's holding his hand screaming, and I'm going, 'You ripped my fucking suit!'"

Don Post Studios was another center of activity for the emerging makeup community. An example of how tight-knit the group was can be seen in a short *Kolchak: The Night Stalker* parody employee William Malone made on reel-to-reel videotape around 1973 called *The Night Turkey*, starring Robert Short as Carl Korncheck.

"Don Post Studios had provided a couple of hands to the original series," says Short. "We all agreed to make a spoof on our favorite show. Bob Burns plays my boss at the newspaper. I'm playing the Night Turkey as well. We asked Rick Baker to do the Night Turkey itself, so Rick did the head as a one-off cotton and latex build-up hand sculpt. When he'd get an assignment on a film, Rick would run into Don Post with whatever it was... the baby from *It's Alive*, like, 'Here's my newest baby!' That was the *Octaman* period, John Landis... a lot of makeup effects people came out of Don Post. Even if they didn't work there, they had a connection because we had foam latex supplies, big barrels of raw materials for people to use."

Foam latex eventually became the lifeblood of the industry, especially after Dick Smith made a name for himself with astonishing work on *Little Big Man* and *The Godfather*. It was originally invented by George Bau in a lab and sold in five-gallon kits from his house.

As Baker explained on the *Creature Geek* podcast, "Foam latex was amazing, better than anything we have today... The problem was only Dick Smith and me were using it. This was at a time when big films weren't happening. I'd buy five gallons a year, maybe, and so would Dick. It didn't seem to be a very good business for George."

An alcoholic, Bau eventually dumped all his supplies and committed suicide by, according to Cellitti, disemboweling himself with a screwdriver on his lawn. Fortunately, the day before he did so a prolific makeup artist named Charles H. Schram had visited him and was able to extract the general formula and milling process. Schram founded Windsor Hills Foam Latex, eventually taken over by the Burmans.

Baker (*left*) and Griffin Dunne (*right*) prepping for a scene in *An American Werewolf in London* (1981).

The year 1973 was fortuitous, with Baker assisting Smith on *The Exorcist* while also manufacturing the ape suit for an indie comedy by first-time director John Landis called *Schlock*. Because it was a fly by night production, Landis himself wore the ape suit while calling the shots. Having worked his way up as a stunt man and gofer on many European sets, Landis was hoping to direct a script he wrote at age 19 called *An American Werewolf in London*, about a young backpacker who becomes a lycanthrope after being attacked by a wolf along the moors. While making *Schlock*, Landis and Baker began thinking up how to create cool werewolf effects for that script. Baker called one of his ideas for a werewolf head that changes structure a "change-o-head."

Baker distinguished himself on films like *The Autobiography of Miss Jane Pittman* and 1976's *King Kong*. When George Lucas was unhappy with the cantina scene in *Star Wars*, he hired Baker to come up with a menagerie of aliens to add in pick-ups, including the cantina band. It became one of the most talked about scenes in the 1977 megahit.

"Post-*Star Wars,* everything exploded," said Chris Walas, another Don Post vet who became a makeup effects guru. "Every single project wanted a cantina scene, science fiction or not. They had to figure out some way to make a scene with a bunch of aliens."

More physical effects gurus emerged (Stan Winston, Tom Savini), though a gold rush for fantasy and monster movies meant rivalries were minimal.

"It wasn't all that competitive because there was so much work," says Walas, who cut his teeth at ILM on Matthew Robbins' *Dragonslayer*. "Maybe you didn't get the project you wanted, but there were five other projects in the wings to cash in on this creature boom."

"In the '80s, so many amazing makeup effects films happened because they were being done by fanboys who loved this stuff," expresses Baker.

Rick and wife Elaine Baker worked briefly for Lucasfilm again on an early mockup of The Emperor for *Empire Strikes Back*. Elaine played the part for a test where chimpanzee eyes were superimposed into the shot. Beswick was brought in to create stop-motion armatures for the AT-AT walkers as well as the puppet for a phallic space slug.

As jobs got more complex, Baker went from a one-man-band to a full-fledged company of multi-talented young artists. One of his first true protégés was a kid from El Monte named Rob Bottin, who at age 14 sent Baker a fan letter with an intricate drawing. Like Baker and Smith, the two struck up a friendship and eventual collaboration. By 1982 Bottin executed the myriad grotesques for

John Carpenter's The Thing, considered by many to be an all-time high-water mark for makeup effects.

"Right place at the right time," Bottin told *L.A. Times* in 1990. "No one knew who Rick was. This stuff wasn't celebrated. The thing that changed all that was *Star Wars*."

Says horror scholar Shellie McMurdo, "Rob Bottin lived with Rick and Elaine for a little while as well because he was really young."

Celliti adds, "Bottin was underage when he met Rick, and for a while Rick was talking to Elaine about them adopting Rob. Elaine put her foot down and said no, he was too old."

Eventually Baker and Bottin began building the werewolves for Joe Dante's 1981 picture *The Howling*, including the change-o-heads. When John Landis found out Baker was attached to *Howling*, he told the makeup artist *An American Werewolf in London* was greenlit and he had to jump ship from Dante. Bottin remained to finish the *Howling* job.

Says Dante, "I think they're both geniuses, in a way, but Rick was an entrepreneur and very logical about his career. Rob was more of an artist and a perfectionist. Even on *The Howling*, which was a $1.98 movie, one night we didn't shoot anything because Rob wasn't finished. His standards were very high, but he wasn't particularly realistic."

"More than anything else, my legacy is probably going to be I created Rob Bottin," Baker laughs. "Rob wouldn't exist if it wasn't for me taking him under. He'd never have done any makeup whatsoever. Was very talented, has an amazing imagination, but *The Thing* never would have happened... not the way it did, anyways. I don't think anybody else, including me, would have done what Rob did in *The Thing*."

Jokes Cellitti, "If you get to know Rob Bottin, he is exactly like *The Thing*. It's *All About Eve*. He is Rick, but imitation Rick. It's like he absorbed Rick."

Adds McMurdo, "They were sharing what they were doing. Later Baker said, 'I kind of wish I hadn't shared as much of what I was gonna do.' Their master-student relationship is really interesting."

"This is a very incestuous business... I saw *The Howling* at a cast and crew screening in Westwood, and most of the *Howling* crew worked on *American Werewolf*," confirms Cellitti. "Rob was not supposed to take any of the things Rick had worked out for *The Howling*, and he took all of them. We were watching the movie and all I can hear is Elaine Baker going, 'I hate him. I hate him. I hate him. I hate him.'"

"It took years for money and technology to catch up to what Baker wanted to do, but you'd be hard pressed to find a movie where a makeup effects artist had years to think about how to do the effects," says *Fangoria*'s Phil Nobile. "Landis tells Baker about it on the set of *Schlock*, and he let the back of his brain cook."

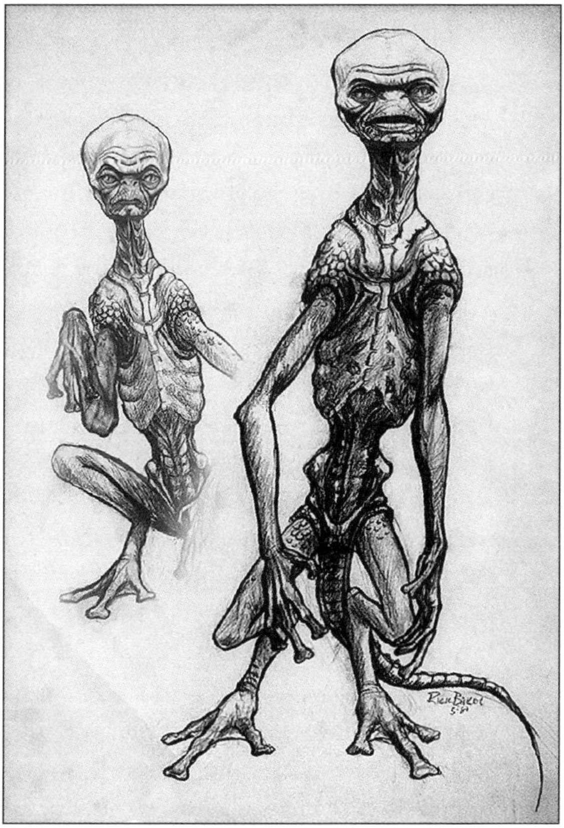

Hoodoo (*left*) and Skar (*right*) drawn by Rick Baker in May 1980.

Even after *Werewolf* began early prep, Landis recommended his pal Baker to Spielberg as the ideal alien maker for *Night Skies*. Baker and partner Doug Beswick had long discussed taking onscreen aliens to the next level, so this was a dream opportunity.

"It was fucking Steven Spielberg, the great American filmmaker," Baker says of his excitement at taking on the project. "Mind you, I was concerned because *Werewolf* was happening at the same time. I liked the idea of making individual characters, not everything out of the same mold, and that's what Steven wanted. I found the whole concept really exciting, but I did say when we first talked, 'I'm doing *American Werewolf in London*.' He said, 'I know, John told me, and he said if you think you can do both at the same time and do them right, then we can do it.' I said yes, but then I was like, 'Can I?'"

During this meeting at the Egg Company, the *Night Skies* story was described as "*Straw Dogs* with aliens," with each alien having a unique persona. Baker proposed an initial estimate for executing Spielberg's vision at $3M, which was not balked at considering the contained farm-set story would need a fraction of *Close Encounters*' scope. Instead of movie stars, the aliens themselves would be the draw.

Baker was shown Bud Ledwith's sketches of the Kelly-Hopkinsville aliens based on eyewitness descriptions, but had no intention of executing "a triangular head and body, and weird hard angles." Instead, he went in a vaguely humanoid direction with reptilian color/textures, still conforming to what J. Allen Hynek expressed as the median witness description: About four-feet tall, spindly body.

The team continued tinkering away on *American Werewolf* when work kicked off on *Night Skies* around March of 1980, without a finished script or even much input from Spielberg beyond the aliens needing to have "unlimited" capabilities. Once the company EFX Inc. was formed to take on these two projects (and more afterwards), Baker brought in David Cellitti, a monster fiend and wax modeler who studied under Katherine Stubergh.

Remembers Cellitti, "I had met Rick at Forey Ackerman's place on Sherborne. Rick had Polaroids of the Baby Monster from *It's Alive*, and his work was obviously years away from anything anybody else was doing. I was impressed. I was at Movieland Wax Museum at that time, and worked with Rick on the pre-production suit for '76 *King Kong*. Then we had a falling out. Years later he came to visit me when I was at Wolf & Vine Mannequins and told me he had two films coming up: *American Werewolf* and *Night Skies*. He poached me away from Wolf & Vine to be the vice president of EFX Inc. When I came on board I was working out of Rick's home. My duty was handling day-to-day business to leave Rick time to sculpt and create."

According to Baker, "David said, 'You're the artist. You shouldn't have to deal with business stuff. I'm good at that stuff, could take a lot off your plate, free you up to create more.' Gave me a whole line of bullshit that sounded good to me, because I hate dealing with that part of the business. That's how he got involved with all this stuff. Also, it was helpful that he could make molds and sculpt too."

Baker's studio at his house on Hortense Street in Studio City was essentially a workshop taking up the back of the home as well as the garage area. At the time it was mainly Baker and wife Elaine, along with mold maker Gunnar Ferdinandsen as well as Rick's right hand man Doug Beswick. In the midst of all this, a friend of Baker's introduced him to a young sculptor named Tom Hester in his early '20s.

"I had no idea who Rick Baker was," says Hester. "I liked monster movies, but wasn't following them as a fan. I met him when he was gearing up for *American Werewolf*. He asked if I would be interested in working on that. I said,

'Yeah, sure.' I started with him in the summer of 1980 and, just before we really got going on werewolf stuff, he asked me if I wanted to help with this test he was doing. That was the *Night Skies* test."

A lot was riding on the Skar test conducted on July 1, 1980, since Spielberg's reaction would keep the Columbia seed money flowing for R&D. They could also firmly establish the EFX facility in preliminary set up on Farmdale Avenue. The producer had been wowed by Baker's initial design of the lead 4-foot-tall alien Skar, whose humanoid facial features were offset by a bizarre body with a dog-like ribcage, frog-like legs, and a ridged tail. The creature's posture was "hunched like an ape" when walking, giving it a proper stalking stance. A reptilian green-hued fiberglass sculpt of Skar's upper body got Baker the okay for a test build of the functional character he described as "a real badass."

Baker explained his inspiration: "The way the arms join on was based on an Indian rhinoceros, which has these weird fleshy folds where the arms fit in. I also collected a bunch of tadpoles at one point, had them develop into toads in my office. The very first casting I did in resin of the *Night Skies* alien I painted up in greens and grays and yellows. Then-when I got the prototype put together-I decided to paint him more in fleshy tones."

After four months of work and $70,000 spent, the "crude" prototype alien had only been constructed from the torso up, thus rested on a table with slave servo mechanisms (also known as "Waldos") for the wrist, elbow, and arm run through the body from underneath. Lever action routing control cables were responsible for head and finger movement. Instead of bone mechanics moving underneath rubber like his ape creation Sidney in *The Incredible Shrinking Woman*, Baker experimented with rubber "flesh" sliding over stationary bone. He referred to this process as "anatomation."

"David Cellitti was saying, 'You know, you should come up with a bullshit name for what we do,'" according to Baker. "On the prototype head I had cables pulling an attachment to the foam, and it would actually move over the bone. The bone remained in place as it really would. I had an actual jaw joint cast from a human skull, the way the jaw fits into a little socket there, and it could move from side to side just as well as up and down. That's why we came up with the name 'anatomation,' but it was just a BS thing."

The test itself is a marvel to behold. In the edited 10-minute MOS version sent to Spielberg, it begins on a wide of the half-finished Skar with its arms outstretched and fingers moving Nosferatu-like against a black backdrop. It then cuts to a closeup, with Skar doing all manner of expressions from snarling to screaming, then smiling as a hand pets its head, showing the versatility of the puppet's "unlimited" ability.

We then cut to a medium shot where the missing lower torso is out of frame. Here we see similar expressions combined with articulate hand and arm movement, such as when it fights Baker who is trying to strangle it. Notably, we see the neck extend considerably when a punch is thrown, confirming a similar aspect to E.T.'s ability. This stretch-and-retract motion would be demonstrated many more times.

According to Baker, part of the reason this prototype came off E.T.-like is "it wasn't necessarily supposed to be Skar, just a generic alien. The design I did for Skar was a little more mean looking than this one."

Again like E.T., it drinks a can of beer and acts drunk. Outtakes show it pouring liquid from one cup to another. For the hell of it, it also blows bubblegum, then looks surprised when the bubble bursts. Closeups emphasize emotions like scheming and confusion alongside subtle fluctuations of the throat, throbbing of the brow, fluttering of eyelids, even a sneeze. The eyes dart here and there. Skar's skin is shiny with glycerin, some of which rubs off on a hand interacting with it. Veiny arm muscles flexed while the stomach expands and contracts for breathing. The final images show its E.T.-like four-fingered hand curling into a middle finger salute. There is no question: Skar was light years ahead of anything else in the movie creature field of 1980. It felt truly alive.

The crew felt alive too. In the hour-long unedited version of the test with sound, the group of artists are having a blast, hyped by the magic of what they were making happen. At one point, a jaunty Baker squeaks out, "Hi Carlo!"

This author had a digital scan made to preserve the VHS test, which was presented to Baker: "Looking at this video, which I haven't seen in many years, the worst part about it is that was the first time we even played with it. First time I got enough people together to work it. It could be so much better if we actually rehearsed, and they had some experience with it. You can hear me saying, 'Do this! Do that!'"

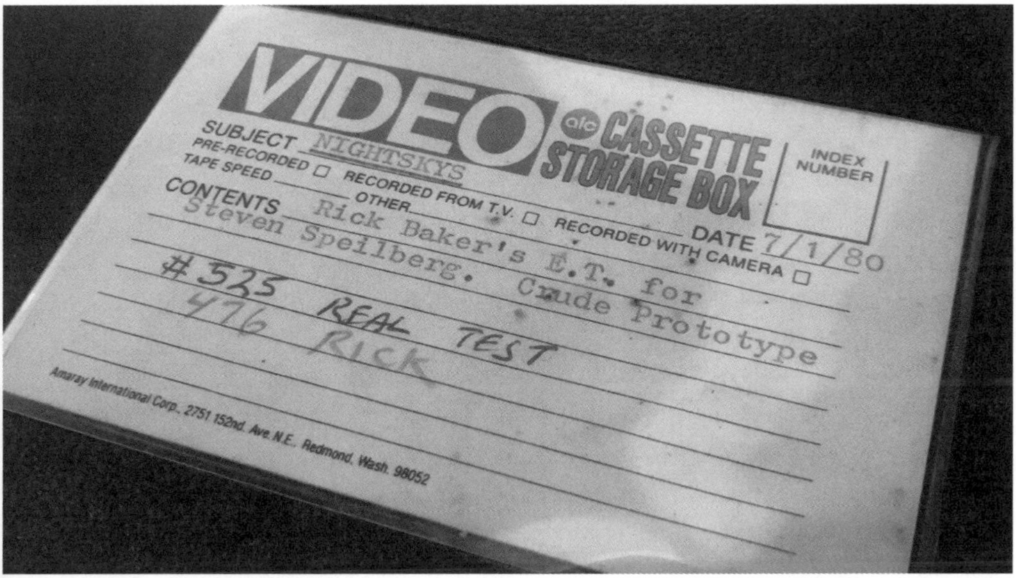

The weekend *Disclosure Day* came out in 2026, Baker released his own edit of this digital scan, stating, "I just turned on the camera and everybody started operating their parts. There was one monitor and the operators were under the puppet struggling to see what they were moving. I regret not planning out what we were going to shoot, but was excited and wanted to see it move."

"When I came to help on the day of the test, that's when I met Doug Beswick and Bill Sturgeon," remembers Hester. "Bill had been building the mechanical stuff with Doug. We were all at Rick's place to help puppeteer this thing. I was puppeteering an arm."

Remembers Craig Reardon, "I drove over to Rick's place, accidentally discovering the test in progress, and he put me to work operating one of the arms! It was a clever contraption that Rick's buddy Doug Beswick helped out with in regard to the mechanical aspects, though Rick had a very good grasp of that himself. We all looked at playback and were caught up with enthusiasm for it. The alien utilized radio-controlled servos for the facial expressions, but a lot of it was done with slave mechanisms, where a puppet is motivated mirroring what you do with your own hand or arm."

"It was primarily about different facial expressions," continues Hester. "Doug had cable mechanisms in the arms. The arm would come into frame and come back. It was amazing to see this thing because it was brand new to me. I was blown away, to say the least."

Says Cellitti, "When Tom Hester joined, everybody made fun of him because he was very insecure, but he made the most progress as a sculptor in the shortest amount of time of anybody I've ever seen. He went from being laughed at to a main sculptor overnight."

Explains Hester, "Seeing Rick's sculpted face and the detail he had on the arms… just seeing that upped my own ability. 'Oh, wait a minute, you can do all this stuff? That's cool.' It's a matter of focusing on those details. It was quite an eye opener."

In a brief email exchange, Bill Sturgeon added, "As you can imagine, I saw Rick's aliens when I was 19 so they had a huge impact on me. I only made finger parts for Doug Beswick at his house for the prototype."

Kathy Kennedy reportedly left an answering machine message telling Baker it "made Yoda look like a toy."

"We did the test and then he sent it to Spielberg, and Spielberg evidently was over the moon… calling it 'movie magic' and all this other stuff," confirms Cellitti.

Baker opened the video with the following intro, taped after the test was filmed:

"Hi, Steve and Kathy. This is the tape of the crude prototype as promised. I might add it was done on time and under budget. There's a few things I want to tell you first, before you see the tape. The black background you see here isn't really a necessity to shoot this guy. You could shoot him from any side or the back or whatever. We had the black up so you could definitely see him, wouldn't get lost in the background. They wanted to make real clear his movements so you could visually see that. I noticed afterwards, looking at the tape, it looked kind of like we had guys dressed in black suits working it, maybe, but it's not the case. Just wanted to fill you in that things are going real well. The shop's just about set up. We weren't able to move in July 1 yet. There's still some work to do, but it's come along nicely. We'll be doing all right. Is there anything else I should say? Everything's going fine, yeah, and I just wanted to add that this is the very first time we photographed this at all. It's the first time it's been put together. We never even had a chance to test it out before this. The people who are working it haven't worked it before and it's all new to them. There's some scenes where he looks a little spastic, and that will be easily taken care of with a little rehearsal time. I hope you like the tape and I'll be anxious to hear from you. Something I forgot to add was that Carol, the secretary, and Richard Weinberg are really working out nicely and we're real pleased. The situation there is really good. Situation with Columbia is really smoothing out. At first we weren't hitting it off that well, but now it's taken care of and things are working out and they're doing their best to get us in the shop right away. Hope you like the tape."

Baker elaborated to this author what the "situation" was with Columbia Pictures: "Shel Schrager was the guy I would have to go talk to, saying, 'I need to set up a shop now!' They go, 'Well, we're not gonna be filming for months.' It's like, 'Yeah, and I need every one of those days to make this stuff, and I can't do it until I have a studio.' This is an emergency which they don't see, all valid

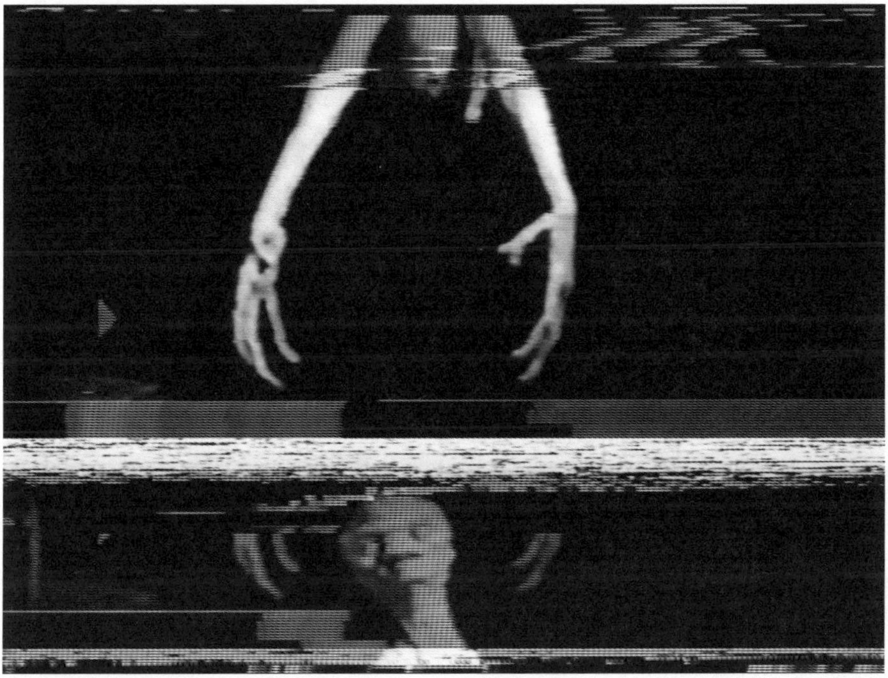

things I was asking for. Instead of going, 'Why do you need this or that?' they just didn't want to spend the money."

On July 6 Baker was taking notes during a call with Kennedy: "Time is the biggest problem... need four months at least. Steven says, 'No time to waste.'" While still at the house on Hortense, Baker had created a quick lower body sculpt in carved foam in order to properly assess the proportions of Skar before they built the full body, including a small tail and legs with two separate joints.

According to the Baker of today, "There's a lot of really stupid things in my design. I wanted it to not appear in any way to be a man in a suit, so we had arms like a praying mantis in the front, but in that video test the prototype couldn't even bend far enough to get him in that position. After working on the project some, it was like, 'We really got to move these arms in a different place... and maybe we shouldn't have the ridiculously skinny waist.' Was considering major redesigns before the whole thing went belly up."

Columbia acquired a facility for EFX to set up shop in the San Fernando Valley on Farmdale near North Hollywood. Un-air-conditioned (with only a swamp cooler to make it tolerable), it was intended entirely for *Night Skies*, though one area was blocked off for *American Werewolf*. *Close Encounters* models were also being stored near the site.

Baker explained that he "had to have one shop where I do both of them, because I can't be spending my time driving between two different locations."

"Once it got going, Rick set up a whole different team doing the *Night Skies* thing," says Hester, who was on Team Werewolf. "He had an arrangement. Spielberg was aware he was working on this other film. I don't know if they were aware, necessarily, that *Werewolf* was actually at the Farmdale site as well because the main shop was based on being for *Night Skies*. We were cloistered away in a room or two doing werewolf stuff, but meant to stay fairly quiet, don't crow about it. Keep your head down. We were working in a secret lab."

"Rick assembled a crew of eager young guys and put me into the mix on the werewolf movie," adds Reardon, who had returned from working on Tobe Hooper's *The Funhouse* in Miami. "There was an entirely separate crew working on the aliens-from-space movie. Rick, far as I know, bootlegged the werewolf project into the building. I don't think he intended for Columbia Pictures to know about it. It was one building divided in two, with the larger portion dedicated to the aliens."

From Farmdale, Doug Beswick turned out a detailed 14-page document titled "BUDGET: Mechanical ET Construction." Some of the figures he came up with included 100 hours to build each alien's close-up head (eyes, eyelids, eye control, jaw rigging, etc.) for a total of 500 billable hours. Also detailed were estimates for "HALF FIGURE," "HALF FIGURE STANDING (BELT RIG)," "FULL FIGURE STANDING (CABLE RIG)," and "STOP MOTION PUPPET ARMATURES" for all five creatures. For just the stop motion, a specialty of Beswick's since his Clokey Films days, it would run $9,570 for construction alone.

In the era before CGI came into its own, stop-motion animation was the go-to for any shot that would be too costly or unfeasible using live-action builds. In the case of creature work like this it would be essential to have shots earmarked for stop-motion execution, predominantly full figure work unsuited for cable-controlled puppets like...

—Buddee and Skar fighting as they roll down the hillside.
—Various aliens following the fight down the hillside.
—Various aliens running towards the barn.
—Buddee running off in the distance.
—Klud and Hoodoo pushing the trunk at the foot of the stairs.
—Klud running towards the shed.

Presciently for the eventual *E.T. the Extra-Terrestrial* puppet, Baker & Co. knew the hands were going to be a problem since the fingers were so delicate/thin and could only pack so much cable. Hence, stop-motion forearms and hands were earmarked to be built for a few of the aliens, possibly full-sized.

"*E.T.* had go motion puppets, so there could have been something like that for *Night Skies* too," adds Mitch Suskin.

Among the list of tools to be purchased specifically for the production were a "2nd lathe" ($6000) and a "2nd mill" ($12,000), with the total for all tools coming to $30,000. This became a bone of contention with Columbia.

"Doug wanted a metal lathe, and it was quite expensive." said Cellitti. "There was a certain amount of attachments too. Shel Schrager handled the finances; he was who I dealt with a lot. I used to have to go in and argue about why we needed a metal lathe."

Adds Baker, "It's like, 'Okay, I've got three or four guys that are machinists, but we don't have a machine. We're wasting money.'"

Prior to this project Baker had actually been inspired by how simple Carlo Rambaldi's mechanical techniques were on *King Kong*, and began tinkering with "sloppy" home-made inner mechanisms using simple tools like drills and files. For *Night Skies,* he and Beswick would have to up their game, which is why the lathe and mill were necessary.

Beswick's final estimate for the mechanics was...

10,928 man hours = 273.2 weeks = 5.464 years
Crew of 8 = approx. 8 months

Crew of 8 @ $800.00/wk for 34.15 wks	$218,560.00
Plus 4 weeks preparing for shot	25,600.00
Plus engineer @ $1000.00/wk for 38.15 wks	38,150.00
Plus supervisor @ $1500.00/wk for 38.15 wks	57,225.00
	$339,535.00
10% margin of error	33,953.50
	$373,488.50
Stop motion puppet armatures	9,570.00
	$383,058.50

In terms of underlying machining for creatures on both *Werewolf* and *Night Skies*, Hester says, "It was primarily Beswick and Sturgeon. A lot of us were doing mechanical stuff as well, but Bill was putting together those change-o-heads and coming up with really cool effects. Years later, mechanical stuff for films became high tech with polished aluminum parts done on a CNC machine. Back then, it was fly by night, whatever would work."

Baker himself additionally drew up a "BUDGET: ET Construction" that folded in all of Beswick's needs plus necessities for molds ($37.5K), sculpture ($72.1K), casting & clean up ($129.6K), paint & make-up ($35.8K), materials ($162K), stop-motion photography ($12K), and stop-motion miniature sets ($6.4K). This totaled out to $868,689.50, excluding other essential utilities like rent, phone, Xerox, trash, etc.

Says Baker, "We were buying the materials that we needed for the whole show. It was like, 'Let's get everything, so we can just keep going.'"

Of course, this was all before the time-consuming process of making these creatures work on 35mm film. Columbia was pouring in money for EFX to work out techniques that simply did not exist at the time.

Says Cellitti, "Kathy Kennedy and Spielberg were off in Tunisia doing *Raiders of the Lost Ark*, right? I was supposed to do a weekly report to Spielberg that was sent from his offices in the Egg Company directly across from Universal."

"It was weird because we were kind of on our own," remembers Baker. "Steven was gone, Ron Cobb was gone. There weren't a lot of people to talk to about it or get answers from. That made it difficult, you know? Disconcerting."

According to Cellitti, one errand he ran involved Spielberg eyeing a potential replacement director for *Night Skies*, presumably while Ron Cobb was ensconced in Spain building markets and temples and villages for *Conan the Barbarian*.

"Never saw him," claims Cellitti of Cobb. "At that point there was no director, because Spielberg didn't want to direct *Night Skies*. When I was working for Rick, they sent me over to New World Pictures to pick up a copy of *Piranha*, because they were talking about Joe Dante directing *Night Skies*. I remember very clearly going over and getting it on half-inch videotape, there were two of them. I think it was Landis' suggestion they contact Dante, but I remember picking up the copy because Spielberg wanted to watch *Piranha* before he made up his mind."

While Spielberg had already seen and loved *Piranha* when it came out in 1978, it could be he simply wanted to rewatch with his team before replacing Cobb, prior to the advent of video stores (*Piranha* hit VHS in 1983). If this story is true, it shows Spielberg had an eye toward bringing Dante into the fold years before calling him up to bat for *Gremlins*. Cellitti's assertion lines up with Polaroids of early Skar sculpts sent to Cobb before the first video test was shot as well as the timeline of early *Poltergeist* development in March 1980 dovetailing with Tobe Hooper being queried about taking over *Night Skies*. Robin Love and others assert the project was generated by and for Cobb to helm, but by mid-1980 Columbia may have been looking elsewhere.

"I was always told that Ron was going to be the director, which I thought was interesting," says Baker. "Ron did some unique designs for *Star Wars*. He could really draw, and he was great, but he was doing *Conan*. We basically had no interaction, at least that I remember. At one point he did drawings of what he thought the aliens might look like, but I had already made the prototype."

Another go-between from the studio was Richard G. Weinberg, a project coordinator at the time. Now president of investment firm Judd Enterprises, Inc.

and a prominent angel investor on Broadway, when reached for comment Weinberg stated, "I was a very low man on the totem pole back then and wouldn't have any pertinent information."

Remembers Cellitti, "Richard was the businessman from Columbia that was on premise. Richard was in hot water at one point because there was some kerfuffle and Richard took Rick's side of the argument. He got called on the carpet and basically told, 'If you want to still work for us, you better knuckle under.'"

While Baker had clearly pulled off fluid expressions for medium shots or close-ups, the process of making the aliens walk was a challenge. A full-body Bunraku-style Skar puppet had rigs the operators would wear not unlike a Steadicam. As Cellitti says, "The way these aliens were going to walk was to be done like shadow puppeting, manipulating the feet." An ET that moved with the puppeteer was the next hurdle to vault over, with more extensive use of Beswick's stop-motion abilities considered if this technique could not do the job.

How puppeteers would be successfully hidden given '80s technology is/was also a mystery, with Baker explaining, "The Bunraku thing was only going to be used for some shots. When you're making puppets, you can't make one puppet that does everything. Bunraku was more for trying to get it to walk. It was going to be a matter of black suits and branches. Stuff to hide things, shit like that. Doing it now digitally would be easy."

A similar technique was realized on a 1987 Chevrolet Corsica commercial directed by Douglas Trumbull. Titled "The Collector" during filming at Culver City's GMT Studios, the ad featured tall spindly alien puppets made by Screaming Mad George that were too skinny to be men in suits. As seen in Japanese doc *Film as Experience*, medium or close shots of these aliens were done on an articulated half-torso figure with lots of cabling running from the bottom, while full body walking shots were accomplished through shadow puppeting. The operators wore harnesses and helmets similar to photos of *Night Skies* development at Farmdale, connected to the puppet (head, arms, feet, body) via thin rods. They created movement while obscured in black sheets.

Said Trumbull, "This Showscan television commercial needed aliens that seem to be alive. Using the Bunraku puppet technique which has been used traditionally in Japan for hundreds of years, we developed a full-size version so the creatures very realistically move in direct proportion to the movements of the operators. When the operators are optically removed, the effect is very believable."

Other *Night Skies* personnel included Baker regular Gunnar Ferdinandsen working on the union side of the shop as a mold maker.

"Doug made the arms separately, I did everything else, Gunnar made the molds," Baker said of the initial test. "I did the initial sculpture of the torso, head, neck, and chest… all one piece. Then I said, 'Okay, we've got to break this up, remold the head and neck as one thing and the body as another thing.' Fortunately, Gunner was available, one of the few union mold makers that were really good."

Then there was Dave Kelsey and Guy Faria, in charge of all the physical effects.

Baker stated, "The problem was most of the people I knew that were really good at this stuff were non-union, but I'd worked with Dave and Guy on *Incredible Shrinking Woman*. They helped operate the Sidney face, and I liked them. They were good and they knew my work, so I hired them. We also had to have a so-called nurse. Kind of seemed like he was an alcoholic that just sat in the front office all day, bored, but if someone hurt themselves he would be there to put a band aid on it."

A storyboard artist who had contributed to *Raiders* named Ed Verreaux was brought in to draw out sequences like the kitchen scene with Squirt.

Verreaux told *E.T.* unit publicist Lyla Foggia in 1982, "In the middle of the summer they called me up from London and said, 'We really need to have this *Night Skies* thing boarded out in the next three weeks.' There apparently was a problem with the story. When you do a special effects film with opticals or puppets, it's just like an animated film, you have to storyboard what everything's going to do. Steven hadn't given them any specific idea of what he wanted with these characters. They were trying to get the financial stuff worked out so they could come up with a budget. I sat down with Rick and Doug and several other people for the next three weeks and we basically storyboarded the movie as we thought Steven might go with… 'If we shoot it this way, this is how much it would cost.' We boarded all the effects shots in the film, then I went on vacation and they sent the stuff off to Steven and whatever else happened."

"I thought Ed was great," Baker said. "We would board stuff, and then I'd say, 'This one, we have to work on.' There was one in a bathroom with an alien climbing up a wall. 'Well, we can control the puppet through the grout lines in the tile.' Just trying to figure out how we're gonna do it."

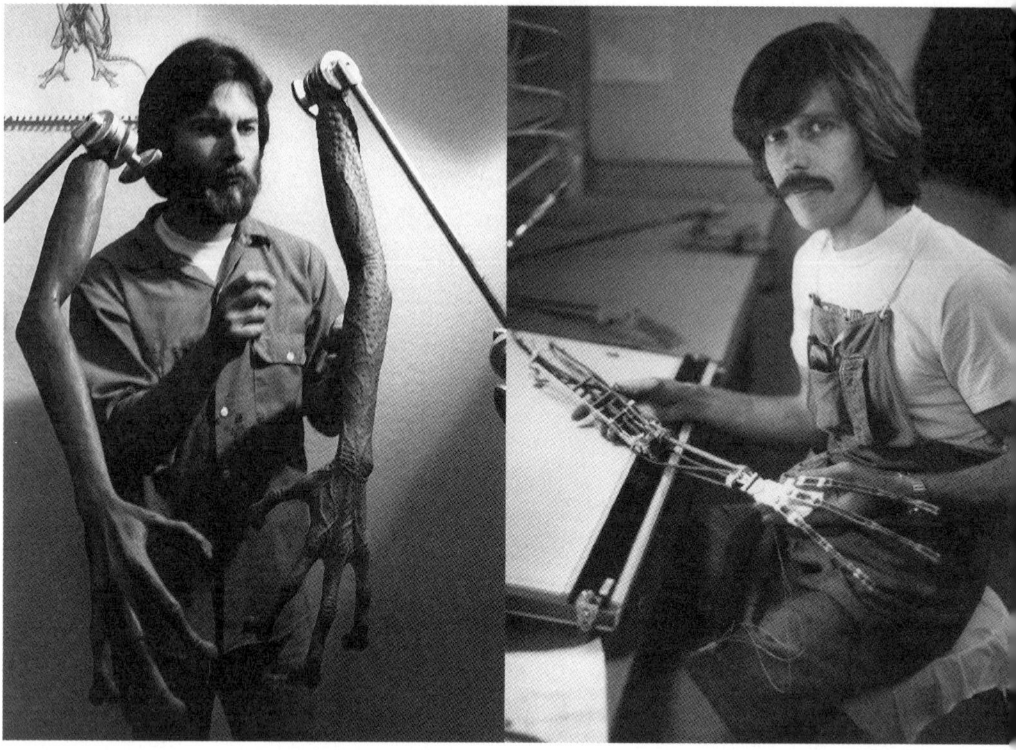

Baker (*left*) and Doug Beswick (*right*).

"Some of those guys crossed over and were working with us as well: Beswick, Cellitti..." Hester remarks. "As far as I knew Craig Reardon was working primarily with *Werewolf*, but I wasn't really focused on what was happening on the other side of that wall."

"Although the shops were divided, I was permitted to wander around a bit on the alien picture side more or less at will," Reardon explains. "There wasn't time to do that often."

Cellitti's secretary in charge of payroll, Carol Byron, was hired by Columbia but generally sympathetic to EFX's concerns. According to Baker, "Carol had a button under her desk that would ring a bell so we'd know if the union business rep showed up, so the *Werewolf* guys could be real quiet."

"A man by the name of Lefty Fletchmeyer was the head of the plasterer's union, and that's where they threw the sculptors and mold makers into," adds Cellitti. "If the light was lit, all the *American Werewolf* people were supposed to go into their part and close the door. The only people that were supposed to be out were *Night Skies*, because *Night Skies* was supposedly a union picture, and *American Werewolf* wasn't."

According to Reardon, "David was there working on sculpting the lower portion of an alien body under Rick's supervision."

"I sculpted the legs for the giant Skar, but my task, as presented to me, was to act as a middleman between Rick and reality," claims Cellitti. "I was supposed to handle the day-to-day business and leave him alone in his studio so he could create these aliens."

"He had a private room he could lock himself away in and just work," Hester recalls of Baker, who would oversee progress in the mornings for both departments before sequestering himself, playing music as he worked uninterrupted. "He would be off in there doing paintings of *Night Skies* aliens or roughing out sculptures of *Werewolf* stuff. When he didn't have to be managing, he wanted to be doing the artwork, understandably, because that's what motivates the whole thing... the desire to create. We'd each have different focuses, and he could come in to take a look and say, 'Okay, keep going with that... Tom, you do this... Bill, you do that.' He let me go to town with the sculptures, letting me come up with ideas myself. I felt very free to create. He would pat me on the shoulder, 'Oh, come on, Tom, if there's anybody who can do it you could do it.'"

"There was a Screen Actors Guild strike, so we didn't have any actors for *American Werewolf*," explains Baker. "I used that time on the werewolf side to train the mostly inexperienced crew. Like, 'This is how I do a life mask. Now you take a life mask of Tom, and Tom takes a life mask of Steve, and Steve takes a life mask of Kevin..."

Says Nobile, "The reason Rick has a career is when he was a kid he wrote to Dick Smith, and Dick Smith had him come to his house and said, 'Okay, ask any questions you want.' When it came time for him to be that person for another generation, he's like, 'Let me learn up these kids.' He needs a special makeup effects team for the first time. Where do you get your *American Werewolf* team? It's a bunch of super interns, mostly 18-year-old kids. He cultivated what was required: a new generation of makeup artists. He wasn't thinking, 'I'm going to change the face of the industry,' but he did."

"Rick was great to work with: articulate, soft spoken, perfect notes," says Mitch Suskin. "He had a way of looking at something, saying, 'You know, we really should make that do this.' He was never like, 'Oh, that's no good. That's not gonna work.' Always constructive. I didn't know what the long-term plan was, but it was going to be genius."

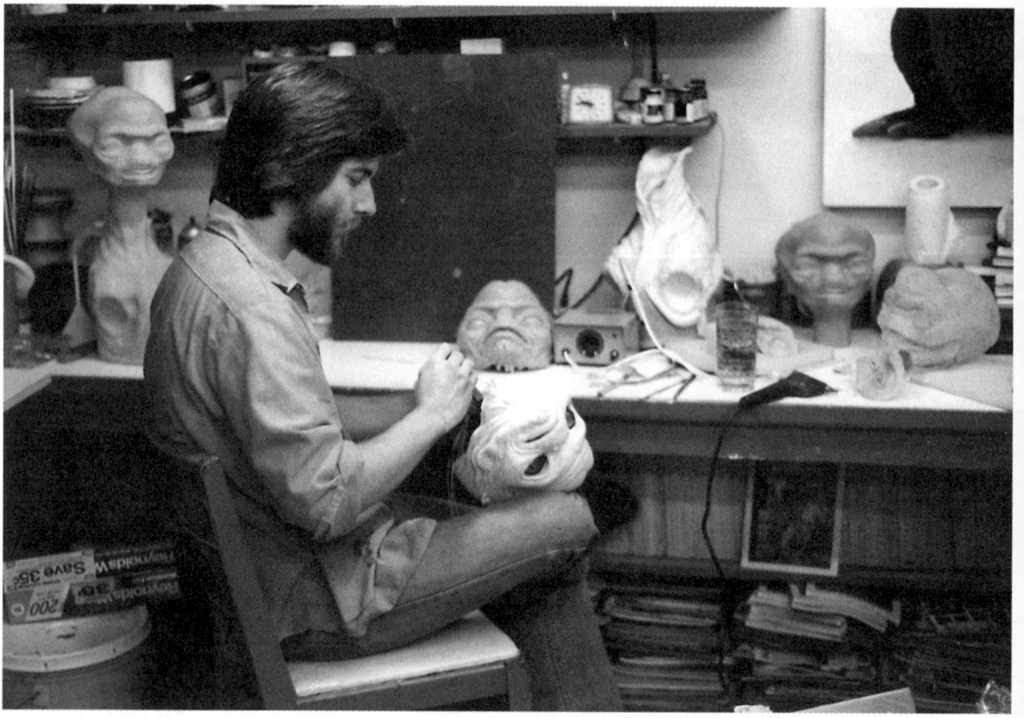

Adds Baker, "I was concentrating during that period on the *Night Skies* work, because there wasn't that much to do on *Werewolf*, right?"

Cross-pollination between *Night Skies* and *American Werewolf* extended to staff and techniques as the lines between creature makeup and special effects blurred. Baker told *Cinefex* in 1984, "The thing that's so attractive about puppets and mechanized creatures is that you're no longer limited to the human structure or what a man can wear. It gets you into more interesting and creative designs."

"He's got this self-taught knowledge of anatomy, which is amazing," adds Nobile. "In genre stuff there's a lot of hand waving and lighting tricks, people drawing attention away from work that's lacking. That *American Werewolf* transformation sequence, Baker said it made him sweat that he had to do it in bright light. I think that rewired him to make all his work stand up to full light. You look at these *Night Skies* designs and it's all there. Nothing wonky, no 'We'll just cover that.' It's a fully realized creation."

Adds Baker, "One of the union regulations was you had to have this laborer guy who would clean up and stuff. When we were playing with our quick, thrown together Bunraku *Night Skies* puppet we needed another set of hands to move something, so we put him to work there. That was the crew at that point. I was planning on really ramping up when it became more real. At this point we didn't have a start date or anything."

"They were experimenting with the puppet alien, Bunraku sticks controlling the legs and so forth," explains Hester. "We did similar things with the main werewolf suit, where it's like a wheelbarrow and somebody's holding the back legs. We ended up having the performer lying on a diving board thing on wheels. Their front legs were moving but the back legs were done Bunraku puppet-style."

"It was a combination of puppetry and animatronics," Cellitti says of Baker's newfound focus on what was termed "special effects makeup." "I remember Rick and Elaine coming back from Lucasfilm having seen footage of Yoda. They were gobsmacked because Yoda was the first thing that wasn't totally animatronics, wasn't really puppetry. That's what started the whole physical effects revolution of mixing different things."

An important member of the team was Elaine Baker herself, whose work as an "extra pair of hands" often entailed hair, repairs, and cable operations alongside general business details. Dr. Shellie McMurdo is a senior lecturer at the University of Hertfordshire, currently at work on a monograph titled *Splatter Matters: Gore and Practical Effects in American Horror Cinema*. One of her chapters focuses on how women have been largely overlooked—or "rendered structurally peripheral"—in the makeup effects industry, with publications like *Fangoria* emphasizing male artists and terms like "makeup man" at the expense of important women in the field like Elaine Baker.

"In his company at the beginning she was a key person," McMurdo says. "You can find photos of Elaine on the set of *American Werewolf in London* getting her hands dirty... literally blood-covered hands as she's touching up the makeup on the wolf. Her and Rick were together for a great many years before they got married, and she worked as his assistant on a lot of things. Because her last name is 'Baker,' there's a danger of looking back and going, 'Well, she was his wife. She was helping him on set. She was probably cooking him dinner while he was doing this.' She was a much more integral part. They were kind of like the mum and dad of EFX, lots of people underneath them went on to make their own effects houses."

"Elaine was helping to coordinate the business aspects," adds Hester. "She was also doing seaming on things. She helped him on *King Kong*, was always running the foam latex. She was very helpful."

The general atmosphere of EFX was loose and fun. A gregarious Landis often brought donuts for everyone, plus what Cellitti calls "this whole thing of marijuana, everybody stoned out of their gourds. There was a contest about who can spend the most on an ounce of marijuana, and the person who won spent $400 at that time." Whether drug use had any adverse effect on the work, Cellitti claims, "I don't think it had any direct effect. It certainly had an effect on me, because I joined AA shortly after things blew up."

Extra scrutiny may have been paid to *Night Skies* development by the studio since from July 21 to October 23 of 1980 a massive labor strike involving 67,000 performers from both SAG and AFTRA ground production to a near standstill. Said Cellitti, "We were the only thing in Hollywood during the strike... the focus was on us." With EFX's internal budget estimates for the five aliens starting to climb as summer 1980 drew to a close, Columbia saw fit to bring in another outsider to Baker's world.

"Doug Beswick pulled me in to Rick Baker's studio," says Mitch Suskin. "Ron was supposed to direct it, so I had the script. They were really great times."

"Towards the end we were forced by Columbia to take in Mitch Suskin," Cellitti claims. "Spielberg had just done the Special Edition of *Close Encounters*, on which Mitch was 'instrumental,' is what I was told. My secretary Carol said, 'Oh, you mean Mitch the snitch?' He was presented to me by Carol as the insider to Columbia that was going to report what was going on in the facility."

Baker adds, "Suskin was recommended to me by somebody at Amblin, or whatever it was called at that time. I thought of him as a spy."

Spielberg did not help this perception when later discussing Suskin's work as "effects watchdog" on both *E.T.* and *Poltergeist*, stating, "Mitch was my spy."

"More his eyes and ears," laughs Suskin at the insinuation. "I don't think it was that clandestine, because I hate to be cast in that role, but I knew a little bit about both sides, knew enough about building the stuff that he trusted me to tell him, 'Yeah, that's gonna work... No, that's not gonna work.' Rather than 'spy,' I would just say his evaluator."

"We had nothing to hide, but he was working for them, reporting back," adds Baker. "In reality, he was a clever guy. He ended up making a really good eye mechanism, something very close to what everybody does now, a three-cable thing, very much like the way side view mirrors work on a car."

While assisting the EFX crew as a creature engineer, Suskin also submitted a detailed progress report going right up to the overhaul of the project (7/80-

10/80). The stated objective was to "create mechanical extra-terrestrial creatures based on designs by Rick Baker and the requirements of the script by John Sayles." The extensive use of said ETs meant the five characters needed to be "reliable, reproduceable (i.e. mass produceable), and adaptable to different characters." There was to be a great deal of component interchangeability between different aliens built into the designs.

Sculpt of Buddee (*left*) and Baker painting of Klud (*right*).

It appears that most of the development in these three months was spent on improving the Skar functionality from the initial test, with an eye towards applying all they learned to the other four ETs (Buddee, Klud, Hoodoo, Squirt). Baker has no recollection of developing the larger Cypress creature, cow carcasses, or other additional makeup effects in Sayles' script. Here were the design parameters for an alien head via Suskin's document, for which he was chiefly responsible for internal mechanisms (written in the past-tense, presumably after the project was shut down):

1. **Eyes**—Both eyes were to be controllable from a single joystick, and have complete freedom of movement: up/down, left/right, or any combination thereof.

2. **Eyelids**—There was to be an upper and lower eyelid on each eye, and each individual lid was to be separately controllable. The lid itself was to be of latex foam and the mechanism was to move the leading edge of the lid.

3. **Brow**—The brows were to be controllable to form the expression of anger, sadness, and surprise. This would entail individual rotational control of each brow, and a means of raising the two brows together (surprise).

4. **Jaw**—Open, close, and side to side motion was to be controlled.

5. **Additional Expression**—Space was to be budgeted in the skull for additional cables to operate the lips, nose, and other areas to be determined by Rick Baker.

"It was going to be cables and servos, we had a lot of technology we were exploring," says Suskin. "A lot of what Rick would design, what was near and dear to his heart, was to make creatures that could not be guys in suits. Even though he was brilliant at guys in suits, he did something that would fool your eye into believing it wasn't a guy in the suit. But these creatures were intended to never be able to be guys in suits. To some degree, that was what drove the *E.T.* design, which is why it's short and has a long neck. Steven wanted to make sure everybody knew it wasn't some guy in a suit, even though, later on, we did have some little people in suits."

Suskin wrote at the time of the *Night Skies* company's biggest R&D challenge: hiding all cables and controls used to operate the aliens. At least 20 cables were needed for the Skar head alone, and the most serviceable sheathing they found was aircraft cable with the same coiled steel used for bicycles, 1/8 inch in diameter. Once you combine all the cables needed for the head, neck, torso, and arms, the filmmakers were going to be stuck with a mass of metal coming out of any given ET. The longer the cables (to keep operators at a distance) the more drag would build up in the works, making the control of these creatures a minefield of on-set delays.

He wrote, "We were going to try to cut down sheathing (and hence, drag) by running cables without sheathing whenever possible, and setting up the bending points only where necessary. This was literally on the drawing boards when we stopped work."

Observes the Suskin of today on Baker juggling two monumentally complex projects, "We were in a building where there's a wall down the middle, and Rick would walk back and forth. Rick was having the time of his life, but it was a little bit stressful for him and for everybody. Steven would come in and want to see stuff, and Baker was like, 'I told him I've got this other movie!' The timing was unfortunate."

"I met Rick Baker once," says John Sayles, "Steven was fighting with the special effects people about how expensive it was going to be. For instance, E.T. doesn't have legs along the ground because having legs—before CGI and other things—was gonna cost an arm and a leg. A lot of time and boredom on the set getting it to move right."

"The budget for the special effects for *Night Skies* was $1M," Cellitti claims, a number which did not include the near-million spent for development. "Rick wanted more than that, $1.5M or $2M. During this Rick and I got called over to do a maxillofacial demonstration at UCLA. There was this lady with half her face missing from cancer. Rick would work on this clay sculpture, then they would take it over. I managed to look at the invoice for her prosthetic and it was budgeted at $500. This is what killed my career. I'm looking at this invoice for $500... this poor lady is going to walk around with this thing for the rest of her life. Her face, slowly disintegrating from cancer, she's got $500 for the appliance, and we're arguing over a million dollars for rubber aliens. It didn't make any sense to me. I thought, 'What is wrong with this picture?'"

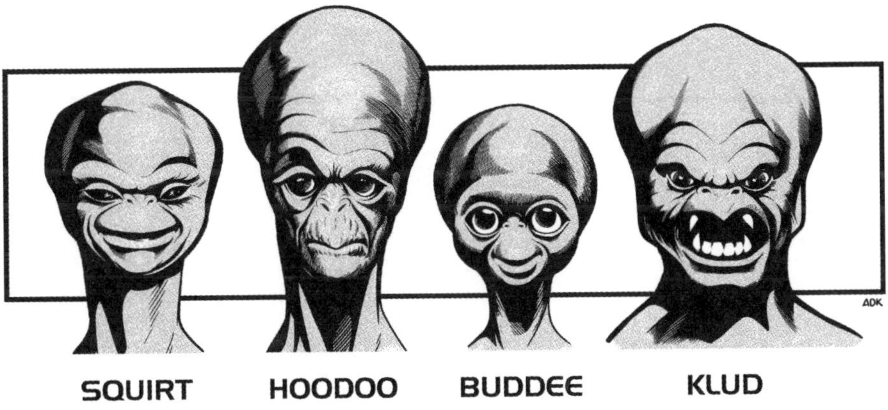

Fan art illustration by Adam DeKraker.

By the mid-2010s Baker finally felt comfortable revealing *Night Skies* photos to the public. Besides Skar these included Buddee and the other baddies in the extraterrestrial clan worked out in clay. Baker posted, "I was so excited to be working on this project, to be able to design different alien characters of the same race."

That excitement would be short-lived.

CHAPTER 8

After School: The Other Childhood Romp

"Frankly, I would very much like to make a small human story next."
—**Steven Spielberg**, *Pittsburgh Post-Gazette*, 1977

Immediately following *Close Encounters*, Steven Spielberg began tinkering on a project alternately titled *After School* or *Growing Up*, meant as a coming-of-age film with an edge. Aspects of it were later folded into *E.T.* just as *Night Skies* was.

"I don't want to make a movie about children that's dimples or cuteness," Spielberg stated at the time. "It's my first vendetta film. I'm going to get back at about twenty people I've always wanted to get back at."

To make his adolescent revenge movie, Spielberg recruited two budding young writing talents touched by a level of madness he could only admire: Bob Gale and Robert Zemeckis. While attending the University of Southern California's film school in 1973, Gale and Zemeckis (colloquially known as "the two Bobs") had their first fateful encounter with Spielberg when he came to show *The Sugarland Express* to students.

Robert Zemeckis (*left*) and Bob Gale (*right*) in 1978.

Said Gale, "Bob and I were amazed this kid, not much older

than we were, made this movie with 250 million police cars in it and all this production value. It was really an amazing picture. Bob then made an appointment to show Steven his student film *Field of Honor*, which Steven loved. They said, 'Well, we'll just keep in touch,' because Steven was certainly not in a position to give Bob a job of any sort."

The two Bobs began their career in earnest pounding out a few TV scripts (a *McCloud* spec, the *Kolchak* episode "Chopper"), while also developing the features *Bordello of Blood* (a vampire sex movie eventually made badly in 1996) and a satire called *Tank*. Their next rendezvous with Spielberg occurred in the spring of '75 when the pair snuck into a 10am distributor screening of *Jaws* at the Cinerama Dome on Sunset Boulevard.

"We managed to get ourselves in there, and our heads exploded," recalled Gale of *Jaws*. "We immediately decided, 'Okay, we got to go bust into Steven's office at Universal and tell him how great this movie is.' The next day we go into Steven's office and he's playing back an audio recording of the audience so he can hear where all the scares were. We told him how much we loved the movie and when the shark ate Robert Shaw we started laughing because it was so great. He goes, 'It was you. You were the guys laughing. I couldn't figure out who would be laughing at that.' That was a bonding experience."

Spielberg began regularly hanging out with the two Bobs, who were in business with John Milius writing the script for *1941* (then titled "The Night the Japs Attacked") about Los Angeles wartime hysteria in the aftermath of Pearl Harbor. When the four of them got together they were said to reach "critical mass," egging each other on with boundless enthusiasm, ideas, and ribald jokes. The four routinely spent Thursday nights at the Oaktree Gun Club in Newhall shooting skeet and trap, followed by an inelegant dinner at Tommy's Hamburger in Panorama City. It was at one of these pig-out sessions that Milius began regaling Spielberg about the *1941* scene where a Japanese submarine shells Pacific Coast Ocean Park and a Ferris wheel rolls down the pier.

Gale says, "They tell you when you're writing your first script, 'Don't make it so expensive that it's prohibitive for anybody to make it,' right? Well, we didn't get that memo. We said, 'Wouldn't it be cool if we did this? Wouldn't it be cool if we did that?' We wrote all this insanity into it. When Steven reads it, he's saying, 'I've never read anything like this. Nobody puts this stuff.' Fortuitously, this screenplay ended up in the hands of the only guy in Hollywood with the ability to put that stuff on screen."

As they developed *1941* for him to direct, Gale and Zemeckis went from Spielberg's gun buddies to protégés as they met for script conferences during evenings after he got off the set of *Close Encounters*. Spielberg found working on the madcap script in the midst of the intense UFO film a relief, plus it scratched his itch to do "a comedy like *Hellzapoppin*, which I must have watched a hundred times on television late-night movies when I was a kid." The three of them brainstormed wild *Mad* magazine-esque ideas like the opening *Jaws* parody with Susan Backlinie. When they weren't spitballing, a print of Stanley Kubrick's *Dr. Strangelove* was often spun for inspiration.

The Bobs were also developing a comedy at Warner Bros. about '60s Beatlemania...

As a student Zemeckis once approached fellow USC alum George Lucas to ask him how to become a director. Lucas responded, "Somehow." That "somehow" turned out to be "Steven Spielberg," who responded to the script for *I Wanna Hold Your Hand* enthusiastically, insisting 27-year-old Zemeckis direct. The problem: Warner Bros. had an ironclad rule against backing first-time filmmakers. On the other hand, Universal's Sid Sheinberg was willing to roll the dice on Zemeckis. In a testament to his clout at the time, Spielberg convinced WB's CEO Frank Wells to simply hand the project off to Universal.

This was to be more than a simple power-flex to help a budding director, though. Because Universal demanded Spielberg be planted on set throughout shooting as insurance on the newbie filmmaker, it became the *Jaws* director's first time as an accredited producer, including his own movies. Spielberg called it "seven boring weeks on the sidelines because they never needed my advice," although at one point he put around $1000 of his own cash for extras and stunts after the studio balked. He continued this hands-off approach in his productions after... for the most part. The late '70s press referred to him as a "baby mogul."

"I'm producing *I Wanna Hold Your Hand* because I believe in the young director, Robert Zemeckis," Spielberg told *Reporter Dispatch* in '77 of the $2.7M film. "He should have every opportunity to show what he can do and nobody was giving it to him, so I did."

According to author Jason Bailey, Zemeckis' mastery of his craft was on display from this very first movie on: "Jesus Christ, what a giant production for a feature debut! To do a period movie about iconography, big crowd work, huge scope... no need to do a first movie that's four people in a room, I guess. The filmmaking is so impressive we overlook how many people are doing all-timer performances. Nancy Allen in *I Wanna Hold Your Hand* has to do so much by herself in those hotel room scenes, and you're riveted to her."

E.T.'s descendants of *After School.*

After this experience, Spielberg planned to continue nurturing his two pet screenwriters by bringing them in on a smaller-scale movie he planned to lens as a kind of "working vacation." Alternately titled "Growing Up" or "After School," the tween comedy grew out of a suggestion by François Truffaut on the set of *Close Encounters*.

"Truffaut had just made this film called *Small Change* and he had the best time working with children," Spielberg told a press conference at the 73rd Berlin Film Festival in 2023. "He said to me, 'You have the heart of a child... you need to make a movie with keeeds!'"

In 1978 the filmmaker was a little less wistful, telling *Starburst* that Truffaut "nagged me to make this movie," meaning *After School*, which he later referred to as "*Small Change American Style*." Riding high on spectacular previews for the now-completed *I Wanna Hold Your Hand*, Spielberg entrusted Zemeckis and Gale to concoct this script for him to direct prior to the titanic production of *1941*.

"We were looking to figure out what our next movie was going to be," remembers Gale. "Steven really liked working with us, and he said, 'Guys, I want you to write a movie for me about kids growing up in the suburbs.'"

"It's a world that hasn't been explored that much in literature or film," Spielberg said at the time. "Movies have told the stories of those 16 or 17 and up but never the microboppers."

"*After School* was a jocks versus nerds type of story," Bob Gale told this author. "Steven didn't really have a focus on it more than that. He said, 'You guys are nuts. Go to town. Come up with something here.' And we did. We went crazy with this thing. After we thought about it for a while, we said, 'Look, our take on this—if we really want to do this and be crazy—is it should be R-rated, because 13 and 14-year-old kids swear like truck drivers.' Even in 1978 they swore like truck drivers. When I was a kid in the '60s we swore like truck drivers. These kids need to be kids and do that stuff."

Spielberg told Bernard Drew in 1977 that the project was "an Our Gang comedy of the '70s, a story of the 8-to-12-year-old kids of today as they grow up, showing what they do between the hours when they come home from school and go to sleep."

In *Starburst* Vol 1 #5, the director further explained, "It's about suburban children in America, gangs of kids... They're really young adults, becoming street smart, making love at 11, discovering drugs at 10. A lot of it will deal greatly with the influence of TV on children today. How they lived out the fantasies of *Charlie's Angels*, how that becomes the most important thing in those after school hours."

States Gale, quite accurately, "I'm sure the Duffer Brothers never thought of doing anything like this!"

Gale provided this author with a copy of the 144-page first draft when it was titled *After School* and still set in Zemeckis' hometown of Chicago, Illinois before Spielberg changed the title to *Growing Up* and started scouting the Arizona locations where he himself grew up. Dated June 23, 1978, the script immediately draws a line in the sand signaling its irreverence with the two Bobs credited as "Meyer Klingman and The Lakeville Road Boys From Cleveland."

Gale cleared up this allusion: "The pseudonyms we used were gangsters mentioned by Hyman Roth in *The Godfather Part II*."

As the 2000s comedies of Adam McKay would later do, the *After School* script begins with an epigraph, in this case from none other than Adolph Hitler:

"Universal education is the most corroding and disintegrating poison that liberalism has ever invented for its own destruction."

A second epigraph is credited to an eighth grader from Chicago: "School sucks."

The story kicks off introducing us to our suburban 7th grade lead Jules Webster, whose nickname is "Dooper." He attends Otto V. Kerner Junior High School, coined after the infamous ex-governor of Illinois who was imprisoned for his part in a horse racing bribery scandal. Jules/Dooper is described as average, not athletic, but somewhat attractive to girls and clearly in need of some confidence.

Dooper is chief among four nerdy friends who form the Our Gang of the movie, similar to the four Dungeons & Dragons-playing pals in *E.T.* (Michael, Greg, Steve, Tyler). One of the *After School* gang is named Benjy Sheets, a.k.a. "Vision" because he's introduced watching a mini-television inside a hollowed-out textbook in class. He wears earphones, like the radio headphones *E.T.* character Greg (K.C. Martel) brandishes.

Another member of the group is Steve Ellis, known as "Weeze" because of his cough and perpetual runny nose. Besides being health-conscious, Weeze presents as the typical nerd stereotype with high water pants, pens/protractors in his shirt pocket, and thick glasses, not unlike River Phoenix's nerd Wolfgang in 1985's *Explorers*. He is introduced in the boy's bathroom getting his head dunked in a toilet (a swirlie) by the movie's primary bully Mower, a precursor to Biff Tanen in *Back to the Future*.

Finally there is Douglas Cooper, a.k.a. "Buster," a little guy whose hair covers his eyes. Buster has a kind of "superpower" where everything he touches breaks. This is shown immediately when he tries to get a drink of water at a fountain and inadvertently busts off the faucet. From another fountain the bully Crusher shoots a stream of water at Buster, humiliating him. This character was partly based on Gale's own brother.

"We all knew kids like that, right?" asks Gale... rhetorically. "'Give me your new toy,' and 10 seconds later it's broken. We did a scene where they had a Stretch Armstrong toy, and they were going to try to see if this kid could break it. They ended up getting onto a construction site and hot wiring a steam roller and tried to break it apart like that."

Said scene climaxes with the steam roller doing no harm to the Stretch Armstrong, but continues to roll forward and knock down a half-constructed house, then crushing a parked ambulance to the point that two interns can't fit a body on a stretcher into it.

After School is full of wild vignettes like this, usually involving some kind of prank or mishap with our nerdy heroes. Things get even more interesting during a school P.E. class where the jocks (Mower, Shades, Crusher, Lomax) as "shirts" face off against the nerds who are "skins" in a game of "slaughter-ball" (essentially dodgeball). The shirtless nerds—described as looking like "refugees from Auschwitz"—are predictably getting creamed when they are saved by new kid William J. Nails, or just "Nails." He is the same "wrong side of the tracks" figure that Matt Dillon made a career of playing in the early '80s. Nails manages to deflect every ball until he is the last man standing, refusing to throw back at the jocks who outnumber him. Mower says, "What's the matter? You chicken?" This echoes the antagonists of *Back to the Future Part II* & *III*.

Choosing to align himself with Dooper's nerd squad over other cliques during lunch at the cafeteria, Nails joins them after school at the mall where they hang out at the arcade. Much of the story takes place in the shopping center, showcasing the burgeoning youth culture that didn't get a proper onscreen treatment until the mallrats of 1982's *Fast Times at Ridgemont High*. After Dooper gets pantsed by the jocks in front of mall onlookers, there is an arcade faceoff between Nails and Mower centered on Midway's pistol-controller video game *Gun Fight*, with Nails invoking John Wayne's *True Grit* line, "Fill your hand, you son of a bitch." Scenes revolving around the similar pistol arcade game *Wild Gunman* were folded into the *Back to the Future* sequels.

There was also a love interest for Dooper... or, more accurately, a crush interest. Like Lorraine in *BTTF*, the good-looking middle school girl JoAnn seems aggressively horny in pursuing the oblivious Dooper. In fact, she is introduced

Back to the Future (1985).

when Dooper gets pushed into the girl's bathroom by the jocks, with our tween male hero staring up at her in a stall, panties around her ankles. After she pulls up her Dittos and emerges from the stall, she tells him, "Dooper, if you want to see it, all you have to do is ask."

Later on, JoAnn startles Dooper—by himself in his backyard eating Pop Rocks—by very forward-ly asking him to the school's upcoming Halloween dance. Again, shades of *BTTF*'s Enchantment Under the Sea Dance, which Lorraine asks Marty to. The 1985 movie's "parking" scene is then invoked when JoAnn invites herself inside Dooper's family garage and into their Volvo station wagon. Inside the front seat she tells Dooper, "I can't wait till you're old enough to drive because then we could park." She tries to kiss him but he squirms back awkwardly, sitting on/activating the garage opener which reveals JoAnn's friends Laura and Karen, giggling. Despite her disappointment, JoAnn makes the date with Dooper... after which it's revealed that Nails has been suspiciously sleeping in the garage inside the Webster family's boat, indicating he's sans home.

Like the Marty/George dynamic in *BTTF*, Nails makes it his mission to instill confidence in Dooper (and the rest of the gang), admitting he has his work cut out for him. There's a scene in Weeze's chemistry lab basement where Nails encourages the boys to swear by saying "dammit" instead of "dang it," echoing Marty McFly's line "Goddammit George, swear!" *After School* being intended as an "R" leads to an escalation from "goddammit" to "goddamn son of a bitch" to "goddamn son of a bitch shit-ass motherfucker." As Gale confirmed, the potty language had to be present "for accuracy and novelty."

Nails' anti-social escapades start with a simple prank in which he and Dooper call in a midnight pizza order from a pay phone to the bully Mower's house, which instigates Mower's dad to slap the hell out of his son and force him to eat the entire anchovy pizza.

Things escalate when the five of them concoct an elaborate revenge plan on the jocks, requiring they get explosives from a dweeby 17-year-old computer geek nicknamed The Wizard (absolutely should have been played by Eddie Deezen). Because the lanky bespectacled creep gets everything from his mom, The Wizard does not want money for the six M-80s, but rather that they acquire some extremely filthy pornography for him.

Off the gang goes to Sid's Adult Bookstore, where Nails lights the proprietor's car on fire to distract him while the gang steals the dirty magazines. As the nerds pour over these mags ("Look what she's doing to that dog!") with wide-eyed innocence, a drunken Nails decides to give these boys a taste of the real thing in arguably the script's most heinous scene. Nails takes them to a dark make-out spot near the airport where they peep on folks in their vehicles giving blow jobs or getting it on, explaining missionary position ("You won't find this one in any of those porno magazines.") and so forth.

After spying two (script character-described) bearded "fags" in one car, they peek in through a van's skylight at a drunken hetero couple having sex. The man stops mid-coitus to get out and pee, giving Nails the opportunity to sneak into this van and fondle the intoxicated/passed out woman's breasts. He then gets Dooper to give her a mild kiss and encourages him to put his mouth on her breast, which a hesitant Dooper is about to do when the woozy woman—mistaking him for her grown-up lover—climbs on top of him, crushing the 7th grader under her naked body. Suddenly, the woman's lover gets in the driver's seat of the van and takes off, with Nails running to get back in and rescue Dooper. The two boys and the naked woman wind up falling out of the speeding van into a ditch, leaving her there as a 747 passes overhead.

This was written a month before John Landis' ribald smash *Animal House* sleazed into theaters, featuring Tom Hulce as a college kid in a relationship with a 13-year-old, among other debauchery. Spielberg was a huge admirer of the film, telling *Rolling Stone* in August '78 (while wearing an *Animal House* t-shirt) he had seen it three times: "I like it because everyone gets fucked in every sense of the word. It had no cheap moralistic ending like *Barnaby Jones*. It was socially irresponsible... I like the movie because it reminded me of my own college days at Cal State Long Beach. That's what I was like then. You know, Ken Kesey did one of his acid tests at a toga party we had. We filmed these pledges stealing traffic lights, and all my best friends ended up in the hospital."

"Socially irresponsible?" Landis responds in the piece. "If that were really true, he wouldn't have liked it."

It is mind-boggling now to imagine the family-friendly Spielberg—"America's director"—filming a scene this over-the-top. This is a first draft of *After School* and would possibly have been toned down. However, the counterpoint to this is a comedic scene in the Zemeckis-directed/Spielberg-produced *Used Cars* where a screaming model's breasts are accidentally exposed and then fondled by a cameraman during a live commercial.

"This was Bob and me in our most 'socially irresponsible' phase," confirms Gale.

The second act brings the script's most memorable scene as our heroes pack a remote-control car with a container of dog shit and Wizard's M-80s rigged to explode with a long fuse. Dubbed "The William J. Nails Shitmobile," they bring it to the mall, communicating with Walkie-Talkies like a tween edition of *Mission: Impossible*. Vision removes the car from a carrying case while Weeze lures the bullies out of the arcade by yelling, "Johnny Mower sucks!" Mower & Co. emerge, Weeze lights the fuse with a Bic, Nails hits a stopwatch. Dooper operates the Shitmobile in their direction via remote control.

Elsewhere in the mall, a Radio Shack salesman demonstrates a C.B. radio to a customer, which suddenly makes the remote-control truck go wildly off course. With 15 seconds before the explosion, the salesman lets go of the C.B. button and the Shitmobile is back in Dooper's control. Then the customer depresses the C.B. button and the truck veers into an arc. Nails exclaims "Jesus Christ!" when he notices what's happening at Radio Shack, running like hell down the ramp toward the main level. With 5 seconds left the truck heads towards a lingerie boutique where JoAnn and her friends emerge. With no time left on the clock, Dooper breaks his cover to scream at JoAnn to get away from the truck now approaching her. In the nick of time Nails snatches the C.B. from the Radio Shack customer, Dooper regains control of the car, speeds it towards the jocks where the dogshit explodes over all six, covering them with globs of excrement.

Gale details, "There was a sequence in a shopping mall where the nerds wanted to get revenge on the jocks, so they built this radio-controlled car that had a dog shit bomb in it. Covering bad guys with shit... we clearly carry this over into *Back to the Future*."

But that's only the half of it. Although the jocks are humiliated, Dooper gave himself away to save JoAnn, so now he is the hunted as jocks head up the escalator after him, getting shit on people in the process. They hop on their skateboards and chase Dooper through Sears, where our hero gets cornered in Sporting Goods until he spies a 10-speed bike and swipes it, evading his enemies. The jocks abandon their skateboards to grab bikes (one of them a girl's bike), as they ride through shoppers, smashing a display of vases. The jock Scanlon uses a belt to whip Dooper as they ride side-by-side à la *Ben-Hur* (a gag later redone with a chain in *Used Cars*), but then the bad kid smashes his bike into a railing and flips over into a fountain. Dooper rides his bike down an escalator, followed by five biking jocks, with some standing riders jumping over the sides to avoid them. A mall security guard tries in vain to stop them, but slips on a dropped Slurpee then falls backwards through a pet store window, unleashing dogs and birds into the mall.

As Dooper exits the mall on his 10-speed with five jocks in pursuit, he jostles through parking lot cars into a busy street and then onto an expressway with 55-mile-an-hour traffic. Our hero rides on the grass divider to avoid cars, which screech and swerve to avoid the biking jocks, all while being pursued by two Illinois State Troopers in their squad car. Dooper cuts across oncoming traffic towards the entrance ramp, causing a (famously ignitable) 1972 Ford Pinto to crash into the police car before being rear-ended by a Mack truck and exploding, the driver running out of the car engulfed in flame.

With Dooper off the expressway and back onto a regular road with Mower, Shades, and Lomax in hot pursuit, he heads down a steep 45-degree embankment at 30 MPH. Now in his own neighborhood, he rides to the backyard behind his own house where neighbor kids are racing Hot Wheels down a 2 X 6 board. Dooper jumps the board, sending him and his bike into the air over the fence "in a stunt Steve McQueen would be envious of!" This certainly puts to rest where Spielberg got the idea for the sequence in *E.T.* of kids on bikes getting pursued by squad cars, buttoned with a bicycle launching into the air. Unlike in *E.T.*, Dooper and his bike land in his backyard swimming pool as Mower and Shades smash into the fence.

This whole 10-page sequence is a classic Two Bobs set piece, right up there with Marty McFly on a skateboard being chased through Hill Valley streets by Biff… if not better. The suspense, escalation, and constant pushing of the envelope would have been tremendous in the hands of Spielberg, certainly the modern grand master of cinematic chase scenes.

Gale concurs, saying, "Yes, the dog shit bomb sequence was us at our best!"

Although the bike landing in the pool feels like the end of this sequence, it is not. As Dooper catches his breath and downs a glass of water in his kitchen, the doorbell rings and Dooper's father answers it, letting in the shit-covered Mower and Shades. The two bullies ignore the dad and throw Dooper against the wall, wailing on him until he's bloody. Neither the victim nor the dad do anything to stop the beating, until Nails arrives and the two bullies drop him on the floor, telling Dooper he will get more of the same if he comes back to school. They leave.

Nails begins a tirade, admonishing Dooper for not fighting back while the dad counters that violence is not the answer. Blaming the dad for Dooper being such a "wimp," Nails gives him the most basic fighting tip: fake with the left, hit with the right. The tough kid then hops on his bike, leaving the battered Dooper behind.

Back at school, the trio of Weeze, Vision, and Buster have a newfound post-prank confidence, even swearing to a teacher. Meanwhile a still-bruised Dooper is staying put at home, silently stewing in his room where hippy-ish dad tries to instill that violence breeds violence while the mom talks about possibly moving, afraid her son will be assaulted again. It should be noted that despite all the lunacy, the script's depiction of the emotional toll all the bullying has on Dooper is inherently serious and forms the emotional core. Even before his brutal beating, a forlorn Dooper is shown depressed in bed listening to Linda Ronstadt's version of "Poor, Poor Pitiful Me."

His dad mentions that he could be moved to the rowdy inner city Warren G. Harding school through the bussing program, which upsets Dooper but gives him a brainstorm.

"Bussing was coming into the school district," Gale explains. "Our nerd characters were real clever, and one of them figured out how to reprogram the school's computer so that their enemies, the jocks, would be sent to this inner-city school."

When Dooper tells Nails this plan, the tough kid is not impressed, calling it "pussy shit," explaining that a computer cannot change the fact that Mower knows he's afraid. With Dooper still absent, Mower feels free to pass JoAnn a lewd note with a drawing of him squeezing her breasts. JoAnn is disgusted and crumples the note, which Nails finds.

There is a scene between Nails and the principal where it is explained they cannot find his school records, and the number he gave for his parents is actually a pay phone. Knowing he's toast at this middle school, Nails gets money from Wizard to supposedly acquire a prostitute for the 17-year-old in exchange for programming the school computer to get the bullies bussed. Nails then uses the money to buy a plane ticket, while Dooper calls JoAnn to tell her he can't come to the Halloween dance with her after all, feeling miserable about it.

On the night of the dance the pranks begin with Buster, Weeze, and Vision blowing up a pumpkin on Mower's porch, then chainsawing a telephone pole which knocks out the power to his house. Meanwhile, Dooper gets second thoughts about the dance and tries calling JoAnn from a pay phone, but she's left already. Then by chance the pay phone rings: American Airlines trying to reach Nails about his flight to St. Louis. Realizing what's happening, Dooper pedals his bike frantically to O'Hare airport.

Once he arrives Dooper makes his way through security and the terminal, commandeers an electrical cart with an old "invalid" woman rider, steals her boarding pass, then gets on board the 727. While confronting Nails, the tough kid again insists Dooper has to learn to fight because there will always be "some punk like Mower who'll fuck with a pussy like you." He then shows him the lewd note Mower gave to JoAnn. Dooper gets furious, fakes with his left before hitting Nails with a right, then runs out of the plane to save JoAnn. Nails rubs his bleeding mouth and grins.

Escaping the airport by sliding down a baggage claim chute, Dooper hops back on his bike and heads towards the school. In the gymnasium at the Halloween dance, the bully Lomax pours his own urine into the punch bowl (similar to Biff spiking the punch bowl with alcohol in *BTTF 2*). He gets two teacher/chaperones to drink it. Dooper arrives and points out to the teachers that their car is on fire, which it is, and this distraction lets him and the rest of the nerds secure the door for the final confrontation.

Echoing *BTTF*, Dooper sees Mower harassing JoAnn and yells out "I said, get your hands off her." In response Mower grabs one of JoAnn's breasts, which provokes Dooper to rush forward and smash Mower's nose, the bully falling backward as the piss-tainted punch spills all over him.

It's hard to state how important this idea of the meek character coming into his own and fighting back is to the early Zemeckis/Gale world. We saw it first in *I Wanna Hold Your Hand*, with Marc McClure's Larry declaring, "Get your goddamn hands off her..." before clobbering a pervert attacking Theresa Saldana's Grace. Then there's the climactic scene between George McFly and Biff in *Back to the Future*, where George opens the door on the bully about to rape Lorraine and says, "Hey you, get your damn hands off..."

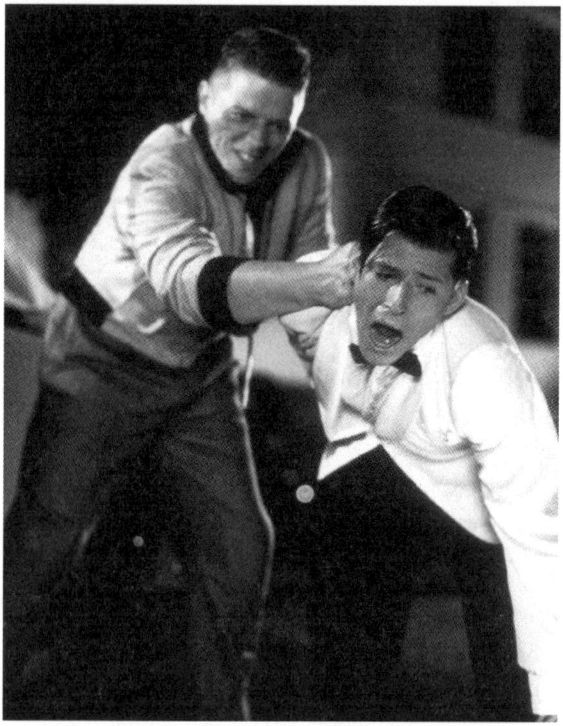

"I actually don't think the movie is about getting the kid in the car back to the future," Biff actor Thomas F. Wilson told Michael Rosenbaum in 2026. "I think the movie is about, 'No, Biff, you leave her alone.' I think that's the core of the movie. It's him standing up for himself and saying, 'No. This isn't going to happen.' Then he hits Biff. Everything changes. Of course, we're in a Hollywood movie. The car has to get him back and then everything's changed with his family and all that stuff happens and the lightning and everything. A lot of fun... but the meaning of the movie is stand up for yourself."

Once *After School*'s Dooper knocks his bully down, Mower gets up and begins wailing hard on Dooper, the other jocks having to pull him off. When Mower tells his guys to pants Dooper, it is time for Buster, Weeze, and Vision to swoop in, pulling out a screwdriver, hammer, and crowbar. The jocks are too scared to pants the nerds. Then, in an act of non-violent defiance, Dooper and his geek gang volunteer not only their pants but their shirts, throwing their clothes at the bullies with glee. The other kids at the dance also start throwing their clothes at Mower until half the kids in the gym are nude. Dooper caps this off by telling Mower to kiss his ass. The jocks all flee, and the nude band begins playing music for the nude kids to dance to. Outside, police and firemen deal with the flaming car and Mower gets arrested for it.

The nerd group puts their clothes back on and quietly exits the dance, only to find Nails has returned. He is proud of the boys, and was ultimately good on his word to get Wizard a prostitute in exchange for sending the jocks to the inner city. In a final goodbye, Dooper thanks his mentor, to which Nails replies "You're welcome" before disappearing into the darkness.

We cut to a school morning as Mower and the rest of the jocks board a police-escorted bus covered with graffiti, bad words, and bloodstains. The nerds watch in satisfaction. Now as they stride down the halls of Otto Kerner Junior High, Dooper and his friends walk with bravado... even a bit full of themselves as Dooper shoves a wimpier kid into the girl's bathroom. No one oppresses like the formerly oppressed.

In one final bit of irony, our heroes head to gym for a game of Slaughter-ball but are confronted by a newly-arrived multicultural group of tough inner-city kids from Warren G. Harding with knife scars, missing teeth, and tattoos. Dooper & Co. do not look happy...

As Gale says, "The kicker was that then those kids from the inner-city school got transferred to the suburbs, and they were going to be the new harassers of our heroes. That was the ending of it."

While a great deal of material from the *After School* script, both specific and thematic, was admittedly pilfered for *Back to the Future,* it is also clear that elements like the suburban setting, the gang of nerdy kids, a scene revolving around pizza delivery, the Halloween setting, the big splashy bicycle chase with a flying bike, and even specific pop culture references (*Star Wars*, Elvis Costello) were ported over to *E.T. the Extra-Terrestrial.* Gale confirms, "Steven got talked out of doing it, and the 'kinder, gentler' movie he made about little kids became *E.T.*"

In early 1978 Spielberg told an assemblage at AFI that, "a movie I'm making called *After School* is really about the essential dilemma we all have in growing up—the wimps versus the jocks... About forty percent of the cast has never been in front of a camera. Can I go back to the streets I came from, with a union crew, and make a movie that doesn't involve fifty technicians and millions of dollars in pre-production work? Can I make a small movie?"

Some prep had been done earmarking a shopping center in Chicago for the mall scenes. Then, on March 1 of 1978, *Variety* announced that the *After School* project was now called *Growing Up*, and would begin shooting for Universal in Phoenix, Arizona, where he spent 11 years of his childhood. *Rolling*

Stone added that *Growing Up* had now integrated "tales of his suburban glory in places like Scottsdale, Arizona and Haddonfield, New Jersey." A month after announcing the retitled project, Spielberg clarified in an April 1978 edition of *The Arizona Republic* that, while some elements of the movie were autobiographical, "it won't be a diary of my life... that would put most of the world to sleep." The box office reception of his autobiographical 2022 film *The Fabelmans* proved this statement prophetic.

"As we learn from *The Fabelmans*, in school Steven was a guy running around with a camera," said Gale. "Bob and I were doing that too, but we knew the character who's an observer is not as interesting as the character who goes out and tries to get the girl or do stuff, right? That seemed too inside to do that. That never seriously crossed our minds."

Not that Spielberg was any kind of angel during his own childhood years. In the pages of *Penthouse*, he recalled going to Arizona's Chris-Town Mall construction site and throwing rocks through windows, causing thousands in damage. The director's mother Leah has said, "His badness was so original that there weren't even books to tell you what to do." He was a self-described terror to his sisters growing up, saying "I loved terrifying them to the point of cardiac arrest." Pranks included locking them in closets, tearing heads off Barbie dolls then serving them on a lettuce platter, et al.

He recounts (with a twinge of embarrassment) during a 1981 Dick Cavett interview a prank he pulled during a movie theater screening of the 1960 version of *The Lost World*. The 13-year-old and his buddies smuggled a container of creamed corn and Parmesan cheese into the balcony, then pretended to wretch while pouring it onto the attendees below, who promptly started actually vomiting. He told a laughing Cavett that the gag "created an enormous chain reaction, upstaging the entire movie and the lights came up in the theater, they stopped the movie... it was an enormous fiasco." He and his friends fled via a fire escape. Upon learning this, a more cynical fan might be surprised that 1997 was not the first time Spielberg made a mess of *The Lost World*. This exact story was later told almost verbatim by the character Chunk in *The Goonies*.

The director planned to lens *Growing Up* in Phoenix over a 28-day $1.5M dollar shoot to begin on May 15, "right in the heat of prostration." The cast was expected to consist mainly of 8-to-14-year-old unknowns, except perhaps for (possibly) *Close Encounters'* Cary Guffey, who would have been 6 that summer. Casting director Sally Dennison (*I Wanna Hold Your Hand, 1941*) began posting notices for talent in *The Hollywood Reporter* and *Variety* by early February of 1978, looking for boys and girls who were "bright, creative, witty, unique, all ethnics, characters will be created from the cast." Sadly, Sally Dennison passed away at age 83 on August 29, 2025, only a few months before this author discovered her involvement in the project.

With the exceptions of *CE3K* editor Michael Kahn and DP Caleb Deschanel (*The Black Stallion*, *Being There*), Spielberg told *Variety* most of the crew would also be "untried."

"Steven wanted Caleb Deschanel, the great director of photography, to shoot this," Gale said. "Caleb read this and he was appalled. He said, 'Steven, I don't want to work on this. This is just so out there, so seamy.' Caleb was appalled that Steven would even consider making a movie that was so mean spirited and had so much bathroom humor. It was an R-rated movie about 12-year-old kids. That was the overall concept of it. This was not something the world was ready for in 1980 or 1981, right? I think Caleb kind of talked Steven out of doing it. So, Steven said, 'Okay, I'm going to figure out this *E.T.* idea.'"

By the time *1941* came into production in October 1978, Spielberg had expanded the cast to dozens of speaking parts for comedians from *Saturday Night Live* (John Belushi, Dan Aykroyd), *SCTV* (John Candy, Joe Flaherty), as well as most of the cast of *I Wanna Hold Your Hand* (Bobby DiCicco, Nancy

Allen, Wendy Joe Sperber, Eddie Deezen). Gale and Zemeckis questioned why Spielberg was peppering his movie with major talents like Broadway's Patti LuPone when there was nothing in the script for her to do.

"This was the kind of weird stuff that Steven was doing because he could," Gale suggests. "Why not? There's a whole lot of good reasons why not. This isn't the movie I started off to make? Maybe it would be a good idea for me to make the movie I started off doing instead of adding all this stuff? 'Let's have John Belushi spit up more food.'"

In his autobiography, Jerry Ziesmer writes of being called in to immediately replace first assistant director Steve Perry, arriving on set that night to find an outrageously improvised production where every brainstorm was catered to. John Belushi and Dan Aykroyd drove to set in an authentic NYC taxicab the two owned, then started rat-at-at-ing ideas for the arrival of an Army tank in the middle of a 1940s L.A. shopping district. Belushi, who was not in the scene, suggested the tank crush a parked car, while Aykroyd added the idea of his Sergeant Tree character popping out of the tank and machine gunning the area to get people's attention for his speech.

As Ziesmer wrote, "Steven was laughing, and the cast was excited. As the assistant director I was in cardiac arrest." It would be his job to find multiple 1940s cars they could demolish, then figure out safety for that as well as Aykroyd firing rounds of blanks with so many extras on the set. Spielberg told Ziesmer to call him when the just-invented action sequence was ready. A half-hour later, the chuckling director emerged with his cast from another brainstorming session, now telling Ziesmer of several new "special shots" to add to the sequence...

—Belushi wanted to appear as Marlon Brando munching pasta in an Italian restaurant as a car drives through the window.

—Aykroyd wanted a Marine in a department store having his face hit by an electric train.

—John Candy wanted a fire engine ladder to hoist an MP up.

All these scenes were somehow put on film over what Spielberg claims was a 175-day shoot. Journalist Jason Bailey recently leafed through late actor Candy's personal files for a project: "I found the call sheets for *1941*, and the extent to which Candy was on that set... longer than he was ever supposed to be. Just looking through the schedule it was clear how much of an out-of-control production it was. So far over schedule and budget, which I think everyone was willing to indulge because the same thing was true with *Jaws*, but it didn't work out quite as well this time."

Also executed was the incredibly complicated shot of Belushi's full-sized P-40E military plane landing on Hollywood Boulevard and crashing into a giant statue of Santa Claus. With the descent later married with miniatures in the final film, the SFX crew spent many nights on the Burbank backlot reshooting this one shot to the director's specifications, continually resetting the plane to be launched from a catapult and slid across the soundstage. In some ways it was the fulfillment of Spielberg's original vision for *Close Encounters*, which according to Willard Huyck had the spaceships landing on Robertson Boulevard in West Hollywood. John Veitch confirmed that when special effects wires holding the plane were visible in a shot, they had to redo it for $300,000.

As off-the-reservation as things seemed, some ideas were a bridge too far. For example, Robert Short was making remote control cars to drive down the street on Greg Jein's Hollywood Boulevard miniature for shots where Belushi's plane flew overhead.

"I did a custom car in military colors, but it was a *Jaws* shark," reveals Short. "In rehearsal we drove the shark car down the street with all the other cars. Steven was not amused, I'll put it that way... we barely skimmed not getting fired."

With speaking parts multiplying like rabbits alongside blindingly elaborate added set pieces, *1941* was a red flag in movie form. Buoyed by success, Spielberg put his bulletproof reputation to the test with a project that—alongside *Heaven's Gate* and *One from the Heart*—became Exhibit A of New Hollywood folly.

"I found the whole thing of *1941* to be a not pleasant experience, because we had a meeting just before going into production and Sid was there," says Frank Price, referring to MCA/Universal chairman Sid Sheinberg. "They'd come over to Columbia, and he said, 'Well, we know you're gonna go at least 10% over budget.' Columbia didn't have the money to be careless. I had a very good head of production, John Veitch, who was trying to make things for what the budget was and anticipate everything."

"If we hadn't stayed on top of it, it could have gone over by another $10 million," Veitch admitted to Marilyn Beck in 1980.

One tactic Veitch took to stanch the bleeding on *1941* was to enlist the two Bobs in creating a cost-cutting script document of specific scenes to eliminate from the shooting schedule in order to save at least half-a-million dollars from the spiraling budget. John Milius insisted that Veitch give each of the boys a Mercedes as compensation for their work, so these became known as "The Mercedes Rewrites." Spielberg ignored the suggested cuts, shot all the scenes in the document, then wound up eliminating them all from the theatrical cut of the film. It's no wonder that most of the star-spangled cast were hired for 14-weeks but wound up shooting for six months.

Says Mitch Suskin, who worked on VFX, "Spielberg made us all t-shirts with his quote from when he pitched it that said, 'I will not make this picture if it costs a penny over $11 million.' They wrapped the movie. It was done. They weren't going to do any more, then they came back three weeks later and did the scene where the tank goes through the paint shop, because Steven thought that would be a funny gag. He had a lot of power at that point, but it was interesting to see the old studio heads tearing their hair out."

"I find myself staring at the bedroom ceiling in the middle of the night and thinking, 'How did I get into this mess?" said Universal Studios President Ned Tanen in 1980. "What do you do, change directors in midstream? It could cost a studio $6 million to $10 million to scrap a movie in mid-production. How could a studio do that?"

"When you've got two studios involved, you've got no control," Price explains. "As Steven was making *1941*, I think he felt certain things weren't working, so the budget kept expanding while he was reshooting. It went from $27M up to $35M... those numbers would be much bigger today. At Columbia that money prevented me from doing another picture. It was siphoning away my budget. When we got through all that, *1941* suffered from the problem that it wasn't funny, even though it had a lot of good comedy talent in it. I don't think Steven has ever been comfortable with a straight comedy."

Gale had such misgivings over how *1941* turned out that he

wrote the official novelization himself so there would be a record of he and Zemeckis' original intent. Spielberg may have longed to be doing the smaller-scale *After School* instead of this runaway behemoth, but he did manage to sneak in that project's primary inspiration.

"Steven had an allusion to *Our Gang* in *1941*," reveals Gale. "In the extended cut, when Bobby Di Cicco comes out of the café, he's got these little kids standing on the street and they look just like *Our Gang*."

Even as *1941* was going pear-shaped, Spielberg once again called on the boys to develop an idea he and Milius had about rival used car lots in Arizona. This became the summer 1980 release *Used Cars*, an extremely audacious dark comedy starring Kurt Russell as a sleazy huckster pulling scams to keep the lot he works at in business while battling Jack Warden, who plays both the "good" and evil car lot-owning Fuchs brothers. Nurturing its relationship with Spielberg, Columbia greenlit the R-rated comedy.

Said Gale, "When we pitched *Used Cars*, Frank Price was totally receptive because Frank sold cars at some point in his early life. He understood there was comedy here."

Zemeckis orchestrated the chaos as director, including an ending chase involving 250 cars, while Spielberg and Milius executive produced this sophomore outing.

As Milius told Nat Segaloff in the biography *Big Bad John*, "On *Used Cars*, when Steven was out of town, they called me in and I went down and got them back on budget—gave them 'a stern talking-to.' I told Zemeckis he'd gone over budget and that was dishonorable. He said, 'Yeah, but what are you supposed to do when you go over budget and it's not your fault? If it rains?' I said, 'Bob, if you go over budget, rain, shine, whatever—there's always the knife.' He said, 'What do you mean?' I said, 'Seppuku, Bob. It's dishonorable to go over budget. Those guys on Tarawa, it wasn't their fault that twenty thousand Marines landed, but they still lost the battle.' Going over budget is an offense that can only be reconciled with Hara-kiri... you've got to think that way or else you don't discipline yourself."

Used Cars might be the raunchiest, least socially responsible movie Spielberg ever attached his name to, spiritual kin to what *After School* could have been... assuming Spielberg would not have botched Gale/Zemeckis' script with constant improv... improv which was part of the plan before shooting was cancelled on the middle school movie. This period from 1978 to 1980 was the most punk rock Spielberg would ever get.

Says Eric Vespe, host of *The Spiel* podcast, "That *Used Cars* period of Spielberg is so interesting because he has this edgelord era where he's the new bad boy in town. You watch him in interviews post-*Jaws* and he's a little bit full of himself. I don't know how much he's playing into a character there, but he's almost like wrestler heel in some of these interviews. He's like, 'Check out my arcade. I got an arcade in my house now... Amy Irving stop talking because I'm talking right now.' You know, 'I'm the important one.'"

Says Dan Harary, who worked publicity at Columbia in 1980, "My boss was in charge of New York field promotions. I had to wear a suit and tie, and my boss gives me a fucking trash bag filled with oil caps and distributors and dipsticks... greasy, disgusting used car parts. He goes, 'Dan, gift wrap these and send them to the top critics in New York.' I had to gift wrap disgusting, oily, dripping distributor caps in tissue paper, put them in boxes with bows, and have them delivered by messenger. The critics were incredibly pissed."

Given this gimmick, it is not surprising reviews for Zemeckis' second film were scalding. Box office ($11.7M) was not ideal either, though it has become a handshake movie among cult comedy devotees, including *Superbad* director Greg Mottola.

"I saw it when it came out," says Mottola. "My association with Kurt Russell was watching Disney films, a very G-rated actor suddenly showing up in this super cynical movie. That movie was so irreverent... really dark in places, really silly in places. I thought, 'This movie is really fucked up. It's great.' Putting dead bodies behind the wheel of a car and this ridiculous war between used car salesmen. I liked the rough and tumble vibe. Wasn't a super slick movie, sort of in the vein of *SNL*. It felt counterculture, thumbing its nose at things you're not supposed to make jokes about."

"The thing about *Used Cars* is the protagonists are villains! That's the whole point of the movie," says *Important Cinema Club* host Justin Decloux. "Kurt Russell's goal in *Used Cars* is to become an elected official who could be corrupt and can be bribed. That is his dream in life. That's why it rules."

Nat Segaloff says, "The characterizations are something you don't expect. They are so extreme and so wonderful. As with *I Wanna Hold Your Hand*, which I also love, Zemeckis has a way of pushing to the extreme and yet not going into burlesque. Those characters were real in a strange way, even though they were doing unreal things. I think his control of tone shows throughout all of his films, where he really knows how far he can go with something and make it work."

Says Bailey, who wrote a 40th anniversary piece in 2020 about *Used Cars* for *The Playlist*, "While I was watching *1941* I thought, 'There's nothing inherently funny about things blowing up.' The scale and ambition of that movie is astonishing, watching practical sets being dismantled. I'm impressed, but never laughing. When that Ferris wheel starts rolling down the pier I'm shocked, I'm like, 'Wow, that's cool,' but it's not funny. Then you watch *Used Cars*, and when they blow up the Mercedes it's funny! When the Edsel goes into the transformer and blows up, it's hilarious! Both those moments are so intricately prepared and executed with such precision that you laugh because it's funny, narratively, and also with a kind of delight at the ingenuity of the filmmaking."

"*Used Cars* disappointed at the box office, even though we had these absolutely fabulous screenings," laments Gale. "Our problem was, as a result of those great screenings, Columbia moved up the release date thinking we would play longer in the summer. The release date they picked was one week after the Zucker Brothers opened *Airplane!*, so everybody was going to see *Airplane!* and that hurt us pretty badly."

"Clearly Zemeckis and Gale were very talented and *Used Cars* was a very funny script," remembers Price, who was known for being a hands-on exec with a flair for comedy. "Had we had what a comedy needs, which is a comedian lead, I think it would have gelled. There's funny things in it. Jack Warden is hilarious, but the audience didn't buy into it. My premise on comedy generally is you need a comedian. I had Bill Murray interested in that before Bill Murray was that known. The executive producers on *Used Cars* were Milius and Spielberg, and what came back from them is they didn't think Bill Murray was a star. We wound up not going with him."

Bailey disagrees that Murray would have been better: "Kurt Russell finding the right note and holding it in that performance is the key to whether that movie sinks or swims."

"After this I always figured if they'd done it with Bill Murray it probably would have been a big hit!" Kurt Russell said, laughing, during the *Used Cars* DVD commentary.

During the *Used Cars* casting there was also a serendipitous meeting with future *E.T.* star Dee Wallace, as the actress explained to this author: "It was kind of a strange little audition. I met Mr. Spielberg in an empty office room in a building at Universal Studios, and that's where the audition took place. Steven worked very far ahead, and I think when he met me he saw exactly who he envisioned for the mom in *E.T.*, so he saved me for that role."

Adds Decloux, "What's fascinating about *Used Cars* is the support Spielberg shows to Bob Gale and Bob Zemeckis. He meets them, they write *1941* for him. Huge flop. Anyone else would be like, 'We're done, get out of here.' He pushes them to make *I Wanna Hold Your Hand*. Flop. Again, does not work. And he's like, 'You know what? *Used Cars*.' Again, does not succeed, yet... *Back to the Future*. I love the idea that early Spielberg just loves these guys so much he will continue to give them chances. While the box office didn't return the favor, I think *I Wanna Hold Your Hand* and *Used Cars* are so much fun. Spielberg was right, it's the audience that was wrong during this time. Yeah, put that quote right in the book! 'Spielberg was right, the audiences were wrong!'"

According to Gale, "Despite that hiccup, Frank said, 'When you guys come up with your next idea, come to me first.' Once we had gotten *Back to the Future* in a form we felt comfortable pitching, Frank said, 'Come on in.' Easiest pitch meeting we ever had. He got it instantly. We didn't even have to give him all these details we had thought of. Zemeckis wanted to tell more, and I kept going, 'Stop, stop. He gets it. He's going to give us a deal.'"

As the Bobs developed a knack for comedy, Spielberg could not match his protégés in the hilarity arena. If December 7, 1941 was "a date which will live in infamy," then December 14, 1979 would be infamous among Spielberg aficionados as the date *1941* opened. Vincent Canby of *The New York Times* called it "less comic than cumbersome, as much fun as a 40-pound wristwatch." Certainly not the outright bomb of its reputation, its performance paled in the shadow of *Jaws* and *Close Encounters*, taking in only $34.17M in North America yet nearly $100M globally. With the bulk of its earnings overseas, Spielberg must have been echoing Woody Allen's sentiment as the blind director in DreamWorks-made comedy *Hollywood Ending*: "Thank God the French exist."

Laurent Bouzereau, who directed the definitive *Making of 1941* doc, told *USA Today*, "I don't think it's a bright light in his filmography, but he often said to me, even at the very beginning, he really realized the love for the film when he went to Europe, where people were actually responding to it a lot more than they did here."

"It's supposed to be funny," opines Segaloff. "Spielberg has comic relief in his films, so did John Ford... but Ford never made a comedy, or not one that worked. For all the entertainment value of his work, you don't think of Spielberg as a comedy director. It was flat, I don't care how many people were in it.

It was compared to *It's a Mad, Mad, Mad, Mad World* because of the star roster, but *Mad Mad World* was far more focused."

According to comedian Dana Gould, "In *1941* they threw all the money at this big canvas but didn't have the straight man... You need a setup and a payoff, both of those things. In *1941* everybody's wacky. There's no structure at all. It's not a cake, it's a bowl of flour with an egg in it. You're selling it as a cake, but it just has the ingredients that a cake needs. It's the theory that, 'If a pie in the face is funny, 100 pies in the face will be 100 times as funny.' That doesn't work."

John Milius in a *1941* deleted scene.

Said Milius in *Big Bad John*, "It felt of too much, the wrong approach. Steve was the wrong director. It's just not the type of movie he should have done. It should have been a small, contained movie that had its roots in real experience. If you overdo everything and make it the biggest this and the biggest that, you lose the real experience. Everything in *Used Cars* comes out of a reality. Nothing in *1941* came out of a reality, though the original script was very rooted in reality. It was a real incident that actually happened. A lot of funny things happened, and it was so twisted by the time that it got on the screen that it lost that. The problem really comes back down to a regard for writing. I maintain the fault of that movie can be blamed on the director's interpretation of the script."

Ever the contrarian, director John Carpenter says, "I kind of like that movie."

"*1941* is manic, man," explains Vespe. "It's what happens when you get Spielberg, the Bobs, and John Milius together, right? Those people were edgelords of their own time. Spielberg was the nerdy one sitting there with a Coke, and Milius is shooting an Uzi up in the sky, and the two Bobs are writing stereotype racist jokes and giggling like 12-year-olds about it. *1941* was his fourth movie and it opens with a *Jaws* spoof, right? Such a wild and radical thing to start a movie spoofing yourself. You're not spoofing your classic from 30 years ago... you're spoofing something that just came out four years before."

1941 has its contemporary defenders, including this author. The film's charms go beyond Spielberg emulating the unbridled irreverence of *SNL* and John Landis. It is more the level of sheer audacity on display. As *The Simpsons* writer George Meyer told *The New Yorker* in 2000, "Michael O'Donoghue'—the late writer for *National Lampoon* and *Saturday Night Live*—used to say that humor had to be startling, and I agree with that. It has to reframe reality in a way that is exciting." As an experiment in fast-paced, special effects-laden comedy, *1941* plays much better today alongside filmmakers like James Gunn, who mix massive sensory-overload set pieces with ironic comedic beats. Spielberg's film was one of the first to evoke the startling humor of the Lampoon and nonstop "chicken fat" (background gags) of *MAD* cartoonists like Will Elder.

Says screenwriter Josh Olson, "There's a scene with Tim Matheson and Nancy Allen in the cockpit of an airplane which most directors would have done by just shooting them in the cockpit. It's not like that's the wrong way to do it, it's all very tight, but every now and then you look out the cockpit window behind them and there's an entire military base with jeeps going by and another airplane and 50 troops marching. He's coordinating all this insane action so in the few moments you see outside the window you realize they're really in an airplane."

Spielberg himself gave his own self-aware autopsy of *1941* to the *L.A. Times* in 1981: "It was overdone. It went from a small pepper steak to burned Chateaubriand. I tried hard to season it, and wound up killing the taste... If we don't take chances, who will? If Francis doesn't take his Machiavellian risks, and John Landis doesn't exploit the success of *Animal House* with *The Blues Brothers*, and if I can't try to make the noisiest movie of all time... without some degree of failure, you can't move ahead."

During *1941* filming he told *Christian Science Monitor* the middle school movie was next on his agenda, that it "is sort of about me but not." The plan was to revert back to the Chicago setting and the shopping center that had been scouted there, malls being "central to the growing-up process of my generation." In March of 1979, while attending Filmex to support *1941* star Treat Williams' *Hair*, Spielberg confirmed to *Variety* that he still intended to lens the "small film" *After School* in August of that year, although by that point Zemeckis and Gale had moved on to *Used Cars*. By the time August rolled around producer Howard Kazanjian announced he would produce George Lucas' *Raiders of the Lost Ark* for Spielberg to direct, which *Variety* stated "will probably roll after Spielberg completes his long-planned low budgeter *After School*."

Even though he wanted to make a small, down and dirty movie with first timers—much the same way Brian De Palma did the small-scale *Home Movies* with students at Sarah Lawrence College—it never came to be.

A comment Spielberg makes in Wim Wenders' 1982 documentary *Room 666* shines a light on the economic industry reasoning behind not making a picture like *After School*: "The danger's not from filmmakers, the danger's not from the producers or the writers. It's from the people who are in control of the money, who essentially say, 'I want my money back, and I want those returns multiplied by the powers of 10. So I'm not really interested in sitting here and seeing a movie about your personal life, your grandfather, what it was like to grow up in American school, what it was like to masturbate for the first time at 13, whatever. I want a picture that's going to please everybody.' In other words, I think Hollywood wants the ideal movie with something in it for everyone, and of course that's impossible."

Elements of the script got absorbed into *E.T.*, while the title "After School" was announced in 1986 trades as the moniker of Amblin's unrelated 1987 high school bully movie eventually re-titled *Three O'Clock High*. The concept of a modern-day *Our Gang* was ported over to *The Goonies* in 1985, then to an actual *Our Gang* movie with 1994's *The Little Rascals*, both family-friendly flicks made by Amblin.

Spielberg told *NY Times* in 1977, "I'm very frustrated when I see movies like *The Conformist* and *Small Change* and I haven't taken a position personally on how I feel about the world. I think my films will eventually get around to that, but I never want to stop entertaining."

The writer of *After School/Growing Up* speculates that the jaundiced critical and public reaction to *1941* may have put Spielberg off of anarchic humor.

"François Truffaut says, 'Your second movie is always a direct reaction to your first movie,'" explains Gale. "So, when your movie fails, you say, 'I'm going to do the exact opposite of that.'"

CHAPTER 9

Second Thoughts: Melissa Mathison Switches Gears

"...I couldn't give up hope...
I know the tides...
I went around the Point..."
—***Sunrise: A Song of Two Humans*** (1927)

Born in Los Angeles on June 3, 1950, Melissa Marie Mathison came from a family of writers including her father, *Newsweek*'s L.A. bureau chief Richard Mathison. She attended the Roman Catholic all-girls Providence High School in Burbank, whose religious teachings from nuns would come in handy later. Like Spielberg, she grew up in a family of four children,

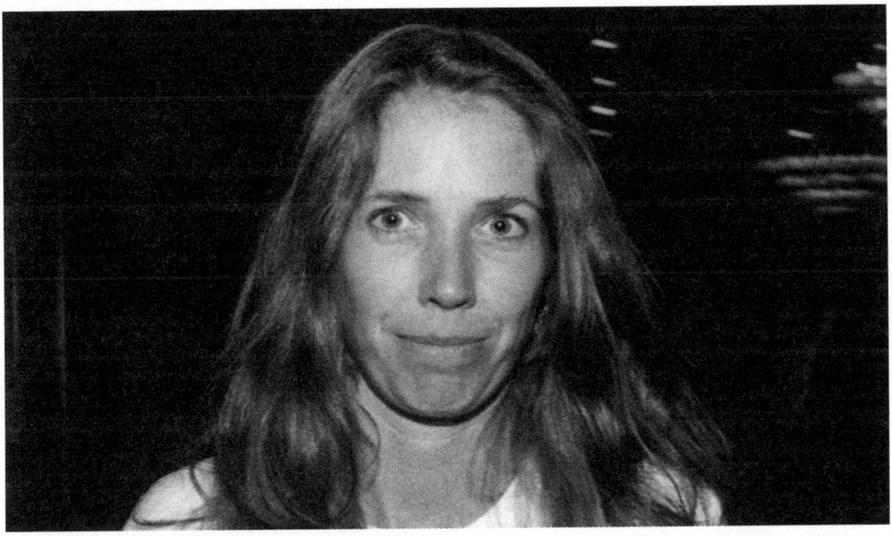

but did not begin speaking until age 3. Their home in the upscale Nichols Canyon neighborhood among the Hollywood Hills was host to a bevy of writers, including Rod Serling and Richard Matheson (unrelated).

Once her sister Melinda aged out of it, Melissa took up her post as a prominent babysitter in the area, known for her quiet and caring disposition. When she was around 18, two of the little boys she looked after were Gian-Carlo and Roman, the sons of an up-and-coming filmmaker named Francis Ford Coppola, hard at work on his small feature *The Rain People*. Even as Mathison left L.A. to enroll at UC Berkley, Coppola encouraged her to write. She admired novelist/journalist/screenwriter Joan Didion and freelanced briefly for the newly-minted *People* magazine. Later she became an uncredited assistant on *The Conversation*, then dropped out of college to earn her first screen credit as a location assistant on *The Godfather Part II*, mostly fetching coffee and sodas.

She was also Coppola's executive assistant during the extended year+ Philippines shoot for *Apocalypse Now*, at one point accompanying him to screen footage at Malacañang Palace for the pleasure of the country's president Ferdinand Marcos and wife Imelda. According to recent book *The Last Kings of Hollywood*, Mathison referred to the palace as a "den of evil." During *Apocalypse* filming, Coppola was constantly changing the script, often simply handing the cast cards with new scenes or basic prompts. Said Mathison, "He'd scribble out some dialogue, and I'd have to type it into a scene for him. That's how I got to know the basics of screenwriting."

She is mentioned during one of Coppola's rants in the documentary *Hearts of Darkness* as he tries to process that his lead Martin Sheen had a heart attack: "Dave Salvin let Melissa tell Barry Hirsch that Marty had a heart attack! What the fuck is that? What the fuck is that? You know that it's gonna be all over Hollywood in half an hour?"

Then came a simple tale of a boy and his horse. Based on the 1941 novel by Walter Farley, *The Black Stallion* was the debut feature of Coppola's UCLA film school pal Carroll Ballard, who had been fired off 1972's *Junior Bonner*, shot second unit on *Star Wars*, and directed an Oscar-nominated documentary called *Harvest*. Also making his feature debut as director of photography was Caleb Deschanel after lensing some Ballard short films.

Like most features, it started on the page. Walter Murch took the entire year of 1975 away from his career as a film editor to focus on writing the *Black Stallion* screenplay based on Ballard's idea of fusing Farley's first two books in the series, the second taking place in North Africa. After a fruitless six months,

Gill Dennis was brought onboard, suggesting simply doing the first book which began with the boy and title horse being shipwrecked on an island, followed by their arrival in American suburbia.

Producer Coppola brought in two newbie scribes to reshape *Black Stallion*. One, Jeanne Rosenberg, was a recent USC grad/horse aficionado who talked her way into meeting Ballard, later acting as script supervisor on *Piranha* and *The Howling* before becoming a full-time screenwriter. The other was the Coppola protégé everyone called "Missy."

As Ballard told DGA's Robert Markowitz, "Francis brought on Melissa Mathison and Jeanne Rosenberg to help do the script, so they did a version. Then a guy named William Wittliff, a really good writer, he came and did a version. Nobody was real happy with it. I wasn't happy with it. I thought it was too much of a stock kiddy animal movie thing, but Francis needed the money, so he sold the project to United Artists, and it entered the gears and finally we started shooting."

Ballard was used to working with small crews and catching things on camera in the moment. A narrative studio feature required adjustment, but he was still "finding the movie" on any given shooting day, kicking off on the numerically lucky 7/7/77.

Ballard told *Gannett News Service* in 1980, "We began shooting in Toronto without a script. I had to walk out and face a crowd of 75 people every morning, not having the fuzziest notion of what I was going to do. Finally, these girls came up with a screenplay—Melissa Mathison and Jeanne Rosenberg—and they would write the lines every night that we'd use the next day."

Rosenberg told *Cowboys & Indians* in 2019, "It was total chaos when I arrived. Melissa Mathison got off another plane. We met and became this writing team *as* we were about to shoot. Carroll hadn't committed to a screenplay. All the actors were there. Everyone! Carroll liked to keep everything open and see what developed. He was driving everyone crazy, of course. There were times when we would actually write in the evenings and hand pages to Carroll ahead of time, but usually we were right there hunkered somewhere in the grass, or in a chair, ripping off pages and throwing them at Mickey Rooney, who would scowl and scowl and then do it. We were writing on set virtually moments before the cameras rolled."

Deschanel told this author of *Black Stallion*, "I really don't know what Melissa contributed to the movie? The script we were using was written by Gill Dennis and Walter Murch. The first forty minutes of the film, what was shot as the second part of filming in Italy, was just 7 pages long. It did not change much as far as I was aware from the first days of shooting. You usually think of a page in a script being about a minute or two of the film... What we shot first in Toronto—the second half of the movie when the boy returns home—did not change much from the draft we started with. There might have been some dialogue polish. The only significant new idea I remember, and I think it came from Bill Wittliff, was the boy breaking the wild black stallion in the water, which Bill picked up in his Texas days."

That section lensed on an isolated Sardinian beach using limited personnel, with only the child actor (Kelly Reno) and horse performing. Ballard kept refusing to let Mathison and Rosenberg actually script the island sequence. They did it anyway.

"Melissa was there," said Rosenberg, who heard of the experience secondhand. "I know it was really hard and really gorgeous. A tough shoot, the kind of shoot that Carroll Ballard loves, out there in the elements with a much smaller crew. Everyone pitching in to carry gear—here, there, and over rocks."

Gill Dennis and Walter Murch's contributions went uncredited on *Black Stallion*. Even though the final movie was critically praised and earned nearly $40M worldwide, Ballard returned from the experience, "flat broke, out in the street, living in a friend's kitchen in San Rafael." He would take a long hiatus between *Stallion* and *Never Cry Wolf*, but his DP was charged up and ready to direct a film for Coppola himself.

After graduating from Johns Hopkins in 1966, Caleb Deschanel's friends Walter Murch and Matthew Robbins convinced him to study film at USC, where they acted as his "mentors into that world." He worked on student films and documentaries in many capacities including directing, but found a knack for cinematography. While lensing docs for Ballard, he also broke into features with additional shooting for George Lucas (*THX 1138*), Francis Coppola (*The Godfather*), and John Cassavettes (*A Woman Under the Influence*). Even before the young cinematographer earned acclaim as the proper DP of *Being There* and *The Black Stallion* in 1979, Coppola had earmarked him to helm a special project about a boy magician.

"Francis brought me in to do additional filming on *Apocalypse Now*," said Deschanel of inserts shot near Coppola's home in Napa to "fill in missing moments. The major part I shot was Marty Sheen's Willard going up river reviewing background material on Kurtz. Marty was much healthier than he had been a few years earlier in the Philippines, so we sweated him up a lot and got away with it. Francis visited on the first day, then decided we got it and left us alone to finish over the next week or so. I think maybe Francis thought I had done a good job with that and gave me the book to read."

That book was David Wagoner's 1965 novel *The Escape Artist*, which Coppola wished to bankroll as Deschanel's $4M directorial debut. It follows talented teenage magician Danny Masters (Griffin O'Neal) navigating an anachronistic town where he becomes involved in a scheme of the mayor's mentally unbalanced son (Raúl Juliá). Eventually Danny learns how his magician father died, all while conning his way into the world of adulthood. Melissa Mathison's writing career would be dominated by similar stories of displaced children, but once again the director says the majority of the work had already been done before she came onboard by first-crack screenwriter Stephen Zito.

"I read the book and really liked it," Deschanel remembers. "I talked to the writer David Wagoner and got some insight into the character. I liked the imbalance of the talented and accomplished child in the world of struggling adults. The 'first-crack,' as you put it, was actually the script we shot. Melissa came in late with some ideas, but the body of the movie had already been set between Zito, Francis, and myself. I liked Melissa. She made some good suggestions which we incorporated into the script."

Taking cues from his work with director Hal Ashby, a master of "off-center humor and insight into a world of unserious people who take themselves too seriously," Deschanel tells a remarkable tall tale with *The Escape Artist*. Master illusionist Ricky Jay was brought in to "advise and inspire" over the entire shoot, helping to fabricate illusions for O'Neill and others with the promise they adhere to the magician's code and not reveal tricks onscreen. Besides some old school faces (Desi Arnaz, Jackie Coogan, Huntz Hall), the whimsey of the Cleveland-shot story is buoyed by a gorgeous Georges Delerue score and Stephen H. Burum's moody photography. While undeniably charming, the movie did not have a charmed history, having been shot in 1980 but not released until 1982 due to extensive post-production tinkering.

Explains Deschanel, "Francis was making *One from the Heart* at the same time, and Wim Wenders was directing *Hammet* for Zoetrope as well... three movies while Francis was trying to hold together a deal to own the studio.

Francis Ford Coppola at Inglenook (2019).

Clearly *One from the Heart* was getting the most attention. *Apocalypse Now* was shot in 1976 and not released until 1979. *The Black Stallion* was filmed in 1977 and released in 1979. It's clearly a Zoetrope tradition. You have to understand that the ultimate decisions were to be made by Francis and he was preoccupied. Francis likes to try things, so the movie went through a number of edits. Francis would try some drastic ideas, and like many movies we decided we needed new material. My friend Robert Towne wrote a short scene between Danny and his aunt, and we tried some narration."

The fact that her next movie was stuck in Zoetrope limbo was apparently one of several factors that had Melissa Mathison down in the dumps about her nascent screenwriting career. She tried to generate a few other scripts on her own which were not clicking, including a book adaptation. She had been introduced to Harrison Ford in 1977 by *Black Stallion* producer Fred Roos while the actor was in Toronto to promote *Star Wars*, and they became an item. Cut to summer 1980 and Missy is accompanying Ford on the Tunisian set of *Raiders of the Lost Ark*. When she met that film's director, Steven Spielberg, she introduced herself as a "failed screenwriter." At one point between set-ups during the sunbaked shoot, the director and Mathison were aimlessly turning up rocks looking for scorpions. That's when he told her his idea for a film about a helpless alien stranded on Earth. She heard it and began tearing up.

There's a deleted scene from *1941* onboard the Japanese submarine where Christopher Lee's Nazi Captain Wolfgang Von Kleinschmidt threatens Slim Pickins' cowboy Hollis P. Wood with a chain-linked weapon, which is revealed to actually be a coat hanger. The film's preview audience did not laugh at this sight gag, but Spielberg recycled it to great success in his very next picture with Ronald Lacey and Karen Allen.

"I was determined to get this gag to work in one of these movies," Spielberg said in 1996's *The Making of 1941*. "I had this bet with myself I would try this gag out in my next ten films and I would stop when it got a laugh. Fortunately, when Toht comes out in *Raiders of the Lost Ark* and takes the torture device and turns into a coat hanger it got a big, big laugh and I was satisfied."

Once you recognize Spielberg's tenacity in chasing the best way to realize an idea, it becomes clear why he took one pet concept that never gelled (*After School*) and combined it with another (*Night Skies*) he now felt a sense of remove from.

His middle school movie seemed to be delving further into autobiography when he abandoned it, telling *The Tampa Tribune* in 1982, "It was to be called *After School*, and I didn't have the heart to make it. You know Elliott's 'This is reality' line in *E.T.*? Well, *After School* was all reality. I didn't want to make that movie yet, so it evolved into *E.T.*"

There are many reasons why the filmmaker may have lost the spark for *Night Skies*, with perhaps the biggest pointed out in his own notes, a line highlighted by Sayles himself: "I know this to be in direct antithesis to my own *Close Encounters of the Third Kind* philosophy." Spielberg had done a great deal with that 1977 film to portray extraterrestrial visitors as inherently benign, since in-theory they would not travel light years through time and space simply to mow us down or dissect us. This darker horror film was an intentionally different take, but perhaps a bridge too far after moving beyond 1950s xenophobic clichés and all-in on peaceful beings.

"It was too violent," stated Spielberg of Sayles' script, even though in his notes he encouraged the writer to up the scary quotient. "It turned me against my own beliefs."

Another possibility lies in the Montana setting, with Utah also possibly being scouted as a backdrop. Spielberg grew up in the suburbs of Jersey, Arizona, and eventually California. Although Arizona has sparsely populated rural areas outside of Phoenix/Scottsdale, the bulk of his experience of rural life and country folk seems to have been gleaned while prepping *White Lightning* and then researching/making *The Sugarland Express*. While that latter film's portrayals certainly carried an authentic flavor by casting local non-actors, the filmmaker probably felt more comfortable within the suburban milieu. Even Melinda Dillon's Jillian in *Close Encounters,* who lives in a secluded Indiana country house, is clearly a coastal transplant as her son Barry's Boston University T-shirt indicates. The decision to place both *E.T.* and *Poltergeist* as firmly suburban feels like a purposeful run towards the familiar.

As Spielberg told *Penthouse* in 1978, "My false poetic dream has always been to meet a female bank teller from Kansas, with hay in her hair, and go off and marry and live on a dairy farm in Wisconsin. Of course, that's the last thing I'd ever want to do… It's a completely dishonest dream. I must have picked it up by looking at too many Norman Rockwell and Andrew Wyeth paintings. Let me tell you, if I were ever given my wish, I'd be the unhappiest boy on the farm."

"A convenient way of dismissing anyone that has a close encounter is to paint them as bumbling, uneducated, ignorant hillbillies or local yokels… that continues to this day," says Aaron Sagers. "If he had moved forward with *Night Skies* with this rural family, the takeaway would not have been sympathetic to rural America. It would have fed into that stereotype: 'Of course this is happening out in the country, in the flyover states.'"

Then there's a third possibility. While grafting the element of cattle mutilations onto extant Kelly-Hopkinsville lore to make *Night Skies* both distinct and topical, those vivid descriptions of mutilated cattle genitals in Sayles' script—as "torn from the pages" of real reports they were—may have harkened back to Spielberg's time struggling to adapt *Cruising* in the early '70s.

"We just couldn't come up with a script that met with my satisfaction," original *Cruising* producer Philip D'Antoni told *IndieWire*'s Michael Gingold in 2017. "Or even how to get around the mutilating of the genitals, which was such a big part of the original story. So we decided to abandon the project."

A huge and perhaps deciding factor was the expense of developing Rick Baker's five heavily articulated *Night Skies* aliens, which at that point had cost $700,000 dollars out of a $3M preliminary VFX budget before a single shot on 35mm was in the can. Whatever the case, John Sayles put it very succinctly in 1983 to *Philadelphia Inquirer*: "Spielberg decided he didn't want to make a movie with hostile aliens, so he did *E.T.* instead."

Storyboard artist Ed Verreaux told *E.T.*'s unit publicist, "The Rick Baker creatures were much more dangerous. They did things that were hostile. Steven said something to me, that he didn't feel it was appropriate to make peo ple afraid of this kind of stuff. He didn't like the idea of making little aliens that were frightening and scary."

"*Night Skies* was kind of a science project," muses Mitch Suskin. "Sort of, 'we want to try to do this,' but it never got to that point of, 'Okay, this is going to work. Here's the money. Go hire.' I never knew who the production designer would be or who the cast was."

"It happened kind of gradually," Kennedy told *Los Angeles Times* in 2012. "We were doing *Raiders of the Lost Ark* together, and we were over in England. Our whole discussion of what our next movie was going to be was something that was a focus of conversation whenever we had time. We had been working on a project called *Night Skies*, which was a different kind of story but in the same realm of *Close Encounters*, and *E.T.* evolved out of those discussions."

The story goes that, while filming *Raiders* for George Lucas, a lonely Spielberg was missing his home in California, his girlfriend Kathleen Carey, feeling like a gun for hire on an impersonal B adventure yarn with exploding Nazis. He wanted to get back to, as he told *Film Comment*, "the tranquility, or at least the spirituality, of *Close Encounters*." Out of this yearning, the director latched on to a specific aspect of Sayles' *Night Skies* story.

Kennedy said in 2018, "We were in the car reading the script and the very last image of the script is a little alien left alone looking at the sky, and Steven said, 'I don't want to make this movie. That's the movie I want to make.'"

Said Spielberg in 2002, "When I read an early draft about the farm family case, I didn't feel it was a movie I wanted to direct. It went against my grain as a filmmaker and storyteller to tell an aggressive, scary story about aliens attacking a farmhouse. That's when everything changed in my mind and I realized I was not going to make that movie, but I might make another movie about an alien who gets left behind on Earth, an idea that came from the ending of *Close Encounters*, when the spaceship door closes."

John Sayles officially backed out of the overhauled project in early September of 1980. Only a few months prior on July 17, Ronald Reagan had accepted the Republican nomination for his successful first run as President of the United States. Sayles was present at that very Republican convention in Detroit, covering the event as a color man for New Republic. Although it would not be put into Hal Riney's marketable words until Reagan's 1984 campaign, the candidate's beacon of positivity coming out of the turbulent '70s (Vietnam, Nixon resignation) truly represented "Morning in America."

As Sayles recounts of the convention in *Sayles on Sayles*, "I said, 'Yeah, this guy's going to win. He knows what he's doing.' It was 'Happy days are here again,' and he never said anything nasty about people on welfare, and he was kind of a cheerful guy," then adding, "On the floor it was a paranoid Barry Goldwater convention… I was pretty aware by that time that the shit was going to turn around."

If Sayles could feel the sea change in the air, then so too likely did Spielberg. No one has more consistently had their finger on the zeitgeist than the *Jaws* director, and it's entirely possible that the nascent rise of Reaganism told him where the wind was blowing. Audiences did not want dread, they wanted uplift.

"I 100% agree with that assessment," says Mark A. Altman. "Post-Watergate, post-Vietnam you have very dark conspiracy thrillers. You have the Pakula trilogy, *Invasion of the Body Snatchers*, all this stuff. In '81 and '82 you start to see the transition. They're still greenlighting these '70s scripts gussied up as '80s movies, and that's where the disconnect comes. That's where you get the *Blade Runner*'s and all these movies which don't perform. Spielberg reads the tea leaves, the Nixon/Ford/Carter era is over. Reagan, whatever we think of him politically, is projecting America as idyllic. We're not going to talk about AIDS, we're not going to talk about the homeless. I think Spielberg gets that, so you start to get movies that reflect this Reagan-esque view of American exceptionalism."

Adds actor Henry Thomas, "As a director and as a person, I think he does always have his finger on the zeitgeist. He knows what's relevant. BMX and D&D in 1980 was very niche, very unheard of and localized to Southern California. He was like, 'Oh, I'm going to put that in the movie because that's what kids will be into by the time the movie comes out.' That's how he's thinking. 'What's gonna happen by the time this movie comes out?'"

"I doubt if it was a political thing," Sayles speculates. "The thing I like about Steven Spielberg's movies, besides that they're so well made, is I never really feel he's watching the box office. It feels like, 'Here's what I'm in the mood to see,' then he gets to make it. It was probably more him feeling his own feeling, because you've got to spend a lot of time with these people. When I write a really nasty character or a nasty thing, it's not always fun to sit down and say, 'Okay, I'm going to deal with this person and their behavior again.' He just felt, 'Maybe I'll take that alien story and go with a different tone.'"

As it were, Spielberg initially extended an offer for Sayles to start over and pen *E.T. and Me* based on he and Mathison's story treatment. Concurrently, Sayles had just been given a plum deal at 20th Century Fox to develop the project which later became *Baby It's You* to write and direct. He was also simultaneously working for the Ladd Company on a satiric film called *Blood of the Lamb* to star Jeff Goldblum as a radio DJ who infiltrates a Christian cult and winds up becoming their de facto leader.

As director he was prepping a small indie film titled *Lianna*, originally set to star Brooke Adams before she "got cold feet about the material" and was replaced by Canadian actress Linda Griffiths. Sayles told *New York Times* it was "one screenplay I'd like total, total, total control on." Partner Maggie Renzi said, "We learned on *Lianna* that you don't celebrate when someone promises you a check. No! You call 10 more people."

Sayles told this author, "I got the money to make my next film *Lianna* and was starting that when Steven felt like, 'I'm going to go in a totally different direction than this.' At some time Kathy may have said, 'Are you going to be available if we want to change this?' I said, 'You know, we're going to be really busy.' I had the Fox deal and was starting my own movie."

Alongside money he earned penning the Cro-Magnon adventure *The Clan of the Cave Bear* and its never-made sequel *The Valley of Horses*, a big chunk of the budget for *Lianna* came from his *Night Skies* writing fee.

"Yeah, oh yeah," Sayles concurs. "We were trying to make *Lianna* for $800,000 in 35mm, and we ended up making it for $300,000 in 16mm. Minimum then probably had gone up to about $15,000 and I think I might even have gotten paid more than minimum on *Night Skies*. It was great to be making some money."

The story of a woman in a flailing marriage who begins a lesbian affair with a college professor was exactly the kind of movie studios were avoiding at that time, or at very least would want to tinker with/homogenize. It makes sense that Sayles would direct another low budget personal movie on his own terms, especially after learning how the "real world" of Hollywood studio development worked. Eventually *Baby It's You* was rejected by Fox (later picked up by Paramount), while *Blood of the Lamb* was derailed by a WGA strike. He told *The New York Times* in 1983 that studio deals such as these and *Night Skies* were akin to "getting drafted by the Red Sox and sent to Pittsfield."

Once informed of Sayles' decision to back out of the evolving *E.T. and Me* project, Kennedy seemed genuinely sad her dream team did not pan out.

Remembers Sayles, "I have a letter from Kathy Kennedy, 'Sorry you can't work on this. Good luck with your new movie.' I have another one where the same thing happened when they wanted me to write the Ninja Turtles. There's usually a good side to any of these things: I had not read the Ninja Turtles, so it turned me on to the comic which was really fun. That was a tough one to turn down, because I thought that concept was so cool and I like the art."

While you are mulling over the alternate universe where John Sayles wrote the *Teenage Mutant Ninja Turtles* movie (having already dealt with sewer-dwelling mutants in *Alligator*), here is Kathy Kennedy's dictated-from-Tunisia "Dear John" letter ending with her hoping they would work together again... which they did.

Kathy Kennedy
Saraha Palace
Nefta, Tunisia

John Sayles
210 13th Street
Hoboken, New Jersey
U.S.A. 07030

September 10, 1980

Dear John,

We congratulate you on the picture deal with 20th Century Fox, yet it is with mixed emotions: we are disappointed that you cannot continue to work on the ET story. I haven't seen Steven so taken with someone's writing style and imagination in a long time. I had anticipated, as I know you had, a wonderful project emanating from the combined talents of Sayles, Cobb, and Spielberg.

The change of concept merely came about because of expense. It was realized after the research and development period and an intensive analysis of the mechanical functions required for the various ETs that we would far overextend the monies originally budgeted just for the effects.

Steven has now come up with a wonderful, more personalized story idea, much more along the lines of Close Encounters. In regards to yourself, however, a writing/directing deal must be a dream come true and I wish you the best; I know you'll be very successful. It was a pleasure working with you and I hope that our paths will cross again.

Best regards,
Kathy Kennedy
KK:mc

By this point the 26-year-old Kennedy had made the lightning-fast ascension from Milius' assistant to Spielberg's assistant to his associate on *Raiders* then his full-fledged *E.T.* co-producer. *Night Skies* was technically the first project she packaged and developed, and although, as Robin Love says, "she had hope," Kennedy ultimately had to navigate a trial-by-fire as one project transitioned somewhat painfully into the other.

"She's just powerfully competent," says Love, who knew Kennedy back from the early A-Team years. "Steven had gone from having an assistant who was very young and very sweet to Kathy the powerhouse. She filled an enormous gap in his professional life. Just stepped up, was fantastic and really well organized."

William Stout concurs: "Kathleen Kennedy was our receptionist, and within about two months she became John Milius' personal assistant, and about two months after that she became Steven Spielberg's personal assistant, then two years later she produced *E.T.*, which is amazing. Fastest rise I've ever seen, but man she earned it. If Steven called her at 4 in the morning and said, 'You know, Kathy, I was thinking we should have elephants in this movie,' her response wouldn't be, 'Goddamn it, you just woke me up at 4am!' Her response would be, 'Do you want Indian or African? And what color would you like those elephants to be?' And they would be on set at 7am, right? She worked her ass off."

After Sayles' exit, Ron Cobb was the next key man on the chopping block.

Says Robin Love, "Ron was very excited at the idea in the first meetings with John Sayles, and then gradually was preoccupied with *Conan*. When it got to the point that Steven was saying, 'Look, this budget is out of control,' Rick Baker had given him a quote, and with so many aliens it was going to be too expensive and not something they wanted to attempt with a first-time director. There was the need to simplify it. Ron was then stuck on *Conan* for the rest of the year. Melissa Mathison was with Harrison Ford in Tunisia, and the project evolved away from Ron at that point."

As Kennedy told the *L.A. Times*, "Once Steven and I had a pretty good idea of what we wanted to do, we would just sit around on the set in between shots and work out a treatment for what the story might be. Melissa Mathison, who was going out with but not yet married to Harrison Ford… I was talking about writers and I had mentioned I loved *The Black Stallion*, and he said, 'Oh my God, she would be perfect.' We pitched Melissa over lunch one day. She said she'd love to do it and the rest is history."

That is something of a simplification, since, despite sparking to Spielberg's pitch, Mathison was not keen on her value as a screenwriter in that moment. She had to be "worked on" by Ford and Kennedy before agreeing to do one initial draft.

Meanwhile, Cobb's commitments to *Conan* in Europe became so extensive he was barely aware his directorial debut was slipping away from him.

"I had some conflicting obligations and it had to be re-written because of budget problems," Cobb told ABC's Robyn Williams. "I couldn't be there for the rewrite, which was very disturbing to me 'cause I was nervous enough and astounded enough that I was being offered this chance. Steven supervised the rewrite and it became *E.T.*"

Rumors started to trickle in that the number of aliens had gone from five to one as Spielberg transmuted the script into something that "wasn't scary anymore."

According to Stout, "Around that time, I thought I should go visit Ron, see how he's doing on his film. I went to his office, and I go, 'Ron, my God, you look miserable. What's going on?' He goes, 'It's Steven. He's finished *Raiders*. Now he's turned his attention to my film and every day he changes something. He's made so many changes it doesn't feel like my movie anymore. I would give anything to get off this film.'"

As Love explains, "Ron's stepfather died, so he took time off from *Conan*. We flew back to L.A. for a week to be there for the funeral and see Ron's mom, and got in touch with Kathy. At this point, Kathy said, 'Look, the project's changed. This is what Steven is wanting to do.' She gave us a draft of the script at that point."

Cobb recounts, "Kathleen Kennedy called to say, 'Steven doesn't know how to tell you this, but... he's decided to direct it himself. What we would like to do when you get back is work out another picture for you because Steven really wants to back your career."

"Kathy had to break the news to Ron that he'd been replaced," recalls Love. "Kathy said, 'When you finish *Conan*, come see Steven and he will work on a project for you to direct, but he's going to do *E.T.*' Ron read the script and he didn't like the script, so he didn't feel he would be the best director for that. I was surprised he wasn't more disappointed, but in fact he really did not like the script. Ron could never work on something he didn't like. I would have pushed him, said, 'Look, just do it anyway because it's a major opportunity.' But there wasn't ever a choice, because Steven was going to do it."

As a token kill fee, Cobb was reportedly offered $10,000 and one profit percentage in what became *E.T.* to walk away from the project. He accepted.

"It never got to the point where we were starting to break down shots or figure out what the sets were," says Suskin of Cobb's involvement. "It was really in the development of the creatures. Ron was delighted but a little bit nervous or overwhelmed with the fact that he was going to be directing a movie. I remember him going, 'Alright, they want me to direct it.' As far as *Night Skies*, we never got to the point where I even knew what Ron was gonna do with the spaceships. It really got cut down in its prime of life before the creatures were actually even done. Steven came back from *Raiders* and reevaluated everything, changed his mind about what he wanted to do."

Says Paul Sammon, "I do not remember any sense of betrayal or anger from Ron. More a sense of sorrow, because that was a benchmark he wanted to achieve in his life. I watched him direct on *Conan the Barbarian*, that entire opening credit sequence with William Smith at the forge, the light flaring up the faces of young Conan and his mom, the whole thing where he sticks the sword in the snow. That's all Ron. He directed bits and pieces of other sequences as well. He seemed to be on a natural progression to become a major filmmaker, but like so many others something happened that derailed him."

"I was friendly with Ron," mentions Mick Garris, who worked with Cobb on *Amazing Stories*. "We weren't close friends, but a very sweet guy and very quiet. It would be hard to imagine Ron in the director's chair, cracking the whip. Directing requires a lot of outward motion, an ability to command forces. Ron probably could have but it's difficult to imagine him with 100 people asking 100 questions every hour and having answers for them, seeing them through, interacting with department heads and saying, 'This is what I want.' And they say, 'Well, how do we do it? Like this or like this?' And not going, 'Gee, I gotta think about that.' You roll with the punches. You plan everything as much as you can, but you can't plan for happenstance, and half of filmmaking is happenstance."

It is possible Spielberg tapped an untried directing talent as a mere "vessel" to explore darker themes on screen, but it may not have worked that way had cameras rolled.

"I don't think Ron would have been sidelined as easily as Tobe Hooper was... apparently," says Cobb's *The Abyss* associate Daren Dochterman. "It's obvious that Ron had the chops to direct something. Honestly, I think Spielberg was looking for someone to shunt off some of these things he was developing so that he wouldn't have to worry about it. 'I want to see this movie but I don't want to go through the shit of making it!'"

Concludes Robin Love of the whole affair, "*Night Skies* would never have been as successful as *E.T.* It would have been very dark, very scary, and would not have been a box office triumph on the level of one of the world's great children's movies. It was pretty amazing that Steven was going to give Ron this opportunity, but it was also disappointing that the script changed so much. Ron couldn't have done *E.T.*, he just wouldn't have done it. It wasn't the kind of project that would engage him."

Spielberg also tried to pivot Rick Baker onboard the *E.T.* train but ran into difficulty.

Night Skies was intended as a roughly $10M film, but Baker had already spent nearly a million of that on testing and infrastructure. More work had been put into experimenting with making the Skar puppet walk and perform various functions, while sculpts for the friendly wide-eyed Buddee and his less-amiable compatriots were also developed. At least three more months of

R&D was in the cards, the outlook starting to come in around $3.5M, at minimum, just to execute the five aliens at the level the script called for. Columbia balked at the cost.

As was learned on *Close Encounters* and especially *1941*, if your budget is rapidly inflating in pre-production, the sky's the limit once principal photography starts. Spielberg returned to L.A. after his budget-conscious work on *Raiders* wrapped in Hawaii on October 12 after 73 days (ahead of Paramount's 85-day timeframe), with his newly-honed "Eye of Sauron" focused on *Night Skies*.

Explains David Cellitti, "The plan was that Rick was going to do R&D on *Night Skies*... he was finishing it up that week, then he was going to turn it over to us and we were going to do the aliens while he went full bore on *American Werewolf*, right? I'll never forget when Kathy Kennedy called and her words were, 'Steven has totally rethought the picture.' She was calling from Tunisia, and what she laid out was *Lassie Come Home*. We were all in shock, because it had gone from a horror movie to a children's movie. We were going back to the beginning. Rick's plans for finishing up *Nights Skies* and segueing to *American Werewolf* had to be scrapped."

"*Night Skies* featured more than one mischievous or malevolent alien," says Craig Reardon. "*E.T.*, then having no name, was a completely different approach, in which one alien was marooned on earth and was by nature benign and naive and vulnerable. Spielberg realized the alien design for *Night Skies* was inappropriate to portray those qualities."

Says Suskin, "Eventually Steven came in after doing *Raiders*, looked at everything and said, 'You know, I've got a different idea for this. Now, we're not going to do this. We're going to do a story about a kid who finds an alien and they become friends.' We're all going, 'Oh God no.'"

On October 21, Spielberg met with Baker & Co. to discuss the new direction, of which Baker wrote in his diary: "*Night Skies* not same. New script. New E.T. to figure out all over again. Will have to spend lots of time that wasn't planning on. Really conflicts with *Werewolf*. I'm in shock... Big change like this is hard to take."

Adds Cellitti, "There was a meeting between Spielberg and Kennedy and the entire crew for *Night Skies* at the Farmdale facility. Spielberg is going, 'I really love the ET, it's really good... I just want a few changes.' I'm sitting there with a pencil and a piece of paper. He's basically describing the values between the ET in *Close Encounters* and this new thing with a little bottom, short legs, tall neck. It's nothing that Rick came up with. That's when he said, 'I want the eyes to be a shade of blue that nobody's ever seen before.'"

"Rick was knocked for a loop by the news," says Reardon. "I remember Rick saying, 'Now he wants the alien to have eyes with a blue that nobody's ever seen before,' fixing me with a look that basically said 'WTF'?"

As Spielberg recounted to Paul Sammon in 1982, "Rick Baker—who, if he is not the most talented man in his field, is at least the equal of Carlo Rambaldi—when he found out I was changing the thrust of the script I'd developed called *Night Skies* into *E.T.* said, 'Hey, you're turning a wonderfully scary movie into nothing more than a Disney film.' In a way, Rick was right. He made a good point. I had told him the new story too softly, in the same manner I might have told it to a small child before bed."

Baker did put some thought into what his E.T. could be: "I was traumatized by that whole thing, so I don't know the timeframe, but I do think there was something about a friendlier alien somewhere in there, and me starting to think about it. Definitely one of the things I would have done is change those fucking stupid arms on the puppet."

"Spielberg and his retinue visited the facility probably more than once, but those particular visits and meetings were kept entirely separate from our continuing activity on the werewolf project," Reardon says. "Nor was Spielberg ever admitted into the big room where we were at work. We were probably requested to keep it hush-hush."

This is emphasized in a photo this author came across of John Landis standing next to Skar in the Farmdale shop, his finger over his mouth in a mock "shhh" pose.

Another issue: Baker wanted an entirely new contract and budget assessment for the friendly alien movie, even if the budget was meant to be in the same $10M ballpark.

According to Baker, "The whole thing fell apart when Steven came and said, 'Yeah, I'm not going to make this movie anymore. It's going to be a movie about a nice alien.' It was like, 'That's starting all over. I mean, that's a whole new deal.'"

Considering the sophisticated mechanisms under development at EFX were meant to be somewhat interchangeable between creatures of the same race, reducing the number of aliens may not have had a substantial impact. In fact, it was later estimated that making the squat E.T. walk without the use of the diminutive Pat Bilon inside a costume would have added a cool million to that film's budget... but Skar (as-developed) could never have been a man in a suit. According to Kennedy, Baker told them, "Talk to my lawyer."

Confirms Cellitti, "What set Spielberg off more than anything when he fired Rick off the picture was he told Spielberg 'talk to my lawyer' when pressed about doing the film. It was a shock to me too, as it was evident Rick already decided he couldn't do both."

Some of this perceived hostility probably had to do with Spielberg's long history of problems with creature makers, like Bob Mattey's malfunctioning shark on *Jaws* or the three separate teams hired to make entirely different ETs for *Close Encounters*, none of which lived up to hopes. On the other side of the table, Baker had been told by parties unknown to be wary of Spielberg as notoriously tough when it came to business. This was still the case by the 1992 *NY Times* assessment "The Man Who Would Be Walt," where an anonymous film editor said, "He doesn't negotiate fees. You work with him because he's so powerful." Spielberg's response? "I am a tough negotiator."

Said Baker in 1982, "Steven is very paranoid of special effects guys... I'd heard that you had to protect yourself."

Speculates Cellitti, "I have nothing to base this on, but there was this kind of rivalry going on at the time between Landis and Spielberg and that whole crew of 'Who's more important?' I got the impression Rick was supposed to show loyalty to Spielberg by dumping *American Werewolf*. Again, I have nothing to base that on other than my interpretation of the situation."

If he was trying to push Baker to chuck his *Werewolf* duties for *E.T.*, that would essentially be the same as Landis pulling Baker off of rival movie *The Howling*. If this extended game of musical chairs continued, Baker would never actually get to fully realize any of his team's hard work onscreen.

Baker adds, "Steven saying 'It's a new movie, we're not going to use any of this stuff' had me freaking out. Now I had my actors and could concentrate on *Werewolf*, and I was very concerned about that. We weren't as far along on *Night Skies* as I would have liked, but we had made a lot of plans, spent a lot of time figuring that shit out. A new design meant starting from scratch."

Suskin adds, "Rick Baker was very committed to doing *American Werewolf in London* and couldn't change gears, so Rick wound up leaving the show. Rick had been very clear that he had this commitment to finish *Werewolf*, and that was filming. *Night Skies* was further in the future. I think the thing that caused the rift was that eventually, when *Night Skies* became *E.T.*, Rick didn't have the bandwidth to start over from scratch again. He basically told them, 'I'll come back to this six months later.' And they couldn't wait. It was unfortunate, because I think he really wanted to do it."

"I can remember sitting down with Rick in his studio at the Columbia facility we were in, saying, 'You can't do both,'" says Cellitti. "Landis and Rick were friends. They've been friends since *Schlock*. No matter who he chose, they were going to be pissed."

Baker's planned compromise to keep the strained relationship with the Spielberg camp alive was to propose Doug Beswick run point on *E.T.* while he went to London making Landis' movie. He was even willing to take a pay cut since he would be largely absent from overseeing the *E.T.* refit... but Baker claims he never got the chance to lay any of this out before Spielberg hit the roof.

At their final meeting at EFX (three weeks after the shift towards *E.T.*), Baker reportedly reiterated how the old *Night Skies* contracts were null and void, deferring to his attorney. Baker says the producer called him "difficult," then, "I told Spielberg that this was like starting over again and it was going to affect my work on *American Werewolf*."

Reveals Cellitti, "There were four people in the room when the blow up happened: Kathy Kennedy, Steven Spielberg, Rick Baker, and myself. Rick started talking to Steve saying he couldn't do both films and do them justice. That's when Spielberg kind of blew up like a little kid, goes ballistic, jumps up and goes, 'I should have gotten Rambaldi.' All I remember is Spielberg running through the building saying, 'I should have gotten Rambaldi!' We knew it was over with."

Baker confirmed as much to this author: "Steven stormed out of the building and said, 'I'm locking this place up. Call Carlo Rambaldi!' as he walked out the door."

Making a show of shouting some variation of "Call Rambaldi!" could be construed as Spielberg twisting the knife in anger, as most of Hollywood knew Rambaldi had assumed credit (and an Oscar) for Baker's majority work on *King Kong*. Almost all accounts of this culminating event at the Farmdale EFX facility have Spielberg being the one who shouts this... except for *The Future Was Now*, a 2024 book by Chris Nashawaty which frames it thusly: "When Spielberg offered him the chance to remake the aliens for his new kinder, gentler version of the film, the irate Baker fired back, 'Call Rambaldi!'" Whether this was written in error, based on the Spielberg camp's telling, or simply to avoid earning the ire of the powerful director, most accounts differ from this reporting.

"Firing Rick was the last thing Steven had on his mind walking into that meeting," Kennedy said in 1981. "But Steven felt that Rick showed little concern with regard to budget and schedule. His work demonstrated some truly innovative ideas, and there is no doubt that he would have given us an extraordinary E.T." Not wanting to get into a heated debate with Baker in the press, Kennedy added, "He needs to understand that there is a business side as well as the creative side. It was strictly an economic decision."

"All I remember was a blowout between Rick and Spielberg," explains Hester. "Rick had said, 'You're asking me to completely start from scratch, a completely new concept... that means that none of these sculptures I've done, none of this stuff is going to be the same... and you don't want to pay any more. That's just not going to work.' Spielberg got very upset and insisted we leave right at that point."

"Steven jumped up and said, 'I should have gotten Rambaldi,' and then left," Cellitti elaborates. "The inference was we were out of there, and better get our stuff out ASAP. I remember Rick panicking and sending somebody out to rent trucks for us to pack up. Elaine took pictures of everything... the Skar head was floppy so I held it up. There's a picture and all you can see is my arm. The *Night Skies* stuff got left behind, so whatever Rick has today was stuff he already had in his house. Richard Weinberg and Kathy Kennedy stayed behind to make sure we didn't take anything. I remember going out front to say goodbye to Carol, and Kathy eating a salad in Richard's office."

"We had *American Werewolf* going on and we had to throw everything in a truck," Baker recalls. "I called my lawyer saying, 'I don't know what just happened, but Steven's locking us out of the building.' My lawyer said, 'Get everything out today, or we may never be able to get it out.'"

In *Metamorphosis*, Bill Sturgeon recalls Baker showing up in EFX's *Werewolf* wing wearing sunglasses, often an indicator of bad tidings. His crew packed all werewolf bodies and tossed them into Sturgeon's truck before heading back to his house on Hortense.

"We had to clear out," says Hester. "From us, from the *Werewolf* perspective, we just hightailed it out of out of there and went over to Rick's garage."

Says William Stout, "Steven locked Rick out of his workspace when he started to get more involved with *Night Skies*. That was another thing that really upset Ron."

"When it got shut down, Steven had Rick Baker's lab locked and everything," recalls Mick Garris. "Suddenly they went to work and it was done."

Continues Baker, "We rented a truck and threw everything in it and parked it in the driveway at my house. We basically couldn't do anything because it wasn't packed up in any organized way. I had to find a new building and it took some time. A lot of industrial buildings didn't want to rent to you just for a few months. It definitely held us up, but I do have to say *American Werewolf* benefitted from *Night Skies* getting shut down because that's the only job I had at that point."

David Robert Cellitti at his home (2026).

A Screen Actors Guild strike which had prevented SAG actors from getting lifecasts for *American Werewolf* resolved on October 23, so the EFX crew was able to rally by going full-bore on Landis' horror film. About a week after the Farmdale collapse Cellitti found a new facility for the company to occupy in North Hollywood, with Baker choosing between two new projects to fill the *Night Skies* gap: An unmade non-Lucasfilm version of *Howard the Duck* (preliminary work eventually done by Stan Winston); or David Cronenberg's *Videodrome*. EFX took the latter.

Soon after, Cellitti was shown the door. As he describes, "When Rick finally let me go he said, 'Both Spielberg's office and my lawyer agreed that you were the primary reason why things blew up.' To this day I don't know why. I was later told that Spielberg's office took umbrage at the fact that I had started all my reports on what we were doing with 'Dear Steve,' like I was supposed to say, 'Dear Mr. Spielberg.' My name was on the memos and reports, but everything had been run by Rick, so there was nothing in those reports that was mine. In the industry, they call it 'the bag person,' the person that's left holding the bag. I got blamed for a lot of stuff that not only did not have my fingerprints on it, it didn't have my fingerprints on it."

Reardon, who wound up uncredited on *American Werewolf*, also parted ways with Baker: "I worked on the werewolf movie through Christmas of 1980 and suddenly Rick canned me. That's a long story, but both of us felt the other guy had double crossed him. Not in a major way, but.... The difference there is only one of those guys held the whip, and it wasn't me! So I was let go. Merry Christmas."

"All those clichés about the movie industry are true," spoke John Landis generally to the *AV Club* in 2004. "Almost everything you read about the business is wrong, but the truth is worse. Still, the product is fantastic. I love movies."

Emerging from the *Night Skies* vortex, the very first line of Mathison's 1981 *E.T.* shooting draft is an almost perfectly literal metaphor of the transition between the two projects:

```
The BLACK SCREEN becomes a NIGHT SKY as, one
by one, stars begin to poke through and come
to life in the darkness.
```

As Kennedy told *USA Today* of *Night Skies* in 2013, "The last image he had was of a little alien standing on this grassy knoll staring into the night sky as his spaceship took off without him. Steven said, 'That's the movie I want to make.' We knew that's where the story started."

That is where Mathison's initial *E.T. and Me* script begins. Hashed out on cards with Spielberg on the floor of Michael Kahn's *Raiders* editing suite, there were very few elements they were not simpatico on, except a few ideas she had like a homesick E.T. watching a bird build a nest outside a window. The director said it was "great for Carroll Ballard," but not him. The first draft follows the final film almost beat-for-beat. E.T. gets stranded while Elliott is introduced as an awkward middle school kid who feels alienated after his parents' divorce. The two meet, become friends, form a psychic bond, and the creature's powers of healing and levitation are revealed. Eventually E.T. becomes sick and is taken to a hospital, later revived and brought to the woods where his cosmic ride arrives to pick him back up.

In fact, the only major plot changes from this initial script were moving the venue where E.T. dies from a hospital to a hazmat-ed version of Elliott's house, as well as the elimination of a B-plot involving Lance, Elliott's weird friend from school. In the story Lance becomes suspicious, then eventually learns of the alien and wants to exploit his gifts for profit, but is rebuffed by Elliott. When the other boys and E.T. head to the woods at the end, Lance tries to snitch on them to government agents, but Mary stops him.

Matthew Robbins reportedly suggested both changes, referring to the character of Lance derogatorily as "Eddie Haskell." Removing Lance (to have been played by Corey Feldman) not only makes the throughline much simpler, it also emphasizes that Elliott is something of an outsider, hence his deep connection to the stranded alien.

"There's a lot of me in Elliott and Elliott in me," Spielberg told *Christian Science Monitor* in 1982. "I only regret I wasn't such a neat kid when I lived in Arizona making 8mm movies and the neighbors thought I was crazy."

As a student, Sam Chown Ahern created an experimental short called *The Dinner Scene* where she took the dinner table conversation in *E.T.* and showed it four times, each time with a different single family member (Elliott, Michael, Gertie, Mary) speaking Italian. It was meant to provoke the audience into thinking "about language and alienation of language," though the triggering incident of Elliott thoughtlessly bringing up his dad's girlfriend Sally to his mom resonated with Ahern's autism.

She says, "For me growing up and trying to understand the concept of friendship, making friends and then sticking to those friends was quite tricky.

In the film we meet Elliott and don't really see him interact with many of his peers. He's quite sidelined from the rest of his class. For me relying on my siblings' friends to have those interactions, then seeing Elliott interacting with his brother's friends... he's wanting to be involved in things. He's wanting to be integrated into some kind of group. In a beautiful way, through E.T. he does actually gain some level of status within his brother's friendship group."

Years of babysitting and a relationship with Harrison Ford's sons informed Mathison's depiction of children, from playing Dungeons & Dragons to the dirty words they say. The phrase "penis breath" came from a child she sat for named Tyler Patton, and one of Michael's friends is named Tyler in his honor. The idea that none of the adults other than Mary would be seen for most of the picture was inspired by a short Carroll Ballard made about a lost cat called *The Perils of Priscilla*.

She told *The Record*'s Jim Wright in 1982, "I like writing for that level, because you can really play with their fantasies—so long as you respect their intelligence. You can never get condescending or cute."

It was also a return to the suburban setting of *Close Encounters*, which Hollywood-raised stars like Richard Dreyfuss and Teri Garr could not connect with on that picture, having to be shown Bill Owens' photography book *Suburbia*.

Spielberg elaborated to *Rolling Stone*: "They have no idea what it's like to grow up in what I consider to be a normal environment: the yelling and the screaming and the mashed potatoes, the television on 24 hours a day, and the radio, the vacuum cleaner, and the neighbors walking on the grass, the fights in the backyard, the kids and the block parties. All that tradition. For the actors who didn't grow up that way, I had to clue them in that this is not in the realm of science fiction, how people live today. I remember several times Teri was mentioning, 'Is this because it's a science-fiction movie that we're living this way?' I said, 'No Teri, this is the way I grew up. You're living my life.' She looked at me and said, 'You had a pretty weird upbringing, didn't you?' Not to me, I didn't. Not to me, I didn't. Not to any of my friends in Phoenix, Arizona."

E.T.'s idea of combining an autobiographical middle class divorce narrative with a genre element was very innovative at the time, certainly an outgrowth of the New Hollywood tendency towards personalizing big studio films. This may or may not have been inspired by a movie from one of Spielberg's closest friends which opened on July 25, 1980, around the time the second draft of *Night Skies* was turned in.

Dressed to Kill is, in many ways, an early autobiography of writer/director Brian De Palma grafted onto the Hitchcockian thriller narrative of a prostitute

Dressed to Kill (1980).

who witnesses a murder. The high school-aged teen character of Peter (Keith Gordon) was modeled after De Palma, who at that age likewise made computer gadgets for science fairs and also used a camera to uncover something nefarious: his father, Anthony, was cheating on his mother, Vivienne. This act of familial surveillance ultimately led to his parents' divorce and Brian being disinherited.

Elaborated the director in the excellent 2015 documentary *De Palma*, "The whole Keith Gordon character came from me and my science fair projects and following people around. I used to follow my father around when he was cheating on my mother. I took photographs of him. I could see a woman going in and out, stuff like that. It was all taking place at his office, which was down the street from our house. I'd broken into the office by ramming my fist through the glass door. I had a knife with me and I threatened him. I said, 'Where is she?' I had to search through the office and I finally found her in a closet on the third floor. He was a bit surprised, to say the least. That is me. I was following around my father for my mother. [Peter's] following around the murderer because his mother got bumped off."

As would be learned years later, Spielberg's background was not far from De Palma's. He discovered his mother Leah's infidelity with his father's co-worker

Bernie Adler while on a family camping trip, accidentally capturing a flirtatious moment between the two with his Super 8 camera, later dramatized in *The Fabelmans*.

As he told *The Times* in 2023, "What was strange was I saw everything with my naked eye, but only believed it when I saw a frame around it later, on my editing machine."

While this adulterous relationship was the cause of the Spielberg family divorce, the director claims it actually drew he and his mother closer.

"That was how I found out about her affair," he continued. "After that I no longer looked at her as a parent. I saw her as a human with all the vulnerabilities I saw in myself. I wish I could have had another ten years looking at my mum as my mum, but that secret brought us together. I was as close to my mother as I've been to anyone."

Keith Gordon and Angie Dickinson's Peter and Kate Miller are a close-knit mother-son pair in *Dressed to Kill*. Perhaps as a concave mirror approach to mask real-life pain, both De Palma and Spielberg swapped which fictional parent was the adulterer, with the mother Mary being the cheated-on party in *E.T.* and Kate being the sneaky cheater in *Dressed to Kill*. In both films the young boy stand-in for the filmmakers finds solace in an unlikely friend, i.e. Peter with the call girl Liz (Nancy Allen) and Elliott with the E.T. alien.

It is certainly possible Spielberg saw *Dressed to Kill*, connected to it on a deep level, and was creatively moved by De Palma's brazen combination of auto-bio angst and loony genre fever dream. While we would have to go to the source to ask whether Spielberg was indeed influenced, there is one other possible clue, i.e. the name of the killer psychiatrist played by Michael Caine in said film: Dr. Elliott.

"Personal filmmaking, as it was defined in the '70s in the United States, is directly evolved from European art cinema of the '50s and '60s," says Matt Zoller Seitz. "The idea of the auteur, i.e. the author of a film, being the director and the director being able to draw on their own life, in addition to all the other things they can draw on, was new to us. I don't think a movie like *E.T.* could have existed before. Could have been thought up before, but it couldn't have existed until Spielberg did it… not on that level."

Opines Dana Gould, "That's the difference between Spielberg and Serling: *E.T.* is a movie about Steven Spielberg surviving his parents' divorce, and Rod Serling didn't write about Rod Serling. Rod Serling wrote about social issues, and I think Steven is a much more personal storyteller. *E.T.* specifically is about a kid in a divorce looking for an island of security, for safe harbor. What you see from *Night Skies* to *E.T.* is him finding a way to make this story about him, and it couldn't be dark."

As Spielberg brought the personal element, Mathison lent universality by integrating arguably the most primal, ingrained mythology in world culture... the story of Jesus.

Said Universal's Thom Mount, "Because I love the script I'd been talking to Melissa as she did a few notes and this and that, nothing serious. Spielberg loved the script too, that was a good sign. I thought if they shot the script, they had a chance of making a successful movie... little did I know how successful. In any event, I was talking to Melissa about where she came from, the angle of attack for this particular story. She said, 'Well Tom, I don't want to tell anybody this but I re-read the New Testament, and it inspired a lot of *E.T.*' That makes a lot of sense if you think about E.T. alongside this strange guy from outside the norms who they were calling Jesus, what he meant to people, and how he dealt with the power structure and society around him. There were big chunks of *E.T.* inspired by that."

This was confirmed by writer Aaron Latham, who in a 1988 piece for *The Washington Post* wrote of meeting Mathison at a Hollywood dinner party and

telling her of several Jesus parallels he saw in the film, including E.T. being found in a shack, teaching children a lesson of love, and that whole death/resurrection angle.

"Of course I did," Mathison told Latham of her integration of classic Biblical themes. "There were lots of other parallels. When E.T. gets sick and is lying in that culvert, that's the Garden of Gethsemane."

A Reverend named Harrison E. Bailey (who also claimed to have had multiple alien encounters), told the *L.A. Times* in 1982 after screening the film, "I don't want to get into a religious discussion, but at one point E.T. tells the boy, 'I'll be with you.' That's just what Christ said to the disciples when he sent them out into the world."

While it may seem strange that America's most prominent Jewish filmmaker would make the most famous cinematic Jesus allegory of our time, all the hallmarks are there from the mother being named "Mary" to the ability to heal wounds to having disciples, right up to E.T.'s final ascent to the heavens.

"You see His Sacred Heart, it's Jesus," says former altar boy Gould. "You can't do a movie where somebody dies and comes back and not think of Jesus... unless it's Dracula."

"We never talked about it on the set," says Mary actress Dee Wallace, who as a child played the Virgin Mary in a church production. "Truthfully, I didn't even know that was a subtext of the movie. From my Methodist upbringing I was always taught that God is love. That's the first thing I learned in Bible school, right? For me, E.T. was love, but did I put that together when I was doing the film? No."

Mathison also reportedly told Latham that she prevented Spielberg from messing with these fundamental parallels: "I would tell Steven, 'You can't change that,' and he would ask, 'Why not?' And I would say, 'Because it says in the New Testament...' And Steven would get mad and say, 'Don't talk to me about the New Testament! I'm Jewish!'"

Being Jewish did not stop Spielberg from telling further Jesus tales after *E.T.*, as *Indiana Jones and the Last Crusade* can attest. Even in *Disclosure Day*, Catholicism plays a major role for Eve Hewson's character, who uses self-inflicted stigmata to avert a psychic attack. If a story works, it works, and he knows all the tricks to game an audience.

Then there's the (possibly-apocryphal) recollection to Julie Salamon in 1994 for *Harper's Bazaar*, where the director told of once wanting Christmas lights on his unlit childhood house in Haddon Township so bad—despite protestations from his parents—that little Spielberg went outside, turned on a bright color wheel, draped himself in a white sheet, and struck a crucifixion pose. If this indeed happened, it was a clear rejection of otherness in an otherwise goy New Jersey community. Spielberg did not want to be in the one weird house on the block, à la the Freelings in *Poltergeist*.

"Being a Jew meant that I was not normal," Spielberg said. "I was not like everybody else. I just wanted to be accepted. Not for who I was. I wanted to be accepted for who everybody else was."

Sean Daniel mentions an additional subtext in *E.T.*, saying, "There was also the inclusion of the American paranoid secret government element, which then, of course, grew and grew in the culture yielding those awful results, but they even had an instinct for that."

Even though Mathison was the only credited screenwriter and was on set throughout production of *E.T.*, Spielberg still called in the aid of his two wild men in residence. They did not just contribute that big bike leap from *After School...* they embellished on it.

Explains Bob Gale, "Steven gave us the script to *E.T.* and said, 'You guys have any notes?' It was Bob Zemeckis that came up with the idea E.T. would levitate all the kids in that very last scene. In the original draft we got, he just levitated Elliott, but Bob said, 'Why shouldn't he levitate all the kids?' 'That would be great,' Steven said. The contribution I made is that E.T. would hide in the closet with Elliott's toys, and his mom would look right at it and not know he was anything but one of Elliott's toys. Steven loved that idea."

While the uplifting tone of *E.T.* is opposed to the sinister nature of Sayles' original *Night Skies* conception, there are multiple ideas ported over. The one element everyone openly admits Mathison and Spielberg kept is *Night Skies*' final page where Buddee has been stranded on Earth by his brethren. His psychic connection with Jaybird could mean salvation, but a circling hawk indicates the friendly alien may not be long for this world. This is essentially the first scene of *E.T.* where he is left stranded by his fellow botanists. One wide shot of the lone creature evokes Sayles' final scene fairly 1:1, even with daylight swapped for darkness and the empty prairie for primordial woods.

As Sayles explains, "I always say the one intersection was that the last page of my script was kind of the first page of their script."

Another key crossover scene in *Night Skies* involves Buddee using some ad hoc jerry rigging to turn Watt's ham radio into a communicator to "phone

home," an SOS message for the larger Cypress aliens to come end the madness of Skar's farm rampage. It is difficult to read this and not be reminded of E.T. reformatting a Speak & Spell, sawblade, and children's record player into makeshift intergalactic semaphore to his pals.

One more keystone visual of *E.T.* from Sayles' script is the glowing hands of the baddie aliens, used during their mutilations as well as one eerie scene where Skar's fingers glow red and melt the window so he can unlock the latch. To Sayles' point, though, it's all a question of tone in that the glowing fingers/hands are used to kill or destroy in his script, while in Mathison's the glowing hands heal. Sayles emphasizes, "Totally different tone, but it was not just tone. The last page of mine was, 'Oh, there's another idea there.'"

Other general similarities include the *Night Skies* script's repeated reference to "ETs" as well as introing a group of visiting aliens, not to mention three children within a family (one older, one younger, one very young), that latter dynamic an aspect of both *E.T.* and *Poltergeist*... and the Kelly-Hopkinsville incident itself.

It is common practice in Hollywood for first writers on a project to get jettisoned during development. If they are lucky, they retain a "story by" credit. Many fight tooth and nail in arbitration to retain credit, but when Sayles saw the shooting draft of *E.T.*, he went out of his way to demure any ownership.

"I really didn't hear anything about it till it had been made," Sayles says. "The way the Writers Guild works, if you were on the thing you get this message saying, 'Do you want to ask for any credit? Here's the script they say they shot.' I got this thing called *A Boy's Life* by Melissa Mathison. It was like, 'Well, this is really good.' I felt like, 'Oh, yeah, there's an overlap of half-a-page. And that's it. Yeah. And this is the best script I've ever been shown.' It really didn't seem like I should ask for any credit. It seemed like, 'Well, they did another thing with it.' It's not even a sequel, in a way. It really is just taking the idea of an alien who's stuck here in a totally different direction. I wrote to the Writers Guild and said, 'I don't want any credit on this.'"

"That's very classy of him," adds Sean Daniel, who later crossed paths with Sayles on an unmade mid-'90s remake of *The Mummy*.

Sayles' contribution is often glossed over or completely ignored in recounting the film's history, as in a recent *E.T.* Blu-ray featurette where Spielberg claims, "I had years of fragments of ideas I was putting together from 1976 until I finally had the story pretty much all in my mind and needed a screenwriter and went to Melissa Mathison, who was with Harrison Ford on *Raiders of the Lost Ark*. I then asked Melissa if she would consider collaborating with me on a script, which became *E.T.* I had all the story, pretty much. I had the whole narrative plot in my head and Melissa helped me flesh out a lot of ideas that were percolating but hadn't really boiled over yet. She was extremely helpful in helping me shape the final story."

Not to indicate anything nefarious on Spielberg's part. He is simply a world class showman who knows what makes a good sound bite, and, as you can see in the text of this book, the complex evolution of *E.T.* cannot be summed up in a digestible 30-seconds. Over the years the director has progressively distanced *E.T.* from *Night Skies*, even while most official books on the 1982 film mention it. Take *Spielberg: The First Ten Years*, where Laurent Bouzereau posits that prior to *E.T.* he "explored variations on the story" with Sayles' script, to which Spielberg replies, "The script that John Sayles wrote for me was a whole different concept." Still, the ejected writer seems happy to discuss the episode without a shade of animosity or regret.

Concludes Sayles of Mathison's work, "Usually, when you're asked to rewrite something, that's because there's a real problem with the script. I said, 'This is a really good story. This is gonna be a good movie.' I didn't think it would be the hit that it was. I thought, 'Oh, it's this nice little Disney kind of movie. It's got a little warm Disney feeling to it, and some really interesting quirks.' Then Steven did his thing to it."

PART III
BRIGHT SKY

CHAPTER 10

A Boy's Life: Making E.T.

"I am the resurrection and the life."

—**The Gospel of John** (chapter 11, verse 25)

In 1978, Frank Price became president of an embattled Columbia Pictures, where—even as *Close Encounters* was helping to lift the studio's stock price—controversy had erupted in 1977 as Spielberg supporter/then-president David Begelman was accused of "certain unauthorized financial transactions" (i.e. embezzlement). The forged check scandal rocked the company, leading to Begelman's leave of absence, CEO Alan Hirschfield's ouster over refusing to reinstate Begelman, and Begelman's ultimate ouster after briefly being reinstated.

It was during this transition period that *Night Skies* began development under the late executives John Veitch and Sheldon Schrager… but Price had plenty to clean up at the studio level before dealing with it.

"The alien project, *Night Skies*, I had never seen a script," Price recalls. "I had the brief outline, seemed kind of routine because of the bad space guys. I knew that wasn't where we'd finally wind up, so I didn't worry too much about it. We'd either get that premise right or not do it. If it became something more material, as it did, then you deal with it. I had plenty of other things I was working on, so that was just a footnote at that time."

Some of those "things" Price was focused on included several projects that would become huge hits including *California Suite*, *The China Syndrome*, *All That Jazz*, and eventual Best Picture winner *Kramer vs. Kramer*. And, yes, the sideways *1941* co-production with Universal.

Night Skies was being developed from 1978–1980 at Spielberg's home-away-from-home Columbia, but there was still a jungle telegraph signaling to Universal.

Confirms Sean Daniel, "Yes, I believe that Sid [Sheinberg] kept as close tabs as he possibly could on what Steven was doing at other studios, with a determination to always bring him back."

Once the overhaul on the project happened, the machinery around it moved swiftly.

Says Price, "A new outline is brought to me by Steven's agent or lawyer called *E.T. and Me*. Totally different storyline. *Night Skies* was dropped. I was delighted, because I didn't think much of the evil aliens. I was told that Steven would like me to register it with the Writer's Guild because he was in Europe, so I went ahead and registered and we developed *E.T.*, put a million dollars into developing the creature."

At least $700,000 of that number likely came from initial *Night Skies* development.

"Rick sculpted and built the aliens, it was on the road to being ready to work," says Mitch Suskin. "There was a major concept shift and it went into turnaround at Columbia."

With Ron Cobb out and Steven Spielberg in as director, a new legality between studios reared its head since there was a promise that the next picture which held the credit "directed by Steven Spielberg" would be a Universal picture.

"I had a very good head of production, John Veitch… Columbia read the script and we were budgeting it," Price recalls. "Then I get this demand from

Steven's agent, which is he's got a contractual obligation to Universal, so we're going to have to split it. I did not want to go through another split after *1941*. I'd had enough of that."

Veitch also confirmed that Sid Sheinberg was willing to "go partners" on *E.T.*, although Daniel says it was not the MCA CEO's preference either.

"I think all that is true," Daniel concurs. "Sheinberg didn't want to do another co-production because it was a spectacular script and a great project. Why should we cut another studio in on it?"

According to Thom Mount, "Steven understood he had a commitment: 'If you direct a picture, the next one would have to be at Universal.' We'd let him out on *Close Encounters*, so he owed us one. We didn't really care what it was, as long as he was directing... at least that was the theory."

Putting that theory to the test just prior to this was a semi-autobiographical R-rated comedy Spielberg co-wrote with TV scribe Gary David Goldberg called *Reel to Reel*. Goldberg had been a classmate of Kathleen Kennedy at San Diego State University, and she recommended him for Spielberg's project as someone good, fast, and cheap. He spent weeks shadowing the director for research on his first draft, then rewrote the *Annie Hall*-ish Hollywood satire while holed up in the same London hotel the director was staying in during *Raiders*. The two would confer in-between shots on set, then Goldberg would write scenes, arriving at Spielberg's room in the evenings with the filmmaker saying, "Okay, where were we?" This was concurrent with Spielberg and Tobe Hooper writing the *Poltergeist* treatment in London, as well as John Sayles' work in Hoboken on *Night Skies*.

The late Goldberg wrote in his autobiography *Sit, Ubu, Sit*, "I loved the way he worked. Open to all ideas. Generous with his praise. Gentle with his criticisms... I remember thinking, 'OK, I get it. This guy's just smarter than the rest of us.'"

Reel to Reel spotlights a neurotic young 20-something, explicitly Jewish filmmaker named Stuart Moss (perfect for *Soap*-era Billy Crystal) who made an unsuccessful art house film called "Blow-Out" (predating De Palma's movie, at that time called *Personal Effects*). Living off his rich architect wife Molly, he is handed an opportunity to helm a $12M MGM musical remake of 1953's *Invaders from Mars* ("trying to combine the success of, say, *Grease* and *War of the Worlds*...") starring a coked-out Willie Nelson-esque country singer named Shane Boudreau.

There are plenty of in-jokes in *Reel to Reel.* At one point, Stuart's beautifully leggy choreographer Pia suggests they use kids dressed in rubber suits for aliens just like *Close Encounters*, which Stuart says "looked horrible." He suggests using monkeys dressed in alien costumes, something which was actually tested on *CE3K* (with an orangutan on roller skates) but scuttled after about five minutes. When the lackluster final alien costumes are revealed to Stuart, the effects guys quickly darken the room and fill it with smoke to hide how crap they are. A European cinematographer named Anatole Kretovic holds up production with hours of lighting setups, almost certainly a stand-in for Vilmos Zsigmond, especially his catch phrase, "I light very good for you. You get all the credit."

As shooting commences the novice director quickly finds himself in over his head *8½*-style as he undermines his department heads, clashes with Boudreau and Pia, and eventually unleashes 15 wild monkeys onto the MGM lot, causing pandemonium. All the while his relationship with Molly deteriorates as he gets lost in his own problems with the sci-fi movie, including a 9-foot one-eyed mechanical monster that falls apart and goes into hydraulic convulsions, destroying the set. With his marriage on the rocks and the studio mulling a replacement director, Stuart goes on-location for six days in Acton, California (where *Duel* was shot). Unseasonable summer rain kills days of his shoot, and then his permits are pulled. Having to get the centerpiece military action scene in one take, the child actor gives his welfare worker one of Shane's "sleeping pills" so Stuart can shoot the explosive night scene before the kid gets pulled.

Stuart and Pia get in a fist fight after an argument, then when he goes back to her house they wind up having sex. That night he has a guilt-ridden dream where Orson Welles is presiding judge in a trial over Stuart not being a real director, including prosecutor Pauline Kael and character witness Mary Tyler Moore. He then comes home and finds wife Molly with another man. They agree to part ways for a bit. Stuart wakes up alone the next morning and cries. On set things get worse as Shane walks off the picture and studio brass offer Pia the chance to take over. Unable to sleep, Stuart has an epiphany in the middle of the night, writes a new scene, rescues Shane from a drug overdose, has a heart-to-heart with the singer, then films the new scene where Shane (as the dad) tells his boy that he loves him and now has a second chance to make things right.

The studio lets a newly-confident Stu finish *Invaders from Mars* over a montage of "Hooray for Hollywood." Cast and crew say their goodbyes, the post process finishes, and the movie is a middling performer with good notices for Stuart. He and Molly reunite and talk about getting back together, looking out at the twinkling lights of the Valley below...

STUART

Someday this will all be yours.

MOLLY

Even if I don't want it?

Although this early draft is absolutely unwieldy at 275 pages, Goldberg's dialogue is crisp with well-timed rat-a-tat Woody Allen-style one-liners. It plays bawdy but deadpan, far less chaotic than *1941*… there's even an old black craft service guy (ideal for Scatman Crothers) giving Stuart a lecture about engrossing the audience with good dialogue instead of frantic movement. *Reel to Reel* was clearly a very personal expression of where Steven Spielberg was in 1980, a "cinemaniac" with workaholic commitments to movies that took over his life while still yearning for a true family of his own. This project would have satisfied his itch for, as he told Nevart Apikian in 1977, "a story where the characters are more important than the event in which I place them."

A major factor in the decision to make *E.T.* at Universal may have been Sheinberg turning down *Reel to Reel* as Spielberg's next directing project, despite (or perhaps because of?) one of the characters being based on Sheinberg, a studio head named Walter Murray. It also could have been post-*1941* jitters over handing Spielberg the reins on another lavish comedy, or simply too inside baseball for mass appeal. (A post-*E.T.* Columbia *Reel to Reel* revival with Michael Cimino at the helm never materialized.) *Raiders* producer Howard Kazanjian stated that after Universal turned down this comedy, Spielberg saw *E.T.* as his chance to make a small movie quickly for the studio in order to satisfy his "moral obligation" and become a true free agent.

Mathison turned in her first draft of *E.T. and Me* after roughly eight weeks of work on December 18 of 1980. Spielberg read it, cried, and immediately found Kennedy in the MGM commissary and told her it was the best first draft he ever read. He could shoot it "tomorrow," but tomorrow was not a day away.

"My understanding was that Melissa Mathison had written a script going under the title *A Boy's Life*," says Daniel. "Columbia had developed a draft of *A Boy's Life* and the John Carpenter movie *Starman*, and Columbia chose to make *Starman*. Spielberg insisted on getting *E.T.* or *A Boy's Life* back in turnaround from Columbia and we at Universal were-what can I say?-sending every signal that it would have a happy home at the studio."

Price, now under the gun, was put in a difficult situation: "I was being pressed because I didn't want to offend Steven, because he's a talented guy and you want to do business with him, but I didn't want to give half of this to Universal."

"At the end of the day, my impression was that Frank lowered Universal's expectations," according to Mount. "In so doing he tried to preserve a relationship with Spielberg, rather than fight the thing in the streets. If there were blood in the streets, Steven would never work there again. I think that had a lot to do with it."

Indeed, Price admitted to the *L.A. Times* in July of 1982, "I could have told Steven to go direct a picture for Universal and then come back to do *E.T.* here, but this was the project he wanted to do next. By blocking him, I think it's safe to say he wouldn't have returned to do any films from us in the future." He added that "Steven did give me an informal commitment to come back and do another film," although the director ultimately did not direct anything with the Columbia logo on it until 2011's *The Adventures of Tintin*.

There is also an oft-repeated story that Columbia had done a marketing survey which indicated the *E.T.* project would have far too limited appeal (i.e. mainly children) compared to the costs they would incur. According to one source at the time, "A wimpy Disney movie" is how it was perceived within Columbia's ranks, though Price countered that he never would have greenlit movies like *Kramer vs Kramer* or *Blue Lagoon* if marketing research was truly the hill they died on.

Daniel explains, "Frank Price had a head of marketing named Marvin Antonowsky, who more than that was really Frank's right-hand man. For reasons that history could never fathom, they didn't get what *Boy's Life* could be. Whatever marketing surveys they did sure steered them in the wrong direction."

Spielberg admitted in 1982 that frequent Disney comparisons were "one of the reasons why the film wasn't made at Columbia. Some of the people there felt *E.T.* was just going to appeal to little kids or to very old people and miss the core audience completely."

For his part, Antonowsky admitted suggesting to Price it was "a more youth-oriented picture compared to *Starman*." Other rumors said Antonowsky insisted the project would only be viable if crassly titled "Close Encounters Part II," or that Spielberg was rankled about development on the studio's rival project *Starman*.

Continues Price, "Eli Horowitz, my terrific head of business affairs who had been at Columbia forever, knew deals backwards and forwards and could always come up with something. I said, 'I don't want to split it. We'll give the project to them... if they give us 10% of the unadjusted gross.' Eli raised his eyebrows, but he went into the negotiation. Ned Tanen and Steven didn't really get along. Steven's relationship there was Sid Sheinberg. I was hoping that Ned would turn it down. Obviously, the split was such an unusual deal that nobody would accept it."

Spielberg (*left*) and Sid Sheinberg (*right*) in 2004.

"I had a very difficult boss who was trying to figure out how to leave the company," explained Mount of Tanen, president of Universal's film division. "He had been at the company all his life. He was unbelievably smart and terrific with a great sense of humor. He was also bipolar. On Monday he would be on top of the world, everything's perfect. 'Go make whatever you want, just call me for the premiere.' By Tuesday, it would be 'Cut the staff you have by 50%, tell everybody they're on waivers. We're not going to spend any money on development, and we're canceling three pictures because I don't want to spend all this money. It's too much risk.' Everything's awful. Then by Wednesday you'd be back in good shape. You had to learn to navigate Ned."

Further explains Paul M. Sammon, "The Machiavellian politics between Sheinberg and Ned Tanen at that time... Tanen was very enthusiastic, but he was spot on, an interesting chess player. You could see the power struggles going on, it was nakedly apparent. Then there was Sheinberg, who everybody was terrified of."

What conspired behind closed doors between the business affairs attorneys of both studios as well as Spielberg's lawyer Bruce Ramer is a little vague, but the result was clear: *E.T. and Me* was now a Universal picture, not Columbia's. The latter got back the $1M it invested in *Night Skies* and *E.T.*, both of which became Universal's property.

Says Mount, "I didn't think it was very hard, but I wasn't in the room negotiating."

"What happened was they did offer 5% of the gross, and Eli had never heard of such a good deal," Price insists. "You take no risk on the picture, and you get 5% of the unadjusted gross! Eli closed the deal, but I had not filled Eli in on my plan so I couldn't undercut him by reneging on the deal. That's how that whole thing worked out."

"My understanding was they ended up with 5%," confirms Daniel. "I didn't do the deal, but that was the discussed number."

Continues Price, "Also around that time, there was a script called *Starman* I bought. In the deal we made to let the project go to Universal, Steven asked that we not release *Starman* before *E.T.*, so I agreed. There was a lot of work to do on that script anyways."

"Columbia had *Starman* in the works," says John Sayles. "Some of them were saying, 'Well, we're not going to make two science fiction movies about aliens. You can go away, Steven.'"

"I didn't think Frank drove too hard a bargain," opines Mount. "If I had owned the material and knew Spielberg was going to direct it, I would have tried to hold out for some larger piece than 5%."

Price later became perturbed about a crucial element of the whole deal...

He said, "There was one thing I discovered I was taken on, after all the dust settled. Guy McElwain, who was Spielberg's agent, had represented that there was a contractual deal with Universal, as had Spielberg's lawyer Bruce Ramer. Spielberg later said it was 'a moral commitment.' I realized I had been lied to because had Eli and I not accepted their word and said, 'show us the contract,' the split wouldn't have happened. They portrayed it as a legal commitment, then after the deal was done suddenly it became a moral commitment. That wasn't what was described to us."

There was even some speculation in the press that the legal gray area of this arrangement could potentially lead to a lawsuit, i.e. if the agency that originally negotiated Spielberg's Universal contract (ICM) did have a hard commitment for one final Universal film, then said agency could be entitled to a hefty commission. According to McElwaine, the 7-year contract signed in 1969 was renegotiated after *Jaws* to give Spielberg profit participation in future projects, and it entailed two more non-consecutive pictures for Universal. *1941* would have fulfilled one of those, while *Close Encounters* was done for Columbia and *Raiders* for Paramount.

By the time *E.T.* had made over $100M, Sheinberg said that "Steven had no compulsion to deliver that project to us, contractual or otherwise," stating the director simply told MCA it was getable from Columbia.

"It wasn't contractual, I know that is true," confirms Mount. "There was no contract that said, 'You have to give us a movie.' The deal he made with Sheinberg said, 'Let me out for this one, I'll give you one.' Sid said, 'Okay, just remember you're going to give me the next one you direct.' And that was it."

"So, we got taken that way," Price adds. "But we made a lot on *E.T.,* that was no risk money. You don't put up anything, nothing's at risk, you just get profit. I've never got an accounting of what Columbia made, but it has been a lot."

The late John Veitch later told Joseph McBride of the 5% net profit participation, "That year we made more on that picture than any of our films."

Mount concludes, "Here's the thing: He could have taken that movie and not made it at Universal, but it would have permanently fucked up his relationship with Universal, and that was his home."

Once *E.T.* was at his favored nation, several high-level executives within the Universal brass were still not convinced this was going to be another *Jaws*-style success. Even though he had two enormous hits under his belt and *Raiders* on the way, the director also had two non-hits in *Sugarland Express* and *1941*. In addition, so far Spielberg's few tries at producing had struck out, i.e. the two Zemeckis pictures and *Continental Divide*. *E.T.* was looking to some like a loss-leader leveraged for some hypothetical future blockbuster from their wonder boy.

Says Paul M. Sammon, who worked in Universal marketing at the time under Gordon Armstrong, "There was a great deal of excitement in house—and, at the same time, a massive amount of ignorance—about obtaining genre product. *Star Wars* ignited the heroic fantasy thing. To get someone of Spielberg's caliber, Universal felt... how can I put this? There was this really weird attitude of, 'This is Steven's little movie,' but they wanted it because it was Steven. In the executive offices there was a great deal of joy that this thing was coming over tied to the fact that the budget was low. *E.T.* coming over to Universal was considered a coup, but a small one."

Mount said, "It was a movie in which children were in the lead, and I could immediately see my senior executives at Universal were not excited about this. They kept saying things like, 'It's going to be another *1941*,' and that's not correct or very nice to be saying about somebody who's actually a good filmmaker."

"*1941* had been such a spectacular failure that people within the company, yes, were gun shy," remembers Sammon. "Not only at Universal, everywhere. People I met from Paramount said, 'Spielberg's dead. Somebody might throw him a bone.' Then you'd hear the other side saying, 'Well, everybody's entitled to misses,' that type of thing. There was a perception within some of the executives at Universal that *1941* had been such a popular disappointment, had confused so many people, that it derailed the locomotive of goodwill Spielberg built up, a catastrophe he would maybe not recover from. The other extreme in house was, 'He's Steven Spielberg. It's a kid's story, but we can do it and, more importantly, we're not spending a lot of money on it.'"

Even Spielberg's *Reel to Reel* writer Gary David Goldberg tried to talk him out of making *E.T.* by telling him, "It can't work... the time for this idea had passed."

"Sid thought it was for kids," adds Mount. "He had another executive or two—all senior guys in their '60s or '70s—who thought this was a children's movie and would lose every dime. There was a lot of pressure on that little movie to be made very cheaply."

Although some at the company were supposedly treating *E.T.* as disdainfully as Columbia had, one exec who claims he did not see it this way was Sean Daniel. He met with Mathison about a script draft over lunch at then-new Studio City restaurant Teru Sushi.

As Daniel lays it out, "Sheinberg was the Universal executive in charge of *E.T.*, but he did bring me in as his executive on the project. It was decided that I get the script from Melissa at this lunch. What a good time it was. She had a particularly infectious laugh. She took me through it, then said, 'but I don't want to give it away,' so I read it literally as soon as I got back to the office. Sometimes you read a script and you just know that something deep in the soul of the movie is working, and you knew that when you read this script. It was very simple, but in its simplicity, there was this incredible power. In Steven's hands a very emotional experience could be created. You never know that a movie is going to come together or be the greatest movie ever made, but you do have a sense that this could really deeply touch people."

Thom Mount (2008).

"The budget had to come down," according to Mount, who began his career working cheap with Roger Corman. "The original that the Universal budgeting department did was high, around $14M, but when you're working at Universal you take whatever the picture costs and you add 25% to it because that's what the labor/union deals do to you when you're working on a traditional lot. Everything costs more than it should quickly. The departments see every shooting picture as an opportunity to recapture some monies for your department. When you get your cameras from the camera department it costs more than just going to Panavision and making a deal, and that's true across the board. Now I had three senior executives saying this is a children's movie we shouldn't be making with a budget that was too high. I decided to do what I would if I were an independent filmmaker: Didn't tell anybody, just started working out what it would cost to do it at a non-union lot, the old Culver City Studios. It had been David O'Selznick's headquarters and now is where Sony is, built by Thomas Ince back in the silent days. It had been Ince Studios, then Pathé, then Selznick, then simply a rental lot much cheaper to work at than Universal. I got the budget down to $12.8M."

Spielberg has insisted the budget was around $10.5M (perhaps not including Columbia's $1M), raised independently though a bond company after Sheinberg "wasn't sure about its commercial viability." The negative pickup deal meant the filmmakers had total creative freedom to deliver the product how they saw fit to Universal, with the promise of distribution. There were stiff penalties if Spielberg went over schedule, though, meaning his points in the film could be siphoned to make up for overages. Essentially, if the film went over budget as *Jaws*, *Close Encounters*, and *1941* had, it would be his ass.

"Oh yeah," remembers Suskin of Spielberg's budget anxiety. "We definitely knew. In a nice way, he let us know. He was cheerful about it, but to some degree his reputation was on the line. I don't know why, he'd done so many big movies at that point, but I think this is one of those where the studio didn't quite see the vision but said, 'We'll humor him, as long as it doesn't bleed us dry.' It was something like $11M or $12M... it wasn't giant."

"I can't recall any moment where there were budgetary restraints," says lead actor Henry Thomas. "We were always pressed for time, but mainly because they were shooting with kids."

"I don't look at making a movie like that," adds co-lead Dee Wallace. "It was very early in my career. The only other studio picture I'd done was *10*, so I didn't have a lot to compare it to. For me it was a big movie, and it was Steven Spielberg. When I do a movie, I go on that set and it's a big movie to me. I give it my all, whether it's a low budget or a multi-million-dollar budget. We were working with a lot of kids, so we worked from 7 in the morning till 7 at night, not extraordinary hours like on a lot of big budget films."

"Kathy was fierce about making sure Steven had absolutely everything he needed," explains Daniel of Kennedy's first time at bat as a producer. "Even though the budget was tight, she was tireless in getting Steven more than what was laid out in the plan. She truly produced this movie."

"I recall a substantial change I made during pre-production," says Matthew Robbins, who was still consulting for Spielberg at the time. "Kathy Kennedy had found a hospital where the set dressers were preparing for E.T. to undergo scientific/medical research. I proposed to Steven the whole investigative thing be transferred to Elliott's house, complete with plastic protective sheeting and hazmat suits. Steven instantly loved this but Kathy was annoyed since money was therefore wasted on the hospital location."

Recalls Suskin, "Kathy was doing *Poltergeist*, then had gone off to produce *E.T.* Kathy called me and said, 'Carlo Rambaldi is making this creature but we haven't seen anything yet, and we're supposed to start filming in two months. Could you take a look and see what they're doing?' I went out there, talked to the guys, came back and said, 'You're not going to start in two months.'"

He wrote her on June 18, 1981: "The current effects crew has been working on this problem for about 7 months. Rick Baker's crew worked on the problem for 5 months before that... I feel an obligation to say that the information that has been presented to me so far does not find a reasonable belief that any E.T. is ready to shoot."

"They wound up having to redo their production schedule to give Carlo more time. I became the go-between with production and Carlo, then eventually the go-between with production and ILM. Kathy called me and says, 'Mitch, we're gonna get on a plane, we gotta go up to ILM.' They'd originally bid the thing on a certain budget, then during prep the budget went up, so we went up to talk to them."

After the big buildup and ultimate letdown of *Night Skies*, Suskin called *E.T.* "a different situation for me. When I came on, it was a real greenlit/going production. Storyboards being created, Jim Bissell doing production design... it was a lot more real. We knew who the cast was going to be, started meeting the kids."

Casting was conducted by a trio consisting of seasoned professionals Mike Fenton and Jane Feinberg (*Chinatown*, *One Flew Over the Cuckoo's Nest*) and one newbie named Marci Liroff. Beginning her career as an assistant at talent powerhouse ICM, Liroff helped put the agency's roster up for network TV series. She would often attend live tapings of shows like *Taxi*, where between scenes Andy Kaufman flirted with her in character as Latka. Gravitating toward casting as a career, in 1979 she went to work at Fenton & Feinberg.

"I was in love with actors and filmmakers," says Liroff. "When I started working with Fenton and Feinberg they were at the zenith of the casting world. There were less than ten major casting offices between L.A. and New York and they were one of them. They cast some of the seminal movies of our time and I was there, smack dab in the middle."

Starting as an assistant with the late Fenton on *Raiders of the Lost Ark*, Liroff got a first-hand view of how an iconic cast comes together, matching men and women up for "chemistry auditions" as actors like Tom Selleck and Sean Young vied for the roles of Indiana Jones and Marion Ravenwood.

Explains Liroff of her mentors, "They had impeccable taste and I learned how not to settle for second best... keep looking until you find the perfect fit for the role. It was a very different time before the internet, cell phones, and video cameras. Live, face-to-face meetings and auditions were our only choice. There was an intimacy that doesn't exist today, a sense of those rooms being sacred. We made strong in-person relationships with agents and managers when they'd come by our office to read the script and make suggestions of their clients for each role. It was networking at its finest."

With Fenton the go-to on the Spielberg account, Liroff was able to "catch the ball when it was thrown to me," becoming a full-on casting director for *E.T.* Since the fantasy film was a relatively small one for the time, and certainly for Spielberg, there were never discussions of name actors for roles.

"We didn't want movie stars because it would steal focus from the story," explains Liroff. "We wanted actors the audience would relate to."

Verified "big kid" Spielberg was enthusiastic meeting with the youngsters auditioning, relating to them through the video game arcade machines in his office.

"He'd talk to them not as kids, but as little humans," Liroff says. "We'd slowly narrow down who we liked and then started reading mock scenes written specifically for the audition. The script was always under lock and key."

Casting on the core group of kids was narrowed, then an impromptu Dungeons & Dragons game organized as a chemistry experiment. During this campaign, it became apparent the prime candidate for Elliott—12-year-old David Hollander (*Airplane!*, *A Small Circle of Friends*)—was not gelling with the rest of the group. This is interesting because the D&D scene at the beginning of the film is about Elliott not fitting in with older boys.

"You know how when you play a game, sometimes your true colors come out?" explains Liroff. "It can reveal itself as being competitive, bossy, a bully with obnoxious behavior. I think that happened with Hollander. Within a few minutes none of the other kids liked him. No slight meant to Hollander, the object of the game is to win so he was doing nothing wrong, but it showed us this group wasn't a good fit, which is the entire point of a chemistry read."

To say the role of Elliott was a lynchpin of the entire production would be an understatement. Whichever child they chose would have to carry nearly every scene, invoking both sympathy and an honesty beyond their years. Poster artist Drew Struzan did an initial promo painting for trades of Elliott as a younger blonde boy.

As Liroff recounts, "Once we had that fateful Dungeons & Dragons meeting, we knew we'd have to start over and find someone else for Elliott. For me, it meant expanding the search and beating the bushes, getting out on the streets in L.A. and other cities across the country. Simultaneously—as if sent by GOD!—director Jack Fisk called Steven to tell him about a kid he just worked with on his film *Raggedy Man*. Henry Thomas was from a small farm in Texas. He urged Steven to fly him in and audition him."

Written by *Black Stallion*'s Bill Wittliff, 1981's *Raggedy Man* is about single mother Nita (Sissy Spacek), the lone overworked switchboard operator in a small Texas town during WWII. She eventually hooks up with gallant Navy sailor Teddy (Eric Roberts), sparking town gossip. Henry Thomas' role as her older son Harry seemed tailor made as a comfortable first feature for the child actor, being shot in Texas where he lived with a husband/wife director and star. He could not have asked for a more accommodating audition piece for *E.T.*, since the story concerned a divorced mom dealing with troubled kids and an outsider who comes in to brighten their lives.

Says Henry Thomas of his *Raggedy Man* debut, "I was working with really great people. Their professionalism, the way they approached everything, that set the mold for me. I was fortunate to have worked with Sissy and Eric Roberts and Sam Shepard. R.G. Armstrong had been around since the '30s or '40s. Everybody on the crew was like, 'Yeah, sure kid, come into the trailer, we'll show you the prop truck and the editing truck.' Back then everything was on film, developed in L.A., then sent back. On set an editor was putting a rough cut together. There would be strips of film hanging from the top of the truck, so it looked like some sort of celluloid slaughterhouse."

At the time Thomas revered Spielberg for the movie he just released in June of 1981, stating, "For me, *Raiders of the Lost Ark* was the quintessential Spielberg film." Fisk had already seemingly convinced Spielberg by sending a reel of Thomas' scenes, but they needed to do a proper audition. The young thespian, alongside mother Carolyn, flew from Texas to L.A. for the first time in his life.

"Henry arrived with his mother, exhausted from getting up around 3am and traveling a long way with many plane connections," remembers Liroff. "We had him read some of the script in the lobby to get an idea of what was happening in the story. Then we had him read the audition scene and he was, to put it mildly, lackluster. This was probably due to exhaustion and being overwhelmed, but he looked exactly like what we all had in our minds' eye for Elliott. Always one to creatively pivot, Steven came up with an improvisation on the spot. He explained to Henry, 'A man knocks on your door and he's from NASA and he's found out that you have a creature in your closet that he's been looking for a long time. Henry, you've had this creature in your closet for 3-to-4 weeks and you've become best friends. This guy has a search warrant and permission to take this creature away and you're not going to let him.'"

Comments Matt Zoller Seitz, "I love that audition reel of little Henry Thomas. He starts crying his fucking eyes out, and you actually hear Spielberg go, 'Okay, okay, okay, all right. Cut. Kid, you got it.' He knew there's no point in continuing. This is the kid."

Liroff continues, "We—Steven, Frank Marshall, Kathleen Kennedy and me—were all standing behind the camera weeping. Finally, Steven tugs on Mike's arm and said, 'Tell him he can keep him!' He did. Steven said, 'You got the job kid!' You see that wry smile on Henry's face. We all finally took a breath and laughed with amazement and relief!"

Although he had been making TV and film professionally for more than a decade, this was the first time Spielberg cast someone "in the room." Liroff suggests that, "Because Steven is truly gifted directing children, I don't think anyone ever worried Henry had limited experience. We wanted kids to be kids. A lot of the 'Hollywood' actor kids are like miniature adults. They are groomed by their parents and bad acting teachers and end up mannered, not natural."

Says Thomas, "I didn't have any reps at the time. Nobody in Hollywood would represent me because I was some kid from Texas. If I did a couple movies while I was a kid, I would have money for college. That's how my parents were looking at it, realists about the whole thing. Definitely a world where we didn't feel we belonged, working on a Spielberg film, a high-level low budget studio film... and I was the lead."

Shortly after *The Howling* was released (for which Spielberg had a poster up in his office), Dee Wallace was given a straight offer to play the mother Mary partly due to her previous *Used Cars* audition.

"When you cast a lot of movies you start to develop a stable of actors that you love and can depend on," explains Liroff. "Dee was definitely part of that group."

She had learned to carry an entire film playing *Howling*'s traumatized Karen White, where she applied self-actualization tools that would later form the core of her self-help practice and several books, including 2021's *Born*.

Wallace says, "To monitor and watch my energy I have a certain method of acting I was learning at the time. It's all-enveloping emotionally, so I really had to watch how I used my energy to make sure I always had enough. My technique depended on the energy I had and still does. It is exactly the same as channeling. When I moved into my spiritual work, I went, 'Oh my God, I know this. I've been doing this in my acting all these years.'"

"Dee Wallace, she had been in *The Howling*, was a great choice," adds John Sayles. "I remember seeing her in *10* and saying, 'Well, boy, who's that?' She ended up being in a lot of horror movies, although she's not exactly a scream queen, just a terrific person and a good actress. I was really happy to see her in it."

Peter Coyote's character of Keys was a challenging one because he presents as an imposing authority figure but could also project empathy and kindness to Elliott. The chosen actor had to dispense with vanity since he would spend half the film being shot from the waist down. Coyote previously auditioned for the part of Indiana Jones.

"Peter was one of the first actors, if not the first, I thought of for this role," says Liroff. "I've always been fascinated by him as a person, as a political activist. We knew it would be a challenge to find an actor who would agree to be faceless until his reveal at the end of the movie. I knew he'd see the brilliance of this and would want to be involved."

Ultimately, the casting director feels that "we cast what Melissa wrote... it was our Bible and we stayed true to it." Thomas did not get that script until a month or two later when he arrived in L.A., only knowing it was a Steven Spielberg movie about outer space. For a minute, he thought it may have been the next *Star Wars* chapter, then was "a little disappointed when there were no laser fights."

"It wasn't till pre-production when we all got together for the first couple times," Thomas says of the rest of the cast including Drew Barrymore and Robert MacNaughton as his siblings. "Robert was great right off the bat. We've been friends ever since. I get on the studio lot and I'm given my dressing room. I meet this guy who's about five years older than me who's done Shakespeare, been on stage, and I can talk to him about acting. It was the first time I can talk to anybody about what I should do and what I shouldn't do where it's on my level, which was helpful for me as a kid. You always feel like, 'Oh, the acting police are gonna come and take me away at some point.'"

"My next film is a small, personal science fiction film," Spielberg told *Prevue* in 1981. "We're working on ways to put visual movement into what is essentially a 'four-wall' movie. The project combines my 'kids' film idea with the *Night Skies* science fiction idea."

In the leadup to principal photography, a veil of secrecy began to form around Spielberg's new directorial effort. He informed one publication that "E.T." did not stand for extra-terrestrial, then told *People* it was "a film about Chicago schoolkids." The *After School* smokescreen continued when *A Boy's Life* was described in the trades as a "comedy about antics and lifestyles of boys living in southern California today."

Remembers Thomas, "Laird was a mid-size studio with six or eight stages. They were filming that fantasy epic *The Sword and the Sorcerer* on the lot while we were filming *E.T.*, so I remember riding my bike around to look at their costumes. Playing D&D and all, I was, like, 'They're making a fantasy movie? They've got, like, swords and stuff!'"

Spielberg made the conscious decision to shoot the movie mostly in-sequence so the children could feel more connected to the E.T. character as they went on. For Thomas, this may have been helpful but not totally necessary, having an innate understanding of the assignment: "It was relatively chronological. We didn't have the goodbye scene in the first week or shoot the middle of the movie at the end, but there were a lot of disjointed things about it. In retrospect that is a luxury to shoot it chronologically, but really, as a film actor, the medium is the disjointedness of it. You have to chart where your character is and know the story well enough that you can jump into Day 3 in the story on the first day, if you need to. Whenever the cameras were rolling, I was in that place in the story. I've always been able to do that well."

As the 61-day shoot went on, the idea that magic was happening at Laird Studios in Culver City began to trickle down to studio brass.

"I went back to Lew Wasserman, the boss of bosses at Universal in the Black Tower, where my office was too," said Mount. "Mr. Wasserman and I had a very close relationship. He counted on me to tell him the truth about stuff. When something was going badly, I just said it was going really badly and here's why. When something had real potential, I tell him that. I don't believe anything until I see it myself. The upshot was the dailies on this picture were looking great to me."

Says Daniel, "When you saw it being made, began to watch dailies or when Steven first had Sid and I come out to see the Rambaldi creature, something special was going on."

Adds Mount, "But Steven didn't want anybody to see dailies. I didn't want anybody seeing their dailies because there were such fractious opinions about the film. I didn't want the studio trying to throw it away with a terrible release."

Like Francis Coppola in the Philippine jungle handing out new cards daily to the cast, according to a 2016 *New Yorker* profile Mathison told Spielberg to "'Leave your script at home and just focus on the day's work.' She wrote out the day's work on three-by-five cards and printed the cards and gave me a copy. 'If you really need to see the script, the continuity person is sitting just over there.'" This may have also owed to the spontaneity of any given Spielberg set.

"There were a lot of revisions happening every day, last minute when Steven or Melissa would get an idea," adds Thomas. "Melissa would come in while we were blocking the scenes in the morning. She and I would sit down and go over the dialogue for the day together, talk about the scenes. That was my favorite part of the day, because she was a lot of fun, Melissa Mathison. We would sit and talk about what had changed and what was new, why the scene was important, where it led to, all of this. Then I would go to set and Steven would be throwing all sorts of crazy suggestions my way, and I would have to, in media res, incorporate it. 'Now, say your line. Say your line. Yeah, say it again.' Melissa was a great anchor for the character because I would get the total rundown from her, then Steven and I would do whatever happened in the moment."

Sean Daniel was one of the privileged few to preview dailies at Spielberg's home in the evenings after filming, noting Mathison's "sheer delight" while viewing the raw footage.

"Melissa was thrilled at her words coming to life on film," he said. "She was giddy on set sometimes, happy in a big way. Like, 'Oh, look, it's coming alive.' Something very real happening on film, every element, everybody who was cast in each role, Steven's feel for the suburbs, which was so much a part of his growing up."

"She had based Elliott off of one of Harrison Ford's sons, Willard I believe... or Ben, I can't remember," Thomas said. "I think Willard, but his fashion sense and everything, the overalls and thermal long johns. When he came to set and I met him, he was dressed the same way I was, and seemed a bit put off. Like, 'Hey, they stole my look.'"

Thomas eventually got to film something with Harrison Ford himself, playing the principal in a scene ultimately cut out of the movie.

Said the actor, "It was great for me, because he was sort of my idol... Han Solo and Indiana Jones, and then he would show up on set because of Melissa. I'd get nervous and want to talk to him, but he was always nice to me. When we had our scene together, that was a big treat for me as a kid. I told my friends I did a scene with Harrison Ford, and then when they cut it and the movie came out, my friends were like, 'You're a liar. Liar.'"

Another set of actors given small roles were Ron Cobb and Mitch Suskin as a pair of orderlies who take E.T.'s casket away after Elliott realizes the alien is still alive. It was a gracious gesture to involve *Night Skies*' original director alongside his VFX man as a nod to that previous iteration of the project.

"We wound up being in a scene together," says Suskin, who was offered the chance to read for his role of a doctor by Melissa Mathison during a celebration of his birthday. "Steven came and listened to the scene. He goes, 'Who's going to do the stuff that Mitch is reading?' I think this was a setup, but Melissa said, 'Well, Mitch can do it.' The next thing I knew I was getting wardrobe. They gave me lines, so I was classified as a weekly screen actor which, surprisingly, still pays residuals today. Then Ron came back from doing *Conan the Barbarian*. He came in to say hello to Steven, and Kathy said, 'Oh, Ron, let's put you in the scene, let's surprise Steven.'"

"Steven just bounded over," Robin Love elaborates. "He was really excited to see Ron. He has a sort of cameo in it."

"I got to carry the little tyke out," Cobb stated.

Adds Suskin, "The Ron thing was kind of a joke to surprise Steven, but once Ron got in the outfit he had to stay for a week and shoot the whole scene and roll in the coffin, tweaking the dials and all that."

Suskin was one of the chosen few who made the transition from *Night Skies* to *E.T.* thanks to his ability to pivot over to *Poltergeist* and then eventually the alien movie.

"I was sort of a little fly on the wall as the giants were working this out," remembers Suskin. "I was tied into it somehow, right place/right time to continue on with the projects. *E.T.* became personal to Steven. In the meetings you could tell he was excited. For us it sounds kind of lame because we had been focused on this really cool dramatic alien encounter with *Night Skies*. It took us a while... I mean, gosh, I remember being at MGM in his offices when we were doing *Poltergeist* and he called us in to talk about *E.T.* and brought in this box... closed all the curtains, closed all the windows and doors. He pulled out the E.T. sculpture from Carlo. I went, you know, 'Ehhhhh?'"

"I was finishing up on *Poltergeist* and fortunately Spielberg liked what I'd done," remembers Craig Reardon. "He had a meeting with me in his office at MGM and showed me the full unpainted prototype of E.T. put together like a dummy. Pulled it out of a cardboard box. I was not very impressed but fully aware of his characteristic enthusiasm and optimism. I feigned enthusiasm for the thing, even though I had very little!"

"But that's just it... in this business, you have to follow the director," adds Suskin. "It's like a military thing: everybody contributes, but command comes from the top. You have to put your faith in the guy at the top knowing what he's doing. Even if we didn't quite see yet, that was the fun thing about him. We all threw ourselves into it."

"A lot of what kills *E.T.* is actually E.T. the puppet," opines Dana Gould. "It's not a great puppet. They did the best they could. It's always in shadow."

"Spielberg's got Baker, the best guy in the world doing this stuff and then, when the pivot comes, he's got Carlo Rambaldi," *Fangoria* editor Phil Nobile explains. "No offense to Carlo Rambaldi, but he's not at that level. He's a guy in Italy doing the *Possession* fuck monster the year before that. Spielberg finds himself in a Bruce the Shark situation where he's got to shoot around a thing that's only kind of working."

Kennedy told *CFQ* of the departed Rick Baker, "We've replaced him with Carlo Rambaldi, who is doing more extensive work than Steven ever imagined for half the money."

While it's true the final costs for Rambaldi's E.T. puppets and accessories were a reported $1.4M ($400K just for electronics) over an estimated 5,000 man hours, the Italian maestro was unquestionably building off what Baker had already done. Other experts were also brought in to compensate for shortcomings.

Says Sammon, "The only halfway convincing thing Carlo Rambaldi did was the tentacle monster for *Possession*... half-finished. The director Andrzej Żuławski pulled that thing away from Rambaldi, put it in the bed and smeared all that stuff on it. Rambaldi's going, 'But it's not finished.' Andrzej says, 'Go away.' Carlo had the embarrassing *King Kong* debacle, with that big damn thing standing there, so awkward. Was it, on Spielberg's part, an active fuck you? I'm sure it was partly that, but you'd have to ask Spielberg."

The filmmakers behind *E.T.* may or may not have recruited Rambaldi out of spite, but they were likely just as aware as anyone that it might not work out. Based on his storyboards for *Night Skies*, illustrator Ed Verreaux collaborated with Spielberg on weekends at the director's Malibu beach house to sketch out versions of E.T. which started out Skar-like but gradually began to take on their own identity. These would form the core of Rambaldi's design and serve as a performance guide as well.

As Verreaux told unit publicist Lyla Foggia, "I'll sit there with Steven and he'll say, 'Well, try drawing something,' and I'll draw something and he'll go, 'Yeah, kind of like that, with maybe a little bit bigger nose or bigger eyes,' or whatever."

Stan Winston was also consulted as a possible alien builder, coming up with his own unique take on the new character that was nowhere near Baker's Skar.

"Stan was the one that was going to do the E.T. after Rick," remembers David Cellitti. "James Kagel did a bunch of clay sculptures for Stan, because Spielberg was obsessed with Disney and he wanted the E.T. to have a bottom like Donald Duck."

The proposed arrangement suggested Rambaldi came with the deal, and Winston did not wish to share responsibilities. Winston would not become Spielberg's go-to makeup effects maven until 1993's *Jurassic Park*, a relationship which extended to *The Lost World*, *A.I.*, *War of the Worlds*, and the fourth Indiana Jones, the latter released a few weeks before Winston's death in 2008. In the midst of this collaboration, Stan Winston Studio (including Scott Stoddard) did create an animatronic E.T. for British Telecom's 1999 "Together" commercial campaign.

The "Donald Duck butt" was later incorporated into Rambaldi's design, and some elements of the head shape in the Winston figure do resemble the final form, although the overall look of Kagel's sculpt is unique unto itself. Rambaldi would later make a big show of saying the shape of his E.T. head was inspired by... himself. Specifically, a Picasso-esque 1952 painting he made called *Donne del Delta* (Women of the Delta) featuring cubist female figures with offset heads. He also made a detailed drawing of his Himalayan cat Kika from which he claimed the face of E.T. was formed, later going on a news show and drawing E.T. over an enlarged image of the cat.

"Imagine how it irked me when I saw that," Rick Baker told this author. "Carlo was great at the bullshit stuff, about selling himself as a genius and doing drawings after the fact. Unfortunately, that is an important part of the business, making people believe the myth. He was great at that."

"Rambaldi's stuff looked crude, primitive," adds Sammon, who wrote an in-depth piece on the film's creation for *Cinefex*, interviewing all involved on set. "You never were sold that E.T. was anything other than some clunky little cable control monstrosity. In the *Cinefex* piece Spielberg says it looks like 'a toad that's been sat upon.'"

Rick Baker's Skar (*left*) and Carlo Rambaldi's E.T. (*right*).

In May of 2014, a respectful two years after Carlo Rambaldi's passing, Baker finally revealed his *Night Skies* aliens to the rest of the world via Twitter posts which rocked fandom, specifically because the Oscar-winner was not mincing words in essentially accusing Rambaldi of appropriation.

"As requested, the *Night Skies* alien. Not finished, no eyes. Cover the top of his head and tell me who he looks like," Baker posted, referring to Rambaldi's E.T. designs. "He does look like Edward G [Robinson] and the others, but painting out the top of the head, adding eyes, and small tweaks... ET's dad."

Baker reveals, "I left all the *Night Skies* stuff there, and Craig Reardon said when Carlo was sculpting my thing was right next to him. Steven was pointing to things on my sculpture and saying, 'Do this. Do that.'"

"The silhouette of the head is intact, that's very much E.T.," muses Nobile. "Skar looks like E.T., but mad. He could be E.T.'s stern father."

"My sculpture is definitely finer than what they ended up with in *E.T.*," Baker adds. "Mind you, there's a lot of stupid things about my design. I think there's a lot of stupid things about the E.T. design too! I remember Craig saying, 'They took a lot from your design,' and at first I was thinking, 'No, they didn't. I don't see it that much.' Then I started looking at pictures. I go, 'There definitely is stuff taken from my design.' They cut my head off at the eyebrows, basically."

Italian makeup specialist Giannetto De Rossi, who worked with Rambaldi on two films, did an interview in 2021 for the Arrow Video release of 1984's *Dune* where he said the following: "Rambaldi had his own vision, so to speak. Think of *King Kong*, for instance, when he won the Oscar... there was a certain Rick Baker helping him there, who I think is truly a beast when it comes to this line of work. [Rambaldi] would create things, like an infant child, and I had to work on it, otherwise it'd look like a plastic doll. Or think of the huge navigator, which all needed makeup because it was all made of plastic."

When asked if, like De Rossi, his basic assignment on *E.T.* was to "fix" Rambaldi's work so it could be camera-ready, Craig Reardon replied, "Yeah, that's exactly what I had to do."

He continues, "*E.T.* was very close to going into production. When those things are set, you can't stop them. It's like stopping a locomotive. Carlo Rambaldi had been given several months to prepare the alien. However, Spielberg was never satisfied with prototypes to suggest paint schemes. I saw them myself and they were, frankly, dreadful. He said 'All I think it needs now is an effective paint job.' He offered me the opportunity. I did it in record time, like a day, working with a head casting provided by Rambaldi... not happily, I might add. His contract with Spielberg gave the latter autonomy, not him."

According to David Cellitti, "Craig Reardon, who painted the E.T., would sneak pictures out—everything was very hush hush at that point—and we used to laugh our asses off at these Polaroids because we thought, 'Oh, this thing is ridiculous.'"

"Steven gave me full reign," claims Reardon. "I did what I felt like doing and brought the head back to MGM. His only comment was the long upper lip might look better if it were more pale... lighter. I took it home to my garage shop, repainted the upper lip, and came back. At that meeting the director Matthew Robbins was there and he chimed in: 'Steven, it makes it look like Muggs the Chimp!' Steven said, 'Put it back the way you had it.' I had only two weeks to do all the alien components at Rambaldi's shop out in Northridge, to paint them and, just as difficult, attempt to match them. It was a marathon."

For the eyes of E.T., Reardon used paint as "makeup" around the sockets and lids to satisfy the director's "desire that it appear 'moist' and 'alive.'" Kathy Kennedy hired Jules Stein Institute's Beverly Hoffman to fabricate those eyes. As for that elusive shade of blue Spielberg wanted? Kennedy proudly told *NY Times* they "are my blue."

"There were a lot of technical issues," Henry Thomas says of performing with the Rambaldi creation. "The eyelids would always stick. It was a very noisy operation when he would blink, and he had to blink. We had to space the dialogue between the blinks for sound, and then the eye would stick shut and we would have to start again. All told, Carlo Rambaldi did a fantastic job. The technical delays we encountered would have been no more than a real actor in its place... their 'technical difficulties.'"

Then came another issue with the friendly alien: His sacred glowing heart.

"They were getting down to the wire and Carlo was having trouble getting the heartlight to work," says Robert Short. "Carlo put the heartlight system in the body, but it wasn't giving them the effect they wanted."

"I was approached about this after I'd managed to paint all the E.T. stuff under the gun," says Craig Reardon. "Steven was infatuated with the idea of the creature's heart glowing through his chest. I was asked to not only come up with that effect, but install it in the existing E.T. castings! The same inch-thick latex rubber torsos worn by little people like Pat Bilon or fitted over metal armatures and used as 1:1 puppets on set."

Reardon came up with a thin design for elastomeric material sculpted like a bas relief to fit within the tight quarters of the existing body. At this time LED lighting was not as developed, and using tiny tungsten bulbs produced too much heat. On top of this, DP Allen Daviau advised that red was the most difficult colored light to photograph. When Reardon came down with the flu, Suskin brought in his pal Robert Short to try to solve the heartlight situation.

Short says, "I took a look at what Carlo was doing, and because I was fresh to the problem I instantly went, 'You guys are trying to do too much on one thing, putting the heartlight in the mechanical body with all its cables and everything. How about we build a chest of E.T. that's just the heartlight?' Everybody went, 'Oh, we could shoot it that way?' 'Yeah.' So that was that."

Short, Suskin, and a few others got together to fabricate a completely clear chest with paint around the area where the heartlight would be. They attached rubber arms to it, leaving room to integrate a mechanical head. Initial drawings of the heart looked too human, until they settled on the idea that E.T. was a botanist and perhaps had vegetable-like organs. The final design resembled gourds, approved swiftly by Spielberg based on Polaroids, and fabricated in the garage of Short's duplex apartment.

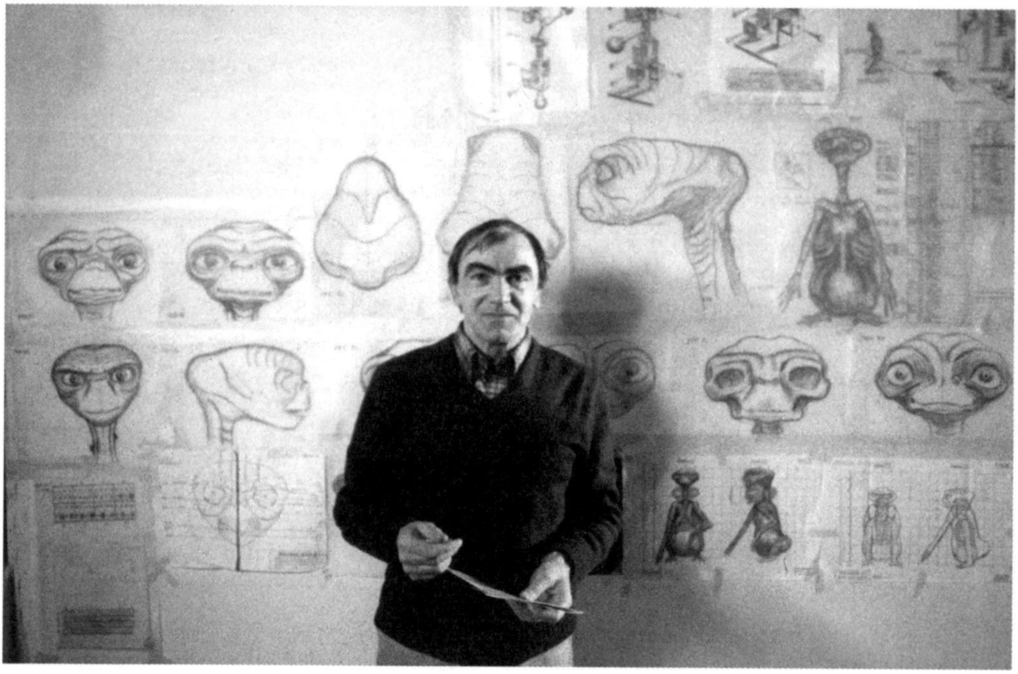

Carlo Rambaldi (1982).

"Craig Reardon had done the paint job on E.T., so I had to match it," Short explains. "I guess Craig took a while to do this multi-layered paint job, but it took me about 10 minutes because of my Don Post background. I was a pretty proficient creature painter when it came to matching and replicating. Spielberg had a very hot halogen light in the back to illuminate the whole thing, with a hairdryer on the base leading up into the chest cavity to keep it cool. Nothing high tech. The heartlight was only going to be in one shot, in the back of the van where the door opens and he's revealed. Once we brought the chest over, Steven made the decision to use it throughout the film."

Counters Reardon, "A guy named Bob Short got the job to do the heartlight and simply made a hollow replica of E.T.'s torso out of fiberglass and installed what looked to me like a party balloon on some copper tubing that inflated and deflated to create a 'heartbeat' while a light was turned up inside. Big deal. This is not sour grapes, though. What I was asked to do was not impossible, but there was no time to do R&D. I like my bas relief a hell of a lot better than what's in the movie, frankly."

For shots of multiple ETs with heartlights synced up, Short came up with another simple solution of chest pieces that strapped to the outside of existing suits with Velcro.

While *Night Skies* may not have reached the point where they were designing spacecraft, for *E.T.* Spielberg went back to his *Close Encounters* mothership creator Ralph McQuarrie to conceive of a circular ship with squat landing gear meant to resemble E.T. itself. Dennis Muren and his team at ILM spearheaded the creation of those shots.

"It was very whimsical," VFX supervisor Suskin says of the ship. "It's like a Christmas tree ornament. It was intended to be more impish. The whole movie had to be cute and child-friendly. Ralph was a wonderful person to work with on that."

As a bonus gig, Robert Short was tasked by production designer Jim Bissell to create the plant life in the ship's briefly-glimpsed interior. These included some of the killer plants from *Day of the Triffids*, as well as a puppeted Green Man specifically requested by Spielberg to root the movie as a fairy tale.

According to Short, "Jim said, 'You want to make the plants?' and I said, 'Yeah, you got designs?' Jim said, 'Design them, build them, just do them.' That's the old days. Trying to get stuff built today you'd have to go through committees and tests. In those days, people gave you an assignment and expected you to deliver and be artistic and craftsman-like and responsible. They cut you loose. The crystal mushrooms in E.T.'s ship was like, 'I'll do some mushrooms. What would make them unearthly? If they were clear and crystal.' I brought them to Jim and he's like, 'Okay.'"

Short then laughed at the absurdity of the movie's overall indie approach: "You got some kid... some kid!... working in his garage under his apartment, building the heartlight and all the plants, and driving them over in his car. I mean, what the hell?"

Having only entered the movie business three years prior as a gofer, Kennedy told *Vanity Fair* in 2016, "I was a kid—I had no idea what I was doing... I got into it, and I realized it was nothing I knew. I was truly overwhelmed... I'd just literally be physically sick, I was so nervous." She has said many times that *E.T.* was akin to an independent movie. Going back to the *After School* plan of having newbies make up the crew, relatively inexperienced *Amblin'* DP Allen Daviau was shooting it after both William Fraker and Vittorio Storaro turned Spielberg down. OG *Close Encounters* collaborators Hal Barwood and Matthew Robbins also contributed peripherally.

"Hal and I visited the set, where I was surprised by the spontaneity of some of Steven's ideas, such as the wilted flower when it seems that E.T. is dying," says Robbins.

"We didn't really do a lot of work on it," explains Barwood. "Watched him do some shooting and made some suggestions when he started editing. George Lucas is this phenomenally terrific movie editor; that's one of his fundamental skills. You're not going to watch a movie that George made that isn't pretty darn crisp, but Steve doesn't have that same instinct. He loves his 'children,' so when he shoots a sequence he wants that in the movie no matter what... so we made some suggestions on *E.T.* about editing."

In fact, editing was one of the tools Spielberg relied on to create a convincing creature, just as he had done with Verna Fields on *Jaws*.

Suskin remembers, "We had a lot of different E.T. puppets and Steven would tell us, 'If I'm filming a Cary Grant movie, I don't need to see his legs in every shot. When I cut in the audience knows he has legs. I can shoot E.T. with one that can walk, one that actually has really articulate face expressions, one that has articulate hands.' You didn't have to have a real walking, talking thing to tell your story since all movie stories are told in cuts."

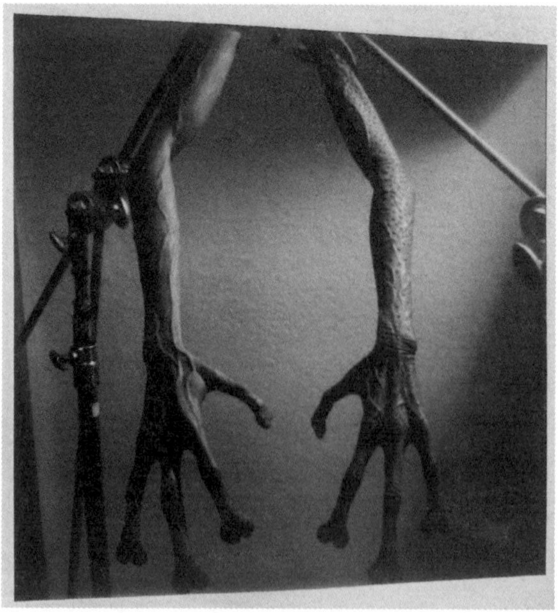

Night Skies arms and hands.

Even the fingers, a source of trouble going back to *Night Skies* due to how tight the space was to pack the wires in, were eventually realized with a low budget solution. Spielberg was frustrated with what he called the ungainly "wogga wogga" movement of the E.T. puppet's arms and hands, so production hired a "movement coordinator" named Caprice Rothe, a mime artist who wore rubber gloves and acted out the alien's more involved hand actions. The director was especially impressed by a moment where Rothe had E.T. wipe a watermelon seed out of his mouth while eating. Rick Baker admits this "was probably the smart thing to do."

Although *E.T.* was a relatively small film, it was a huge gamble for Spielberg both creatively and financially. He has admitted there was palpable tension between he and director of photography Daviau, as there had been with Vilmos Zsigmond on *Close Encounters*. Eventually Kennedy had to step into the breach...

"I was a little bit of a hothead, impatient, and I would be hard on my crew... loving to my cast but tough on my crew," Spielberg told *THR* in 2017. "About 15 days into shooting *E.T.*, [Kennedy] pulled me into her office and sat me down in a chair and gave me the bollocking of my life because she did not like the way I was talking to the crew. She didn't care for my impatience, she didn't care for my sharpness. She said, 'This is unacceptable behavior,' and I hadn't heard that since a teacher in school or my own mom — and that was a big shift in my life. I became mindful because somebody I trusted and respected had called me out."

In 1985 he admitted to *Rolling Stone*'s David Breskin that the process of making the film was "tortuous" and "traumatic," adding—perhaps facetiously?—"My pubic hairs turned gray!" Spielberg said, "At first, I thought I was making this personal statement about the effects of divorce on children. Which is, to me, what *E.T.* was really about. And other times I thought I was making a kiddie show that would be un-releasable in motion-picture theaters and would have to be released on Saturday-morning television, next to *He-Man* and *Transformers*."

"Finally, I'd seen something a little better than a rough cut—not a total rough cut, but not a final cut—and I loved it," enthuses Mount. "I thought it would be a hit movie. Then I had to gerrymander the marketing department. In those days at all studios, but especially at Universal, we took every picture out to preview in two different cities on a single weekend—Friday night in Denver then Saturday night in Atlanta—places where we would get different audiences and learn a lot about who liked the movie and who didn't. In those previews this picture performed brilliantly, and suddenly everybody at Universal shut up about the picture. They didn't know what to do. It was previewing like gangbusters, and then we said, 'Well, let's run it one more time.' Sid Sheinberg is from Texas, and he wanted to have a preview in Texas because he said, quite inaccurately, that more people in America were like Texans than anything else."

Spielberg and Sheinberg's previous good luck theater had been the Medallion in Dallas before the disastrous first preview of *1941* there. For *E.T.*, the big studio preview with all the bigwigs in attendance would be held in Houston.

"The movie had just been finished," explained Daniel. "The audience was recruited. I have been incredibly fortunate to have worked in the movie business during my life, and I've been to some pretty great previews. I have also been at previews of movies that didn't work. Outside of a death in the family, there is nothing more painful, no experience bleaker than a bad preview. But that was not what we went in thinking here. We knew something was working in this wonderful movie that we'd seen a cut of, but—and Frank and Kathy will surely agree with me—it was a preview like none other. It went beyond being a movie preview. The audience in that theater lost their collective mind. When those bicycles went in the air, people levitated out of their seats. Unforgettable. The energy that you could feel from the audience, the depth of their connection to what was going on, their sheer delight that a movie could make them feel like this. Affirming everything you ever thought about the power of a movie."

Mount goes on, "Sheinberg was there. Sheinberg hadn't seen the film. He looked at the film that night with an audience, a cold house, very nice theater in Texas, and came running out, threw his arms around Spielberg, and said, 'This will be a giant hit.' Well, this is the same guy who wanted this cut from the development list just a few months before, so all I can say is 'Great. Take credit for making the movie, whatever you're going to do.' By the way, anybody who takes credit for making a Spielberg movie is lying, because the only person who makes a Spielberg movie is Spielberg."

"Obviously the deep humanity that Steven and Melissa had achieved was... I don't know how to say it," expresses Daniel. "Every audience member was having an experience that went beyond a fun night in the movies. It grabbed people in their souls."

After this through-the-roof preview, Sheinberg and Wasserman took the entire Universal group out to dinner at famous Tex-Mex restaurant Ninfa's. They were flying first class that night, likely unaware *E.T.* was about to take the company on a rocket ride straight out of the stratosphere.

CHAPTER 11

I'll Buy Right Here: The Biggest Movie of All Time

"Movies are art, now more than ever."
—***The Player*** (1992)

"When the movie's a hit, there are many fathers," says Thom Mount. "When the movie's a flop, everybody was a pastry chef during the war."

Mount knows of what he speaks, since he greenlit both *Smokey and the Bandit* and *Xanadu*. A one-time civil rights demonstrator and painter, Mount eventually kickstarted his career in 1975 as a $300-a-week script reader for Universal's Ned Tanen. He quickly ascended to Tanen's executive vice president of production. By mid-1978, *New York* magazine's Maureen Orth dubbed 29-year-old Mount and other former student lefties who became studio execs—Paula Weinstein (32), Don Simpson (32),

Sean Daniel (26)—as "baby moguls." The name also applied to young directors like Steven Spielberg and John Landis. The term "baby mogul" became an albatross for Mount, who bore some responsibility considering he was dating Orth at the time.

"I'm not happy about it," Orth told *Washington Post* that July of the conflict. "I wound up bending over backwards to keep him out of the story as much as possible, even though he has much more power than anyone else in the piece."

Mount told *Interview*'s Cameron Crowe in '85, "The thing that was important about that article, I thought, is that it really did signal a changing of the guard in the studio system."

Fresh-faced Universal execs Mount and Daniel were not only cooking up hits that spoke to the new generation (*Smokey*, *Animal House*). They pushed at least one or two socially-relevant projects through the system each year (*Blue Collar*, *Coal Miner's Daughter*).

Flash forward, with Mount now president in charge of production, as the social conscience of the '70s was nudged aside for the blockbuster '80s, a mentality cemented by a summer of '82 driven by genre fare. Baby mogul Spielberg's *E.T.* would embody the kind of paradigm-changing four-quadrant bonanza that became the Holy Grail every studio sought thereafter... assuming Universal did not fumble the ball marketing this delicate mix of sci-fi and soulful.

"The studio was behind the movie going into the preview," claims Daniel of the May 1982 screening in Texas. "That cemented how all out they could go, but they were going to do that anyway. It's just that they now realize they're doing it in service of a movie so powerful... that's what nobody had seen coming."

Adds Paul Sammon, "It was a low budget picture, certainly did not have the full attention of marketing. There was the one sheet with the moon. I went to conventions and passed out *E.T.* buttons: 'E.T. was here!'... 'E.T. come home.' There was a campaign, but an after-the-fact campaign. Once the preview screenings had such an incredible impact, suddenly more money was coming into promotions."

Neither audience nor exhibitor enthusiasm were immediately apparent. By March of 1982 Marvin Antonowsky claimed research conducted by both Columbia and Universal placed *E.T.* near the bottom in terms of interest for that summer's slate, thus the film was initially booked into a mere 500 theaters. It was later bumped up to 600-700 with plans to expand later in the season. One anonymous exec stated the studio "didn't know what we had" until the preview gave Universal the gusto to knock that number way up to 1,600, which Spielberg supposedly was against. The two sides compromised with something right in between: 1,100 screens.

"Gordon Armstrong was the head of the publicity department, and I had my own little office under the commissary at Universal... I could smell the daily special every day," recalls Mick Garris. "I worked under Gordon on *E.T.*, and there was only excitement about it. Steven came in for a marketing meeting with the first 15 minutes of cut footage, and everybody was hypnotized, mesmerized and thrilled. Steven told me after the meeting, 'I was watching you all the way through Mick,' because I was a fan of the genre and was as entranced as anybody. Nobody thought of it as Disney-fied at the time, until after it came out and became such a huge success, without any of the violence of *Jaws*."

Some in Universal marketing may have noticed in that first 15 minutes a shot of E.T. overlooking a grid of city lights from mountain bluffs after his spaceship has departed. The vista is absolutely identical to the first teaser trailer for *1941*, which featured the same vantage point as the title *1941* erupts from the ground in giant stone letters, which then explode. This setting in *E.T.* is slightly more tranquil.

A similar vista is described at the end of *Reel to Reel* and had inspired the mothership design in *Close Encounters*. That ship was originally a giant black wedge, an image recycled for *Disclosure Day*. After Spielberg visited a village outside Bombay in January 1977 while shooting *CE3K*, he passed a large oil refinery lit by thousands of lights. Immediately after returning to Los Angeles, he was on Mulholland Drive looking down at the night lights of the San Fernando Valley. "A little stoned," he turned upside down on the hood of his car and imagined that vista as the underbelly of the Bombay refinery. That formed the basis for the iconic ship designed by Ralph McQuarrie and now perpetually on display at the Smithsonian National Air and Space Museum.

There was also a demographic question mark of whether *E.T.*, which is largely lily-white in its casting, could reach across the aisle in appealing to POC audiences too.

"I think that was the point," says Mike Ryan. "He's like, 'This is what suburban life is like. You are not exposed to anything that's not like yourself, and then an alien shows up.'"

When this author joked to filmmaker Ernest Dickerson that the only prominent black character in *E.T.* is a Lando Calrissian action figure, Dickerson joked back, "I think one of the FBI agents might be black too. I'll check. He kind of comes and goes."

"Steven wanted some people of color to see it, to see what their response was," recalls Mount. "I got that request, put together a screening, and called Richard Pryor, who was under contract, asked him to come watch this movie. And I called Michael Jackson. They had the advantage of both being black, and they saw the movie and loved it, flipped out over it. They were both crying. That erased worry on the part of marketing that we would have to stay away from black audiences because the movie was so white. I thought, 'Now we have a couple of industry leaders who are people of color who can talk about having seen the movie.' Richard did that for us. Richard did some late-night talk shows: 'I just saw this great movie about this extraterrestrial thing.' He made jokes about it, but you could tell he was really moved by the movie and that kind of commentary could help us everywhere... and it did."

Michael Jackson eventually became part of the *E.T.* tapestry with the November 1982 release of an *E.T. the Extra-Terrestrial* album featuring music from John Williams' soundtrack along with the "Thriller" singer performing an audiobook version of the story, genuinely beginning to cry at one point. A single based on the film titled "Someone in the Dark" won Jackson a Grammy, one of eight for him that year. He told *Ebony*, "When I was doing that recording I really felt that I was E.T., and it was because his story is the story of my life."

Says critic Jourdain Searles, "If they don't have any other trauma, divorce is the big trauma for white people. I feel like for black people, unless you're really Christian, it feels like less of a deal. I don't know if it's that we have other things to worry about? Like, what about it? We're a lot more chill about divorce. My dad died when I was very young, and it was just my mom and my grandmother. Every man in my life was just some guy. 'This guy's not my dad, he's just some guy that's here for five years and now he's not here anymore.' It's a little bit more casual for me. There's this idea of what a happy home is and what a happy childhood is. It's interesting the different ways that Spielberg addresses his divorced parents throughout different films, in contrast to someone like Noah Baumbach who made two movies about divorce: One about his parents and one about his own divorce. Spielberg is like, 'This is about me, but this is a blockbuster… a personal story with mass appeal."

Sean Daniel says, "I'm not trying to put a gloss on it… Take my word for it, everyone was completely bullish about this movie, not knowing that alchemy would result in something just beyond anyone's concept of what a success it would be."

That success was never assured, though. The summer of 1982 was legendarily packed with enormous films, some of which were massive hits out of the gate (*Rocky III*, *An Officer and a Gentlemen*) while others later found a devoted cult audience (*Blade Runner*, *Tron*). That summer Universal alone was responsible for releasing *Conan the Barbarian*, *Fast Times at Ridgemont High*, and *The Best Little Whorehouse in Texas*. *E.T.*'s June 11 release date had it going head-to-head with the opening of Paramount's *Grease 2* following the prior week's *Star Trek II* and Spielberg's own production of *Poltergeist*.

"It's fucking maddening, the summer of '82," says Stephen Scarlata. "It's absolutely insane. I do remember going to see *Poltergeist* and it scaring the shit out of me, this PG movie. I'll never forget passing by in the lobby a giant standee for *The Thing*. People were actually saying *Star Trek II* was good. 'No way that's a good movie, that last one sucked.' You couldn't pass a newsstand without seeing *Tron* on the cover of so many magazines. *Rocky III* was a really big deal, the line was so long that my brother ended up staying on line while the movie played to go into the next screening."

"It was very crowded and we were aware of that," says Mount. "Steven did a great job upselling the marketing people, but what really did it was that preview in Texas because a sufficient number of senior executives were in that preview. Now they're all fucked up because they can't decide whether this is an anomaly or whether this is the biggest picture of the year. Little did they know, it's going to be the biggest picture in history."

According to Daniel, "Sheinberg got hung up on the title, thought it needed to be explained as 'E.T. in His Adventure on Earth.' Frankly, no one else thought that was necessary, but it did end up being in the initial advertising."

As marketing for both *Poltergeist* and *E.T.* geared up, *Variety* reported friction between the publicity units of MGM and Universal, respectively. Both studios wanted Spielberg, Kathleen Kennedy, and Frank Marshall to do separate press junkets for each film, even though they were only bowing a week apart. Kennedy assured exhibitors the two films would not cannibalize each other but rather create cross-attendance through word-of-mouth on "two totally different pictures with the Spielberg touch."

According to William Stout, Ron Cobb "got invited to the cast and crew screening, and he told me, 'I'm so glad I did not make this movie.'" Thankfully, his work on John Milius' *Conan the Barbarian* hit the bullseye when released that May, with audiences eating it up to the tune of nearly $70M worldwide even as critics bemoaned the violent film as "*Star Wars* for psychos." That R-rated sword & sorcery was a key influence on HBO phenom *Game of Thrones*, as well as other filmmakers like *The Northman*'s Robert Eggers, who told this author in 2022 (for */Film*), "I didn't seek to make *Conan*, but it was a movie that I watched a ton as a kid. There were a handful of deliberate nods to *Conan*, but then sometime during filming I watched *Conan* and realized there were a lot of unintentional nods. Fjölnir taking his helmet off is a direct nod to James Earl Jones taking his helmet off, which is a nod to a Teutonic knight taking his helmet off in *Alexander Nevsky*."

Meanwhile, Melissa Mathison's work for *The Escape Artist* was finally being seen, albeit in only two theaters with a token release by Orion on May 28, where it opened to $23K before finishing its run at $143,369 total. With a mixed critical reception, Coppola's American Zoetrope was unable to salvage the release after *One from the Heart* died the death in February of '82. In the time it took for *Escape Artist* to clear release, Mathison had already written another film which was about to come out, although director Caleb Deschanel did not see the irony: "To say that Melissa 'went off and finished a whole other movie' at that time is a strange way to put it. She wrote a screenplay... and Steve Spielberg made the movie." Although Deschanel would direct again for the small and big screen, he went back to more lucrative DP work starting with *The Right Stuff*, which he said "seems like a vacation" compared to *The Escape Artist*.

By early April the marketing budget for the $10M *E.T.* was around $8M, both numbers posing minimal risk. Expectations rose when it was chosen as the closing night film of the 1982 Cannes Film Festival on May 26, where it was rapturously received.

"The biggest audience hit was Steven Spielberg's *E.T.*, his companion piece to *Close Encounters of the Third Kind*," wrote Ron Base of *Toronto Star*. "*E.T.* is badly-needed evidence that the best movies come from the heart and the mind... It is also the sure-fire box office hit of the summer."

A few days after that, major studio sneak previews on the evening of May 30 helped stoke word-of-mouth from the public, who came away cheering.

Journalist Sharon Johnson reported "subdued sniffling" from typically stoic New York critics screenings. *NY Daily News*' Rex Reed stated, "No other film is even in the same league this summer."

Martin Kent of *The Hollywood Reporter* wrote out of Cannes, "Perhaps the greatest wonder involved in *E.T.* is that it was reportedly brought in for around $10.3M. Judging by what's already been released, and what's poised to come forth this summer, *E.T.*, to be released June 11, will make its money back many, many times over."

Sugarland Express cheerleader Pauline Kael honed in on the film's screenwriter for *The New Yorker* review: "Mathison was one of the scenarists for *The Black Stallion* and is a co-writer of *The Escape Artist*; it probably isn't a coincidence that all three of these films have young boy heroes who miss their fathers... Henry Thomas, who plays Elliott, and Kelly Reno in *The Black Stallion* and Griffin O'Neal as the boy magician in *The Escape Artist* are not Hollywood movie kids; they all have an unusual—a magical—reserve."

"Thomas is astonishingly convincing, especially when one considers that he was required to respond emotionally to an actor made entirely out of steel and foam rubber," opined *Daily News*' Kathleen Carroll, adding, "Dee Wallace is quietly touching as the newly-separated mother who must cope with the mysterious activities of her children while struggling to conceal her own sense of loss."

Variety's Todd McCarthy wrote, "Rarely has a picture so completely evinced a kid's p.o.v. and shown the complicity of youngsters against adults. It's been said that the only people who don't like Disneyland are late adolescents who feel too hip to enjoy the pleasures of their earlier years, and the same will probably hold true for *E.T.*"

Gary Arnold of *The Washington Post* said, "Spielberg knows how to transform the raw material of his childhood into an appealing popular fable. There are sequences that touch you to the quick in mysteriously casual ways: Elliott explaining the functions of his toys to E.T.; the mother reading *Peter Pan* to Gertie while Elliott and E.T. also listen from a place of seclusion; Mike taking refuge among Gertie's stuffed animals and falling asleep on the night when it appears that E.T.'s life may be flickering out."

"The girl of my dreams is the sweetest girl
Of all the girls I know
Each sweet co-ed, like a rainbow trail
Fades in the afterglow"

— "The Sweetheart of Sigma Chi" (1911)

Some found nitpicks, though. Future Spielberg biographer Molly Haskell preferred *Poltergeist* that summer: "By contrast, the ending of *E.T.*—an unendurably prolonged goodbye between Elliott and E.T. —is softer and more sentimental. It reminds me of what I don't like about Spielberg, his Peter Pan-ism, the let's-be-boys-forever fantasy that inspires so much of his work."

NY Times critic Vincent Canby's otherwise positive review finishes thus: "At the end of the film, there is an all-out assault on the emotions that depends, it seems, more on the rising volume of this music than on the events portrayed. *E.T.* is good enough not to have to resort to such tricks."

Chief in that bag of tricks is the symbolic rainbow trail the spaceship leaves as it flies off beyond the stars.

"Yeah, it was a bit much," Henry Thomas said of the rainbow's inclusion. "In Spielberg movies there's always a Spielberg moment where it goes too far, and the rainbow was a step too far in *E.T.* But, at the same time, with the John Williams score and everything... even if you're scoffing at it, you might be doing it through a veil of tears, right?"

The initial image of the rainbow is what sticks out in many cynics' minds, but the actual visual language of the film when broken down shows...

A) the rainbow trail as the ship departs to the stars

B) varied emotional reactions from Mary & Keys/Tyler & Greg & Steve/ Michael & Gertie

C) the rainbow in the sky fades away

D) Elliott looks resolute

The real ending message is not a "happy rainbow" but more the true meaning of the film, which is about learning to live with loss. Elliott has stepped over the threshold into manhood because he has learned, as Max Fisher says in *Rushmore*, "Sic transit gloria" (glory fades). As final grace notes go, it is an elegant one, expressed without words.

This penultimate image of the film (as well as E.T. being referred to as a "goblin") was likely inspired by the Kelly-Hopkinsville incident. As Geraldine Sutton Stith told this author, "Billy Ray said the ship had the colors of the rainbow falling behind it."

"You feel like you're carried along in this current of consciousness with *E.T.*," says contemporary critic Adam Nayman. "You access these things in the collective... who isn't going to respond to this movie? You have to become like Elaine May."

Journalist Don Shewey overheard filmmaker Elaine May (*A New Leaf*, *The Heartbreak Kid*) talking about seeing *E.T.* in a Los Angeles theater: "All around me, people are sniffling, and I keep thinking, 'When is this fucking puppet gonna die?'"

When *E.T. the Extra-Terrestrial* opened on June 11, 1982 into 1,101 locations, it grossed $11.9M in first place at the box office ahead of holdovers *Star Trek II* ($9.4M), *Rocky III* ($8.2M), and *Poltergeist* ($5.37M), giving Spielberg two films in the Top 5. It also crushed the debut of Paramount's *Grease 2* at #5 ($4.6M). Then... it did better. In its second frame *E.T.* stayed on top of the charts with $12.6M, beating the debut of Clint Eastwood's high tech thriller *Firefox* ($8.15M). In week 3 it earned $13.38M at #1, taking down the debuts of *Blade Runner* at #2 ($6.15M), Universal's own *The Thing* at #8 ($3.1M), and *Megaforce* at #9 ($2.35M).

Spielberg's film was beginning to suck all the oxygen out of the room. By week 4 it jumped a nearly unheard-of +29% raking in $17.25M from 1,323 screens, its all-time peak weekend. It also became the first movie to make $100M in its first 30 days of release. *E.T.* remained the #1 film in the country for a record six straight weekends in a row until Universal's own musical *The Best Little Whorehouse in Texas* took it down during the July 23 weekend, but just barely.

E.T. bounced back to #1 in frame 8, then frame 9. It would sit at the top of the box office for 16 non-consecutive weekends of 1982, going all the way to the Dec 3 frame. Peak theater count was 1,709 during the August 13 weekend when, appropriately, it was beaten by *Friday the 13th Part III*. Theatrical play went way beyond 1982, lasting a full year. The movie finally left screens after its 52nd weekend on June 3, 1983, just outside the top 10 at #11.

Daniel felt, "a particular euphoria ran through the company, but everyone who'd been in that preview was not surprised at the numbers."

Although the fear-soaked haunted house thrills of *Poltergeist* proved profitable for MGM ($74.7M domestic), the unapologetic hopefulness of *E.T.* struck a chord across the whole world. The financials bore this out. Even though George Lucas' original *Star Wars* had been given an 8-week re-release in the summer of '82 that brought its total to $322.8M, Spielberg's tear-jerker would surpass it by ending its 52-week run at $359.19M domestic. *It was the most successful movie ever released in history.*

Says Sammon, "If the analogy is a multi-stage rocket from NASA, *Duel* is the countdown to firing the rockets. *Jaws* is lift off. *Close Encounters* is the first stage separating. *E.T.* is the one that decides this rocket is headed out to blanket the cosmos."

"I saw the movie and quite liked it," relates John Sayles. "I think I remembered in Melissa Mathison's script there was more of the Corsican Brothers thing, where the kid is at school and E.T. gets drunk. They had this connection that it was happening to the kid, and he didn't know what's happening to him. I think they cut some of that out, but her script is pretty close to what they shot. Steven Spielberg did it so well, and the music and everything lifts up what she started."

Says screenwriter Ashley Miller (*Thor*, *X-Men: First Class*), "I go back to *E.T.* all the time. It's his actual masterpiece. It was the movie that demonstrated his complete mastery of filmmaking, showed off everything in the most subtle ways imaginable. The choices he made were advanced things that would never occur to someone else. You don't even notice they're happening. He so clearly yet so emotionally states the theme, the theme of every Spielberg movie: 'Damn it, Elliott, you got to learn that other people have feelings too.' Every scene... every scene is about the fact that other people have feelings. For Spielberg, film is empathy. My favorite cut from any film is when Elliott is saying goodbye and hugs E.T., and anybody else would have stayed on that kid and that alien. Spielberg cuts to Dee Wallace, who falls to her knees and looks at Elliott, who looks at her. It's beautiful. It's perfect."

Adds Dee Wallace, "I think that's very important in the film because it's a completion moment where the audience understands that Mary's heart recognizes the friendship and the importance of that relationship her son has, and the loss of that friendship. For all the parents in the audience, that's an important moment, that bonding. Saying, 'I understand, sweetheart, how important this person is to you. I'm not judging you. I'm not in fear for you. I see you have a friend and I love him also.'"

As Ingmar Bergman once said, "We have an ability to affect each other. We make each other alive. It doesn't make a difference if it hurts."

Vanity Fair's Adam Lance Garcia thinks the E.T. creature being the galvanizing force at the center of the film adds another autobiographical aspect: "Look at Spielberg's life when his parents are divorcing. He uses filmmaking as a way to process and escape his reality. One can argue—and I do not think this is intentional—that E.T. represents the filmmaking Spielberg used to escape the circumstances of his life. He used filmmaking to make friends and learn to adjust through all the places that he lived. Then you look at E.T. and how that helps build out Elliott's friends and family and literally physically escape the circumstances of life. You can almost say that E.T. is a metaphor for Spielberg galvanizing the people around him. One of my favorite stories in *The Fabelmans* but also in his biography was he'd have these bullies make films with him… 'Here we are, we're all in this together to make this one thing… to get this thing home.'"

Screenwriter Andrew Barrer adds, "You can overlay that theory onto the movie. A kid has this fascination with something magical and it slowly loops in the siblings, then the neighborhood kids. Everyone's engaged in this project together that adults don't understand. From what I know about his filmmaking as a kid, it did seem like he was putting together crews, so I think that's a totally valid theory."

"I saw *E.T.* opening weekend, June 11… I was 8-years-old, so that was the sweet spot," laughs Mike Ryan. "By opening weekend everyone had to see it, and yeah, I bawled. It was the saddest. If you asked me at the time, I'd say, 'Well, that's the best movie ever made.' I still like it a lot."

"*E.T.* was the greatest movie ever made if you were a certain age when it came out," adds Phil Nobile. "Without equal. Before that I didn't know a movie could make you cry. I remember being embarrassed that I cried, hesitant to tell anybody. My friends at school were split into, 'Oh man, I was crying so much,' and then, 'I didn't cry. I didn't cry at all.' It was all the wonder of movies about science fiction and space, but with this emotional component we had never seen before. That was the secret sauce of *E.T.*, not special effects or an alien. It was about the emotion."

Because Spielberg once again went with benevolent aliens after *CE3K*, some UFO experiencers believed the filmmaker knew more than he was letting on. Were his movies a form of soft disclosure, paving the way for first contact to the general public?

"This is a true movie, not a romance," speculated an unnamed photo research technician—whose family purportedly experienced an alien encounter while desert camping—to the *L.A. Times* in 1982. "It's part of a conditioning process to prepare us for the arrival of alien beings."

Says Hollywood Disclosure Alliance co-founder Dan Harary, "In '82 Spielberg showed *E.T.* to Ronald Reagan at the White House. Wasn't a huge audience, family and friends, a private showing. At the end of it, Reagan went up to the screen and said from the front of the room, 'There are probably five or six people in this room right now who know that what we just saw on the screen is real.' Spielberg said Reagan was not joking. He wasn't smiling, didn't wink at him. He said it as a statement of fact."

This conspiracy built around Spielberg and perpetuated for years after would later be parodied by the director himself during a short cameo in the movie *Paul*, where the titular alien (Seth Rogen) is feeding the director ideas for the *E.T.* movie.

Explains another Paul, J. Allen Hynek's son Paul Hynek, "I have no evidence to go with that. To me, the Occam's Razor simple explanation is he just got interested in this and wanted to make a movie. I don't see the need to read more into it. It could be true for all I know, but there's nothing I've seen or heard that really lends credence to that."

The theory—similar to all the "faked moon landing" rumors around Stanley Kubrick—starts to fall apart when you take into consideration that a studio spent nearly $1M developing an evil alien movie with Spielberg called *Night Skies* before it evolved into *E.T.* Then there are later Spielberg films such as *War of the Worlds* or *Kingdom of the Crystal Skull* which seem off-message in terms of paving the way for alien acceptance. If this book shows anything, it is Spielberg's ambivalence towards the "true" nature of extraterrestrials, utilizing them from *Firelight* on as a vehicle for whatever artistic mood he happened to be in.

"It doesn't seem to jive," Hynek adds. "Even *Close Encounters*, why have them abduct? Why not have them be nice, happy aliens who are really sweet? And why not portray the government in a really positive light?"

Spielberg was very aware *Night Skies* would have been a sharp shift away from *Close Encounters*' messaging, which may be why it's explained at the end of Sayles' script that Skar and the gang are merely the bad apples who spoil the bunch. Still, it is fascinating to speculate on what would have happened if he stayed on that path, perhaps directing *Reel to Reel* instead of *E.T.* while producing *Night Skies* instead of *Poltergeist*.

As Joe Dante says at the very beginning of this book, "If he'd done a gritty horror movie it wouldn't have been as successful as *E.T.* The industry would not be the same but it wouldn't have been as good."

Says Aaron Sagers of the potential impact on the UFO community, "We're creating these alternate universes here, but I think if he had done *E.T.* and then done *Nights Skies* that would have been considered a betrayal: 'You gave us this cute, cuddly alien then terrified us!' Or maybe *Night Skies* first, and then he had to cleanse the palate with *E.T.* If we had done *Night Skies* after *Close*

Encounters, assuming it had experienced the success of *Close Encounters*, it would have changed the cultural conversation, changed our idea of the alien that's coming to visit us."

John Carpenter told *The Guardian* in 1994, "When you make a movie, you're a prisoner of whatever is around you at the moment you're released. Whatever is happening in the society, whatever is happening in the world, and whatever movies are released."

"Would *Night Skies* have connected?" asks Mick Garris. "In 1982 *The Thing* did not connect but *E.T.* did. I did *The Making of The Thing* documentary and worked publicity on *E.T.* so I was around and saw that stuff."

"It was a grim movie in many ways," Carpenter told Robert Rodriguez of *The Thing* in 2014. "The whole theme of it, loss of identity and the end of the human race... I just dove right into that, you know? 'Let's do that.' That didn't make the audience feel too happy at the time. They wanted something that was an up cry and they got that with *E.T.*, not with my film. I thought, 'This is my best movie.' Part of me still thinks it is."

"Had *E.T.* stayed as *Night Skies* and had *Night Skies* come out... would *The Thing* have done better?" questions Mark Altman, who made a documentary titled *1982: Greatest Geek Year Ever*. "Would people want to see something else, like *Night Skies* had been? There's a famous story where John Carpenter and Adrian Barbeau get off a plane from Hawaii and see that *Rolling Stone* with E.T. on the cover, right before *The Thing* opens, and Carpenter is like, 'Oh, we're dead. We're finished. Nobody wants to see a scary alien that wants to kill us after they've fallen in love with this cute alien.' And he was right. Two weeks later, *The Thing* opens and it bombs along with *Blade Runner* and *Megaforce*."

"You act like there's a grudge match between *E.T.* and *The Thing*, and that's kind of a specious way of looking at movies," says Carpenter's wife and producing partner Sandy King. "These are people that admire each other, and you don't worry about whose film opened bigger. When somebody does a good movie and it's successful, you cheer for cinema, and if it's your movie, you get happier."

Carpenter added, "Steven made the movie that everybody wanted to see. Boy oh boy oh boy did he get it. He knew. He knew it and it was amazing!"

Remembers Dana Gould, "I graduated high school in that classic summer of 1982 and I was an usher at a cinema and at a drive-in, same company. I saw everything 40 times. I saw *E.T.* like everybody else and thought it was amazing like everybody else, but—as I get older and look back on all of these movies—it's one of my least favorite films of that summer. I'm a dark person, so my favorite movies that summer were *Blade Runner* and *The Thing*, both released on the same day. They both bombed, critics and audiences hated them, but today they are both a lot more timeless than *E.T.* I think *E.T.* is very much of its time in a way those films aren't."

"Anytime anybody says anything nice about a movie that I've made is wonderful, okay?" Carpenter said in response to the notion his movie aged better than others. "Anytime anybody says something bad, it's not good. Obviously, I'm very proud of *The Thing*. I'm happy I made it and God bless it."

Recalls Henry Thomas, "It shows in the fact that Universal released *The Thing* and *E.T.* at the same time: 'If they want the bad alien, they've got the bad alien... if they want the good alien, there's a good alien.' Always hedging their bets. I think *E.T.* was kind of a favor film to Spielberg that Universal was doing, because it was a movie he was making with his friends, right? *Poltergeist* was the horse they all had their money on to be the big blockbuster hit. *E.T.* was 'his little sentimental alien movie, his kids movie.'"

Poltergeist screenwriter Mark Victor agrees with that assessment, stating, 'Our film was far more tangible and genre-oriented. We were the first suburban ghost story, instead of haunted houses with lightning in the dark. Doing a movie that's designed to scare... that's a more proven audience than an alien lost in the suburbs. Unfortunate for us, because *E.T.* was in the box office records. *Poltergeist* did great, and I believe it would have done a lot more if it had its own non-Spielberg competition. Anybody would be happy with the results, but it certainly missed a larger opportunity."

Says David Cellitti, who was part of the second of three makeup FX teams hired by Rob Bottin for Carpenter's horror movie, "The word was out when I was working on *The Thing* that it was going to be a blockbuster and *E.T.* was going to be Spielberg's Waterloo. Of course, the complete opposite happened."

Adds Sandy King of the Carpenter oeuvre, "For a long time, every time we made a movie they'd say, 'What happened to the genius that made the last movie?' David Ansen said *The Thing* was pornography of violence then turned around and rewrote his review when *The Thing* got declared a masterpiece. You can't take it to heart."

Explains Gould, "I'm much more fascinated with *Night Skies* than I am with *E.T.* Maybe I'm just the wrong person because I have a more plangent view of the world. I will watch *The Thing* over *E.T.* any day, even though everybody—

myself included—cried leaving *E.T.* Nobody wanted *The Thing* or *Blade Runner*. *E.T.* was hopeful, sweet. *Rocky III* was 'scary black people lose.' It was Reagan's America."

Even though *E.T.* was a perfect swing towards a right-leaning USA, that does not mean Spielberg himself was a conservative the same way his friend John Milius was. In fact, the character of E.T. itself is a kind of progressive beacon: Hippie-ish, gentle, in love with nature, and deliberately without clear male/female identification.

"I think that's where he's so far ahead of all of us," Laurent Bouzereau told *USA Today*. "Yes, E.T. can be a boy for a young boy, can be neutral for someone else, can be a girl for a girl, and it doesn't change anything. That is the power of Steven Spielberg."

Says Altman, "Spielberg has given a lot of money to Democrats over the years. He's very political, but he's smuggling these messages in crowd-pleasing films that appear Reagan-friendly. If you look closer, there's a lot more to them. Spielberg actually believes in the Statue of Liberty. 'Give me your tired, your poor, your huddled masses yearning to breathe free.' That's something in America we believed in... even in the '80s. The demonizing of immigrants and xenophobia common to our culture now didn't really exist in the '80s. *E.T.* is the ultimate immigrant story. He's the one who can heal people. He has all these magical abilities, can make things fly... he's special. If you look below the ugly veneer, 'Oh my god, this guy is a gift, he brings something, he's healed the family unit that's been damaged by this divorce.' He's the catalyst for change. Spielberg was aware of where the country was going with the rah-rah patriotism, but at the same time he was making sure what he believed in was represented in the movies he made."

To an even greater effect than *Close Encounters, E.T.* functioned as a cinematic revival tent, dazzling audiences who craved hope and meaning. One such individual was The Beach Boys musician Brian Wilson. The "Good Vibrations" rock star had nearly died of an alcohol and drug overdose, weighing in at over 340 pounds. In 1982 he began undergoing radical rehabilitation under unethical psychologist Eugene Landy, who isolated Wilson in Hawaii to dry out via a strict diet and exercise regimen. In an autobiography titled *Wouldn't It Be Nice: My Own Story*, the singer recounts an anecdote in which the therapist took him on a March '83 movie outing in Kona...

"Like the millions of people who saw *E.T.,* I was sucked into the story within a few minutes," recalled Wilson. "By the time I glimpsed the lovable alien,

I felt a certain kinship with him. He and I were both outsiders: we had trouble communicating, being understood. I tensed after realizing he'd been left behind, applauded when the kids adopted him. I nearly jumped out of my seat in the scene where the kids hide E.T. in their bedroom closet, a place I would've hid. As their mother, searching for whatever it was her kids were hiding, begins her snooping, I clutched the armrest and leaned forward. As she went toward the closet, I put my hand over my eyes. Finally, when she opens the closet door and looks inside, the scene where the audience sees E.T.'s head among all the stuffed animals, I bolted up from my seat and yelled, 'Watch out, E.T.!'"

Another famous singer/songwriter profoundly affected by *E.T.* was Neil Diamond, who caught an early screening of the film then co-penned the tribute song "Heartlight" with Carole Bayer Sager and Burt Bacharach, off his 1982 album of the same name. The song reached #5 on *Billboard*'s Hot 100 (his last top 10 hit), but the lyrics were a little too close to Spielberg's film, leading to a $25,000 dollar settlement with MCA/Universal...

"Turn on your heartlight
In the middle of a young boy's dream
Don't wake me up too soon
Gonna take a ride across the moon"

"I was thrilled," says heartlight effect creator Robert Short. "All of a sudden it came on the radio. 'What the... What do you mean Neil Diamond's latest release? Are you kidding me? Why would...' I guess it's immortalized. It's amazing, like, 'I don't know where I go from here, but hey...' Now they do Neil Diamond retrospectives and 'Heartlight' always shows up. Who would have thunk? Right around that time, we were on the cover of *Rolling Stone*, you couldn't turn around without E.T. being somewhere, so it all kind of fit. One more notch in the history of *E.T.*"

Jokes Dana Gould, "The weirdest thing about *E.T.* was Neil Diamond's song 'Heartlight.' Neil Diamond saw the movie and wanted to write a song about it. I used to do a bit in my stand up about that, like, 'Has this ever happened before? After the movie comes out...'

[*singing like Neil Diamond*]
'It's a boat called the Poseidon, but it's upside down now.
We gotta go to the top but that's the bottom
because the boat is upside down.'

'I'll ask you to do me a favor,
and you can't refuse
because I'm the Godfather.'

'Anyone who says that a shark can't jump onto a boat
has never met me.
That's why my name is Jaws.'"

Diamond was only the tip of the iceberg when it came to tributes. Says superfan Wesley Boutilier, moderator of Facebook's Official E.T. Fan Club (16K members), "There's all sorts of cool random *E.T.*-specific songs from back in the day, especially in the '80s, from all over the world. There's an Alvin and the Chipmunks song about *E.T.*, a song in Spanish called 'Dónde Estás ETE.' It goes pretty deep, the amount of *E.T.* fever people had."

Before *Jaws* was released it only had one merchandising license, but two weeks after it had 55 such deals. By April of 1982 *E.T.* already had 11 licensing deals firmed up by MCA VP Steve Adler, based mostly on the track record of the filmmaker. These were done with great secrecy, and in some cases vendors did not receive art of the title character's likeness until close to release.

Wrote *Variety*, "The public will be confronted with E.T. bicycles, E.T. pajamas, E.T. candy, and E.T. electronic toys aside from the slew of posters, ac-

tion figures, bubble gum, and iron-on transfers." There were cross-promotions with in-movie product placement, including Hershey's Reese's Pieces and Electronic Instruments' Speak & Spell, as well as a storybook from Putnam and novelization from Berkeley. Spielberg had personal approval over every item pitched.

"The promotional potential is most important," said Universal's marketing and distribution president Bob Rehme. "You have to remember, every time there is a piece of merchandise, a store display, there is free advertising for the film."

By August of that year, after the movie became the fastest to cross $100M (Spielberg earning $500,000 a day with his profit share), UPI reported "43 manufacturing firms have been licensed to produce *E.T.* items ranging from rubber facsimiles of the bug-eyed space creature to underwear, from heart-warming posters to shoelaces, from lunch boxes to story books... Other products include night lights, brush and comb sets, clocks and watches, bedding, T-shirts, footwear, tableware and greeting cards." Sales on Reese's Pieces rose 45%, and most new items were being readied for retail by late '82 to meet Christmas demand.

There was also the official *E.T. The Extra-Terrestrial* Fan Club, which *Starlog* assistant publisher Ira Friedman ran for Amblin' Productions and Universal Studios. By September 1982 more than 10,000 letters and drawings arrived for the friendly alien at Friedman's New York headquarters, including 10-year-old Allison Silverman from Florida, who declared June 23 "Steven Spielberg Day," adding, "P.S. I'll give you $150 to be in one of your movies." In exchange for the adoration, fans were provided with photos, a newsletter called *E.T.'s Communicator*, and a vinyl record featuring various sound clips.

In 2012 for MTV, this author interviewed Nick Gjoka, described as the biggest *E.T.* fan in the world during its 30th anniversary. A working set decorator, Gjoka's claim to fame was having more memorabilia from the 1982 movie than anyone on Earth. He owned 50 copies of the film on VHS and the rare E.T. Big Wheel bike for kids. He claimed to have "everything" with the alien, including "original sketches of the spaceship. I have a piece of E.T.'s actual foot that they used to make Halloween costumes. A couple props. I'm really into displays and costumes and storyboards." Universal paraded him around to promote a new Blu-ray release in 2012, just as his wife was pregnant.

Gjoka said, "We were watching it the other day. As soon as Elliott and E.T. took off on the bikes, he started kicking. I'm not just making that up for the interview! He sorta watched it already. One year old, six months old, he's gonna watch it as early as possible."

Fourteen years later, this author reconnected with Gjoka, who by now had two children. When asked what happened when he finally showed his kids *E.T.*, he said, "I don't even remember. I can't remember. I feel like my son had questions, like, 'What's happening here?' He was scared."

Gjoka has since sold off most of his collection, except for six boxes and the talking E.T. toy he got from his grandfather at age 4, "one of the reasons I have such a strong connection with the movie."

"Around our interview we had just moved into our first house," he said in 2026. "I moved the rest of the collection down from New York to Atlanta and thought, 'What the hell am I doing?' Just keeping it in storage... it couldn't be done. I was like, 'I should be selling this to make memories with this money, or it will continue collecting dust.' At flea markets I started selling E.T. stuff. People were paying $10 bucks for a figure, and I can't even sell those for $1 on eBay. It worked out."

By 1998 *E.T.* had generated over $1B in merchandising sales alone, and while an *E.T.* gift shop still graces the exit of the movie's ride at Universal Orlando, the market is no longer saturated with product.

Says Wesley Boutilier, "By the time you get to the 20th anniversary, it's like there was no presence. In my lifetime everybody calls it a classic, but I keep going back to Snoopy and Charlie Brown or Bugs Bunny or Mickey Mouse... stuff that you're gonna see in any store, on any shelf, on any given day. It's not that *E.T.* didn't have a cultural impact, because it did. It had a huge one, but it's interesting that it was such a massive hit with stuff everywhere. I still get shocked by the amount of merchandise I'll find online, like, 'This existed too?' But you don't really see *E.T.* stuff everywhere anymore."

"It's still an icon," says fellow superfan Peter de Mooij. "There are still young people who become fans. That said, in this modern age the film might be a little too slow for the youngsters. I'm sure if they take the time to watch it, they can feel the same as I did so many moons ago."

Spielberg had briefly dated *One Day at a Time* star Valerie Bertinelli in early 1980, and (according to her autobiography *Losing It*) when he ran into her at the Universal commissary in 1982 she blurted out, "'Boy, congratulations on *E.T.* You must be really rich now!' It was one of the few times I remember Steven being speechless."

Think about that, though. Put aside all the corridors of money and power *E.T.* opened up for Spielberg and think about the road that got him there. How nerve-wracking it must have been to take a project like *Night Skies* with nearly a million already sunk, that everyone around him seemed sure would be a hit, and completely catastrophically rethink it based on what his gut was telling him. For someone as empathetic to artists as Spielberg is, imagine how difficult it was to cut his collaborators loose while experiencing two studios' lack of enthusiasm expressed through outright rejection or a lack of major funding. Even when *Raiders* made him a hitmaker again, he navigated the production of *E.T.* with a lot of doubt about the way it could be received or even if he would pull it off with a fairly green cast and crew. Going into a crowded summer where initial interest in the movie was near the bottom of the pack. For an odd blend of broad genre appeal and deeply personal storytelling, the fact that *E.T.* was embraced at all was remarkable, but the chord it struck with the world was a miracle. Truly.

"Extraterrestrial, running over pedestrians in a spaceship while they're screaming at me, 'Let's just be friends.'"

—Eminem

Here you can see a fan art painting by Samanthuel Louise Gillson of E.T. being pelted by pinecones. She explains it thusly...

"I was thinking about this lineage of horrible withered-looking freaks in cinema that the filmmakers expect you to find endearing... your E.T.'s, your Yoda's, your Dobby's, etc. This resulted in a really vivid mental image of this painting I needed to create because it made me laugh. There's a fierce, inhuman quality to the people assaulting E.T. here, as if witnessing such an otherworldly creature has reduced them to something primordial because they refuse to accept or understand him, becoming more distorted as the small crowd trails into the distance. I went into this feeling cynicism towards E.T. as a character, but afterwards felt an incredible amount of pity for him."

In 1982 Spielberg had an avalanche of success with *E.T.*, *Poltergeist*, and the afterglow of *Raiders of the Lost Ark*. Even though he was feted by politicians and CEOs, there was an undercurrent of nastiness he had to navigate amid the cute alien's rise to cultural prominence. E.T.'s neck stretched just high enough for tall poppy syndrome.

Still lingering was the resentment of shunned *Night Skies* makeup FX artist Rick Baker, who the press portrayed as cruelly cast out of paradise. When hired by Spielberg in 1980 he was still an up-and-comer, but by March of '82 Baker was the inaugural Oscar-winner for Best Makeup on the groundbreaking *An American Werewolf in London*, the first year makeup was honored by the Academy as a main category.

Accepting the award from presenters Vincent Price and Kim Hunter, Baker thanked filmmakers John Landis and George Folsey, stars David Naughton and Griffin Dunne, and his EFX crew of Doug Beswick, Tom Hester, Steve Johnson, Shawn McEnroe, Bill Sturgeon, Kevin Brennan, and Elaine Baker. He added, "I'd like to thank my parents Doris and Ralph Baker for their love and support, and last but not least I'd like to thank a man who's been a real inspiration to me, Dick Smith, for all that Dick has contributed to the art of makeup. He deserves an Academy Award more than any makeup artist I know."

Fred Clarke's popular fan magazine *Cinefantastique* (a.k.a. *CFQ*) billed itself as "the magazine with a Sense of Wonder." During its run as a glossy quarterly publication from 1970 until Clarke's stewardship ended with his death in 2000, *CFQ* could also have been dubbed "the magazine that's a thorn in Hollywood's side." Clarke's network of insiders providing him with dirt and spoilers on genre fare pre-dated the internet reign of Harry Knowles, rankling filmmakers like George Lucas, Joe Dante, and Steven Spielberg. The latter, who once praised the magazine for their "super job" covering *Close Encounters*, could not have been pleased by a pair of neg-slanted '81 and '82 articles chronicling Baker's experience on the aborted *Night Skies*.

In the 1982 piece, Baker refers to the following *Time* magazine profile of Rambaldi: "The E.T. who appears on the screen is a highly evolved creature. One special effects crew tried to make the spaceman and failed, spending a reported $700,000 in the process. Then Spielberg turned to Carlo Rambaldi, an Italian painter and sculptor."

Baker called the remark "upsetting" after devoting long nights and weekends to the project. He told *CFQ*, "I did some of the best work I've ever done on that picture. The thanks I got was saying I wasn't competent... there are an amazing number of things taken from my design. Some of the mechanics are exactly in the same place, and I can point to wrinkles in exactly the same place... If Spielberg and Rambaldi are claiming the thing I did was no good, why don't they okay me to publish pictures of it?"

"Those puppets are goddamn gorgeous," says Steven Awalt, "I've talked to Rick about it, and he told me it is—out of such an amazing, storied career—still the most painful thing that ever happened."

"I came back from doing *Greystoke* in England and saw *The Thing* and *E.T.*," Baker explained to this author. "When I saw *E.T.* I just wanted to cry because it was such a great movie... and that could have been mine! But yeah, it was heartbreaking. First, I get this message on my phone machine from Kathy Kennedy saying, 'Steven is over the moon' and 'It made Yoda look like a toy' and blah blah blah blah blah. I went from that to a guy who didn't care about the budget and whose work was no good. That was really hard to take. Definitely one of the dark days of my life."

According to a 1986 piece in the *Los Angeles Times*, producer Kathleen Kennedy had to go into damage control mode, framing the flare-up between Baker and his then-boss as "personal and economic differences." Clarke allowed Kennedy to tone down the piece, but claimed she tried pivoting him toward a story on *E.T.* instead.

According to Paul Sammon, who wrote for Clarke until a falling out in 1984, "The film business resembles every other kind of business: It does not thrive on controversy. Business does not thrive on disruption. Business wants everything running smoothly and calmly and under control. It doesn't want eruptions of personalities and battles about credit and backstabbing going public... it's bad for business. Fred Clarke always cast himself in the role of the little David out there in Oak Park, Illinois fighting the big ugly Goliath of Hollywood. Coming from an ethical standpoint, he would say, 'Look, the truth is... and all the rest of this is Hollywood obfuscation and crisis control.' Fred's agenda was to find out what was really going on. Fred loved scandal, but he had this absolutely pure devotion to the genres and thought they were worthy of intelligent discourse/examination. It wasn't just dirty linen, it was more about the process. It was about, 'How did this work of art actually come into being?'"

Ever the gentleman, '82 Baker conceded it was the right call to overhaul the project, saying, "I would have loved *Night Skies* and so would people who like science fiction and horror, but I doubt if it would appeal to as many people as *E.T.*"

Another controversy: Two plagiarism disputes arose around *E.T.*, the first brought by playwright Lisa Litchfield who filed a $750 million dollar lawsuit against Spielberg, Mathison, and Universal. She claimed her one-act play produced in 1978 titled *Lokey from Maldemar* had been mined by the studio, for whom it was proven she had pitched the project. This is the plot of the play, as stated by *UPI* in 1984: "The story of two aliens, Fudinkle and Lokey, who are stranded on earth near the North Pole. They meet Lisa Marie, her younger brother and father, a scientist at the North Pole."

Litchfield ultimately lost a bid for a summary judgment by the United States District Court in May of 1983, then in July of 1984 a three-judge panel of the 9th Circuit Court of Appeals sided with Spielberg and Universal in the case, stating the play and film were not "substantially similar" and that "Any similarities in plot exist only at the general level for which (Ms. Litchfield) cannot claim copyright protection."

"It is amazing to see the amount of material that gets dumped on the man every day," one Spielberg associate told *Fangoria* #24. "It's put into mail sacks, unopened, and sent to the Writer's Guild. It's something the man has to do to protect himself, because every time a film makes over $100M, these people come out of the woodwork."

While Lisa Litchfield was an unknown, another claim was more unfortunate because it came from respected Bengali filmmaker Satyajit Ray, whose 1955 *Pather Panchali* (the first of his Apu Trilogy) made him a world cinema leader held in the same esteem as Kurosawa, Fellini, or Bergman. He claimed key elements of Spielberg's 1982 film resembled his 1967 screenplay *The Alien*, to have been produced by Columbia Pictures in 1968 with Marlon Brando and Peter Sellers starring.

Ray's script follows an extraterrestrial spaceship landing in rural Bengal, which is subsequently worshipped by locals. A creature nicknamed "Mr. Ang" emerges to cause mischief while forming a relationship with a young boy named Haba ("dumb") through mental communication. Similarities to E.T.'s powers include making flowers grow and healing wounds. Both are introduced with an image of their fingers moving out of frame.

A major science fiction fan intrigued by the possibilities of '80s VFX, Ray announced to Ela Dutta in 1981 his thoughts of reviving *The Alien* (possibly under a new title, "Avatar") with an American lawyer in San Francisco named Leonard Tillem, who said "this was psychologically the right time to do it."

Ray was quoted in a February 15, 1983 *India Today* saying the aliens in both *Close Encounters* and *E.T.* would not have been possible without circulated copies of his script containing drawings. The sketches bear a minor resemblance to Puck, but Puck was a generic composite of numerous experiencer reports. He claimed his friend Arthur C. Clarke phoned him, "saying I should file a copyright case." Clarke later wrote Ray clarifying he did not encourage a suit, rather simply writing Spielberg "a polite letter."

This led graduate student Aseem Chhabra, calling from his dorm, to speak to Clarke and the Indian filmmaker for the Columbia News Service. Ray said he conferred with his lawyers but there was "nothing one could do about it," emphasizing he was not "vindictive" and that Spielberg was "a good director."

The *L.A. Times* circulated this in March '83, a week later reporting this: "Chhabra's story surfaced in the middle of final balloting for the Academy of Motion Picture Arts and Sciences annual awards presentation. Given that Universal's *E.T.* and Columbia's *Gandhi* are top competitors, allegations were immediately flung from the upper echelons of Universal that, somehow, Columbia Pictures was behind the story. Columbia officials, on the other hand, said they knew nothing of the story."

Martin Scorsese told *Times of India*'s Ranjan Das Gupta in 2010, "I have no qualms in admitting that Spielberg's *E.T.* was influenced by Ray's *Alien*. Even Sir Richard Attenborough pointed this out to me."

Alien visitors were very much in the zeitgeist from the post-war period on. Even *5-25-77* filmmaker Patrick Read Johnson claimed to this author that he coincidentally had a similar (albeit sillier) concept when he was a teenager: "While I was in high school, I was writing something called *The Visitor* about this high school-age alien. It's *E.T.,* but the alien is of age and a little more humanoid, and gets hidden by these high school students, made up by a kid who knew prosthetics into something vaguely human. He's brought to school, rejected, turned into the weirdest kid of all. Meanwhile, the government's searching where it crash-landed... it was *E.T.* beat for beat for beat. I didn't know anything about *E.T.*, this was back in 1977 or '78, right?"

Spielberg never indicated the tempest in a teapot over *The Alien* tipped the Oscar scales against *E.T.*, and even visited Arthur C. Clarke in Sri Lanka with Harrison Ford while filming *Temple of Doom*. When the *non*troversy was reperpetuated by *The Times* in '84, Clarke wrote the editors: "Encounters between children and friendly E.T.'s are an old concept in science fiction; notable examples are Theodore Sturgeon's *Mewhu's Jet* (1946) and Robert Heinlein's novel *Star Beast* (1954)." Scorsese and Spielberg were instrumental in getting the Academy to recognize Ray with an honorary Oscar in '92.

Twilight Zone: The Movie (1983).

"He's kind of in the Twilight Zone. His Twilight Zone is our Twilight Zone, it's America's Twilight Zone."

—**Francis Coppola**, *Hearts of Darkness*

The biggest seismic catastrophe for Spielberg occurred on July 23, 1982, a mere month and change after *E.T.'s* release...

Time Warner CEO Steve Ross (along with new WB head Terry Semel) was attempting to woo Spielberg to his studio to make movies. MCA had already secured the services of the director's girlfriend/Warner music producer Kathleen Carey while beginning construction on the lavish Amblin Entertainment offices on the Universal backlot. Ross worked hard to cultivate a relationship with the director, including wildly overpaying on behalf of Time Warner's Atari with $23M for the rights to an *E.T.* video game cartridge. The catch? Spielberg wanted it out by Christmas. The result was a botched/rushed game no one wanted, with unsold cartridges occupying a New Mexico landfill, as depicted in Zak Penn's documentary *Atari: Game Over*. It was another black mark for Spielberg to button the year, albeit a lucrative one.

Then there was *Twilight Zone: The Movie*.

Before his death in 1975 at the age of 50, Rod Serling was haplessly shopping a movie version of *The Twilight Zone* inspired by British anthology *Dead of Night*. It would have contained a trilogy of stories hosted by Serling, shot in black and white, costing less than a million dollars. According to widow Carol Serling in a 1983 issue of *Twilight Zone* magazine, stories developed for the proposed film included "Eyes," the segment eventually made by Spielberg for *Night Gallery*. Another titled "The Theatre" was produced in 1994 for TV movie *Twilight Zone: Rod Serling's Lost Classics* starring Amy Irving, Spielberg's ex-wife.

Carol Serling wrote, "At some later date, Rod sent out another memo along with a story about an alien who lands on earth and is hounded and hunted by adults and befriended by a child. (Sound familiar, E.T.?)"

A deal was struck at Warner Bros. for Spielberg and his friend John Landis to develop *Twilight Zone*, serving as producers while each directed segments in the $10M picture, with roughly $2.5M to $3M set aside per story. Buzz was initially sky high, the idea being a new *TZ* anthology could be made annually at the studio. The runway for the picture was laid in *E.T.* when one of the kids hums the TV show's "doo-doo-DOO-doo" theme song, which Gene Siskel said, "Always brings a laugh from the audience."

Landis' segment, titled "Time Out," focused on a bigot named Bill upset at being passed over for promotion in favor of a Jewish co-worker. During a drunken rant to his friends Ray and Larry at a bar, he raves about Jews, blacks, and Asians. Upon leaving the bar he goes on a harrowing odyssey through history, put in the place of a Jew in Nazi-occupied France, a black man in Jim Crow era American south, and a Viet Cong during the Vietnam War. It ends with Bill being thrown onboard a train with other Jewish prisoners headed to a concentration camp.

Tasked by the studio to redeem Bill, Landis crafted a new arc where the main character encounters two Vietnamese children whose village is being strafed by a US helicopter. In a script draft dated July 22 of '82, he tells the children, "I'll keep you safe kids, I promise. Nothing will hurt you. I swear to God." The little girl hands him a naked Barbie doll. He grabs both kids, heroically carrying them across a river as explosions decimate the village, the helicopter's door-mounted gun firing on them. He gets them safely to a shed, which turns into a shed in the south as the KKK head toward him. When he is snatched, the Klansmen turn into Nazis putting him onboard the concentration camp train. As it pulls away, he sees the bar he originally exited from. We see Bill before the time odyssey get hit by a car as his friends Ray and Larry look on. Ray cradles his head, trying to help. Bill looks down at the broken Barbie in his hand.

Besides *E.T.*'s Peter Coyote and country singer Glen Campbell, one actor seriously considered for the role of Bill was Ronny Cox of *Deliverance* fame. In 2019, Cox detailed on his blog a meeting with Landis where he said, "Ronny, you're the person I want for this... The role is yours... It's a done deal." The next day the actor got a call from Landis: "Ronny, I'm so embarrassed. I know that I said the role was yours, but over the weekend Steven Spielberg met with Vic Morrow and offered him the role and Vic had accepted it."

Spielberg confirmed (via *Starlog* #17) his first post-*Firelight* writing escapades were spec scripts for Morrow-led '60s TV show *Combat!* By 1982, *Twilight Zone* was just the break Morrow needed after years of appearing mainly in exploitation pictures.

Cut to the final night of production. After shooting two previous scenes with a Bell UH-1B helicopter, it came time for shots of Morrow's character rescuing the two kids on July 23, 1982 at 2:20am. Everything went wrong. As the helicopter's searchlights hovered over Morrow, the scent of gasoline in the air, the actor grabbed the two children, Renee Shin-Yi Chen (age 6) and Myca Dinh Le (age 7), then proceeded to lurch across a shallow section of the Santa Clara River as underwater squibs went off around them. Massive explosions of 11 huts in the village settings behind them (including shrapnel from a 5-gallon pot of glue with a steel lid haphazardly left near the incendiaries) apparently damaged the tail rotor mechanism of the low-flying copter, which spun out of control and crashed into the river. Morrow and the two children were killed.

Further details of the three on-set deaths at the Indian Dunes film ranch in Valencia, as well as the injuries sustained by all aboard the helicopter and the witness' trauma, are better left to others. Spielberg went on record to the National Transportation Safety Board that he was not on set during the night of the incident.

In a strange, little-discussed parallel, writer/director James Glickenhaus filmed a Vietnam prologue to his 1980 movie *The Exterminator* in the exact same Indian Dunes location as the ill-fated *TZ* production, but no mishaps were recorded. When watched back-to-back with *TZ* crash footage, it is hard to tell the scenes apart.

Still close friends with John Landis, Mick Garris said the lost friendship between Spielberg and Landis in the wake of the tragedy effected both men "a lot, and in very terrible ways. I went to the trial a couple of times and it was painful to see John going through what he went through. Obviously, the people who suffered the most were the parents of the children. It definitely ended the very close friendship between John and Steven, quite abruptly. I understand it and never wanted to be in the center of that. Fortunately, I was not caught in the crossfire."

Warner Bros. knew they had a hot potato with *Twilight Zone: The Movie*. They also had Spielberg signed to deliver his first film since the runaway success of *E.T.*

"Steven was required to direct an episode," says Mike Finnell, who produced Joe Dante's *TZ* segment. "It was one of the very few things I can say he phoned in because he really didn't want to have anything to do with the movie at that point, but he had to do his episode. That was a horrible event. Actually, Joe and I were going to go to the set that night, and then it was too late, too this or that... thank God we didn't go. Then the aftermath was like, 'Oh my God, how do we proceed?' We did, but it cast a pall over the whole movie."

Twilight Zone: The Movie was originally earmarked as a new opportunity for Spielberg to delve into his dark side. He hired *TZ* vet Richard Matheson to script an idea of his, which the writer described in an October '83 *Twilight Zone* magazine: "A Halloween story about a not-nice young man who went out and tormented these kids while they were trick-or-treating. Then all the things that were make-believe began to become real and turn against him as a sort of cosmic punishment. It ended up like a painting by Hieronymus Bosch. I don't know whether they didn't like it or what; I think it was a very good script. One thing they did say is that it would cost too much money."

The episode would have required not only the construction of a full neighborhood block, but, as Spielberg told *Starlog* #62, "We have all these monsters we have to build." Former Rick Baker associate Craig Reardon was earmarked to create the creatures for this segment, but it was ultimately cancelled.

Reardon elaborated more fully in the pages of *Starlog*, saying the Matheson script followed a neighborhood bully in a Hunchback of Notre Dame costume. Like the anarchic deleted Halloween scene in *E.T.*, this kid "runs amok across the streets… egging houses, leaving burning bags of dog manure on the front porch, stealing bags from other kids, and single-handedly ruining the holiday." Suddenly a supernatural comeuppance begins brewing, with mailboxes lurching at him, or a little girl in a witch costume becoming a large witch out to get him. The streets become hellishly overrun with werewolves, Frankensteins, and vampires chasing the bully. The doorknob of his own house tries to bite him. Once "safe" in his house he looks in the mirror and sees his Quasimodo makeup has become real, that he is now a "monster." Disoriented and scared, the bully limps out of his house where the horde of monsters catch sight of him, chasing him across an empty lot as the camera tilts up to the October moon.

While Reardon suggested the story taking place at night with children was nixed post-accident, other evidence points to it being scrubbed prior due to budgetary reasons. As Matheson explains more plainly in *Fangoria* #31, "They told me it was too expensive to shoot. If this film makes a lot of money, maybe they'll use it in the next one."

After courting this darker *Twilight Zone* story, Spielberg settled on a banal retread of upbeat 1962 episode "Kick the Can," with George Clayton Johnson's original teleplay revised by Richard Matheson and Melissa Mathison (the latter credited as "Josh Rogan"). It is speculated that Spielberg switched gears to something cheerier after the tragedy, but according to an interview for *Twilight Zone* magazine conducted by Paul Sammon a few days before the accident, Landis mentioned Spielberg's segment would be "Kick the Can." Sammon said this was not changed after-the-fact by the publication.

"That's legitimate, exactly what was said" he confirmed. "Spielberg just did this sweet little story *E.T.* and he wanted to do another. Children again, all that stuff. It's the weakest segment in the film."

However, Reardon doubled down to this author that Spielberg's monster-laden segment was dashed due to the tragedy: "After John Landis involved me on that movie to come up with something to scare the audience in his curtain raiser, I thought I was done. I got called in again and saw Spielberg this time, who described a Richard Matheson original written just for this movie, and gave me the script. It was chock full of things that required practical effects, makeups, costumes, etc. Would've been a field day, but then the terrible early day happened and due to the involvement of small children in the Matheson script it was never used."

In a special for Japanese TV which aired in December '82, Spielberg is seen on stage 26 at Warner Bros. directing Scatman Crothers as the magical man who turns members of an old folks residence young again in "Kick the Can." The *E.T.* filmmaker is distracted by visitors brought in to keep morale up, including Richard Dreyfuss and Burt Reynolds. Talking to Crothers and Reynolds, the director says to the latter, "I told Scat he's the black E.T. This is the black E.T." "Cause he's getting shorter every year," jokes Reynolds.

"Kick the Can" shot over a TV-like 7-day schedule beginning shortly after Thanksgiving. Dante's portion had lensed in September of that year, followed by Miller's. Many in the industry had earlier speculated the film would be shut down. At very least it was thought the Landis piece would be excluded, but the filmmakers simply jettisoned everything with Morrow and the children/the redemption arc.

"The reason Warner Bros. went ahead with *Twilight Zone* after the accident, which was an iffy move, was they wanted us," explains Dante. "They wanted a Spielberg movie. He had an office on their lot and they wanted him to keep it, but he was making a deal at Universal to move Amblin. Warners got movies out of him, but Universal got the office."

When it opened on June 24, 1983 to modest business, critics felt the new kids on the block (Miller and Dante) outshone more established hitmakers Landis and Spielberg, exemplified by Roger Ebert's headline, "Super-directors' efforts topped in *Twilight Zone*."

The "It's a Good Life" segment in particular, centering on a creepy little boy who can get anything he wishes for, is pure concentrated Joe Dante. His surreal stylishness is enhanced by incredible cartoonish creatures created by Rob Bottin around the same time the over-extended makeup genius was finishing John Carpenter's *The Thing*.

"On *Twilight Zone* nobody was supervising it," explains Dante. "Once it became a hot potato, the studio kept their mitts off it completely, which gave George

Miller and I an erroneous idea of what it was like to work for a movie studio. George was doing this huge airplane thing and I was doing this bizarre cartoon story with forced perspective sets and all sorts of weird stuff. Nobody said, 'Don't do that' or 'This is costing too much.' We thought, 'This is great. They hire you. They give you money, great people to work with, and they leave you alone. No wonder people want to make movies.' Then we both made another picture for the studio under normal circumstances and discovered that wasn't exactly the way."

"Nightmare at 20,000 Feet," in which Miller traded the open expanses of the Australian outback in *The Road Warrior* for the confinement of an airplane fuselage (where a manic John Lithgow sees a gremlin on the wing), is a tour de force. In honor of *Das Boot*, the crew wore shirts reading "Das Plane." According to Dante, the segment was originally reconceived from the classic William Shatner TV episode to be only 10 minutes long before Matheson said, "This is ridiculous. You can't tell this story in 10 minutes. You've got to have it as long as the other episodes."

As Miller told Anne Billson in 1985, "Spielberg's very generous in that he said 'take this story, it's a good one.' It's his favorite of the old *Twilight Zone* stories... I ended up with the best story."

Craig Reardon created the evil gremlin for this segment, stating it "had been conceptualized between illustrator Ed Verreaux, production designer James Bissell, and George Miller. I had three weeks at most to build this thing, a fraught experience. Shooting was hard as the costume was beaten with thousands of gallons of water from firehoses. Almost destroyed the paint work. George was a great guy, though, and would drop by my house where I was working to provide encouragement."

Miller and his production partner Byron Kennedy were deluged with Hollywood offers after the global success of *The Road Warrior* and critical praise for the *Twilight Zone* piece, but favored working in their native Australia. "We have bought a studio and want to run our own company in Sydney," Kennedy said. Less than one month after *Twilight Zone* opened, Kennedy was killed in a freak helicopter accident, crashing into Lake Burragorang just south of Sydney.

There is speculation that George Miller abandoned the film in post-production, with Dante filling in by overseeing final editing. Dante puts this idea to rest, saying, "No, I didn't supervise post. George had to leave before the end of the movie was shot, with Lithgow going away in the ambulance. I shot that with Frank Marshall because George had long since departed." The decision to position Miller's segment as the finale was apparently made after Spielberg's piece was shot, the last on the schedule.

"This has been the most interesting year of my film career," Spielberg told *L.A. Times'* Dale Pollock. "It has mixed the best, the success of *E.T.*, with the worst, the *Twilight Zone* tragedy. A mixture of tragedy and grief. It has made me grow up a little bit more. The accident cast a pall on all 150 people who worked on this production. We are still just sick to the center of our souls."

Many New Hollywood filmmakers were blindsided with a reality check as the '70s turned over into the '80s. Scorsese burned the midnight oil too hard on *New York, New York* as Friedkin flamed out on *Sorcerer*. Cimino bet the studio farm and lost on *Heaven's Gate*, while Coppola bet his own farm and lost on *One from the Heart*. If *1941* was a light critical and box office spanking for Spielberg, *Twilight Zone: The Movie* was a tipping point that, as he says, forced him into a different frame of mind moving forward. It did not negate the success of *E.T.*, but it tempered any sense that the party would never stop. From *Night Gallery* to *Twilight Zone*, the auspicious early era of Spielberg's career was over, bookended with terrible symmetry by the spirit of Rod Serling.

At first it seemed a foregone conclusion *E.T. the Extra-Terrestrial* would take home the Best Picture trophy at the 1983 Academy Awards. With controversies plaguing Spielberg into awards season, the outlook went from great to not-so-great. Being the "populist" film versus the "important" film *Gandhi* (on top of the optics of Satyajit Ray and *Twilight Zone*) turned the biggest moneymaker in history into the underdog.

Jaid and Drew Barrymore at the 1983 Oscars.

"M.B. may prevent *E.T.* from capturing the Oscar for Best Picture," wrote John Hawn of the *Indianapolis Star* in April 1983. "M.B. in this case stands for merchandizing blitz, the likes of which Hollywood movie makers have never seen before. Is there not a store that doesn't sell an E.T. item? As deserving as the movie is to win the top prize, the oversell of E.T. merchandise has turned many people—and perhaps Academy voters—a bit surly." He added for Best Director odds, "Spielberg, who directed *E.T.*, lost whatever chance he had of winning the award when the *Twilight Zone* tragedy occurred... Though Spielberg was not the director in that particular segment, he is the producer of the film and the scandal was front-page news for several days in the Hollywood trade papers."

Add onto that the general resentment towards giving "too successful too soon" Spielberg an award, which dated back to being passed over for an Emmy or Golden Globe nomination for *Duel*. *E.T.* lost Best Picture and Best Director to *Gandhi*, with Richard Attenborough making it a point to embrace Spielberg on his way up to the stage, telling him, "This isn't right, this should be yours." It was a gracious gesture repaid a decade later with the plumb role of John Hammond in *Jurassic Park* and *The Lost World*. *Gandhi* star Ben Kingsley would feature in *Schindler's List* and *A.I. Artificial Intelligence*.

E.T. did earn Carlo Rambaldi a visual effects Oscar (alongside ILM's Dennis Muren and optical man Kenneth Smith), with the Italian thanking the Academy and "the art and technology which gave E.T. life" as Spielberg and Kennedy were shown looking on blankly from the audience. Rambaldi would not work for Spielberg again, providing creatures for various Dino De Laurentiis productions (*Dune*, *Silver Bullet*) and small Italian films until retiring in the late-1980s.

Says Phil Nobile, "Everybody was selling the thing like, 'effects wizard Carlo Rambaldi.' I don't remember anybody saying, 'Wow, E.T. looks like shit,' and I think that's probably to be credited to a lot of folks doing triage work on a situation. Later you get Rambaldi doing *Silver Bullet*, and you're like, 'Uh, that wasn't as good as the last couple of werewolf transformations I saw.'"

"*E.T.* is a prime case of the shop steward winning the prize when the artisans under him should have shared in the moment of glory," says Paul Sammon. "It was definitely a group effort, jobbed out to different people. Carlo was a glory hound, in a sense."

Carlo Rambaldi passed away in 2012 at age 86.

As for *E.T.*'s Oscar losses, Sean Daniel chalks it up to being, "Too populist, too heart-warming, too uplifting. *Gandhi* was the perfect Academy movie. Yes, there was disappointment. *E.T.* was the best script that year."

"It was really simple: The Academy almost never votes for a very commercially successful picture," expressed Mount. "They find it embarrassing. The truth of the matter about Hollywood is it's all about money, and it's always been all about money, but that means people need to have deniability around that so they feel like they're artists, you know? And I don't mean that sarcastically. There is art in what a lot of people do in the movie business, but for a movie person whose life is devoted to some aspect of filmmaking to say, 'I'm only doing this for the money' is anathema."

Spielberg echoed these statements to the *L.A. Times*, saying, "There's always a backlash against anything that makes more than $50M in film rentals. We were almost precluded from awards because people feel we've already been amply rewarded." He added that Henry Thomas should have been nominated for his performance: "This film would not have worked without Henry. I'm 35—I'm not a kid anymore, but getting that nomination would have meant so much to Henry."

Although Amblin Television produced a few of Henry Thomas' recent collaborations with Mike Flanagan (*The Haunting of Hill House*, *The Haunting of Bly Manor*), a reunion between *E.T.*'s star and director was not in the cards... at least not yet.

"Steven had promised me many things back in the '80s," said Thomas. "I don't think he did it vindictively or viciously or anything. It's just the way it works out. There was talk of *Empire of the Sun*, there was talk of River Phoenix's role in *Raiders* 3, all of these things were kind of bandied around a little bit. Obviously, the only collaboration we ever had was *E.T.* I've seen him often. I've read for him a couple of times since then, for things like *Band of Brothers*. I saw him at auditions over the years when I was a young adult actor. It's just... *E.T.* was it."

On the bright side, one of the most important legacies is neither the merchandising nor even the film itself, but the lasting friendship between the principles, namely Thomas, Dee Wallace, and Robert MacNaughton. The trio are frequently together on the convention circuit, spreading the gospel of the movie Wallace calls "our *Wizard of Oz*."

"It was an impactful experience," Thomas smiles. "Changed my life in many ways. To have experienced that with other people, you stay in touch. For the audience it takes on a different connotative reality. For the actors, we've been through a war together, so to speak. We tell war stories and reminisce about the days of *E.T.*, but you have a history with someone. I've known them all my professional life now."

"We're very close, it means a lot to continue that friendship," adds Wallace. "I don't feel motherly to them any longer, but we have a camaraderie that's going to be there until we're not here any longer. There is never a Q&A that goes by that I don't learn something new from Robert MacNaughton. They did so many things I wasn't on set for. I love him, and we love being together."

"Robert especially," concludes Thomas. "He was always someone I asked advice of. Well read, older than me, knew better music. He became like my brother, because I don't have any brothers or sisters. Robert has been a constant since 1981 in my life. I've seen Dee over the years many many times and she's kind of like my surrogate mother now. They're like my family that I travel with and see more often than my real family."

Wallace has written books and done other work with a focus on healing the self. Many fans have related to her how *E.T.* helped them accept, heal, or overcome.

MacNaughton, Wallace, fan Peter de Mooij, and Thomas (*left to right*).

She said, "This mother came up to me at a convention and said, 'Miss Wallace, you're part of a miracle in my life.' She told me about her autistic son, who was 10 years old and did not speak ever. She took him to see the re-release of *E.T.* and on the way home he started saying every line E.T. said in the film. Another young man from a small town in Texas told me in fourth grade his parents got divorced and all his friends stopped talking to him. That summer *E.T.* came out, where the parents were divorced. That gave his friends permission to bring him back into the fold again. This movie reaches into people's souls and reminds them of a higher truth."

As for the studio head for whom *E.T.* was "the one that got away," even Frank Price admired the film.

"*E.T.* is a good movie," proclaims Price. "I understood its appeal. We'd like to have had it, but I still wouldn't have gone into the split studio thing. Through much of the shooting of *1941* I was responsible for the budget. I didn't like that because I'm responsible for something I can't control. You don't have any control when you've got two studios involved. I had a good enough record of hits that you're not going to win them all. They hired me to run Universal next, so… obviously they didn't view it as some wound."

One person holding a grudge was Spielberg, who—once Price arrived at Universal in late '83—reportedly had it in his contract that he not have to collaborate with the new movie division chairman or his president of marketing Marvin Antonowsky on any projects.

"Frank Price passed on *E.T.* and Steven never forgave him for that," screenwriter Bob Gale adds. "Even though Frank facilitated getting *Back to the Future* made at Universal, Frank was not the day-to-day executive on that. Steven didn't want to deal with him. Steven was still pissed off he passed on *E.T.*, so we dealt directly with Sid Sheinberg on *Back to the Future*."

Another person a little bit peeved may have been Thom Mount, who for *New York* magazine's 1978 piece "After Begelman" stated, "I haven't the slightest interest in David Begelman or who takes his place. What people like him do or how they conduct their business has nothing to do with me or what I do."

Unfortunately, Mount was wrong. After Begelman left Columbia in disgrace in February 1978, he was replaced in May by MGM's head of production Daniel Melnick, who hired Frank Price as president of film production. By March of 1979 Melnick had resigned for a job at Fox, and with major shareholder Ray Stark's backing Price became president of Columbia Pictures. During his successful tenure Coca-Cola bought the company, pressuring Price to vacate, so he jumped ship to become chairman of the MCA Motion Picture Group. As soon as he came to Universal in November of 1983, Price fired Thom Mount, replacing him with creative advisor Wendy Margolis.

"Frank was not well loved in the company," Mount told this author. "He got the job replacing me because they took a look at our executive staff and the guy running the movie division was 30-something... that would be me, and that was unacceptable. I 'wasn't old enough and didn't have enough experience,' even though we did nothing but make money. I ran that position for nine years total, and eight of those years were record years for the company."

He later formed The Mount Company, producing *Bull Durham* and *Natural Born Killers.*

Between its release in 1982 and 20th anniversary re-release in 2002, *E.T. the Extra-Terrestrial* has made $797,307,407 in box office alone off of an estimated $10.5M budget. Adjusted for inflation that's $1.45 billion. In *The New York Times* obituary for the late Price on August 29, 2025 they called his decision to pass on *E.T.* "one of the biggest blunders in Hollywood history."

Famous for his axiom "nobody knows anything," screenwriter William Goldman penned the following assessment in his 1983 tome *Adventures in the Screen Trade*: "They had passed on *E.T.* Columbia had had it, developed it for a million dollars, took a survey, and discovered the audience for the movie would be too limited to make it profitable. So they let it go. (Universal picked it up and may make back the billion they didn't earn by dropping *Star Wars*.)"

Concluded Price to this author, "I went on *Good Morning America*. David Hartman was the host there. He asked me about it, and I said, 'Well, David, I was smart enough to develop it and dumb enough to lose it.'"

CHAPTER 12

Re-Reborn: Night Skies Finds New Life...?

"Strange, isn't it? Each man's life touches so many other lives."
—***It's a Wonderful Life*** (1946)

Steven Spielberg clearly did not believe in Robert Frost's "The Road Not Taken," since he decided to pursue the dark ideas in *Night Skies* after all... just not with visitors from outer space. The spirit of that scrapped project wound up, arguably, inhabiting the corporeal forms of two other Spielberg productions in different beastly incarnations.

"You can sort of see a three-way Venn diagram," muses modern screenwriter Andrew Barrer. "*E.T.* and *Gremlins* are 'a boy and his unlikely friend.' *Gremlins* and *Poltergeist* are '*Straw Dogs*, but ghosts'... '*Straw Dogs*, but monsters.' There definitely is a common DNA running through those three movies."

Spielberg's chain of mainstream success led to unprecedented creative/financial freedom, but Austin filmmaker Tobe Hooper experienced a much rockier road. Like his genre contemporary Wes Craven, Hooper started in academia, first as a University of Texas at Austin student (where he was present for Charles Whitman's clock tower massacre), then as a professor. He began his filmmaking career as a documentarian. A 1966 nonfiction short *Down Friday Street* depicts a creepy house violently brought down at the end, a pattern repeated in both *Salem's Lot* and *Poltergeist*.

His first experimental feature was 1969's *Eggshells*, about a hippie commune encroached upon by a supernatural force. Taking visual inspiration from Andrew Wyeth's stark rural landscape painting *Christina's World*, as well as the infamous mutilations of Ed Gein, his next feature was 1974's *The Texas Chainsaw Massacre*. It follows a group of youngsters encountering a savage family who run a slaughterhouse, including the giant killer Leatherface whose mask of human skin became iconic.

"I knew it was going to get recognition, because it was so different," Hooper told *Interview* in 2014. "The films I had been watching before I made it were Fellini films, Antonioni, and Truffaut. I was at the art house a lot. I had made about 60 documentaries and TV commercials, so I'd developed a style of fast cuts, almost as subliminal as you can get at 24 frames a second."

Not as violent as its title suggests (much of the gore is implied), *Texas Chainsaw* was nonetheless effective, one of the most successful independent films of the decade. It raked in over $30M, led to eight prequels/remakes/sequels (including one directed by Hooper), and inspired major films including Ridley Scott's *Alien*.

"It is very difficult to really scare me," Scott told *The Hollywood Reporter* in 2019. "I watched *Texas Chainsaw Massacre* when I was prepping for *Alien* one Saturday afternoon in the Fox studio in a small theater. It was horrendous, and it scared the shit out of me... Tobe Hooper did a great job, and it was my challenge to say, 'How do I get that scary?'"

"Tobe was a very close friend and one of the sweetest human beings I've ever known," said Mick Garris, who produced Hooper's TV films for *Masters of Horror*. "*Texas Chainsaw* was a big hit, but he never saw any of that because it was a non-union movie. No residuals, no royalties. He got his initial paycheck and that's all you can expect, other than your next job being better. George Romero had ownership in his movies, which Tobe did not. Romero was a better businessman, but I never heard anything but feelings of fortune from Tobe for being able to make a living telling stories."

Hooper found it difficult to ascend from that $90,000 low budget hit. He and *Texas Chainsaw* co-writer Kim Henkel pitched Universal on an unfilmable remake of *The Thing* centered around a sea captain hunting an underwater alien in Antarctica. After failing to finance a murder mystery starring John Travolta titled *Bleeding Hearts*, the young counterculture director made swampy slasher *Eaten Alive*. Released under various titles on the grindhouse circuit (*Starlight Slaughter*, *Death Trap*), it was a failure. The next year Hooper was fired off creature feature *The Dark* after 2 days. He rebounded on the highly successful $4M TV miniseries version of Stephen King's *Salem's Lot*, but then had a nervous breakdown after 9 days filming *Venom* with Oliver Reed and Klaus Kinski, again having to be replaced. He did make a go of his first official studio film, 1981 slasher *The Funhouse*, which was a modest success.

There's a major aspect of *Poltergeist* often overlooked by those assessing its authorship: It was Hooper's idea. His interest in ghosts began in the early '70s when—a few days after his father's death—drinking glasses in the family kitchen exploded while ceramic souvenirs flew, shattering across the room. After the glasses were replaced, they exploded again.

"I did very much believe there's an energy that can manifest itself that's beyond our hearing and sight," Hooper said.

Interest in this area was piqued during his initial development deal at Universal in the mid-'70s, taking over the offices of director Robert Wise. In said office he discovered a book on poltergeists used as reference while Wise made *The Haunting*, wondering why there had not been a major ghost movie in so long. Hooper tried pitching Universal on his haunted house idea about a family who lived next to a cemetery with the support of then-mentor William Friedkin, who championed *Texas Chainsaw* (comparing it to the art of Francis Bacon). The idea was to use Surround Sound to make the audience feel the poltergeist presence with immersive audio effects. Hooper chipped away at it for years until Spielberg came along.

Proprietor of the long-running Tobe Hooper Appreciation Society blog Julius Banzon explains, "No conception of *Poltergeist* as we know it existed before Spielberg, but Hooper was actively formulating a piece about poltergeists, fascinated with the supernatural, the afterlife."

"Bob and I saw *Texas Chainsaw Massacre* when it came out," remembers Bob Gale, referring to he and Robert Zemeckis. "We loved it. We absolutely loved it. We dragged Milius to see it. Milius loved it. We set up a screening so Steven could see it, and as a result Steven hired Tobe Hooper to direct *Poltergeist*."

At one point John Milius collaborated with Hooper on an unmade/more straightforward version of *Texas Chainsaw Massacre 2,* then in the spring of 1980 Steven Spielberg offered Hooper the director's chair on *Night Skies*. Hooper poo-pooed making an alien movie at that time, although he eventually did two with *Lifeforce* in 1985 as well as the remake of *Invaders from Mars* in 1986.

As Hooper told *Fangoria* #23, "When I started shooting *Funhouse*, Steven called me in Florida and asked me to come back—there was something he wanted me to do. I came back, and he wanted me to do a follow-up to *Close Encounters of the Third Kind*, the film that eventually came to be *E.T.*, though what he described to me was very different. I explained to him that really wasn't my kind of thing, but I'd always wanted to do a film about ghosts and poltergeists. He said, 'Fantastic,' and at that point we set about creating *Poltergeist*. We worked on it in London while he was shooting *Raiders*."

"They started the treatment of *It's Night Time* over mail correspondence," says Banzon. "Met in London to finish it up. There's a pretty recent interview with Richard Edlund where he says he met Hooper on the set of *Raiders of the Lost Ark*. Spielberg was touting him as the director of his next producing project."

Hooper told *AV Club* in 2000, "It came down to Steven and myself sitting at his house. He wrote the screenplay, and we gathered around a poltergeist textbook for the research."

"It went back to Hooper having the idea of doing a movie about poltergeists," explains David Furtney who has been running a dedicated *Poltergeist* fan site for decades. "He wasn't interested in the alien aspect of *Night Skies*, so he decided to focus on a ghost story. Then they began collaborating on the treatment."

Furtney tracked down a copy of said treatment stored at the Margaret Herrick Library in Beverly Hills, paying a researcher to transcribe the document titled "Night Time"/"It's Night Time." Credited solely to Spielberg, the first treatment was 11 pages dated March 31, 1980, followed by 15 added pages on July 31, 5 more pages on August 18, and the last pages on August 23. Spielberg's *Night Time* outline is concurrent with his notes for John Sayles' draft of *Night Skies* earlier in Chapter 5 of this book dated August 5, 1980.

The March *Night Time* treatment describes the Freeling family as open and loving, and typical of their neighborhood called Vista. Steven is the real estate agent, while his wife Nora (age 34) was "married at 17, pregnant at 18," something hinted in the final movie when Diana gives her age as 32... meaning she was 16 when her first child came.

The *Poltergeist* House today at 4267 Roxbury Street in Simi Valley, CA.

"Yeah, that doesn't work out the way it should," laughs eventual screenwriter Mark Victor. "I've been asked about that before. I can't remember, 'Did we think about that or screw it up? Was that Steven or us?' They got married early."

There are four kids instead of three: Sweeny (16), Angel (14), Lawrence (12), and Carol Ann (6). Like *After School*, the two middle children are in a Chicago junior high, with much of their activity in a shopping mall. The dog's name is Elmer (after Spielberg's own cocker spaniel), while in the film he's called Buzz after E. Buzz Miller on *SNL*.

Things get going with static-y phone calls in the middle of the night, followed by TV channels flipping, food disappearing, and furniture rearranged. Elmer begins staring at one particular wall. The daughter Angel finds/plays an old record of 19th century pioneer songs. An aviary with many pet birds is mysteriously torn open. Their backyard pool (already built) has something invisible swimming in it. Things escalate as furniture arrangements become more brazen. Doors/windows are left open. Angel is putting makeup on in a mirror when the image becomes someone else's face.

Steven and Nora go out for the night but return to find the babysitter has fled in terror, leaving their kids on the front porch. Nora receives a terrifying "ghost kiss," and the furniture is now completely rearranged with chairs stacked on top of chairs. The family decamps for a Holiday Inn, where Steven is inhabited by a spirit who alters his behavior when he makes love to his wife (which she kinda digs). At breakfast, Carol Ann's voice changes to that of a man, scaring everybody. Her possession trajectory mirrors Sandy Dennis in *Something Evil*.

Steven contacts a Chicago-based parapsychology organization, who invades their home and scares the neighbors. An archaeological dig in Vista uncovers the 150-year-old bones of massacred white settlers, with visible arrowheads and scalping knives. It is theorized by ghost chasers that these settlers' spirits have found a gateway into the 1980s. Amid a deluge of crackpots descending on the house, tabloid-friendly psychic Tagina Barrins arrives. Nora and Steven awaken in their bedroom to find Tagina speaking to television static.

The kids are teased at school for being "haunted people." Neighbors start a petition to kick the Freelings out of the housing division. Soon hauntings spread to the neighbors, with isolated "ghost fires" scorching houses. Ectoplasm and smoky ghost apparitions emanate from TV sets. The climax would have TVs exploding and the town evacuated as ghost fires engulf their homes in a purifying measure so the souls can rest.

"There's a lot of out-there ideas about spirit fires," comments Banzon. "Hooper made a film called *Spontaneous Combustion* about that same poltergeist phenomena."

July treatment notes add more fuel to neighborhood hysteria, with mobs chanting "Free us from the Freelings" as they surround their home. A police officer asks the family to consider moving. This mirrors the galvanizing of Kelly residents in 1955 around the Sutton property, as well as *Twilight Zone*'s "The Monsters Are Due on Maple Street."

By August notes, Carol Ann becomes the focus of the entity. She and her friend Jeanette are playing with dolls when suddenly Jeanette takes a stick pin with a carving of a Native American fire god and drives it into her doll, with Carol Ann saying, "She must die." The doll bursts into flame, as does the door to the room. Firemen come, but only the door and the doll burned, nothing else.

When Steven is on a business trip and Nora is sleeping alone, Carol Ann barges in, gets on the bed and starts chanting "It's night time, it's night time..." The next day Nora installs a lock on her door. That night she gets her son Sweeny to take the other kids to see *Fantasia* at the movie theater, leaving her and dog Elmer alone. Like Tess in *Night Skies* she takes a soothing bubble bath, but is startled to see blood dripping from the faucet. She grabs a towel, then hears

Elmer yelping outside and runs to the backyard in a thunderstorm where the hole for the pool is (now being dug in the notes). What follows is very similar to the final film, with Diana in the hole and mummies popping up.

The kids return home from the movie to find their house covered with mud and the bathtub full of blood. They call their dad and tell him to come home, afraid to tell police or neighbors. Meanwhile Nora drives to a dive café called Indian Palms, where she sees a menu that shows her subdivision was the exact location of a massacre in the early 1800s.

Back at home Sweeny sees a skeleton rising out of the pool hole. Carol Ann darts up from her slumber on the couch singing "It's night time, it's night time..." She tears the head off her bunny, speaking in a man's voice. Steven returns as the other kids try to leave, but the door lights on fire, as does the neighbors' house. Sweeny screams to his dad, "We've got to get out of here, she'll burn the place down." Steve hurls a chair through a window and helps his kids outside. Nora returns as well, and they all beg him to leave Carol Ann behind, which he does. As they flee the entire division burns, Next day we see a "No Trespassing" sign on the neighborhood as a huge archeological dig proceeds.

The final set of treatment additions dated August 23, 1980 change the white settlers killed by Natives trope to simply a normal burial site where the bodies were left by Steven's company. Lawrence is also renamed Robbie, and we get the scene of the dueling remote controls with the neighbor during football.

As released, *Poltergeist* whittles the haunting down to one location (even though the entire neighborhood is built on the burial ground), simplifies the parapsychology team to one group plus Tangina, omits the neighbor hysteria, deletes one of the four children, and adds the crucial element of Carol Anne getting sucked into the ghost world à la "Little Girl Lost." The phrase "For when it's night time" is uttered by Carol Anne when putting her dead pet bird in a cigar box casket.

"The storyline progresses as the months go on from early to late 1980," says Furtney of *Night Time*. "In August the haunting's origin is changed to a cemetery that a developer had gone in and just moved the headstones. That's when the two Bobs... I don't know if they actually wrote it or they just told Spielberg the idea then he wrote it down?"

Says Bob Gale, "When we read the script, we said, 'Steven, there's a lot of great stuff in here but the one thing that's missing is a reason why all this is happening.' Taking a page from the episode of *The Night Stalker* we wrote called 'Chopper,' we said, 'What if this subdivision was built on top of an old graveyard, and they took the headstones out but they didn't move the graves and that's why this phenomenon has happened?' Steven loved that idea, and that's in the movie."

Adds Dana Gould, who paid homage to Kolchak in his TV series *Stan Against Evil*, "'Chopper' is an episode of *Kolchak the Night Stalker* that has a guy in a biker gang in the '50s who was beheaded in an accident. They buried his head separate from his body, and his body wants his head. His body keeps coming back and killing everybody involved in the gang until somebody reunites his head with his body. It's also *Sleepy Hollow*, right?"

Spielberg's first feature film *The Sugarland Express* came out the same week in 1974 that monumental horror author Stephen King's first novel *Carrie* was published. Ever since then the two men have been in a perpetual dance to someday work together, starting with *Poltergeist*, continuing through the decades-long quest for Amblin to adapt *The Talisman*, all the way through King's tenuous relationship with *The Shining* movie being a plot point in *Ready Player One*.

"I wanted him to help me out with the script and sort of write it with me, but he was unavailable," Spielberg told *EW* of *Poltergeist* in 2018.

Added King, "It didn't work out because it was before the internet and we had a communication breakdown... I was on a ship going across the Atlantic to England."

Spielberg ultimately went with a pair of young writers responsible for Charles Bronson/Lee Marvin vehicle *Death Hunt*: Michael Grais and Mark Victor. They also had a hot comedy spec about air traffic controllers titled *Turn Left or Die* gearing up at MGM with Dan Aykroyd and John Belushi attached.

As Victor told this author, "He tried to get Stephen King, and I don't think Stephen was willing to accept some of the terms that Steven wanted regarding credit."

Spielberg had initially been meeting Grais and Victor for a remake of the 1943 Spencer Tracy romantic fantasy *A Guy Named Joe*, a clip of which features in *Poltergeist* and which he remade in 1989 as *Always*.

Said Victor, "That was a remake of a romantic comedy, and we had written *Death Hunt* which was intense. I don't think we felt confident we could do a great job with it. He was telling us about the ghost movie he was interested in doing because Kubrick's movie *The Shining* had come out and he felt it didn't cover a ghost movie. We walked out and said, 'You know, I'd rather do the ghost movie.' He finished up with King and came back to us."

Victor recalls being handed a 5-to-8-page treatment that was "Very loose. There wasn't a real throughline, more of a setting, some names, not a lot of characterization. Wasn't much to work with, just the concept of a family. It was more identifying a project. It was called *It's Night Time*. The word 'poltergeist' came from us. I remember bringing up the word, it wasn't common vernacular in the US at that point."

He also does not recall the bake-off between this and the other "Night" project in Spielberg's stable about a family with three kids under siege: *Night Skies*.

"The writers are the last to know," Victor explains. "If it wasn't coming across our desk, it wasn't on our radar. It may have been a bake-off. When Steven's doing a project, he watches all the movies in the arena, and based on experience it wouldn't surprise me he's maybe going down similar paths with different people. I never felt during the project that we were competing against one because I probably didn't know about it. If that was *Night Skies* then that was already on the path to being *E.T.*"

Explains Furtney, "At that point Grais and Victor did their own draft of what was then called 'It's Night Time,' later retitled *Poltergeist*. But Spielberg apparently wasn't happy with the draft that Grais and Victor did, so supposedly by himself he rewrote that into what became the final shooting script."

Furtney spent $1500 for a copy of this rare draft of the movie which represents the ultimate contributions of Grais and Victor. It is dated February 9, 1981, less than two months after Melissa Mathison's first draft of *E.T.* is turned in and a scant three months before principal photography on *Poltergeist* began.

According to Victor, "We were assigned to write it pretty much from scratch. We weren't following a treatment. We did ghost research, reading things, made a lot of note cards. We put the scenes up on a board, color coded them based on intensity, then moved them around. Day after day coming up with scares: 'What are the outsiders and who's coming?' Steven was not working on the cards with us. We'd have lunch to bring him up to date on what we were doing. We didn't talk to Tobe about scenes."

The pair's original *It's Night Time* draft contains many differences from the final film, including a higher degree of violence: Carol Anne dies, Diane is raped by black goo while dangling from the ceiling, and the neighbor's head is crushed by the station wagon as the Freelings escape the house. Dr. Lesh was originally written as a man, while the whole subplot of the neighborhood turning against the family was included. Even the development Cuesta Verde was originally called West Haven.

"The greater intensity is us saying, 'How do we make it scarier or go for more shock value?'" explains Victor. "We had a lunch with Steven where we said, 'What if we kill Carol Anne?' It caused him to gulp. He came back and said, 'Well, you can do all the other stuff, but you can't kill her,' so there was this 'Little Girl Lost' *Twilight Zone* thing. That's how it was portrayed, she went to another dimension."

It turns out Victor had a strong connection to this aspect of the story, saying, "I had a sibling pass away when I was much younger, and my mother spoke with a medium that had things she was able to say that were rather amazing. It opened my mind to what I call 'non-ordinary reality,' things beyond our senses. If you take the next step on those investigations, all of a sudden you start entering that milieu. They have all these places for stuff like Noetics. In India it's reincarnation. This was a ghost horror movie, so a lot of those things like 'going into the light' are in books. People have experienced things. Falling out of a ceiling. I was in England in my early 20s and got to talk to this psychic lady Ena Twig, a small little lady who had some talent I didn't quite understand."

When this author suggested his sibling's death may have been his "eyes in" to making the story personally resonant, Victor was somewhat taken aback: "Maybe it was there... I'm trying to figure out... I don't know. I'd have to think about that. It was certainly there and part of my psyche, but it's also, 'How's the movie going to work?' I think what you're saying certainly makes sense, even if I wasn't thinking about it while writing it. If you accept/feel/believe anything you bring more to writing it."

"Grais and Victor conceived a number of elements, including the double ending, all the monsters, the clown, the storm, the tree, the closet... it's all in there," Banzon details. "They definitely deserve credit, but the characters and the drama, it's all different. Spielberg helped them create that draft in story meetings. He suggested, 'Oh, a tree scared me when I was a kid,' and then Grais or Victor were like, 'Oh, I remember when a tree branch crashed through my window.' They all agreed to put an evil, living tree in the script. Hooper claims to have created the maquette of the tree, and if you watch David Lean's adaptation of *Great Expectations* there's an identical tree... and it's one of Hooper's favorite films."

Adding to the crossover, there is also a whole subplot in Spielberg's unmade *Reel to Reel* where Stuart the director gets an idea in the shower: "The trees have got to be scary. That's it." He gets his VFX guys to construct a scary tree whose limbs move to grab the little boy as lightning flashes in his *Invaders from Mars* remake. The irony never ceases, since Hooper would direct an actual remake of *Invaders from Mars*.

Spielberg's revised shooting script features many parallels to *Night Skies*, beginning with the central concept of a family being bombarded by mischievous and malevolent forces in their home. As with John Sayles' script, a child (Carol Anne) becomes a focal point for the menacing forces of evil, not to mention two of *Poltergeist*'s most famous lines coming directly from *Night Skies*, i.e. "What's happening?!" and "They're heeeere..."

Adds Banzon, "Grais and Victor wrote their draft, then very quickly Spielberg rewrote it, all within four months of shooting. The impending WGA strike was presumably why they fast-tracked the production. There's also a director's strike looming, and by all accounts the film was fast-tracked in order to make a product for 1982 before the strike."

Explained Sayles to *Starburst* in 1983, "Rick Baker was involved with the [*Night Skies*] mechanical effects, but Columbia rejected his budget which involved inventing a lot of technology. Steven then had a similar row with Rick and promptly got involved with *Poltergeist*, which seems to me got the horror out of his system and then lost interest in *Night Skies*."

One ex-EFX alum lucky enough to get called up to the plate was Craig Reardon, who became head of special effects makeup on the ghost movie.

Reardon told podcast *Mark and Me*, "Mr. Spielberg had a difference of opinion with some of the leading lights in the field back at that time, including one of the newer ones, Rick Baker. Also Stan Winston and Tom Burman, to name some names. The timing couldn't have been better for an x-factor person to step into that breach… Spielberg took the attitude, 'If this is who Tobe says he wants and he's vouching for him, I guess it's good enough for me.'"

Right after *Night Skies* died the death, Mitch Suskin was shifted immediately onto the ghost film. He says, "I remember talking to Kathy right after the meeting where Steven came in and said, 'We're gonna shut this down,' and that's how I got pulled into *Poltergeist* because they were prepping that. I was put in a room at MGM working with some storyboard artists and illustrators. I became optical effects coordinator."

David Cellitti was not so lucky: "When Craig hired me on *Poltergeist*, which I was supposed to work on, I said, 'Have you run my name past Kathy Kennedy?' Because this is after *Night Skies*. He gave me this big speech about, 'They're not going to tell me who to hire and who not to hire, and blah, blah, blah, blah, blah.' The next day, he calls me up, 'Well, I ran your name past Kathy Kennedy, and you're off the picture.'"

Cellitti would go on to work on 1984's *Dreamscape* with Reardon. Shortly after, he left the movie business entirely, stating, "When I left Rick I was really bitter. 'Screw Spielberg, screw Rick, screw everybody.' Then I went to work for all these other people and realized it's not them, it's the industry. 'You're the wrong person for this.'"

Suskin said, "*Poltergeist* was another *1941*… big project, big special effects. My challenge was to keep up with things and make sure nothing got lost between the cracks. I was coordinating between ILM and our special effects unit in production. I wouldn't say spy, but literally coordinating for Steven and Frank Marshall."

The Freeling family were led by JoBeth Williams and Craig T. Nelson as parents Diane and Steve, whose intimate scenes carry a loving spontaneity.

"The married couple in *Poltergeist* are one of the best married couples I've ever seen in a horror movie," says Jourdain Searles. "When people are like, 'Oh, Spielberg shadow directed,' it's like, 'I don't know, the parents like each other too much.'"

The Freeling children Dana, Robbie, and Carol Anne were played by Dominique Dunne, Oliver Robins, and 5-year-old Heather O'Rourke, respectively.

There was crossover between *Poltergeist* and *E.T.*, with Drew Barrymore coming close to landing Carol Anne.

"We were essentially casting both movies simultaneously, which definitely worked to our advantage," says Marci Liroff. "Many kids read for both and it helped us hone in on who the characters were for each. Heather O'Rourke read for both. Steven likes to say he spotted her at the MGM commissary and invited her to audition for *Poltergeist*... but I had already auditioned her and scheduled her to meet him."

"Heather as Carol Anne was great," remembers Victor. "I could be playing with her on the set or talking to her or joking around, then she'd go into a scene and be right there, right into it. She had a natural gift."

As with *E.T.*, *Poltergeist* was set in a suburban area instead of the rural *Night Skies*, connecting it more towards the kind of environments Spielberg himself grew up in. There are publicity photos of Spielberg clowning around with children from the cast of both films at the same time on those idyllic neighborhood streets.

"*E.T.* was shot in San Fernando Valley, California, and then *Poltergeist* was shot in Agoura Hills," explains Furtney. "If you watch them back-to-back you could almost see it happening the next street over."

Universal insisted Spielberg could not direct MGM's *Poltergeist* while fulfilling that position on their *E.T.* project. With shooting on the ghost movie taking place from May 11 to Jul 10 of 1981, then *E.T.* going from September 8 until December, it was a hectic road to the "summer of Spielberg" in 1982.

Says Universal's Sean Daniel, "He was overseeing *Poltergeist*, and there was always a tension that Sid and I would—I guess, naturally—be worried that somehow... There was never an issue of Steven's devotion to *E.T.*, just a chagrin that there was a competitor's movie he was also working on. They both turned out great."

There are certain concrete aspects of the film Tobe Hooper has claimed were his handywork, such as personally designing/building the maquette for the frightening tree outside of Robbie's window. The parapsychologist played by Beatrice Straight was based on a real one, former actress/screenwriter-turned-academic Thelma Moss, whom William Friedkin had introduced to Hooper for his initial research on poltergeists.

Confirms Mark Victor, "Thelma Moss ran a psych department at UCLA that entertained and studied all this stuff. I didn't spend time talking to her."

With Hooper directing the shoot but Spielberg overseeing things almost daily, word began to trickle out who the real "ghost director" on the film was. Hooper's authority on the movie was crippled, both figuratively and literally because he "used a cane through half of the picture" due to a torn ligament.

Explains Suskin, "Tobe Hooper was the director of record, and for a number of reasons he couldn't get up to speed quickly enough from doing low budget to a major studio production at MGM. My earliest memory of *Poltergeist* was being in a little office with an artist doing concept sketches and storyboards. Outside our office was a hallway, one end was Spielberg's office, at the other end was Hooper's. Tobe would walk in chewing on a cigar and say, 'Okay, here's what we're gonna do with the scene.' We'd say, 'Okay, great,' start working it out, he'd go back to his office. An hour or two later, Spielberg would walk in and say, 'What are you working on?' We go, 'Working on the scene.' He goes, 'No, no, that's not it. It's got to be like this.' We'd start changing the scene, Spielberg would go back to his office. Hooper would walk in and say, 'What are you doing? You got it all wrong. That's not what I said.' There was this literal disconnect, like The Three Stooges. They had a different vision from the beginning as to what the movie really wanted to be, or how it wanted to be directed."

"There was a definite division between the influence implicit in a strong producer and a distinctive director, with Spielberg and Hooper fulfilling those roles," confirms Reardon. "No hostility, not ever, but Spielberg is a huge enthusiast, not a money man producer who lets the movie make itself. Tobe was beholden to him for the job and had respect for his dual role as an effective producer and acclaimed director. I don't think it was anything mysterious or sinister."

The speed of Hooper's decision making was noted by William Stout, who did concept art for 1986's *Invaders from Mars*: "Tobe was a really nice guy, but Tobe was the director who could not make a decision, the classic bad client. The worst client is a guy who says, 'I don't know what I want, but I'll know it when I see it.' Well, then the choices are infinite! I can show you stuff till the end of time. That was Tobe's thing. It was like, 'Oh my God.'"

Adds Suskin, "I worked with Tobe years later, when he was in a much better space in his life. He got caught in the wrong place on the wrong project for him. Everybody loved Tobe, so it was a little sad and uncomfortable to be in the middle of that at times."

According to Bob Gale, "I have no idea what the making of *Texas Chainsaw* was like, but I know Hooper was not the type of guy that could direct a studio movie, at least not then. We'd go to the set of *Poltergeist* and Steven would be sitting in the back of the set. Tobe would say, 'I think the camera should be here and the shot should be like this.' We'd watch the director of photography Matt Leonetti look over his shoulder at Steven, who would either nod or shake his head. That's how the story came about that Steven actually directed *Poltergeist*. There may have been some scenes that he did."

First assistant cameraman John Leonetti (brother of Matthew), stated in 2017 to the *Shock Waves* podcast, "Steven Spielberg directed that movie… He directed it in case there was going to be a strike and Tobe was cool with that. It wasn't anything against Tobe. Every once in a while he would actually leave the set and let Tobe do a few things."

Recalls Reardon, "I remember an incident when we were filming the scene with the corpses bobbing up in the pool. There I am down in the water, freezing cold. Tobe leaned near the edge and asked if I could do such-and-such with one of the 'bodies.' It struck me in the moment as a good idea but impossible to implement. Too late. Had he had the idea earlier it could have been done. You can't pull things out of your ear."

Continues Suskin, "Tobe wound up obviously being the director at the beginning. The first thing we shot with the bodies coming out of the ground at

Spielberg and Hooper on set (*far left*).

the house, that was his. He really did direct that. He designed it. He figured it all out. Once it got on stage with a lot of the actors, it started to change. There were specific ideas Steven wanted visually. Little by little, Spielberg started sending storyboards, showing up on set more."

While Hooper worked mainly with storyboard artist Carl Aldana in pre-production, it's possible Spielberg worked with artist Richard Lasley to turn his stick figure storyboards into something more professional as production barreled on through the changes.

"Hooper has a valid claim he storyboarded half the film," says Banzon. "The storyboard sketches by Spielberg cover the first two scenes shot on the sound stage, the living room scene when they contact Carol Anne."

"To his credit, it wasn't that Steven couldn't let go... the movie might not have gotten done," adds Suskin. "It probably would have taken forever and certainly wouldn't have been the same if Tobe had finished it. It would have been smaller, more constrained, without that elegant visual style Steven has to sell supernatural things."

As actress Zelda Rubinstein told Eric Vespe bluntly in 2007, "I only worked six days on the film and Steven was there. Tobe set up the shots and Steven made the adjustments... I'm not a fan of Tobe Hooper. I feel he allowed... some unacceptable chemical agents into his work. Tobe was only partially there."

Continues Suskin, "We'd start to see Tobe's dailies in the screening room and you'd hear Steven's notes. The next day you'd see it come back re-shot. It wanted to be a Steven Spielberg film in the end, not a Tobe Hooper film. Tobe definitely had a sense of the macabre, was a lot of fun to talk to. I think his movie would have been fun too."

A production source told Furtney (who confirmed the person's validity to this author) about an incident where the culture clash got real. Here is the unattributed quote:

"The only time I ever saw him really fight with Tobe was after an entire day of shooting a scene with Beatrice Straight and the other two scientists involving a great deal of gobbledygook dialogue. Tobe just couldn't get the shot. Steven came onto the set and was very upset—there was a lot of ugly yelling—and Tobe just stood there taking it. Beatrice Straight finally stood up to Steven, said that the dialogue—which I believe Steven himself had written for the scene—was unplayable and that Sir Laurence Olivier himself couldn't act such badly-written dreck. She made it very clear that Tobe was not to be blamed. Steven was very quiet and about five minutes later the cast and crew were all dismissed for the day. The next day the actors came back to the set and were handed new dialogue, which again I believe Steven had rewritten. It was 100% better and Tobe shot the scene in about an hour with no problem. But before shooting commenced, Steven got up in front of the entire cast and crew and apologized for the outburst and said Tobe was not to blame for the previous day's delays."

This moment on *Poltergeist* brings to mind a beat in the script for Spielberg's *Reel to Reel* where the director apologizes to a child for yelling at him as things go wrong on set:

STUART

```
Sometimes when you're angry at your enemies
you take it out on your friends. Because you
figure they're your friends and they'll
understand. It's not an excuse, but that's what
people sometimes do. And that's what I did.
```

"There's so much that's a mystery," says Banzon. "Spielberg admitted, 'I wish that production went smoother.' People won't push the fact Hooper was involved. When you say 'slow and hesitant,' that's kind of how Hooper was. He wasn't a classic Hollywood industry director, organized and planned. He'd get on set and change things. It's not as simple as, 'Hooper was slow and wasn't making decisions.' It was, 'What kind of decisions was he making?' That film could have turned any which way without Hooper. It could have turned out a Spielberg way... It could have turned out a Joe Dante way... But it is what it is because Hooper was there."

According to Steven Awalt, "People ask the wrong question. They say, 'Who directed *Poltergeist*?' The right question is, 'Who was the creative force behind *Poltergeist*?' and that's undeniably Steven. I don't think Tobe should be besmirched his directorial credit, but Steven was there all but three days and Hooper wasn't there on post-production at all. He didn't work with ILM. He had his own edit, but then Steven specifically worked with Michael Kahn to the point where Carol Littleton edited *E.T.* because Kahn was on *Poltergeist*. I asked Marvin Levy when he was alive, 'Could I do a *Poltergeist* book?' and Marvin said, 'That's not a film Steven wants to revisit.'"

Explains Mick Garris, who did specialized publicity and assisted Frank Marshall in putting together the short subject *The Making of Poltergeist*, "I was on set and can tell you Tobe directed the movie with a very involved writer/producer named Steven Spielberg, a strong producer who was on set every day. Tobe was calling action and cut and calling the shots, involved every step of the way. I think it was a rough time, but all films are hard to make. The hours suck. It's always pulling the train up the mountain, you never get to ride it down."

One example of how publicity was openly diminishing Hooper's contributions was that very 7-minute Making Of piece, which concentrates almost entirely on Spielberg directing actors on set. Hooper only appears in one single non-verbal shot, with Marshall himself getting more screen time in the doc than *Poltergeist*'s ostensible director.

"Frank directed it, so that's understandable," Garris says of the doc. "He was Steven's right-hand man as a producer, and you go with the name brand. This documentary was not made for buffs, it was made for the mainstream. 'Steven Spielberg' was the biggest name in filmmaking history, so naturally they're going to focus more attention on Steven. I haven't seen the documentary in decades but I do remember that about it."

Adds Mike Ryan, "Every behind the scenes shot is Spielberg pointing at something like, 'Hey guys, I want you to maybe look that way.' All you ever see is Spielberg directing it."

There was debate among publicists during post-production over who should actually get the director credit, to which Garris jokingly said, "How about Christian Nyby?" That is a sly reference to similar controversy surrounding 1951's sci-fi horror classic *The Thing from Another World*, where Howard Hawks had such a strong hand in producing Nyby's film that many question who the authorial director was.

It is quite evident that Spielberg had a major influence on *Poltergeist*, whether it was directing scenes—which he obviously did—or simply having a director who chose to emulate his mise en scène. Yet, to say Hooper had no influence on the movie is folly. If one watches 1981's *The Funhouse*, the clown imagery and strobe lighting effects are very much in Hooper's wheelhouse, as are scenes of mundane community life in 1979's *Salem's Lot*. The intersection of science and the supernatural in *Poltergeist* represented not only Hooper's initial research into parapsychology but also his love of British scribe Nigel Kneale's *The Stone Tape*. His next film *Lifeforce* was also indebted to Kneale's *Quatermass and the Pit*.

Says Banzon, "Hooper doesn't see any difference between his relationship with Spielberg on the set of *Poltergeist* from Spielberg's relationship with Lucas on the set of *Raiders of the Lost Ark*. If you watch the making of *Raiders*, Lucas was there suggesting ideas. Sometimes he'd have a camera and be shooting."

Raiders did run into similar issues, as confirmed by Chris Walas, the make-up artist charged with creating the exploding/melting Nazi heads in the finale: "With the melting head, both George and Steven said, 'Show us what you can do.' The exploding head was a different story, because George and Steven were never in the same room, so I couldn't have the conversation with both to say, 'Okay, from what you're saying, I'm going to do this, this, and this. Is that right?' Steven would go, 'Yeah, that's it. Do that.' I get that shot. Steven's response is, 'I love it. It's good if it's okay with George.' George would see it and go, 'Well, I think we can do this with the background.' I go, 'Okay,' go back and do that. George loves the shot, if it's okay with Steven. Steven's like, 'Well, if we're gonna change the background, maybe we can have smoke...' It's like, 'Guys! Just talk amongst yourselves.'"

Eventually a DGA inquiry looked into what happened on Hooper's set, with Spielberg confirming to *Tulsa World*, "I was there because he wanted me there, but if they accuse me of taking over the film, if they sue me, then I will quit the guild."

He addressed a letter to Hooper in *Variety* on June 2, 1982: "Regrettably, some of the press have misunderstood the rather unique, creative relationship which you and I shared throughout the making of *Poltergeist*. I enjoyed your openness in allowing me, as producer and writer, a wide berth for creative involvement, just as I know you were happy with the freedom you had to direct *Poltergeist* so wonderfully."

The "friction" between Hooper and Spielberg has been overblown. Amblin hired Hooper afterwards for the final episode of *Amazing Stories* and the first episode of 2002 miniseries *Taken*.

During a 2010 interview for the French l'Etrange Festival, Hooper stated, "It affected my career, but he made sure to continue to hire me to work for him. He and I remained best of friends, but it did not... he and I are still very good friends. It did not affect our relationship, and he's done all he can do, but once something like that is out there at a given time, you can't take it back. You can't erase it."

Ten years after *Poltergeist*, Spielberg told *NY Times*, "Producing has been the least fulfilling aspect of what I've done in the last decade. It was frustrating. I found out not everyone is like Bob Zemeckis, as open-minded."

A truly horrible incident occurred on October 30, 1982 when 22-year-old *Poltergeist* co-star Dominique Dunne was strangled by a boyfriend outside her home and never regained consciousness. She was taken off life support by her parents on November 4. At the time her brother, *An American Werewolf in London*'s Griffin Dunne, was producing John Sayles' directorial effort *Baby It's You*, which is dedicated to Dominique's memory.

As for the house where *Poltergeist* was lensed, the current owners now operate it as a movie-themed Airbnb, complete with original 1980 set decorations. Screenwriter Josh Miller (*Sonic the Hedgehog, Violent Night*) celebrated his birthday at the Poltergeist House in Simi Valley, providing all the photos of it for this chapter.

Poltergeist and *E.T.* have always felt like the A and B sides of a 45 record, opening two weeks apart (June 4 and June 11). As Garris remembers, "They were both rated PG, but one was definitely an about face from what *Night Skies* was going to be, and the other one was a no holds barred horror movie that happened not to have an R-rating."

While some of the kids who came to see it were scared out of their wits, others took it as a beacon into the world of fright. One director who achieved enormous success in the contemporary horror field is James Wan, who kicked off his career with the inaugural *Saw* before branching into highly successful scarers involving families endangered by spirits, including the first two films in both the *Insidious* and *Conjuring* franchises.

"*Poltergeist* is definitely the movie that probably left the biggest impact on me, because I saw it at a very young age," explains Wan to this author. "It was my first horror film that I saw in a theater, and it scared me to hell! Ever since then, seriously, I love—and am terrified of—the idea of a haunted house. Your home is supposed to be your sanctuary, your fortress of solitude, right? The idea that something supernatural is within it, invading your personal space, is terrifying for me. The other thing that *Poltergeist* did is it made me terrified of creepy dolls."

Wan transferred that creepy doll phobia into several small-scale icons including Jigsaw's Billy the Puppet as well as the Annabelle doll featured in all nine Conjuring Universe films, including three eponymous entries all her own. The *Poltergeist* appreciation society extends to Wan's protégé Michael Chaves, who has made four of those franchise entries including the most recent and "final" installment titled *The Conjuring: Last Rites*, depicting the real-life Smurl family of Pennsylvania whose suburban home became a focal point for ghostly phenomenon in 1986.

"It was huge," Chaves said of the impact *Poltergeist* had on him. "Because I saw them all on VHS, I saw *Nightmare on Elm Street 3: Dream Warriors* before I even saw *Poltergeist*. That's how messed up the order was. *Poltergeist* is such a better introduction into horror movies for a kid. *Poltergeist* was a great inspiration for *Last Rites*. We even shot on anamorphic Panavision C-Series lenses, the same lenses used to shoot *Poltergeist*."

As Chaves mentions, what Hooper and Spielberg's 1982 film offers is a perfect gateway drug into the genre because it very pointedly aims for a broad audience that might not have cottoned to the *Friday the 13th* or *Halloween*-style slashers of that era. This is a skill Wan has honed particularly well over the *Conjuring* series, which despite R-ratings, are oriented towards family values and jump scares rather than torture porn.

Adds Wan, "*Poltergeist* was designed to scare you, but it was also an entertaining thing, right? It remembered that it's an entertaining movie and it still has to do that particular job. I definitely grew up with a steady diet of classic Steven Spielberg movies, especially from the '80s and '90s. A lot of that personality and that mindset went into me as I became a filmmaker."

The other "vessel" the spirit of *Night Skies* inhabited was director Joe Dante's 1984 summer blockbuster *Gremlins*, which is appropriate since he and John Sayles made two films prior in 1978's *Piranha* and 1981's *The Howling*.

"Tone is something my friend Joe Dante does very, very, very well," says Sayles. "It's been nice to write for him, because I can say, 'Joe will get this because he understands tone.' One of the things Joe does is make a movie that is self-aware, funny, but scary at the same time without getting campy."

A movie mad kid who aspired to be a cartoonist before dabbling as a critic for publications like *Castle of Frankenstein*, Joe Dante entered the world of filmmaking in 1968 with an oddball 7-hour compilation feature known as *The Movie Orgy*. It featured a psychotronic assortment of clips from vintage TV shows, cartoons, serials, commercials, educational films, and other ephemera juxtaposed to maximum hilarity.

As Dante told audiences at a 2016 showing at Brooklyn's BAM that this author attended, "The Schlitz beer company found out about it and said, 'We will pay you guys to take this film and show it in college campuses and we will sell beer and give you a couple of bucks.' A couple of bucks is always good, especially when you're in college, so this became a traveling show. It was a work in progress from 1968 to the mid-'70s. Then I went to work for Roger Corman and I was too busy to do it."

The Movie Orgy was edited in conjunction with Dante's pal Jon Davison, an avid 16mm film collector. When Dante found his way to Los Angeles, Davison had already scored a gig in 1972 as director of advertising and publicity for B-movie king Corman. He brought Dante into the New World Pictures fold in 1974, initially as a trailer editor on films like *Caged Heat*. Dante and fellow editor Allan Arkush banded together to co-direct the ultra-low budget Corman-produced feature *Hollywood Boulevard*.

Says Beverly Gray, Corman's assistant during the early '70s, "In that era I would never have pictured Joe as someone who was going to be an international celebrity filmmaker. He was a trailer cutter, a quiet, sweet guy whom I liked and everybody liked... but I didn't picture him beyond that world. If you were an editor, you were a bit of a hermit, holed away. He was definitely a quiet, mild guy, and suddenly he was a director. You've got to be telling people what to do. He dug deep and discovered he could do that."

"When I made my first movie for Roger I wasn't even sure I was going to be a director," admits Dante. "I was happy being an editor. Then I discovered on set that I really liked the input. I liked the camaraderie of people putting together a show. Directing was even more rewarding than editing, but the editing stood me in good stead. I learned what you can get away with, what you don't need to do, how to save time and money. It doesn't matter how big a budget—you got to use those lessons."

When Dante made his second New World feature *Piranha* solo, it nearly suffered the same fate as Enzo G. Castellari's Italian-made *Jaws* knockoff *Great White* (a.k.a. *The Last Shark*), which Universal sued over. After a successful month in theaters, *Great White* was pulled from distribution by a federal judge over similarities. What stopped Universal from reading *Piranha* the same riot act? Steven Spielberg.

"Spielberg's on record saying he thinks it's the best *Jaws* rip-off," says Dante. "It's also self-aware right up front: 'Okay, we all know it's a *Jaws* rip-off, so let's get over that.' Steven was instrumental in getting the picture released, because Universal was going to injunct it like so many other *Jaws* rip-offs and keep it from seeing the light day. He intervened and said, 'No, this is a parody. This is not a rip-off,' which, of course, it was. That was very helpful. I had no idea about this until long after."

After that project both Dante and Sayles made the leap away from Corman to mini-major Avco Embassy for werewolf movie *The Howling*. Dante's Corman cohort Mike Finnell had already been brought aboard to co-produce the adaptation of Gary Brandner's supermarket paperback. After initially hiring a director who did not work out, Finnell acquired Dante, who in turn hired Sayles to rewrite the script by Terence H. Winkless... except *Jaws* nearly got in the way of werewolf history.

"Since *Piranha*, Joe was now the fish director," recalls Finnell. "The only offers he was getting was either Dino De Laurentiis' *Orca II* or *National Lampoon's Jaws 3/People 0*."

John Hughes and Todd Carroll had written the latter spoof sequel to Spielberg's original hit, being produced by the *Jaws* team of Zanuck and Brown as well as *Animal House*'s Matty Simmons. Dante developed it until he realized he would have very little input, including storyboards being handed to him. Conflicts between producers along with the studio's eventual cold feet killed the project, paving the way for the reviled *Jaws 3-D*.

As Finnell recalls, "Eventually Universal said, 'We don't want to do this comedy version, we'll kill the franchise.' The timing was perfect for it to fall apart and we were able to bring Joe in. He said, 'Well, this script is terrible.' We agree. John Sayles was the obvious guy to rewrite because Joe knew him. We threw out the first draft, hardly kept anything except the names of some of the characters."

Sayles came up with his own story satirizing New Age self-help organizations like EST by putting them in a werewolf context. Dee Wallace's reporter Karen White is drawn into the lycanthropic world after being invited by the benign Dr. George Waggner (Patrick Macnee) to his colony, where werewolves are taught to suppress their urge to kill by eating cattle instead. Sayles and Dante layered the film with lots of in-jokes, including characters named after horror directors (Terry Fisher, Fred Francis, Erle Kenton, etc.).

Oscar-nominated screenwriter Josh Olson, Dante's current co-host for *The Movies that Made Me* podcast, says, "Sayles was such an effortless master at genre. *The Howling* blew my mind, a mix of very dark, real, scary, nasty, funny, and smart, all at the same time. I had seen *Secaucus 7* because Siskel & Ebert championed it, so I was interested to find out someone who had done that film had written this blood and guts werewolf movie. It was a thrill to see he connected with a director as good at his job as John was."

After *The Howling*, Hollywood started to perk up to Dante, who along with Finnell was occupying a rat-infested office on El Centro Avenue in Hollywood.

They were developing *The Philadelphia Experiment* for Avco (a project which already vexed John Carpenter), and, according to J. W. Rinzler's official book, Dante was on a list of considered names to direct *Return of the Jedi*.

"I never knew that," Dante told this author. "How would I know that? They didn't ask me. I guess I was getting profiled. I was oblivious to that stuff, just making movies and watching them, wasn't really paying much attention to the biz."

The biz was paying attention to him, though. As mentioned earlier, Spielberg had possibly looked at Dante to replace Ron Cobb on *Night Skies*, and now he wanted him to perpetrate some mischief with a new set of little green monsters.

"Our agent David Gersh calls and says, 'Steven Spielberg wants to send you guys a script," Finnell recalls. "The script shows up. Every page is stamped with a number so they'll be able to trace it, all top secret. Chris Columbus had written it at NYU and had gotten an agent at CAA based on this. It landed on Steven's desk, and he said, 'I want to make this. I don't want to direct it, but I want to produce it.'"

"I figured it was a mistake, that it had gone to the wrong address," Dante thought. "I figured this guy doesn't know who I am. The first time I met him was outside the mixing stage at Todd AO. He was mixing *E.T.*, but I wasn't allowed to go in and see that, so we met in a parking lot. I showed him my storyboards that I had done, and I think that's what got me the job. Which, by the way, depict children, because in the original script of *Gremlins* the kids were 12 years old, and that's why Billy has an 11-year-old friend who's a holdover from the original version."

"The character was much younger," confirms Finnell. "We wanted to make it a bit more teen friendly, although the weird thing is Billy's friends with this little kid played by Corey Feldman."

A week after this initial meeting, Dante and Finnell were summoned to the office of Warner's executive VP of worldwide production Lucy Fisher, who was excited about *Gremlins* but concerned about the violence in Columbus' spec, including a scene where the monsters eat all the customers in a McDonald's but leave the burgers untouched.

Says Finnell, "What Steven liked about *The Howling* was the combination of horror, complex special effects, and humor. That's exactly the tone he wanted for *Gremlins*. We had to tone down the violence and rewrite it to make it produceable."

While the rewrites would change a great deal, Columbus' 1982 redraft for Amblin still has many of the elements which make it a classic, including the "oriental market" opening (originally in Hong Kong), *Snow White* screening, Christmas setting, and the infamous Santa Claus monologue. What was not yet on the page was the Looney Tunes sensibility or, most crucially, the character of Gizmo. The original relationship between Billy and the generic Mogwai he gets as a gift had the young man showing disdain for the creature.

"The only way this picture was going to get made by Warners is if it was a movie for teenagers and families... and the idea of mom getting her head cut off and bounced down the stairs wasn't really going to play to that audience," Dante adds. "The whole warm family dynamic with the inventor father ended up pushed to the fore, because if the audience doesn't like the characters they're not going to think much of the movie. A lot of that had to do with Steven."

Although *Twilight Zone: The Movie* was produced by an uncredited Amblin, the first official Amblin Entertainment release would be *Gremlins*. It would build off Spielberg's initial conception of a "children's crusade of filmmakers" to give up-and-comers their shot, kicking off the peak era for the company whose logo was branded with Elliott and E.T. soaring across the moon. Universal spent $3.5M building Amblin's permanent offices, something the then-36-year-old called "the most amazing gift I've ever received."

Said Sid Sheinberg in December 1982, "I am convinced that anything Steven set out to do he would do very well. If it had to do with running a company or something in the business world as distinguished from the creative world he would do it well 'cause he's one of those people that learns what he has to learn, listens very carefully, absorbs it, and very soon thereafter becomes a master of it."

While Spielberg had been dabbling as a producer for a few years—sometimes hands off (*Continental Divide*) and sometimes hands extremely on (*Poltergeist*)—the unprecedented success of *E.T.* drove him into full-on moguldom. Amblin' Productions was transformed into Amblin Entertainment, which developed a flurry of projects at different studios across town. That "no-strings" element of the deal must have rankled Universal: Of the roughly 30 films Spielberg has directed in the decades since *E.T.,* only 7 have been for Universal, including *Disclosure Day*. However, the relationship has yielded a Best Picture winner in *Schindler's List* as well as the studio's cornerstone *Jurassic* franchise, not to mention lucrative Spielberg productions like *Back to the Future*.

Spielberg and Dante on set (*left to right*).

Explains Sean Daniel, "The long history between Sid and Steven and the joyous success of *E.T.* made it an absolute priority to have Steven headquartered at Universal, where he is to this day. It was more than a deal, it really did have to do with a relationship."

Says Mick Garris, "*E.T.* was the first film Spielberg himself had ownership in. Amblin Entertainment became a different sort of company from what originally was, basically a banner. It became an actual living and breathing entity with *E.T.* and beyond. It was a great place to work. They had their own building at Universal in that Southwestern Santa Fe style popular in the '80s. They called it 'the Taco Bell.'"

"Well, that's kind of cruel," Dante adds of the nickname. "It was a very attractive place. Lots of wood. There was a big tree that was in *Leave it to Beaver's* yard. The great thing is Amblin was a shield against whatever studio they were making the pictures for, because you had Steven to run interference. He was always on the side of the filmmaker. That didn't mean he didn't disagree with you, or you couldn't have an argument with him, but you never felt some preposterous studio demand was going to be insisted on. There was always Steven to say, 'No, that's stupid. Don't do that.'"

Adds Garris, "My office was in the building next door, but there was a beautiful central open area in the middle where you could have lunch. He'd insisted I storyboard my *Amazing Stories* episode I directed so I knew what I was doing. I was sitting out in that patio with Steven Spielberg for two hours going over these storyboards, looking around going, 'Have I been tapped by the sword of King Arthur?'"

In Chris Columbus' second draft of *Gremlins* for Amblin, Billy was an aspiring fantasy novelist obsessed with Arthurian chivalry... hence the swords on the wall, which remained in the film as evidence of development. This, and many other things, changed partly thanks to ghost writer John Sayles. Dante's go-to scribe was hired briefly to draft a ten-page treatment that radically reimagined *Gremlins* from top to bottom, much as he had on *The Howling*. The director has little memory of this, saying, "I never really thought of John as part of that," but his producer did recall bringing Sayles in.

Some of the oddball changes Sayles put in his *Gremlins* treatment included changing Billy Peltzer to Danny Raymond, an aspiring comic book artist who lives in his parent's attic and works in a sporting goods store. (Both of those settings and the cartoonist aspirations were integrated into the film.) His birth father was a dreamer who ultimately killed himself, and there is a fear that Danny could crack up too. Instead of Pennsylvania it takes place in heavily-forested northern Michigan, where hunters are finding deer torn apart in the woods, much like the cattle mutilations in *Night Skies*.

Danny discovers two furry gremlins (not called Mogwai) in an antique shop where they do not remember stocking them, thinking they are stuffed dolls. Danny gives one to a little girl named Rosie and keeps the "broken" one. Missing its arm, he calls it "Lefty." Later his mom finds something has raided the kitchen pantry, and Danny returns from work to find ink spilled on his drawing table, black footprints leading to Lefty. He leaves then returns to find the ink cleaned up while Lefty now has two arms, making him think he's crazy. After getting fired from his job the next day, Danny takes a conciliatory ride with the sheriff to the site of another deer carcass found stripped of meat.

Danny goes home and Lefty begins eating chips with him. Surprised but curious, Danny gets the creature water and more food. Lefty understands everything he says, and they shake hands, agreeing not to let anyone else know. Danny's love interest Megan comes over; they drink wine and trauma bond. Later that night they are in bed and she rises to get aspirin from the bathroom, where Lefty leaps out at her from the cabinet. After she screams and it scurries away, Danny is relieved someone else has seen the thing. Megan eventually finds a book containing a photo of a Native American totem pole with a creature just like Lefty carved at the top.

Two redneck hunters named Chester and Rick shoot a deer while poaching at night. Then, Chester is shot by his own gun and Rick screams at glowing red eyes. During the day, Danny and Megan ask high school biology teacher Mr. Feeny to stop by the house and examine Lefty. He returns home to find his mom's parakeet killed, its blood smeared on drawings of Chester and Rick. He digs through his father's sketchbook and finds a drawing of a gremlin, realizing his dad had seen them too. He puts Lefty in a metal bird cage so Feeny can examine him, but then Danny is arrested under suspicion of killing Chester and Rick. The caged Lefty metamorphosizes into a black pod stuck in the cage, a visual used in the movie.

Danny meets up with a Native American high school friend named Rueben Bird, whose grandmother recognizes Danny's sketches of Lefty as one of the Fox People, a fable of little creatures who found game for the tribes. "Whatever dreams the tribe had, the Fox People would make them real," until one day the creatures turned on the tribe and killed them all, disappearing up north. She points lower on the photo of the totem pole to a different grinning creature with razor sharp teeth.

Pods begin hatching all over town. Danny's co-worker Vicki is surprised by a red-eyed gremlin splashing into her bath, just like Buddee into Tess's bath in *Night Skies*. She is then chased by multiple gremlins and killed, but Danny cannot be blamed since he was in custody. The transformed reptilian Lefty has now emerged from the pod and killed Feeny. Megan finds Danny and they are given a ride by Rueben in his snowplow. They break into the sporting goods store and fight off gremlins with anything available (tennis rackets, baseball bats, etc.), all of which wound up in the produced movie. The couple drive a snowmobile through the front window, racing to the antique barn to warn townspeople at a Christmas pageant.

The vehicle runs out of gas and Megan is attacked by a gremlin in her sleeping bag. By daylight Danny is dragging the wounded Megan through the snow to the barn where the townspeople remain trapped. Descriptions of folks fighting off gremlins who make their way in from the rafters evokes the 1951 Val Lewton western *Apache Drums,* where a town fortifies itself against an attack inside an old church for the last third of the movie. Said gremlin siege reaches its peak when murdered Rueben's plow breaks through the barn with the monsters at the wheel, likely the seed of Mr. Futterman's scene in the film. With a hole in the barn, the reptilian gremlins—standing apart—begin to freeze to death, while the humans—huddled together for warmth—shield themselves from the beasts.

By morning the gremlins are frozen corpses. Danny goes out in the snow to investigate but gets pounced on by the last remaining gremlin, who kept itself alive under a body. It attacks Danny, but then out of nowhere Danny's dog Atlas takes the creature down. Dying, the last gremlin reaches out to shake Danny's hand, acknowledging it is Lefty. The final shot shows Rosie, the little girl with the other gremlin from the beginning, still holding her little furry friend, whose eyes move mischievously.

"I'm not sure why we did that," Finnell said of Sayles' treatment. "We wanted a different take, then came up with something so different it was like, 'Well, no, this doesn't really work.' Because we had a good relationship with John we thought, 'Maybe we need another pair of eyes on this.' Ultimately didn't use anything of that, I don't think."

"That was fun," Sayles recalls of his treatment for *Gremlins*. "I liked it. Joe wanted to go a little darker with it, and I went a little darker with it… at least the treatment. I don't think Spielberg wanted to go there."

But wait, there's more. According to author Steven Awalt, who has been hard at work for years on a definitive book about the making of *Gremlins*, Sayles was also tasked with some rewrites on an actual full script draft dated October 1982.

"At the very least, Sayles rewrote an opening scene set in Texas, to replace Chris' scene in Chinatown," Awalt told this author. "Possibly to remove Chinese stereotypes, although the Mogwai are still of Chinese origin. I can't verify if he did this entire rewrite or only the Texas sequence. I talked with both, and Columbus only found out about Sayles' work after the fact. He said he got it, 'fledgling writer, that's how it goes,' but it surely sucked for him. He only did a single rewrite before Sayles came in. Chris came out okay: Sole credit and three more Amblin scripts after, two of them, *Goonies* and *Young Sherlock*, produced."

The general tone of mischievous monsters was a huge part of *Night Skies*, as one could easily imagine a gremlin riding the cow and other monkeyshines in that script. However, two scenes in *Gremlins* feel specifically elaborated on from the earlier project: The kitchen scene where the mother grinds a gremlin in the blender (something verbally referenced in *Night Skies*, along with the scene where Gram fights Squirt in the kitchen), and the section where Mr. Futterman is run over by his own plow (like Skar trying to drive Ed's cultivator into the family). The kitchen scene is in Columbus' April 1982 redraft with Billy instead of his mom, but the plow scene is not, and neither are the iconic "Three Rules" (no bright light, don't get them wet, no food after midnight). Columbus' original spec is not currently available.

Awalt sheds more light: "'Mr. Futters' appears in Chris's April 1982 draft, next door neighbor to Mrs. Deagle. He's not the character we know, though. By the October draft he has a wife, he's a rah-rah USA fella, and he's killed with his own plow. Same with the kitchen sequence, could've been something Steven loved in *Night Skies*, might've put the bug for that in Chris' ear after the spec."

Says Finnell, "I don't know of any connection between *Night Skies* and *Gremlins*, because Chris had written it when he was still in college. It was its own thing with no crossover. I remember reading *Night Skies* and saying, 'Oh, this is great.' The more commercial version was what Steven ultimately did with *E.T.*"

"I don't think it was conscious," says Dante of the similarities. "There may be things that were in that script, which I haven't read in 20 years, but personally I see more of that script in *E.T.* That's the nice version of *Night Skies*."

"I see elements of *Night Skies* in other movies, but you never know," concludes Sayles. "I think there's just stuff in the zeitgeist. I watch the same movies a lot of other screenwriters do, so I don't ever feel like somebody took something of mine. I say, 'Oh, really? You know, that's almost exactly what I did in some other script.'"

"I never thought about it," Rick Baker said of a possible *Night Skies* influence on *Gremlins*. "I wouldn't be surprised. That shit happens all the time."

"*Night Skies* reminded me all over again of *Gremlins*," exclaimed Geraldine Sutton Stith. "The way one was in the pantry and she was trying to get him out with the broom!"

As for the idea that *Night Skies* influenced the gremlins themselves, that is a lot more tenuous. Within the gremlin design one can find elements of Rick Baker's Skar creature (eyes, brow), Ron Cobb's unused *Night Skies* sketches (teeth, jawline), and the eyewitness sketches from Kelly-Hopkinsville (ears, chin). The green skin with white belly coloring of Baker's initial build is similar as well, but both creatures are reptilian so that is a common element from nature.

"No, not at all," says gremlins creator Chris Walas of any influence. "Maybe between Steven and Joe or something like that, but I certainly didn't see it. *Night Skies* was closed down fairly quietly, because it was kind of a secret project to begin with. Not everybody heard about it for quite a while. I remember Rick was pretty upset about that."

There is zero evidence any of these elements were discussed during extensive *Gremlins* creature development, yet Walas' wonders represent perhaps the most accurate cinematic depiction of what the Sutton family claims they saw that night in 1955. The movie does end, after all, with a reporter describing the creatures as "little green men."

After his stunning work realizing the werewolves in *The Howling* and the Big Daddy Roth-influenced creatures in Dante's *Twilight Zone* segment, Rob Bottin was highly favored to create the gremlins. His schedule fabricating Tim Curry's iconic Lucifer in Ridley Scott's *Legend* did not allow him the job, so Chris Walas—who had worked with Dante on *Piranha* and Finnell on *Airplane!*—was brought in. Alongside Dante and Finnell, he had been attached to a 3D remake of *Creature from the Black Lagoon*.

"I was really looking forward to that, because Creature is my favorite Universal monster," said Walas. "That fell through because they decided they're going to do *Jaws 3-D* instead. Adrian Lyne's *Starman* also fell apart, and I just bought a house. Mike calls up and says, '*Creature* has fallen through, but there's this other project we want you to take a look at called *Gremlins*.' He sent a script up, and I'm reading hordes of thousands of gremlins running through the town. Mike calls back and says, 'What do you think?' I'm going, 'Well, it's impossible. Let's do it.' I didn't have an option."

Dante was initially conceiving the creatures for stop-motion, but Walas suggested puppets as the better route. The director then, like Spielberg on *Close Encounters*, considered monkeys in costumes like the Mickey Mouse in 1934's *March of the Wooden Soldiers*. After a "trained" monkey ripped apart his office and crapped on his floor, Dante called Walas back saying, "Yeah, puppets sound better."

Finnell remembers, "This was before CGI, so the whole thing had to be done practically with puppets. Chris Columbus had drawn little sketches of gremlins with big ears and spindly legs, so that was kind of the jumping off point for Chris Walas."

According to Walas, Columbus only drew one brief rendering based on his work during the scattergun design process: "What I brought to it was the big ears, the wider face, and basic body proportion. I was designing based on puppets, so they have long forearms and short legs, proportions with the biggest opportunity for puppeteering success. Chris's rendering was based on all that, but it wasn't the final gremlin at all."

Adds Dante, "Even when Chris Walas came on and had to literally make the gremlins, it was pretty close to what Chris originally said with big ears, big teeth, and reptilian. Them being anarchic, that Marx Brothers quality, was because there were so few things they could do physically. The only way to tell the story was to have them as anarchic as possible and meet as many gruesome deaths as we can visit on them."

Based on reading Columbus' April draft, Walas' statement that "there wasn't a lot of character in the original script" rings true. He suggests the antic nature came out of a meeting with he, Dante, and Spielberg: "I'm saying, 'I think they walk around like this, because that's easy for us to do and it's creepy.' I'm walking around the coffee table hunched over, then Joe gets up going, 'Yeah, then maybe he bounces around!' Then Steven gets up and it's the three of us walking like insane goofballs around a table, acting like 2-year-olds! We all got on the same page."

Walas found it difficult to imbue his sketches with that personality, so he built a small maquette of a gremlin, photographing it in various places including his garden. It passed the standard for good design, readability and relatability, as well as striking a recognizable silhouette. Dante approved. As for the first stage gremlin, the cuter furrier Mogwai, Walas was inspired by the Italian children's puppet character Topo Gigio, who graced American screens on *The Ed Sullivan Show*. He also drew from the galagos (or bush baby), a primate native to sub-Saharan Africa, wanting to create sympathy with big eyes, a small face, and overall moppet appeal.

When it came to fabricating the many gremlins with varying abilities, Walas' team took the route of vacuum forming which is, as explained by Adam Savage on *Tested*, "Basically taking hot plastic and using it to make molds to do the detailing." Sheets of styrene are the most common plastic used, and the process is relatively cheap and durable.

Says Walas, "You can vacuum form forty shells in the time you can do two shells with fiberglass, and vacuum forming is so much less obnoxious. I hate fiberglass so much, and polyester resin, but a lot of times that's what you have to do for one-off stuff. But if you're cranking out a bunch..."

As seen in Walas' 2020 documentary *Gremlins: The Puppet Story*, his team of mostly fresh talent from the Bay Area filmed dozens of puppeteering tests on video to work out gags like a gremlin riding a trike or being ground in a blender. Even with all this impressive footage, it nearly became another *Night Skies* scenario of getting cancelled.

"There were big questions about whether the puppets would hold up," Walas admits. "I'm not sure Warners wanted to make the movie so much as they wanted a Steven Spielberg production going on the lot."

"It was almost half-a-year to build these things," adds Finnell. "We didn't have a greenlight, and everything was like, 'Okay, we need X dollars to keep Chris Walas working.' The studio said, 'Okay, but we're not there yet in terms of making the final decision.' We went off with Allen Daviau, Steven's go-to director of photography, and shot a bunch of tests with Gizmo. That got Terry Semel to say, 'Okay, I can see how this is going to work.' Lucy Fisher calls: 'Please come up to my office.' Me and Joe go, 'Oh God.' We go up there and she's got this cardboard box. She opens the box and there's a light bulb painted green."

Dante claims, "Steven finally got Warners to pony up as a favor to him, which is the way they looked at it... 'Spielberg's folly,' they used to call it."

Production ramped up on the Universal Studios backlot around Courthouse Square, with the fictional Kingston Falls' town movie theater marquee touting two inside joke films: A BOY'S LIFE and WATCH THE SKIES. Zach Galligan took the lead of Billy, while Corey Feldman played his young friend Pete, a role given to him by Spielberg to make up for cutting his *E.T.* character Lance. Shooting on the backlot drove up costs on what was intended as a low-budget project, but Dante knew the puppets would clash with too realistic a locale. The budget eventually hit $11M, also rising due to constant improv with their monstrous puppet theater troupe.

Walas says it was "the most evolutionary project I've ever worked on. Joe's like, 'I'd like to do this and I'd like to do that.' I'm going, 'Okay, we can do that, but you have to do it this way.' Chris was amazing, because we'd come up with all this stuff in a morning meeting and the next day he's got 10 pages of new script ready to shoot. I'm starting to tear my hair out. I go to Joe with storyboards for the day and he's like, 'Throw it away, we're not gonna use those.' I'm like, 'Give me a chance here.' I would get a call to the set and they're shooting something where there's no gremlins in the script, and suddenly we have 12 gremlin puppets in the shot, off the cuff. No prep time, just, 'Get some puppets out here and we'll figure out what to do with them.' That level of insanity never let up."

The most catastrophic change came from Spielberg very late in the day. The filmmakers had already catered to their power producer by giving Gizmo the same coloring as his cocker spaniel dog (upon which he approved it), but now he had another request: Gizmo should not turn into a gremlin... he should be the hero of the movie.

"I remember distinctly the day Joe came to me first thing in the morning as we were filming, and I could see he was upset," remembers Walas. "He says, 'I just had a conversation with Steven. He says, 'One of the Mogwai should stay and be Billy's friend. What do you think?' I'm like, 'That's a terrible idea. It's gonna ruin the movie.' Joe's like, 'Yeah, I know. I think I'm gonna have to do it.' Of course, it made the movie. Gizmo wound up being the big star. Steven has this intuition about stuff that did not make the job any easier but certainly made the product better."

"That wasn't decided until they saw the dailies," adds Dante "In the original script, Gizmo turns into Stripe, the bad gremlin. The Mogwai we made was this little bucket of bolts we were hoping to get away with for 20 minutes, and now he had to be the hero. We totally panicked and ended up having to build a giant Gizmo because the only way you get expressions from them is if you had something big. To see this giant Gizmo head walking around was the strangest thing, but the reason that movie is so popular is because of that one decision Steven made to keep Gizmo around."

This "added surprise" started with a foam mockup of Mega Gizmo to work out movement. The big guy would be cable-controlled, but the initial instinct was to do this (and much of the other puppetry) in a Bunraku style similar to what was planned for *Night Skies*, with the operators behind the puppet in blue suits then optically removed.

"I saw the potential there to do a better job," says Walas of this ahead-of-the-curve technique. "Opticals cost a fortune back then and didn't always work. Straight practical stuff in front of the camera looks better because it's there, there's no trick other than not showing the operator."

The person who wound up finally using this technique on a Mogwai turned out to be Rick Baker himself when he did the puppets for *Gremlins 2*. As explained in *Cinefex* #46, Baker and Dante both wanted to see Gizmo moving around on his legs in the sequel, and they used Bunraku combined with the way Walas' inspiration Topo Gigio was done.

Baker explained, "Our idea was to have the puppeteer's hand hidden behind the Mogwai body with his fingers down inside the legs. Another puppeteer would use rods to move its arms while still another would operate its head from behind using a gimbal mechanism to move the neck."

His team improvised Topo Gizmo doing a dance, and after Warner execs saw the video test they insisted he dance in *Gremlins 2*. When the chroma key element did not work on 35mm film, Baker pivoted to shooting against black instead. *Night Skies* lives!

While the first *Gremlins*' puppets are not nearly as articulate as Skar was, in some ways their Muppet-like limitations are what make them so funny and appealing. While shooting the creatures tearing apart the local bar, Dante resorted to soliciting crew members to throw out ideas on a chalk board.

Said Walas, "My heart almost burst when he put that list up and tells the crew, 'Hey, anybody! Come up with a funny idea for the gremlins to do! Just write it down.' I can't keep up with the day, and he's adding all this stuff. Just insane. More and more. Crew members shouting out, 'Hey, how about this?' I'm going, 'Shut up, everybody!' Somebody would say, 'How about Gizmo drives a radio-controlled car?' Before I get a chance to say, 'Hold on,' the prop guy's got three Barbie cars ready to go."

Principal photography began in April of 1983, with Walas only responsible for scenes involving gremlin/human interaction. After wrapping in August, he was given three months to refurbish all the torn rubber, then went into six weeks of non-stop gremlin mayhem. Eventually, this frantic pace drove him into the ground.

"*Gremlins* almost killed me," the artist says bluntly.

Considering Rob Bottin had been hospitalized for exhaustion, double pneumonia, and a bleeding ulcer after the year-long marathon creating the title creature(s) for *The Thing*, it's a good thing he did not do *Gremlins* given what happened to Walas.

"That was my introduction to kidney stones," remembers Walas. "Woke up one morning feeling bad. My crew drove me to the only medical center open and they were like, 'You got a kidney stone.' Then Mike showed up and we went to Saint Joseph's."

Recalls Finnell, "At one point I actually took Chris to the emergency room in the middle of shooting at Saint Joseph's Hospital in Burbank, near the studio.

He was exhausted, having kind of a mini nervous breakdown. His heart was racing or something, and I drove him to the emergency room and he calmed down. Everything was fine."

"I finally passed the stone that same day," Walas continues. "We went to work the next day and it was the worst day on the whole show. We tried to shoot a bunch of stuff we shouldn't have. Didn't go well. We didn't get our day. Then I broke my ankle during one of the shots that didn't have any gremlins in it, Billy's friend in the window firing his slingshot. Initially, it was just the kid in the window, period. Then Joe's like, 'Get Chris over here.' I'm literally running, trying to keep up. He's going, 'Maybe we can get a couple gremlins in the foreground.' I'm like, 'Okay, great, we can do that.' Sure enough, as this shot grows, now there's a gremlin hanging from Christmas lights and all this. We're working out of a trailer on the stage, and I had a cold so I was on medicine. Groggy. I stepped off the stairs and went down on my right ankle, broke it. That was no fun. The medical department sent me to the hospital again, did X-rays, said 'It's going to heal itself. You have to stay off it.' Like I could do that."

Rick Baker says, "I remember visiting Chris at Warner Bros. and he was on crutches at the time because he had fallen off the back of the truck on the stage."

"I was on crutches for at least a week," Walas confirms. "Towards the very end, I got anemic, dead on my feet. By that point my crew was in top form, three steps ahead, so they covered my rear end."

Fortunately, all that hard work done across over 100 days of filming was about to pay off as the biggest name on the film returned from London to view the fruits of their labor.

"Steven went away to do *Indiana Jones*," remembers Dante. "A lot of things changed because of the vagaries of working with puppets, things they could and couldn't do. A tremendous amount of improv: 'They can do this, let's do more of that!' By the time Steven saw the movie, it was a revelation... it was so unlike what he had expected."

According to Finnell, Spielberg had one big note: "At the very end of the movie, when they're in this department store and Stripe is duplicating in the water, originally Billy opens the window so light comes in and melts Stripe. Steven said, 'No, Gizmo should do that.' We reconstructed part of the set and had Gizmo pull the cord. We then spotted the movie with Jerry Goldsmith. He had a studio in his Beverly Hills house with a state-of-the-art electric piano. I went over, Steven and Joe were already there. Steven said, 'Listen to this...'

Jerry plays what became known as 'The Gremlin Rag.' It was completely different from what any of us expected. We thought it would be horror movie stuff, but it was like demented carnival music. We said, 'You know what? That's perfect.'"

Despite nearly killing himself pulling off the job, the movie's puppet maestro was rewarded with an above-the-line main title credit: "Gremlins Created by Chris Walas."

"Rick got so ticked off when I got a head credit," exclaims Walas happily. "He's like, 'How did you get a head credit on a picture?' It was a big deal. That's how much pull we had at the time, because there weren't that many of us doing it. We got highly valued very quickly, moved from cheap Roger Corman movies to major studio productions. Rick and everyone, we became names attached to the project to bring something to it. We were riding pretty darn high, I gotta tell you. I got treated like a rock star."

"*Fangoria* was a big part of my life in my adolescence, and Rick Baker, Tom Savini, Rob Bottin, and Chris Walas were rock stars of makeup effects," concurs modern *Fangoria* editor-in-chief Phil Nobile. "They'd be on the covers of these magazines with their creations, idols for a generation of horror fans. They had long hair and beards, looked like they rolled out of a van to do a gig, except the gig is making monsters and blowing people's heads up."

As exec producers, Kathy Kennedy and Frank Marshall were very supportive, often fielding script issues or running interference when Finnell could not quell studio meddling. They insisted Dante get to preview his cut before making changes, and "his cut" meant almost all elements finished including Jerry Goldsmith's completed score. George Lucas and other names were present at the Sacramento test screening.

"Directors would be lucky to get a preview like this once in their life," beams Dante. "They tore the roof off the theater. You've got to remember this was a movie nobody ever heard of. No famous people in it. It was, 'What is this?' It was a surprise."

"The movie was released and was a big hit," says Finnell of the $153M domestic gross, proving "*E.T.* with teeth" had bite. "The second weekend actually made more money than the first, which was rare."

Adds Sayles, "When Joe finally came up with *Gremlins*, it had that nice turning point. It's like an *E.T.* movie—'Aw, isn't it cute?' —and then it's like, 'Oh no, don't put them in the water.' The violence is not that scary because it's so broad and comic."

Concludes Dante, "The Looney Tunes-ness came from me, but the script had a solid story. The tone, which I've often been criticized for in my career, is probably one of the things that's most salient about it. This remained with people because it was an unusual tone. They expect it to be one thing, and it turned out to be another."

"I love working with him," Frank Marshall told this author of Dante in 2018 (for Coming Soon). "If I look back, all the directors I work with have great senses of humor, and he's no exception. He's really fun, funny, steeped in the history of movies and the language of filmmaking. That's why, when you see his movies, you go, 'That's a Joe,' because he knows what he wants. He's not just going, 'Let's get 10 shots. Let me get the coverage here.' He has a point of view, the same as Zemeckis. We had great filmmakers back then and I'm honored to have worked with them, but Joe in particular because he has such a quirky sense of humor."

"I always liked Joe Dante," comments Greg Mottola. "His stuff was really funny and a little gonzo, a little B movie. Very irreverent but filled with a love of old movies. As a kid who grew up watching black and white '50s horror films and sci-fi movies on television, I knew all those references. There was so much affection in every frame of what he did, but he also wasn't afraid to be naughty and dark and go there with gore."

Contemporary screenwriter Andrew Barrer (*Ant-Man and The Wasp*, *Transformers One*) describes *Gremlins* as a useful comp when he and partner Gabriel Ferrari are pitching material that treads the line between kid and grown-up sensibilities:

"Right now we have a movie in... let's call it pre-pre-production because there's a lot of practical effects, but it's based on a YouTube short called *Gnomes* that is absolutely brilliant. A jogger goes out to the woods. She steps on a mushroom which triggers the anger of a group of little gnomes who emerge with man-killing machines and devour her. It's a shockingly violent short about killer gnomes. We pitched the concept first to 21 Laps, the company where *Stranger Things* was born, and you'd be hard pressed to find a show more Spielbergian than that. We couldn't come in with this hard-R blood and guts gnomes movie, so we're like, 'How do you take what's special about the notion of gnomes in your backyard and make it make sense to a studio that wants to do the PG-13 version?' Spielbergian says it all. You tell a story about a human who moves into a house that is adjacent to these woods. Yes, there are bad gnomes out there, but they're not all bad. There's a friendship to be had and there's wonder and discovery. Once we said we wanted to do this Amblin/Spielberg version, everyone was like, 'Oh.' It just clicked and made sense. Hopefully, fingers crossed, we get to make that movie. It will be our homage to *Gremlins* and *E.T.* in particular."

"Come back again
I want you to stay next time"
—Neil Diamond

Steven Spielberg told UPI in 1983, "There will be an *E.T.* sequel when it's time for one, and when the story is ready. I'm not interested in creating a cottage industry just for the sake of hard currency. *E.T.* came out of my purest intentions as a filmmaker, and I'm not about to join the Wall Street generation. A sequel will evolve naturally, not because of the pressure to create more fury at the box office. I'm not dialing for dollars here."

There was never a sequel to the all-time top grosser. For a town whose biggest currency is—shockingly—money, this was an odd turn of events. It is not as if the filmmakers did not consider a more open-ended conclusion... in fact, they shot it, but it wound up on the cutting room floor.

"The script originally ended after the spaceship leaves," Henry Thomas explains. "It fades out, as it does, but then it comes back and we're in Elliott's living room. They're playing D&D but now Elliott's the Dungeon Master and he's got absolute power, relishing in the role. We pull out and reveal the communicator on top of the roof clicking away. It left room for a sequel, an open ending. Steven edited it out and ended it at that moment. It's great because it says all that the scene we shot said, but leaves it for the audience. That's the best way you can leave it."

"Everybody's talking about a sequel, but I hate discussing it because I want this movie to stand on its own," said Mathison before *E.T.*'s release.

"I don't think any of us were really involved in that decision," says Dee Wallace. "At one point toward the end of filming, Steven happened to say to me on the set, 'You know Dee, they're already talking to me about making a sequel. What do you think?' I said, 'Steven, I think you should let it be the classic that I know it's going to be.' That was my answer."

"There was talk," says Thomas of a potential *E.T. II*. "There was a huge incentive for him to do that. Definitely Sid Sheinberg and all the guys there were like, 'We need a sequel. We need something else.'"

"I just did not want to make a sequel," Spielberg told an audience at the TCM Festival in 2018. "I flirted with it for a little bit—just a little bit to see if I could think of a story."

This resulted in a 9-page treatment document titled "E.T. II: Nocturnal Fears," dated July 17, 1982. To put it in context, this is a little over a month after *E.T.* had been released, having grossed $129.67M by then.

"No, I never saw it... or if I did, I might have blanked it out or something," Thomas admits. "I don't know. I've heard of this, though. It's like, there's a bad alien who comes looking for E.T., and then Elliott and E.T. have to fight the bad alien, or something?"

One of this author's greatest joys in putting this book together was telling Henry Thomas the story of *E.T. II* and watching him laugh himself silly: "It's extremely depressing. It starts with everyone sitting around moping because E.T. doesn't come back. Then the evil aliens come and they're, like, albino E.T.s and they're looking for him, and you find out E.T.'s name is Zreck. Then they kidnap the kids, they torture them on a spaceship, and then E.T. comes in the last five minutes or something and rescues everybody and then goes away again."

Laughed Thomas, "So after working with the kids, Steven and Melissa decided in the next instance they would have to torture the kids!"

The aforementioned "EVIL" aliens in the treatment are "carnivorous," fanged, red-eyed albino mutations of the same squat species as E.T., led by the nasty Korel. Obvious parallels with the malevolent aliens of *Night Skies* are made more direct with the following random line: "There have been numerous reports of unexplained cattle mutilations in the surrounding countryside."

"I remember they're turning it in, and I remember Sheinberg turned it down," Thom Mount recalls of the sequel treatment.

Cynicism certainly shines through in how brief and unstructured it is, or lines like "E.T. is as popular today as he ever was!" and sign-off note "Dreams can come true!" One envisions this being tossed off to a transcriber at Amblin' Productions as the creators giggle like Zero Mostel and Gene Wilder.

Whether or not this sub-par idea—barely featuring E.T. at all—was a deliberate sabotage job on the parts of said creators, Mount thinks that's a possibility: "I wouldn't be surprised at all, because Steven and Melissa were not fans of sequels. I have always been constitutionally opposed to sequels. There was a lot of pressure to do sequels to *Smokey and the Bandit*. I gave in to that pressure and regretted it because those are fucking dreadful. There was a lot of pressure to do a sequel to *Animal House*, which I refused because I thought, 'This is a one-off, an anomaly, perfect in its little universe. All you can do is diminish it.'"

Said Josh Miller of *Best Movies Never Made* podcast, "We were theorizing that was actually Spielberg's way of not doing an *E.T. II*, because it is so hard to accept that he thought these ideas were good at any point in time. Who knows? Maybe Spielberg was like, 'Yeah, torture Elliott!' Once somebody suggests the idea that was his attempt to tank doing a sequel... to come up with a thing that even Universal would be like, 'Yeah, we like money, but I don't know...'"

"Maybe Sid gave it to me to read," thinks Daniel. "The question is... was Sid leaning on them to see some kind of sequel? I remember the mindset was, 'This is not a movie that should have a sequel.'"

Drew Barrymore recalled to Spielberg at the 2018 event, "I remember you saying, 'We are not making a sequel to *E.T.*' I think I was eight. I remember being like, 'Okay, that's a bummer, but I totally get it.' I thought it was a smart choice."

It speaks to the amount of sway Spielberg had at the time that he could convince the powers that be to not go down that road, even though they were theoretically leaving hundreds of millions of dollars (in box office alone) on the table.

"That's ultimately what they decided," said Mount. "This guy just gave us the biggest windfall in the history of the studio. Is somebody gonna say, 'Hey, you gotta make a sequel or we're gonna shoot you'? If you want to be in business with Steven Spielberg, you're gonna listen to him. If you make *E.T. II* without him then all you do is alienate Steven forever. He would have become either Columbia or Warner Bros.' captive as opposed to Universal's captive. I mean, we built him a fucking office building in the middle of the lot, right? We did everything we could to make an environment at Universal that he liked and he controlled."

"He was going to be left alone, because they didn't want to mess with the lucky charm," adds Thomas.

Said Spielberg, "Before *E.T.* I had some rights, but I didn't have a lot of rights. I didn't have what we call 'the freeze,' where you can stop the studio from making a sequel because you control the freeze on sequels, remakes, and other ancillary uses of the IP. I didn't have that. I got it after *E.T.* because of its success."

"There is a long Hollywood tradition of sequels to certain movies," says Daniel, one of the stewards of Universal's *Mummy* franchise. "That was a different time than today, when movies are IP. That wasn't the order of the day, right? It was understood and accepted that *E.T.* was really special and there wasn't a sequel to be done. Frank Marshall and I were talking about this the other day, that it was a time when each movie stood on its own. It wasn't an industrial process of any kind."

Says Mike Ryan, "That ending is so powerful to this day because there's nothing else. It's not like, 'Well, let's see what happens when he comes back! Now Elliott goes to E.T. world!' Unless you want to count *The Phantom Menace* as a sequel... or a prequel, I guess. E.T.'s species does appear on film again."

Adds Dana Gould, "It would have been funny if they did it like *Aliens*… 'E.T.s'… and it's 40 lost E.T.s, 40 lonely kids…"

On the promo trail for *Disclosure Day* in 2026, Josh Horowitz asked Spielberg point blank, "Did Elliott ever see E.T. again?" The director replied, "No, never saw him again… but he did dream about him. There was the psychic link between the two of them. If you noticed, E.T. touched Elliott right here [*head*] and said, 'I'll be right here.' Touches him right there. That is for the rest of Elliott's life."

In 1985 Spielberg decided to funnel some of his more fanciful notions of an E.T. sequel into *E.T.: The Book of the Green Planet*, which elaborated on the movie's Dr. Seuss-esque ship interior and took it to the next level. It follows E.T. back home to a planet dominated by sentient fauna. Due to a time jump, Elliott is now 14, and E.T. attempts to send several clones of himself to Earth to rejoin his human friend, who is distracted by girls. There are adorable creatures called Flopgopples.

"The only thing I could think about was a book called *The Green Planet*, which was all going to take place at E.T.'s home," said Spielberg. "It was better as a novel than I think it would have been as a film."

Chosen to pen the YA sequel book was William Kotzwinkle, whom Spielberg previously appointed to write the novelization of *E.T.*, having been a fan of his 1974 novel *The Fan Man*. Kotzwinkle's novel version was its own unique animal, mostly told from the point of view of the title alien. That 1982 book has now had 19 printings to date, and the author even received a kind thank you note from screenwriter Melissa Mathison.

As Kotzwinkle told *The Collidescope* in 2023, "When we first discussed *The Book of the Green Planet*, Spielberg was thinking of filming a sequel, but then he changed his mind. There were just a few things he wanted in the book and one of them was a character who 'looked like a bunch of floppy socks.' This set the tone, which was playful, and let me invent some remarkable extraterrestrial characters."

"You can't mess with perfection," says superfan Nick Gjoka. "There was a children's book written back in '85 called *The Green Planet*, and part of the E.T. ride was based on it, but if they went in that direction, it wouldn't match up. The first movie was shot very dark, but *The Green Planet* was bright and poppy. I'm glad there's no sequel."

E.T. Adventure is an attraction where you ride on a suspended bike through a forest flanked by government agents, then are sped through the stars to E.T.'s planet of whimsical plants and creatures. To make the experience as "personal" as the film, each rider gives their name at the beginning, and then an animatronic E.T. shouts them out at the end. It opened at Universal Orlando in 1990, Universal Studios Hollywood in 1991, and Universal Studios Japan in 2001. While only the Orlando E.T. ride remains, part of Spielberg's rich exclusive consulting deal dictates that it is not allowed to close. His piece of every park entry reportedly earns him $30M annually.

Rick Baker and Steven Spielberg had a falling out on *Night Skies*, then let bygones be bygones half-a-decade later when the call of Bigfoot was heard at Amblin Entertainment.

Harry and the Hendersons started in the late '70s as a TV pilot spec by writers Bill Martin and Ezra D. Rappaport, with *The Munsters*' Fred Gwynne envisioned as a sasquatch who moves in with an average American family. While working with the writers on a sketch comedy film called *Elephant Parts*, director William Dear told Martin "This is way bigger than a TV show." He bought the concept from them, expanding it into a feature. With the first 40 pages and a proof-of-concept sculpture of Harry the Bigfoot, Dear went to the one man he thought could effectively realize his title creature.

"I found out where Rick Baker lived," Dear said. "I knocked on his door and said, 'My name is Bill Dear blah, blah, blah. I'm writing this script on Bigfoot, and want you to make the Bigfoot. No other person can make it.' He looked at me like I was crazy. He said, 'I don't want to be a jerk but you can't afford me.' I said, 'I'll work on that part. Would you like to read what I got so far?' He said, 'No, no, I don't want to get...' I'm sure there were legal reasons why he couldn't get involved."

Baker later had a change of heart and wound up doing preliminary sketches of Harry to complete the sales package: "He wanted me to design Harry, saying 'You give your characters a soul,' all these things I liked hearing, which is how he got me to do the drawing for free."

A cinematographer Dear worked with on several commercials, Allen Daviau, had a huge breakthrough as DP of *E.T. the Extra-Terrestrial*. He was working with Spielberg on several projects, including a sci-fi fantasy anthology TV show called *Amazing Stories* where opportunities to climb the ladder were abundant.

While shooting a *Making of the Goonies* doc in Oregon, Mick Garris was telling Spielberg of his screenwriting aspirations when he got hired on the spot to write an episode of *Amazing Stories*: "I turned it in and he asked me to do another one. A day-and-a-half into that, he asked me to be story editor on *Amazing Stories*. I literally went from food stamps to an office in the Spielberg building."

With the most successful movie ever to his name, Spielberg used his premium clout to launch *Amazing Stories* at NBC through his deal with Universal. Every episode of the first season was made from a story by Spielberg, with ample budgets ($1M per 22-min episode) and a two-season network guarantee. It would be a talent farm for potential writers and directors that Amblin could make features with. Helmers who got their start on the show included Lesli Linka Glatter (*Now and Then*), Thomas Carter (*Swing Kids*), Phil Joanou (*State of Grace*), and Brad Bird (*The Incredibles*).

"Allen said to me, 'I can introduce you to Steven... *Amazing Stories* is all about him finding new directors,'" Dear remembers. "They sent me a script for 'Mummy Daddy.' The premise was a guy playing a mummy in a movie gets a call that his wife has gone into labor and, rather than get out of his costume and makeup, he rushes to the hospital. One day during the edit of my *Amazing Stories*, Steven came down and said, 'Let me see what you got so far.' I ran what I had on the Moviola and he said, 'You got anything else? You got a movie or anything?' I said, 'Yes, it's called *Harry and the Hendersons*. I am doing a final polish on the script. I'd love to show it to you.' He said, 'No, tell me the movie right now.' I told him the story. He said, 'Why don't you come to my office tomorrow? I think we might be able to make a movie. I know some people.' I love that line, 'I know some people.' Naturally, I brought Daviau on as director of photography, because he turned me on to Spielberg. All this was dream come true stuff."

The deal with Amblin to develop *Harry and the Hendersons* would enable Dear to go back to Rick Baker and say, "Now I can afford you." However, Baker brought up the unresolved *Night Skies* feud: "Bill called and said, 'Good news, Harry's gonna get made at Amblin.' I said, 'I guess you're gonna have to get somebody else.' He goes, 'No, Steven said he thought you would be the right person to do this.' This surprised me, but I said, 'I need to talk to Steven because I need to find out what the fuck happened. I went from being the golden child to the bastard son. I want to be able to show pictures of what I did because I want to prove my stuff wasn't crap.' Bill was a little bit worried about that."

Dear told Cinefantastique in '87, "Baker didn't know how that was going to affect the working relationship with Spielberg. I just told him, 'Well, here's the opportunity to make a movie in the best of situations, but I'm not going to turn on you because I have an opportunity to make a movie here.' Baker and I were working on this from the start. If nothing could be resolved, then Baker and I would have gone somewhere else to make the movie. The industry is full of enemies one day/best friends the next. Those things are reparable with a conversation."

A convenient thing to say to the press, 2025's Bill Dear sees that situation differently.

"I would never say I wasn't going to do the project without Rick," Dear told this author. "I would have been out of my mind to want to take the project anywhere else, because of the offer and someone wanting to make the movie like Steven, who really understood it. I would like to reread that article and go, 'What the hell?' I would have been very foolish to take it somewhere else, but I was pretty adamant there was nobody except Rick to do it. I can see where, in my mind, I would go, 'Rick, if you're not doing it, I'll leave the Spielberg situation and we'll find a place to do it.' Very naive on my part, because it isn't that easy to get somebody to support your idea, especially a new filmmaker. There was probably a meeting where I appealed to Steven, 'Please, can we go with Rick?' Whatever they worked out between them, there never seemed to be any residual animosity."

According to Baker's biography, Spielberg's explanation was, "I'd decided many months before that I wasn't going to make this film, and I'd been working for months on the *E.T.* script with Melissa Mathison. I was mad that you weren't excited about my new movie."

While he did wonder why no one informed him months earlier of said change, Baker added, "Steven was saying, 'You know, we were both younger, we both made mistakes, water under the bridge. We're older now, let's just forget about it and move forward.' I said 'Okay.' I didn't ask about the photos at that point, because I wanted to do *Harry*."

Says David Robert Cellitti, "You could have knocked me over with a feather, because I thought for sure Rick would never work for Spielberg again, or vice versa."

Recalls Tom Hester, "We were doing a shot where Harry is behind a chain link fence looking out at the freeway. That day Spielberg had come to the set and was talking with Rick, so I think they must have, you know... they were talking. It wasn't a fist fight, as far as I could tell. I think Spielberg had to acknowledge the talent that was Rick. It was undeniable."

Harry's getup worn by Kevin Peter Hall was a costume with thousands of hand-punched hairs. Baker's original idea for the head was an entirely remote-controlled servo helmet, not unlike his work on Skar. The director described this head with fake eyeballs as being appropriate for "some kind of *Care Bear* movie." Dear says he convinced Baker to incorporate Hall's actual eyes into the head, "where the soul of the actor can come through." Baker initially put yellow contacts in Hall's eyes, which Dear claimed "made Harry into a monster," so they settled on the performer's actual blue-green peepers.

As Dear says, "To Rick's credit, you hear about actors going in five hours early to get their makeup ready with all the prosthetics. Harry could be ready in about 20 minutes because the head had servos and it was mechanical. The main work they did was makeup around his eyelids."

This decision to carefully integrate Hall's eyes within the mechanical apparatus later became crucial to the Academy of Motion Picture Arts and Sciences' decision to allow Baker's work to be considered for a 1988 Best Makeup Oscar... which he won, his second such statue after *American Werewolf*. It also cleared the way for future Baker work on Spielberg productions like *Gremlins 2* and the *Men in Black* movies.

"My relationship with Steven after that was fine," Baker admits. "We worked on numerous projects together, he as an executive producer. I never did a film where Steven directed. I wish I would have, so he could really see what I could do firsthand. When we did *Gremlins 2*, we used to put on puppet shows for

Max Spielberg. Steven would bring Max to the set. He goes, 'He really wants to meet Gizmo.' We'd set up a thing in a corner of a stage where our puppeteers were hidden and Max would come up and Gizmo would be there waving to him and responding to him. We did that a couple different times with Max."

"He is such a gentleman, such a talent," Dear says of Baker. "He regards Harry as one of the finest pieces he's ever done. I was so proud of the work he did."

The movie itself shot from May 28 to September of 1986, with production running smoothly with the exception of Daviau: "I don't want to say anything negative about anybody, but there were instances where Allen Daviau was taking quite a while, and I was getting notes. Sid Sheinberg, head of Universal, said, 'Bill, you're a day-and-a-half behind, what's going on?' Allen was taking more time than necessary to light. At one point Steven came down and said, 'Allen, we gotta speed this up, man.' Allen ultimately shot *Empire of the Sun* for Steven, but I don't think he shot one after that for Steve."

"He really wanted to get the right mood, the right shots," Hester says of Daviau. "They took their time getting things lit, but it was worth it. It's a guy in a creature suit but a very intimate story, feels warm and friendly. I thought he did a beautiful job."

According to Baker, "Allen Daviau was going, 'I can't believe how easy it is to shoot this character compared to what it was to shoot E.T.! There were so many times we would start filming and then something would break, and we'd have to sit around and wait for the day to fix it.' That never happened on this because we built all these extra spares, we could just change heads. I was glad somebody appreciated that."

Claims Dear, "When *Harry* was done, I remember Kathy Kennedy saying, 'This was so much better than I thought it was going to be.' She didn't have day-to-day involvement, or she would have seen what it was evolving into."

Sid Sheinberg begged Dear and Spielberg to show Harry in the advertising, but the pair went the *E.T.* marketing route and kept Baker's creation a surprise. When the film came out to so-so business in 1987 it was compared to *E.T.*, especially elements like a family accepting a strange creature into their home while keeping it from nefarious forces. Dear not only agrees with this comparison, it's precisely what he was going for.

He says, "People saw that as more of a negative than I did. One of the reviews said 'Harry aped E.T.' I saw *E.T.* many times, cried every time. I wanted to entertain the best I could. 'Hope you learned something, hope you remember it, hope you talk about it, hope you feel good.' That's the kind of movie I wanted to make. It goes against the norm of perception, since Bigfoot was perceived as a monster. Aliens were perceived in most science fiction movies as malevolent creatures, not kind sweet creatures. In that respect, it did draw a lot. I was influenced heavily by *E.T.*, but I always knew I wanted Harry to be a soulful creature who would teach the family a lesson."

The actual Bigfoot community apparently holds Dear's movie in high esteem. A self-proclaimed Bigfoot hunter named David Eller, who founded a research group called P.U.R.S.U.E. (the Paranormal Unit for Research and Study of Unexplained Events), told this author that *Harry and the Hendersons* is a movie every cryptozoologist has seen.

"It's one of those films you have to watch if you have any love for the subject," said Eller. "The other film is *Legend of Boggy Creek*. Virtually everyone I know who is into this subject has seen that, and many of them say it's that film that started their love for this. That film and *Harry and the Hendersons* are pivotal in our society for getting this type of thing to be acceptable."

Amblin's track record of making films full-steam-ahead in this early era was tremendous, in 1987 alone releasing *Empire of the Sun*, *Innerspace*, *Batteries Not Included*, *Three O'Clock High*, and *Harry and the Hendersons*. The latter two signified the company's willingness to take chances on fresh talent, but also a certain fickleness since Spielberg had his name removed from both. The company's ability to roll the dice on modestly-priced product could be compared to what Roger Corman was doing in the '70s, though with greater prestige and family-friendliness.

"With Kathy Kennedy and the gang, everybody had the feeling this is the team, this is the place to be," said Chris Walas of Amblin. "The most relaxed office I've ever been in the business. It wasn't hierarchical. Anything Steven said was law but, in terms of everybody being available to everybody else, Amblin was more open than most companies. The only other company that open was Corman's New World Pictures."

Today Amblin Entertainment is one of the most successful production companies that has ever existed inside the studio system, with just the theatrical releases (not including television productions or home video) amassing over $16 billion in grosses.

Whether elements of *Poltergeist* or *Gremlins* were hatched from Spielberg's previous work on *Night Skies*, the important thing is both films fulfilled some promise of what that unmade movie could have been.

John Sayles is perfectly sanguine about all the elements of his script that have appeared elsewhere. This has always been his style, going back to *Return of the Secaucus 7*, which many claim Lawrence Kasdan stole the essence of for his own 1983 generational ode *The Big Chill*. Sayles points out that *Big Chill* is about yuppies who gave up their ideals, while *Secaucus 7* follows working-class friends who continue to believe in the radical notions of their youth.

"I never feel like anybody has stolen things from me," he says matter-of-factly. "It's just that it's out there and it's based on the same information and every once-in-a-while you get an idea from somebody and say, 'Oh, that can be useful in what I'm doing.' *The Big Chill* is called *The Big Chill* for a reason, people realizing they have lost their ideals or maybe never had them in the first place. That's a very different thing than *Return*, which is like the rebirth... they're coming back."

Josh Olson directed 2002's low-budgeter *Infested* starring *Gremlins*' Zach Galligan, whose premise is "What if the characters from *The Big Chill* got murdered by killer flies?"

Said Olson, "There's a line during a party scene where one character says to another, 'I'm just saying Sayles did it first and it was better.' *Secaucus 7* was a great film about characters I grew up around as a kid and never saw in a movie before. Usually when Hollywood does 'politics' they take all the politics out of it. The Hollywood version is *Big Chill*, where you'd think the '60s was just about dancing to Motown. The characters in *Secaucus 7* are actual radicals grappling with real questions of growing old."

"'Oh, this is ripped off,' you hear that all the time," waxes *Inglorious Treksperts*' Mark Altman. "Did they both go to college? Yes. You look at your life and think, 'What's an interesting story to mine for material? Oh, all my friends I went to college with! We had grand dreams then sold out.' It doesn't come from, 'I saw *Secaucus 7*, I'm going to do a movie just like it.' They had similar experiences, dreams deferred and all that. I'm always amazed when Star Trek fans say, 'Oh, they stole my script.' If you have one good idea, you're in the wrong business. Not to say people never steal, but it's rarer than you think."

The Wrap's Drew Taylor sees it differently: "It feels like Sayles is just comfortable being ripped off, because I feel like he's been ripped off for 50 years. Maybe he's not giving himself enough credit in terms of being someone who influences the popular culture in the ways he does."

CHAPTER 13

Dissected, Probed, & Mutilated: Influence

"Whenever cannibals are on the brink of starvation, Heaven, in its infinite mercy, sends them a fat missionary."

—Oscar Wilde

Even in the absence of a direct *E.T.* sequel, a virtual industry of kid-meets-alien rip-offs (*Flight of the Navigator, Mac and Me*) as well as movies that took a page or ten from Spielberg's 1982 classic (*Cocoon, The Iron Giant, Lilo & Stitch*) were plentiful. Yet somehow, elements of the original *Night Skies* project—knowingly or unknowingly—crept their way into major films... including a big one by Spielberg.

The Brother from Another Planet (1984)

The most left-field answer film to *E.T.* was made by the *Night Skies* writer himself. John Sayles' 1984 sci-fi satire *The Brother from Another Planet* casts Joe Morton (*Terminator 2*) as a non-verbal alien from a distant galaxy who crash lands on Ellis Island and has an adventure through New York City which mirrors an immigrant's assimilation journey. This extraterrestrial with magical powers resembles an African American male in all aspects except his three-toed reptilian feet.

The idea came to Sayles over several dreams. In one he was writing a script for Joe Dante called "Assholes from Outer Space," then another of a black man from another planet walking around Harlem. After the dreams, he hammered out the script in six days.

Sayles says, "One of the things with *Brother from Another Planet* is I'm going to go different places than science fiction usually does when aliens come to Earth. That was the first of a whole bunch of fish-out-of-water movies like *Moscow on the Hudson*, *Coming to America*... it became a popular genre. He was one of the early guys who showed up not having a clue what goes on in a very familiar world."

Morton had been a stage and screen actor for well over a decade—ironically, known for his singing in a Tony-nominated role in *Raisin*—when he landed his breakout role of the mute title alien in Sayles' film.

"I knew who John was," remembers Morton. "We met at the audition. He asked about my background. I told him my father had been in the army. Until I was 10 I lived outside the country. My dad's job was to integrate the Armed Forces overseas. We were usually one of two black families brought on to any post. That night John called me to say the part was mine."

The actor was able to utilize those early memories of being stationed in far off locales like Germany and Japan as his character navigates the overwhelming environment of New York City. The Brother meets a wide variety of characters, from a single mother to a video arcade owner to a bar full of salty characters.

"He wasn't so much a fish-out-of-water as someone who was outside looking in, which is what I was using from my childhood," Morton says. "I was being that kid that had to be very careful about where he went and what he said and who he hung out with. For The Brother, it was, 'Where do I land? How do I literally negotiate a place I can feel safe in?'"

Capturing this sensory overload on film was young cinematographer Ernest Dickerson, who had been the director of photography on Spike Lee's NYU student short *Joe's Bed-Stuy Barbershop: We Cut Heads*. Recent Tisch School grad Dickerson was "doing the occasional music video" when his wife got pregnant with their first daughter. Pressure for more steady income led him to contemplate getting a taxi driver's medallion, until Sayles' production manager Peggy Rajski gave him a call out of the blue.

Recalls Dickerson, "Peggy asked me if I knew John Sayles and I said, 'Whoa, yes.' At that time, Sayles was the premier independent filmmaker with *Return of Secaucus 7* and *Lianna*. She said he was doing a Roger Corman-esque science fiction film called 'The Brother Who Fell to Earth,' and wanted to talk to me about shooting it. He saw *Joe's Bed-Stuy Barbershop* at the New Films/New Director series in New York. His film was gonna be in Harlem, so he figured it would be good to have as much crew of color as possible. He told me the whole story. I've been a reader of science fiction since I was much younger. The idea of combining science fiction with social commentary... I loved it. He asked me if I'd ever shot anything in 35mm. I lied and said, 'Yes.'"

A week after that initial meeting Dickerson began assembling his crew for the guerilla-style 24-day shoot. The budget was only $300,000, cobbled together with money Sayles earned from writing jobs and his MacArthur Fellows "Genius Grant." Cast and crew were transported to set in "an old bread truck."

"We were all working deferred," Dickerson says. "I remember Spike tried to get on as an assistant director, and John wouldn't hire him. John said, 'Well, Coppola wouldn't hire Scorsese as an AD.' Turning Spike down was actually paying him the ultimate compliment, even though Spike was a little hurt."

The assistant director hired was Craig Rice, frequently mistaken by onlookers for the director. Dickerson says this was because Rice had a more authoritarian persona, whereas "John really likes to fade into the background." That unobtrusiveness was part of Sayles' stylistics with the camera as well: "He wanted a very simple style, not a showy camera." The DP later became known for his dynamic cinematography on Lee's movies like *Do the Right Thing*.

Says critic Adam Nayman, "I think it's very significant to the DNA of *Brother from Another Planet* that Dickerson shot it. It matters beyond the fact that it's well shot."

Because of the low budget/fast paced nature of the indie production, Sayles entrusted Morton to carry nearly every scene with minimal input.

According to Morton, "He knew I had done a lot of Shakespeare and theater and was looking for an actor who could take care of their own emotional life within the movie, that he would not have to wet nurse in any way. We'd get there early in the morning, talk about that particular scene, then I wouldn't talk for the rest of the day. John would tell all the other actors, 'He's not going to talk.' The interesting thing for me was people started telling me stories, because they think you're never going to repeat them. I could use that, because that's what happens in the film. I also decided he wouldn't understand the handshake. Every time people did that, it was like, 'What am I supposed to do with that?' People would say, 'Where are you from?' and he would [points up]. He meant from another planet, they thought he meant from up north."

Dickerson says of Morton, "Joe really created this great character, this vegetarian, this *stranger in a strange land*. He did that perfectly. Walking down the street with a head of cabbage, eating as he goes. The little touches we came up with, like the eyeball that comes out and spying on the guy."

Many of those Roger Corman-esque "lo-fi sci-fi" flourishes were concocted by production designer Nora Chavooshian, who later designed Sayles' *Matewan* and *Eight Men Out*... and also became Morton's second wife.

"We met on the film in '83, then we got married in '86," Morton confirms. "All the low-grade sci-fi was Nora. She made the eyeball that I put into the plant. I wish you could have seen the outside of the spaceship; it was like something The Little Rascals put together. It was boards and boards, then she had a turntable with the light on it so that light would pass in front of me. It was hysterical."

Laughs Sayles, "We made the special effects at the beginning so primitive that it was telling people, 'This is the $1.98 version of a science fiction movie. That's going to be the tone.' There's a shot of the rocket arcing in, then you hear a big splash. It was made with construction paper and a pin. You always have to be conscious of your audience."

Dickerson knew this movie was the opportunity that would accelerate him to feature DP status without working his way up as an AC. However, the first day of shooting almost spelled the end for him. They shot a whole sequence of Morton walking east from the Hudson River, including The Brother in front of the 125th Street sign shot from a specially built platform. When Dickerson arrived on set Day 2, he caught Sayles in a huddle with producers Rajski and Maggie Renzi. They said call the lab.

"The movie lab liaison said, 'Ernest, baby, I hate to tell you this, but you're gonna have to reshoot everything you did yesterday. Your HMIs, man, they're flickering all over the place,'" Dickerson reveals. "We couldn't afford HMIs. That's a light that has a pulse to it, and the camera would be synced into the pulse. I said, 'Everything I did yesterday was with reflectors bouncing sunlight.'

I go back to Peggy and John: 'Something doesn't feel right. Have them reprint everything.' They did, and everything was fine. The guy doing the printing that night—I don't know if he'd been tippling—had the wrong shutter setting in the printer, so that's why everything was strobing. For a moment, I thought I had blown my chance."

That wasn't the only Day 1 near-catastrophe, according to Morton: "The very first day we started shooting was supposed to be in this bodega in Harlem, and somebody told the owner she could make more money. She tried to charge John more for use of the store. He couldn't afford it, so we had to find another location. It was crazy. A lot of the scenes at the end of the movie, when I'm on the subway, those were all stolen."

Something else production got off the streets of New York? The film's title. In Strivers' Row, a random person approached Morton: "I was waiting to go on and this brother walked up to me and said, 'Ain't you the brother from *Another World*?' I had been on the soap opera *Another World*, playing twins. I looked over at John, who winked at me. That's where the title came from. He changed 'Another World' to 'Another Planet.'"

Sayles' *Night Skies* experience certainly paved the way for one aspect of *Brother*: the Men in Black, over a decade before Spielberg produced his own movie on the subject.

"The *Night Skies* script was based on research Spielberg had done for *Close Encounters*," remembers Sayles. "It's where I got my idea about the Men in Black who appear in *Brother from Another Planet*, right? They're part of the literature."

Dickerson, who later graduated to the director's chair on films like *Juice* and *Demon Knight*, got his first real taste of calling the shots during scenes when David Strathairn and Sayles play the oddball Men in Black. The pair, hunting the runaway slave Brother across the galaxy, often shot their scenes backwards to give them an otherworldly feel.

"It puts the cinematographer into the director's chair," says Dickerson. "I've got to be his objective eyes, to tell John if it's working. The trust was there. He would work with David directing it, then I would shoot it and tell him what adjustments needed to be made."

"It felt like a family," Morton says of the experience. "Everyone was accommodating everybody else. We knew we had something. We knew it was going to be inexpensive, and we had to make it real with what little there was."

"It was a pretty fun set," Dickerson agrees. "Maggie and Peggy and John were great to work for. We all worked for deferred payment. Back in them days, if you're working deferred, forget about it. You're not going to get your money, but for us it was a way of breaking in. What was amazing was the cast and crew were invited to the opening night screening and John and Maggie were standing outside with envelopes for all of us. They paid us off. They were so pro-crew, made sure we were taken care of."

The movie opened in 9 theaters on October 26, 1984, playing steadily into summer 1985 and ultimately making $3.7M. In *Sayles on Sayles* the director said, "Until *Lone Star* it was probably our most successful film in terms of the money we made back over its budget. Our production company actually made money."

Then there's the big question: Was *Brother from Another Planet*—consciously or unconsciously—made as an answer film to *E.T.* by the man who had silently contributed part of its inspiration?

"The film turns out to be a bit of a cross between *E.T. the Extra-Terrestrial* and *Starman*." —John A. Douglas, *Grand Rapids Press*

"E.T. was lucky. He was stranded in a cushy California subdivision. No such luck for *The Brother from Another Planet*." —Mike McInally, *The Missoulian*

"In the years since *E.T. the Extra-Terrestrial* opened, several other escapist films have offered views of what happens if friendly aliens found themselves stranded in modern society. But it takes an odd movie like *The Brother from Another Planet*, an escapist film with a social consciousness, to show what those other pictures have been leaving out." —Jay Boyar, *Orlando Sentinel*

As *Hollywood Reporter* journalist Jourdain Searles told this author, "It really is, when you think about it, a counterpoint: 'What if an alien comes down and it looked black? How would it be treated?' In Spielberg's world there is this ideal way to live, this ideal family. You know what's missing and what you need, whereas John Sayles is just like, 'Well, here's what it looks like. Here's what everybody is dealing with.' *The Brother from Another Planet* is a movie that's definitely more relatable than *E.T.* for me."

"*Brother from Another Planet* is a great companion piece to *E.T.* in the sense that it's without the fantasy," says Mark Altman. "That's the thing about John Sayles: Even though he could find the fun in outrageous premises, he was always a clear-eyed realist."

Adam Nayman wrote a 2023 piece for *Downtime* about the film, and his Twitter handle is "brofromanother." He says, "Three films serve as answers to *E.T.:* The satirical answer of *Gremlins*... then *Mac and Me*, which is like the

Reese's Pieces product placement if it's an entire film... then *Brother from Another Planet*. What if it's urban, not suburban? What if he can't go home? What does it mean to assimilate? Instead of saying, 'I'm gonna live right here in a little boy's heart,' it's, 'Let's get a fucking white drug empire pusher arrested.' In *E.T.* the only sex is this weird kiss in class while they're watching *The Quiet Man*, but The Brother gets laid. All the things tying it to *E.T.* show its connection and difference. The whole world can embrace a deracinated genderless puppet, but the best The Brother can do is an Indie Spirit Award. All the things that make *E.T.* great I don't think are accessible to Sayles in the way they are to Spielberg... not just the budget, but the purity of emotion and the child's-eye perspective. Sayles does what he's good at, mapping an urban ecosystem and putting words in lots of different kinds of mouths. It's one of the funniest things anyone's ever done with a MacArthur Genius Grant."

Neither Dickerson nor Morton were aware of Sayles' connection to *E.T.*, with varying thoughts on whether it exists in response to Spielberg's opus.

Said Morton, "The things they have in common is both E.T. and The Brother can heal by touch. Certainly can fix electronic equipment by touch. There's no speech. Both are literally aliens in environments they don't know anything about. The difference is *E.T.* was accepted as this lovable, wonderful sci-fi film. With *The Brother from Another Planet*, a lot of black people in particular thought it was a black exploitation film and didn't see it until it hit television. That's when it became the cult favorite it is today."

"People can call it an answer film to *E.T.* if they want," says Dickerson. "There have been a lot of films about aliens dealing with this world, starting with *The Day the Earth Stood Still.* The idea of an alien coming in and dealing with America is a great dramatic setup, because it's a way of seeing our society through the fresh eyes of an innocent."

Admits Sayles, "The one conscious thing in it is at the very end, when Joe Morton's character meets the other people from his planet and he goes like this [thumbs up]. They go like this [thumbs down]. It's, 'Are we going home?' 'No, E.T. stays here. Our planet is so fucked up that we had to escape.' I was very conscious of that."

Starman (1984)

While Columbia may have chosen to make *Starman* over *E.T.*, the rider Steven Spielberg added making sure their movie came after his certainly made for "sloppy seconds" in terms of expectations for a benign outer space visitor.

"When *E.T.* came out, what it was, in many ways, was *Starman*," director John Carpenter told *The Atlanta Journal* in 1984. "It was disheartening to the studio. They thought they couldn't do it now. That they'd been ripped off or whatever."

But do it they did. This Johnny-come-lately, about a woman named Jenny (Karen Allen) taken on a cross-country road trip with a stranded extraterrestrial (Jeff Bridges) who assumes the form of her dead husband, proved to be less Spielbergian than a charming sci-fi twist on *It Happened One Night*.

Starman (or "The Star Man" as it was initially known) spent a great deal of time in development at Columbia Pictures after the script by Bruce A. Evans and Raynold Gideon was first purchased by producer Michael Douglas as a starring vehicle for himself. Originally Douglas had Mark Rydell lined up to direct, then Adrian Lyne.

Says makeup artist Chris Walas, who worked on Lyne's take, "It was more visually oriented, which is not that surprising given Adrian and John's differences. We were working on a transparent alien, did a bunch of tests that came out great. I was working with Jon Berg on that, and we did a three fingered arm that was translucent so you see all the veins and blood circulating. It was fully mechanical, very cool. Then Adrian took some other project."

A version looked ready to go in September '82 with Tom Conti in the title role for director John Badham, but the latter got cold feet because the movie was just too damn close to *E.T.* The studio then gravitated towards Tony Scott, fresh off his debut *The Hunger*, followed by Peter Hyams, until finally acquiring John Carpenter (*Halloween*, *The Fog*) after his remake of *The Thing* had been burned by *E.T.* at the summer box office. If you can't beat 'em, join 'em.

"I was just offered the job and said yes," Carpenter told this author. "I got the script and I read it. It was really simple. I just loved it. I'm a horror director, and I love being a horror director, but this was my one chance to do a big budget road comedy and a romance. 'Aw hell, I'm doin' it!' This one didn't like it so much..."

"This one" refers to Carpenter's wife and producing partner Sandy King, whom he first met when she was a script supervisor on *Starman*, delightfully mirroring the love story they were making.

"I thought it read like Mork and Mindy go across country," King laughs.

Egged Carpenter, "Tell him what you told me the first day: 'I'm not gonna be your friend.' She was just rough! I thought, 'What is this?'"

Explains King, "I asked him why he didn't have a regular script supervisor. He was mumbling about, 'Well, people always try and get too close.' I understood what happens to celebrity directors where everybody tries to get closer. I said, 'I'm not trying to be your best friend, I just need to get inside your head to work.' He spent the next couple of weeks saying, 'Why don't you want to be my friend?' I said, 'I didn't say I didn't want to be your friend. I just need to understand where it is you're going.' At that time, John was surrounded with a bunch of people who wanted to be the only one next to him. They would try and say, 'Go through me.' Like fuck I'm gonna do that. I need to have direct contact with the director, understand what he needs, or I'm not doing my job. You don't shoot in continuity, and the idea is to know when we're getting off track. It's not just matching which hand the cigarettes are in. It took us a while to get past, 'You don't want to be my friend.'"

Suggested that this was a perfect "meet cute," Carpenter quipped, "She wasn't that cute."

While *E.T.* had inadvertently crushed *The Thing* and slowed the momentum of Carpenter's career (thrown off *Firestarter*, kicked off the Universal lot), Spielberg himself still saw a lot of potential in him, telling *Rolling Stone* in 1982 of directors he thought might have a major commercial breakthrough,

"John Carpenter will get there." Would a good-natured story like *Starman* be Carpenter's final ascent to the big leagues?

The script went through many overhauls, including a pass in the wake of *E.T.* that focused less on the supernatural aspects and more on the tender love story.

"I thought *Starman* could be a great picture," says former Columbia head Frank Price. "I got one of my favorite writers on it, Dean Reisner, who had done *Rich Man, Poor Man* for me, had written all the lines in *Dirty Harry*. In rewriting he came up with some very good lines, like the alien explaining his understanding of driving: 'Red means stop. Green means go. Yellow means go very fast.'"

Continues Carpenter, "It was all there when I read it. I didn't do anything to it. Dean Reisner rewrote the script based on the original authors. He kind of softened it from their view. According to him, he wanted to write a woman's picture, but Jeff Bridges made it his."

For the title alien, Carpenter at one time considered both Tom Cruise and Kevin Bacon, deadpanning, "Bacon didn't want to do it and he turned me down... the piece of trash."

Likewise, youthful Mariel Hemingway and Diane Lane interviewed for the female lead. Once Carpenter honed in on Karen Allen to play Jenny, he knew he had to cast someone opposite in their early-to-mid '30s. Carpenter's frequent leading man Kurt Russell was "too pretty for Starman," so he gravitated towards Jeff Bridges, especially after he asked him if he was "afraid to make a fool of himself and do some really absurd things?" The *Tron* star replied, "Hell no."

"Jeff is incredible," Carpenter beams. "That was the best thing, the casting. I'm just really happy with the cast. Jeff had a picture of a bird on the front of his script. If you look at it, that's what he based all the moves he did on."

This author spoke to Bridges about the film briefly in 2017 (for *Coming Soon*), where the Oscar-winner said of Carpenter, "Yeah, he was terrific. I always had these ideas, and I would come up to him with my ideas and then he would look at me sometimes with an implacable expression on his face and say, 'Yeah, but what do you know?'"

Says King, "John gets actors' trust and he communicates very clearly what he wants to see, where they're going. It's why he and Kurt Russell do so well together. It's how Jeff Bridges wound up with an Academy Award nomination for *Starman*. There's trust and an ability to have a fully realized character, without deviation."

As Carpenter took control in early 1984, Douglas stepped aside as the primary producer to become merely a supervisory executive producer, telling Marilyn Beck, "I haven't sensed an adversary relationship between us. He's seemed open and receptive to my suggestions, and I've had no sense of being replaced. It was just a matter of my spreading myself too thin, and things have worked out best this way. I'm still working on *Romancing the Stone*." Larry Franco stepped in to wrangle the production.

"Larry was a producer who worked with me since *Elvis*," Carpenter explained. "I just wanted him around. I wanted him to do it. Douglas was still there, he was just in the background, and he was a little scared of it because of *E.T.* Everybody was scared of *E.T.*"

Filming on the $25M production involved numerous effects, 17 helicopters, five states, and one massive forest fire. At the mercy of the weather, with whole days lost to issues like rain, King still insists it was a smoothly run show: "I'd worked for Coppola and Michael Mann, and the biggest deal is communication. I'm good at puzzles, at organization. Working with Larry Franco and John was an ideal situation, because we all communicated well. Franco worked double duty as producer and first AD."

A tender scene in a truck bed where Jenny tells Starman she is barren was shot in Monument Valley, the site of numerous John Ford westerns. Carpenter says filming there was special, "but not for the reasons you think... but yes, it was. Every shot was really ugly and cold. I never really got the shots that I wanted. We just got it done. I would have preferred a less cold, less grim day. Visually it wasn't much, it flattened."

Adds King, "It was snowing and we thought we were shut down, all went back to the hotel. Then suddenly Franco called it and we were back out in the truck, bundled up in a million down jackets, uncomfortable. Kayenta is a beautiful place, though. You can't really take away from its majesty no matter what."

In terms of special makeup effects, *Starman* was historic in that it was the first and only time Rick Baker, Stan Winston, and Dick Smith worked on a sequence together, namely the opening "birth of Starman" scene. Baker specifically supplied the glowing Baby Starman, which somewhat resembled the mutant child from *It's Alive*.

Says Tom Hester, "We worked on *Starman,* and Rick did a quick popsicle stick and hot glue mechanism to show how you could move something from underneath the set. It does the job, doesn't have to be a super high-tech polished aluminum masterpiece. For the baby, Doug Beswick just had a child so we did lifecasts of his kid's hands and feet, quite small. I sculpted the body to match those, and Rick sculpted the head."

One issue came with Smith's morphing of Jeff Bridges' face as he rapidly ages, accomplished in stop motion with 100 different sculpted heads.

"Rick was great, Stan Winston was great," says Carpenter. "Each of them brought something different to the program. Dick Smith was the only problem. He animated his change, and it just looked phony. ILM had to smooth it out because it was jittery, and Dick wasn't happy. Well, I wasn't happy because it didn't look good, right? That wasn't the right technique."

"Unfortunately, I had to leave *Starman* behind when I went to Universal," says Price. "The script still needed more work. I was able to get *Out of Africa* and *Back to the Future* back to Universal, but I couldn't get *Starman* because they were going ahead. They wound up with a more B-picture director, John Carpenter, and Jeff Bridges is not a romantic lead. He's a very good actor, but the key to that one was romance. They got an okay picture, but I think that could have been so much better."

Starman opened in December 1984 against other big sci-fi movies *Dune*, *2010*, and *Runaway*, likely cannibalizing each other. When asked why he thought the movie failed at the box office, Carpenter said flatly, "I have no idea. Maybe advertising. Maybe the movie stunk. I can't ever tell. People either do or don't respond."

The movie's ending certainly leaves the door open for a sequel, partly realized with a short-lived TV series, but never as a film.

"I was kind of surprised they never did one for *Starman* because it was all set up for one," Bridges says of a *Starman II*. "Karen Allen is pregnant with the 'Star Baby' and there's a silver ball with the kid. Whenever I see Karen, we always jam about different ideas for a sequel. I heard there were talks for a remake, but I still think they should have made a sequel and stuff."

That remake was in development at Sony with director Shawn Levy, who told this author in 2016, "To me, I think it's brilliant. It's thick with ideas, rich with romantic feelings, and those are the things I'm going to carry over into this updated version. I don't know why it's kind of separate in the canon of Carpenter, but I think it's magnificent. It fits less neatly in his genre legacy. I think it's absolutely one of his finest films. I am going to try to be faithful to the romantic spine of the story but also the fish-out-of-water humor, which is genuinely charming and winning in the way Carpenter and Bridges filmed it."

Bridges and Carpenter have never worked together again, with the director admitting, "We never brought it up. We never talked about it, but we're friends to this day. Jeff was fantastic. I really think he was wonderful."

It would not be right to end this capsule without one more fun piece of trivia. Carpenter's father Howard moved his family to Bowling Green in 1953 to teach music theory at Western Kentucky University. Little John would have been 7 years old when the Hopkinsville Goblins arrived in 1955, an hour away from campus. Years later, while a student at WKU, Carpenter toured a psychiatric facility where he spotted a 12 or 13-year-old mentally disturbed boy. He described the look in the patient's eyes as "completely evil," and used him as the inspiration for a character in a certain 1978 film. In 2021, when a Kentucky *News-Democrat & Leader* reporter asked Carpenter if the psychiatric hospital in question was Western State in Hopkinsville, Carpenter played coy: "I'm not gonna tell ya where that was." Would it not be fitting that the character of Michael Myers was also born in Hopkinsville?

Endangered Species (1982)

Cattle mutilations were a hot button topic in the early '80s, leading to several pictures on the subject including Greydon Clark's *The Return*, a strange mishmash of *Close Encounters* and a slasher film starring Jan-Michael Vincent and Cybill Shepherd as a star-crossed pair investigating mutilations in a dusty New Mexico town. The effects are sub-par, with classic character actors like

Martin Landau, Raymond Burr, and Neville Brand all slumming, but the movie frames itself intriguingly as one big cosmic experiment.

Then there is *Endangered Species*, which takes place in rural Colorado and, like *The Return*, follows the relationship between a local cop and an outsider as they investigate cattle mutilations. The explanation for these animal deaths turns out to be quite terrestrial: silent government black ops helicopters choppering the dissected cows to fields as a smokescreen for more nefarious activity. It is an unusual film for the genre, perpetrated under duress by one of cinema's truly eccentric auteurs.

"I started in the best place you could start when Robert Altman threw me in the deep end and said, 'swim,'" director Alan Rudolph told this author. "I got to make two movies with him where nobody told me what to do. The second one, *Remember My Name*, nobody wanted. It's never been streaming, never DVD-ed, a total failure. I couldn't get arrested, as they say. Then producer Carolyn Pfeiffer said, 'We've got two projects and we'd like to work with you. They're studio films.' I said, 'Oh man, I don't want to do that. Do they pay?' I was flat broke. She said, 'Yeah, we'll get some money.' So, we made those two films. One was *Roadie*, which was a big dumb comedy, but fun to make. The other one was *Endangered Species*, which I really wanted to get into."

Some of Rudolph's nightmare included the replacement of lead actress Nancy Allen with *Poltergeist*'s JoBeth Williams as small-town cop Harriet opposite Robert Urich's ex-cop trying to uncover why cattle mutilations are falsely blamed on both UFOs and satanists.

"Turned out it was the worst shooting experience I ever had," Admits Rudolph. "Not because of the actors or anything, but the studio shut it down twice, fired everybody. I tried to quit, but contractually couldn't. They wanted a romance or something."

Endangered Species was buried at the box office when it opened on September 10, 1982, with *E.T.* still the #1 movie in theaters. The film's release was hampered by incoming MGM president Freddie Fields, who failed to hire anyone to run publicity on the picture. Due to a staggered opening over two weekends, the movie never cracked the top 10. It made $1.47M on a $7M budget, a sacrificial lamb of a new studio regime.

"It opened around the time of *E.T.*, quickly buried," sighs Rudolph. "I thought it was a fascinating look at something, and we could blame it on the American government, which was always a good thing. It didn't work out."

Signs (2002)

"A sharp fingernail eases out of the alien towards the young boy's head as he lays on the ground." Is this a description from *Night Skies* or a scene in M. Night Shyamalan's *Signs*? Well, it's both. Not a surprise, since both projects were overseen by Kathleen Kennedy.

As Geraldine Sutton Stith says, "The one I like best, which I have heard was based loosely on the Kelly story, is *Signs*."

Just as Spielberg was declared to be Hitchcockian before he was Spielbergian, M. Night Shyamalan wore the albatross of being "the next Spielberg" for many years before staking out his own identity as a crafter of reliably surprising chillers. Like Spielberg, Shyamalan is a student of the Rod Serling school of ironic twists used to great effect in *The Sixth Sense*. The Kennedy/Marshall Company had produced that smash, then set out to deliver another hit with 2002's *Signs*, which examines an alien invasion of Earth entirely from the point of view of a broken family living in an isolated farmhouse.

Shyamalan told *SFX* in 2002, "This movie is all on a farm, all one family, in one place, and so when you leave it you'll know what it felt like to be on this farm, and be with this family, during this very horrific time."

That magazine later stated, "Set among the whispering cornfields of rural Pennsylvania, *Signs* took inspiration from the Kelly-Hopkinsville encounter of 1955, in which a remote Kentucky farmhouse was allegedly menaced by extraterrestrial 'goblins.' Spielberg nearly brought the incident to the screen as a horror movie called *Night Skies*, which eventually mutated into the far sweeter *E.T.*"

Mel Gibson led *Signs* as an Episcopal priest who has lost his faith after the death of his wife. He lives on a Pennsylvania farmstead with his two small children (Rory Culkin, Abigail Breslin) and ne'er-do-well younger brother (Joaquin Phoenix). Suddenly crop circles begin to appear, then noises on the roof at night...

Shyamalan stated "the air was supercharged" when shooting on *Signs* began only two days after 9/11 occurred. The whole movie carries that paranoic charge, with the director utilizing his penchant for quiet dread as the farm is stalked by nefarious ETs. Released in August of 2002, it earned $408M globally.

Already an *X-Files* fanatic, critic Devindra Hardawar of *The Filmcast* could not have been more ready to receive these *Signs*: "It blew my mind. Whatever Shyamalan was doing, he was on my wavelength. He bragged about cracking the Spielberg code: broken families going through some crisis, hints of some supernatural force you never quite see. In *Signs* it's all hinted at, right? Glimpses are scarier than showing something upfront. Spielberg was always the guy that knew exactly where to put the camera, and I think Shyamalan chased that in every setup. Often you start with one character in one location, then in one take you follow them to another conversation... the purposeful camera."

"It's the creepy factor, the unknown," says Stith. "Just like the ones that were at Kelly. What were these things that were popping up everywhere and trying to get in the farmhouse? It's scary."

"The Kelly-Hopkinsville story is a good setup," says Hardawar. "It's *Home Alone*. It's *Straw Dogs*. The inspiration is certainly there. I'm sure somebody was talking about *Night Skies* like, 'Oh man, Spielberg almost made this alien thing.' If Shyamalan was looking for his next thing, as somebody who grew up in the '80s and '90s in the height of UFO interest, I'm sure that idea stuck. That was the decade of *The X-Files* and the idea of extraterrestrials was everywhere. *Signs* was the ultimate expression: 'This is what we're actually afraid of, an external force invading our secure family.' It really boiled down the nature and the terror of it, and that's why we haven't really seen much alien invasion pop culture up until Jordan Peele's *Nope*. *Signs* cleared the way for two decades."

Explorers (1985)

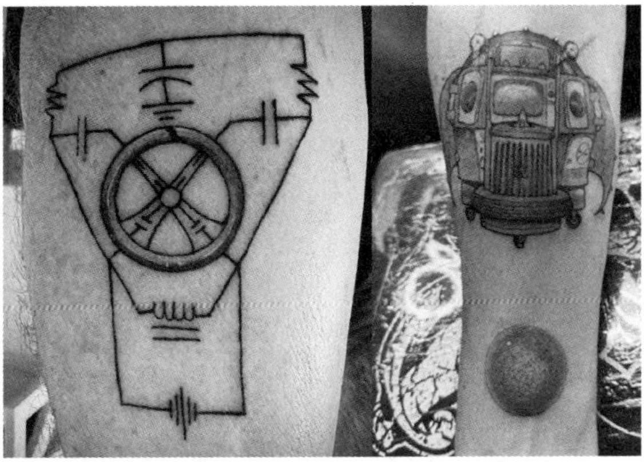

"What if, instead of an E.T. coming here and befriending a child, the kids went there?"

That's the leap of logic Eric Luke made in 1982 which led to *Explorers*, one of the most fondly-remembered box office bombs of the '80s. Luke graduated from UCLA film school and snagged his first agent from a student short he made called *Dark Ages*, about a fantasy hero accompanied by a computerized stick which dispenses advice. While working as a clerk at sci-fi bookstore Change of Hobbit, the fledgling screenwriter penned a couple specs: A horror entry *Nightmare* about a babysitter battling monsters inside a house, as well as '50s-inspired sci-fi-er *Attack from Outer Space* about a hot-rod kid drag racing with aliens.

"My career wasn't going anywhere," he told this author. "I was driving home one night, saw the moon out the car window and thought, 'What if three kids build their own spaceship and fly to the moon and beyond?' We were first going to the moon when I was a kid and I pretended we built our own spaceship. The impulse was, 'What if that could actually come true?'"

Luke penned a screenplay involving three outsider boys who band together to construct a ship based on circuit diagrams they receive in dreams implanted by extraterrestrials. Turning *Explorers* into a viable movie was fraught with cliffhangers: Most agents turned Luke down as a client except for Brenda Beckett, and she in turn sent the *Explorers* spec out as a weekend read which only producers David Bombyk and Edward S. Feldman responded to, and they got turned down by every studio except Paramount.

"Once Paramount picked it up, the doors opened," explains Luke. "In *Los Angeles* magazine I was on a list of the 10 hottest writers. Then the pattern continued: All the directors they sent it to passed except Joe Dante. If Joe passed, I think that was it."

Lawrence Kasdan was one of the filmmakers who passed, while Wolfgang Peterson was seriously considered until Paramount execs were unimpressed by footage from *The Neverending Story*. Dante's eyes-in on the project probably went back to being a movie-mad kid in New Jersey who was hospitalized with polio for a year, spending most of that time isolated reading comics. Luke theorizes, "Joe responded to it because of his feelings of being outside the mainstream as a child, living in the world of imagination."

Spielberg revealed to Luke during a general meeting that he too was interested in making *Explorers* before Paramount swooped it up. The studio put Luke on the payroll as an in-house studio writer for projects like a failed *Jetsons* movie.

"I went over to Amblin on the Universal lot and there I was, sitting with Spielberg in his dimly-lit office throwing ideas back and forth," says Luke. "It turned out he'd seen *Dark Ages*. I was surprised he took the time. Nothing came of it. He said, 'Well, if they ever let go of you, come see me.' But Katzenberg and Eisner moved over to Disney and I moved with them. Years went by and a call to Spielberg at that point would have been sort of, you know... so much had changed with him too."

The scripts for both *Explorers* and Robert Zemeckis' 1997 *Contact* have the same issue: they spend two-thirds of their runtime building to first contact with aliens, then have to show their hand. Luke's initial third act conception owed a great deal to H.G. Wells' *The First Men in the Moon,* with the three kids marooned on Mars where a resident alien civilization is dying and they have to help them while also trying to get back home. For symmetry purposes, said three kids were originally supposed to meet three aliens named Pinn, Neek, and Wak, but only the latter two made it to shooting.

"The first two acts of *Explorers* are solid, but the third is interchangeable," explains Luke of the issue. "Once they get in the spaceship, the whole third act was rewritten again and again and again with all these different concepts."

Dante recalled at a 2009 screening that Luke's script "was very entertaining, but it didn't have a third act. The first two thirds of the script were great, but at the end the kids went to the planet, play baseball, then go home. That was the plot. That wasn't quite enough."

The December 1983 draft of *Explorers* does feature Darren and Wak playing with a glowing sphere while standing on anti-gravity discs:

```
                    PINN
    Rules. Must catch on the first bounce.
```

Dante's producer Mike Finnell elaborates: "The two big problems were the ending... the script had no ending... and we had to start shooting because the studio had a hard summer release date that was not negotiable. We winged it."

When Finnell says "no ending," he likely means Luke's ending was far too expensive, featuring an otherworldly setting of wild flora/fauna, a menagerie of creatures, flying vehicles, underwater environments, etc. What they ultimately landed on was more contained (set in the alien spaceship) while also providing opportunities for satire. Dante's left-field pop culture angle posited that these aliens the kids encountered were not only teenagers themselves but had learned everything about humanity from old television broadcasts. Pop culture montages presented by the aliens in *Explorers* have the exact same content and energy as Dante's '60s roadshow film *The Movie Orgy*.

"I knew that was a part of his history, juxtaposing images and all the ephemera," admits Luke. "He really got into supervising those montages, the big projections around them. He was emotionally involved in that concept; that wasn't just an intellectual exercise for him. The aliens watched American media and cartoons Joe loved when he was a kid."

One aspect relating to *Night Skies* is the ending of *Explorers*, which was dashed together on-the-fly: A larger cypress-shaped alien appears to stop the smaller aliens from interfering with humans.

Says noted screenwriter Josh Miller, "At the end of *Night Skies* the good alien shows up. It feels like the reveal at the end of *Explorers* where it turns out our two aliens are just teenagers. Their dad shows up like, 'What are you kids doing?' My God, the fingerprints from this fucking script just go everywhere... things Spielberg didn't even work on!"

"I don't think so," says Finnell. "I read the *Night Skies* script decades ago and I don't remember a lot about it. It mostly takes place in a house, right? These aliens invade this house, but I don't recall us pulling anything out of that script for *Explorers*."

"There was never another set of eyes," explains Luke of the rewriting process. "Joe was really respectful. He would come to me at the end of the day and say, 'This scene tomorrow, I could use something like this...' He'd talk to me about an overnight rewrite, or keep working with me. He didn't have to do that, it was great he did. The John Sayles script was never mentioned. I remember *Night Skies*, but it's not a strong connection."

Ethan Hawke made his movie debut as the dreamer of the group, Ben. To portray the science geek Wolfgang, Dante cast intense River Phoenix against type, while Jason Presson played the more James Dean-ish "wrong side of the tracks" kid Darren. *A Christmas Story*'s Peter Billingsly was one of the actors up for the Wolfgang part.

"Ethan, River, and Jason were great," beams Luke. "All their ad libbing was hooked onto those iconic ideas for the characters: the head (Wolfgang), the hands (Darren), and the heart (Ben). Once the kids had that, they could improvise in-character."

Confirmed Dante, "We'd shot the picture under very hurried auspices, with the paint on the sets literally wet. When the kids stepped in the spaceship, they sunk into the cement because it wasn't dry."

Perhaps because of how rushed it was, the movie has a fairly off-beat nature stemming from Dante's canted angles and cartoonish sensibilities, all the while maintaining a tone that feels of-a-piece with the suburban fantasias of '80s Spielberg. It has one of the all-time great Jerry Goldsmith scores. The visual effects by ILM are outstanding. The Thunder Road spaceship designed by Nilo Rodis-Jamero is a thing of ad hoc beauty that should be as remembered today as the DeLorean time machine in *Back to the Future*.

"*Explorers* is the most Amblin-y movie that isn't actually Amblin," expresses Josh Miller. "I always forget that Spielberg had nothing to do with *Explorers*, because it feels like it slots right in there with *Goonies* and all the '80s stuff."

Explains Finnell, "Joe wasn't trying to emulate Steven in any way, but they have the same influences, being from the same generation. They grew up watching movies and cartoons and reading comic books. That's why there's an overlap between their styles."

"It's supposed to look like a Spielberg movie, apparently, but it's an unfinished Spielberg," Dante adds. "We were told to stop working because the people who hired us went off to Disney. New people came in and said, 'Okay, what do we got here? A bunch of pictures made by these other guys who are gone. Let's dump 'em.'"

Incoming studio heads Frank Mancuso Sr. and Ned Tanen replaced Eisner and Katzenberg as *Explorers* was slated for an already-rushed release, which got moved up. Luke felt the shifting winds during the regime change: "They didn't understand it, wanted to get it out of the way. There was real care taken with the first regime, then crickets, then a really fast release, then pulled from theaters."

Dante nearly resigned in post and has talked about his frustration at how truncated both the shoot and final editing process was, to the point he introduced a screening at the New Beverly saying, "Welcome to the rough cut of *Explorers*."

Adds Finnell, "It was really a nightmare that the studio wouldn't budge on the release date. We had to send it out before it was totally finished. Not a happy experience."

"We took it to Arizona for an audience test screening, and it did not go well," laments Luke. "People were on board for the first two acts, then having the rug pulled out in the third was a disappointment for some. There was the sense of, 'Okay, we've got more work to do, but how are we going to get that done in this situation?' I remember going up to my hotel room and *Citizen Kane* was on TV. That was one of the big misunderstood films, considered a failure. I went over to Joe because we were feeling pretty down and said, '*Citizen Kane* was on and you know the story of *Citizen Kane*?' He put his hand on my shoulder and said, 'Thank you, but this is not *Citizen Kane*.'"

Quick aside: While it may not have been *Citizen Kane*, this is the movie where Dante was given one of the three known surviving Rosebud sleds. The prop from Orson Welles' immortal film was brought to him by a member of the crew charged with throwing it and thousands of other props from the RKO side of Paramount into dumpsters. The rescued Rosebud appears in *Explorers* as well as several other Dante films, and it was sold at Heritage Auctions in July 2025 for $14.75M. Another of the three Rosebud's was sold in June 1982 for $60,500 to Steven Spielberg, during the week *E.T.* was released.

Dante told this author in 2018, "It only takes one screening to see what you need to do to a movie, but in this case the one screening was like, 'Okay, lock it.' Things we took out were a big mistake. There was a party scene in the middle of the movie where Ben gets a kiss for the first time, then he gives her this hideous moon rock ring, which she tries to say is nice. At the end of the movie, she's wearing the ring when they're flying. The idea is, 'She's wearing my ring now,' but it didn't make any sense, so we had to take it out. A lot of stuff like that in the movie makes it hard for me to watch."

At the time it came out, *Explorers* was part of a glut of movies about the confluence of teenagers and technology, including *Back to the Future*, *D.A.R.Y.L.*, *Real Genius*, *Weird Science*, *My Science Project*, and *The Manhattan Project*.

"It was part of the zeitgeist," Dante says of the "whiz kid" trend. "How many movies were about teenage scientists? It was a genre. Unfortunately, mine was one of the last ones and the viewers were fed up. They just dumped on it."

Expected to be one of the big movies of that summer, *Explorers* debuted on July 12, 1985 at #6 to only $3.6M, finishing its run around $10M on a reported budget of $25M. An unnamed Paramount executive told *L.A. Times* of

Explorers, "Here was a wonderful piece of material, but by the time it came out you felt as though you'd already seen it."

"*Gremlins* starts like a monster movie you've seen before, then it goes off the rails," says Luke. "That was successful because of Joe's impulse to pull the rug out from audience expectations. He's so aware of film tropes, of what the audience is thinking, that he wants to get there before them to say, 'Nope.' With *Explorers*, the expectation was *E.T.*, but *E.T.* has already been made. They're thinking, 'This is going to be a cosmic encounter with some alien life.' Joe said, 'No, it's just kids who have been watching TV and stole their father's car!' Ethan Hawke said, '*Explorers* is all about disappointment.' Ben goes, 'Is this all there is?' If Joe had longer to work on the film, to get it right, it would have been, 'Yes, this is all there is, and it's great! We're all the same.' 'We're not so different' is a great message for us all now."

Laments Finnell, "Boy, I tell you, it really flopped. One reviewer called it a 'monstrosity.' I'll never forget that... 'monstrosity.' Nobody liked it. Steven liked it!"

Spielberg has a 35mm print of *Explorers* in his personal collection, according to Dante.

Adds the director, "I remember people coming up saying how much they like it. I had to bite my tongue to not say, 'But this isn't the movie! It's not done.' I appreciate that people like it, and there are nice things in the movie, but at a certain point it becomes someone else's movie if they don't let you finish it. I tried to put it back together a couple years ago but the studio was uninterested and they destroyed all the material."

"I looked at it a year ago, and it's very charming," Finnell says. "The kids are great. It's very funny. The alien stuff that Rob Bottin did is great. It held up."

Luke explains, "On a personal level I saw my life taking off in one direction, then it didn't. Ethan talked about that too. His personal journey was extreme for a 14-year-old kid. People around him in the industry were saying, 'This is going to be the next *E.T.*, you're the next whoever.' He said he took the whole thing onto his shoulders: 'If I'd only been better as Ben this would have been a success.' One thing I want to tell him is I took the whole thing onto my shoulders. If I'd written a better initial script, if my draft had been bulletproof, had the third act not been interchangeable, this would have been stronger all the way to the end."

Despite Eric Luke's mixed feelings towards *Explorers*, he wears it proudly with three tattoos: The blue force field, the diagram from Ben's dream, and the Thunder Road.

"Pain and pride describes it," concludes the writer. "The pain of what could have been, but pride in my young self for believing in that vision enough to follow it through. When it started, I had no career, then that original idea made it all start to happen for me."

War of the Worlds (2005)

In 1982, Spielberg told Paul Sammon of *Night Skies*, "I saw that I was doing nothing more than getting back to the old days of *Earth vs. the Flying Saucers*, *Invaders from Mars*, and certainly *War of the Worlds*."

He spoke of the latter George Pal alien invasion film with disdain, but at some point over the ensuing years a switch must have flipped. Suddenly, he wanted to direct a new version of the movie that, as a child, left him "scared to death and under my chair."

Said producer Kathleen Kennedy in the production notes for 2005's *War of the Worlds*, "When we first started developing *E.T.*, it was a much edgier, darker story and it evolved into something that was more benign. I think that the edgier, darker story has always been somewhere inside him. Now, he's telling that story."

"I did make a movie when I was 15 and 16, my first sound movie on 8mm called *Firelight*," said the director in 2007 doc *Spielberg on Spielberg*. "It was a story of these blue and red, very aggressive firelights that come down and char us into a little pile of cinders. I thought, 'Oh my God, I'm a hypocrite. I've been making these movies declaring I'm the ambassador of goodwill between them and us, and I started out my life making a movie about aggressive aliens!"

At $132M, *War of the Worlds* was the biggest budget Spielberg had worked with at the time, partly owing to how rushed the production was, with only three months prep for a film involving extensive ILM effects and crowds of thousands. Lensed over 72 days from November 2004 to March 2005 before arriving in theaters on July 30, it was hastened in order to fill a hole in Paramount and Tom Cruise's schedule when J.J. Abrams had to push *Mission: Impossible III* a year due to TV commitments.

Adapted by Josh Friedman and David Koepp after Abrams declined writing duties, this contemporary reframe of H.G. Wells' classic invasion narrative featured Cruise as a blue-collar New Jersey guy taking his two kids (Dakota Fanning, Justin Chatwin) off his ex-wife's hands for a week.

"At the beginning of the movie, Ray is truly inept as a father," Koepp explained. "He's not really interested in being a father, primarily because he thinks he's not good at it. And he isn't. He has been a failure. The kids don't like him and they don't like coming to his house."

The bad-dad-osity of the Cruise character is off-the-charts, but once a race of totally hostile aliens emerges from the sky above as well as the earth below, he has to step up and protect his kids at all costs.

Spielberg stated at a press conference for the film in 2005, "There wasn't anything huge that changed in my life that made me do a scary alien movie. I thought, 'Why can't I try my hand at the kind of film that Ridley Scott made when he did the first *Alien*, which is one of my favorite scary science fiction movies of all time?' It's something I had always wanted to do. I told Tom I wanted to do *War of the Worlds* ever since I read the book in college before I became a filmmaker."

A typically effusive Tom Cruise replied that this movie was "E.T. gone gangster!"

When pressed by a reporter at this conference if *Night Skies* was an influence, he replied, "No, nothing from *Night Skies* made its way into this project."

That is not quite the case, though. A scene in *War of the Worlds* features the Cruise character and his small daughter taking refuge in an isolated farmhouse with a deranged survivalist played by Tim Robbins. As in *Night Skies*, the protagonists are forced to hide from nasty aliens along with pulsing tentacle probes from a ship.

The element of tentacles reaching their way into a house may have been culled from Pal and the source material, but John Sayles' *Night Skies* actually describes the visual very specifically the way Spielberg orchestrates it for *War of the Worlds*: A pair of tubes with beams emanating from the ends and light running through them as they probe. Once Cruise exits the farmhouse, we even get a dissected cow splayed on the ground that Cruise jumps over.

The 30-minute farm sequence sticks out like a sore thumb within the body of *WOTW*, as indicated by Richard Roeper of *Ebert & Roeper*: "There's an intriguing but kind of strange interlude with Tim Robbins as a survivalist that seemed like it was from another movie."

"I think *War of the Worlds* is great," says Chris Evangelista of the podcast *21st Century Spielberg*. "It's a very disturbing, unsettling movie. He's using techniques deliberately meant to evoke footage captured on 9/11. That first tripod attack is shot from the ground up because all amateur footage of 9/11 is people on the ground pointing cameras up at the building. When Cruise is getting his kids to evacuate, Fanning's character is like, 'Is it the terrorists?' It's not subtle. Cruise's character is a prototypical Spielberg bad dad, distant from his kids. The movie is about him learning to be a dad again."

After *E.T.*, Jourdain Searles thinks the 2005 film is Spielberg going back to the divorce well to diminishing returns: "*War of the Worlds* is the exact kind of divorce movie I just don't care about. 'It's the worst possible thing to ever happen. Divorce! The family isn't together. We gotta push them together with disaster! You gotta destroy buildings so you know how DRAMATIC it is to be DIVORCED!' I'm not trying to make light of divorce. It's just like, man… I get it. It's rough. If I ever get divorced, it's gonna suck. I'm gonna complain about it. I have complained about much less, but…"

"It feels like a subversion of the classic Amblin movies with a broken family," says Hoai-Tran Bui. "I come away with an appreciation of *War of the Worlds* the more I get away from it. It is jarring at first: 'Oh, this is a different filmmaker than the one I grew up with, a bit more provocative. A little less sugar with his medicine.' When Cruise sees the destruction and chaos after the aliens attack, he's wandering outside in shock. It's upsetting. People were not fond of the ending, because they saw it as hacky or easy. 'Oh, germs killed them.' The son coming back. That's the Spielberg instinct, 'I can't push it too far. I have to please people.'"

Adds Evangelista, "A lot of people were pissed off about that happy ending where the son is still alive, and I get it. There's weird fan theories going, 'Oh, the son's not actually there. He's imagining him there.'"

While a journalist for *Ain't It Cool News*, Eric Vespe got to visit the set in Lexington, Virginia during the big battle scene just before the farmhouse sequence, saying of Spielberg, "He was always manning the camera. That was the big surprise, because he was 60 or something. I saw him do what should have been a second unit shot of random military guys and then a tank fires behind them. Some general barks two lines of dialogue. Spielberg was laying on his back with the 35mm camera pointed up. This is the equivalent of an insert of a hand grabbing car keys. Somebody else should have been doing this, but no, it was him. Then he invited me into the video village tent to show me the playback of the Humvee on fire rolling down the hill."

Explains Devindra Hardawar, "*War of the Worlds* is a post-9/11 movie: 'Oh my god, this can be destroyed at any moment. Our cities are at risk, everything is at risk.' It is his extraterrestrial statement, the alien movie that suited that moment."

Evangelista claims, "*War of the Worlds* is a complete rejection of friendly aliens who just want to help humanity. All these aliens want to do is exterminate us. When *Close Encounters* and *E.T.* came out, everything was great, but *War of the Worlds* was coming out in this era which led to disastrous wars and terrible things. The immediate aftermath of 9/11 was this uneasy American fear, 'we're not safe here.' The truth is we were never safe to begin with, it just woke us up. Making a friendly alien movie after 9/11 would be really weird. How many friendly alien movies have come out in the last few years?"

Paul (2011)

On July 21, 2008 this author attended an event at Village East Cinemas in NYC celebrating the release of the cult TV show *Spaced* on DVD a decade after debuting on the UK's Channel 4. Stars/creators Simon Pegg and Jessica Hynes alongside director Edgar Wright were in attendance, as were several celebrity fans like Paul Rudd, Bill Hader, Joe Lo Truglio, and director Greg Mottola. Unbeknownst to them, the latter three were about to be welcomed into the Simon Pegg/Nick Frost fold, helping usher the comedy duo behind *Shaun of the Dead* and *Hot Fuzz* further into the American mainstream.

Not long after this event, Pegg, who had been a fan of Mottola's 1996 debut film *The Daytrippers*, gave the filmmaker a script he and Frost had written titled *Paul*, an R-rated road trip comedy in which British nerds Graeme and Clive travel across America in an RV with the irreverent title extraterrestrial. It was conceived in a perfect intersection where Pegg and Frost had heat, Mottola had directed the sleeper hit *Superbad* ($169.95M worldwide), and nerd culture was heavily catered to by studios. Still, once Mottola committed there was some hesitancy from Universal Pictures.

"It was shocking to me that movie got greenlit," Mottola admits to this author. "I had an interesting conversation with the top executives at Universal when Working Title was trying to push them toward a greenlight. The question posed to me was, 'Would you make this movie with, say, Jonah Hill and Paul Rudd or Seth Rogen and Jason Siegel instead of Simon and Nick?' I said, 'Look, they wrote it. This is their baby. I love them. I'm a huge fan. You need to find another director if that's the direction you want to go.' I called their bluff, and they greenlit the movie."

Filming on *Paul* took place across the New Mexico desert in summer 2009, with stopovers at downtown San Diego for the Comic Con exterior scenes and the iconic Devil's Tower monument in Wyoming. Although Bill Hader portrayed the grey alien Paul in early VFX tests and Jo Lo Truglio would be the on-set reference, superstar Seth Rogen provided the final voice and performance capture for the foul-mouthed free spirit.

Mottola says, "I had an expensive CG character that I was constantly told, 'Let's keep Paul out of this shot and it will save us $20,000.' Making that movie was a bit like making a medium-budget comedy with a $15 million movie star because so much of the budget went into the animation. I was limited, but I leaned toward wider lenses and things that Spielberg loves."

Besides the central characters along with besuited Men in Black-esque pursuers played by Hader, Lo Truglio, and Jason Bateman, a crucial side character is that of fundamentalist Christian Ruth Buggs. Played by Kristen Wiig, Ruth (note the same name as *Night Skies'* religious fanatic mother) begins as a narrow-minded anti-science creationist under the thumb of her Bible-beating father (John Carroll Lynch), but through exposure to Paul—as a living contradiction to everything she believes—turns over a new leaf and becomes Pegg's love interest. It could be argued that her subplot about veering away from religion towards secular humanism was more daring than the myriad F-bombs and sex jokes in *Paul.*

"I didn't see it as them going after somebody," Bill Hader told this author in 2011. "Yeah, if this guy showed up, it might rock some people's beliefs. It didn't bother me at all."

This aspect which forms the thematic core of Pegg and Frost's script was something Mottola himself could relate to, raised in a Catholic family which attended church every Sunday. Even as he was forced to attend catechism classes, his time growing up a believer eventually ended when he told himself, "'I need more proof. Faith isn't enough for me.' Then I got older and saw people doing things in the name of Jesus that didn't seem very Jesus-y."

Once *Paul* arrived in US theaters in March of 2011, the broadsides against religion hardly caused a flutter of controversy. As the director says, "The people who tended to like it most were not necessarily the obvious. I've had people tell me, 'Oh yeah, my mom loves that movie.' And I'm like, 'Oh, I'm curious, is she religious?' She's like, 'Yeah, she goes to church.' I was like, 'She wasn't bothered with that?' 'Oh, she thought that stuff was funny.' I thought those people were gonna not like it. You can walk away from the movie saying, 'Well, that's Paul's opinion, he's just one intelligent entity in the universe. He could be wrong.' If you're gonna let this cartoon alien make you question your belief system, your belief system must be pretty piss poor."

If there is one true and loving God the film has absolute reverence for, his name is Steven Spielberg. The movie is loaded with gags riffing on *Close Encounters* (Devil's Tower) and *E.T.* (Paul leaving Earth on a spaceship with our heroes looking on). There's even a *Mac & Me* reference, along with in-jokes for hardcore Spielbergians such as a theater marquee with *Duel.*

At the junket for *Paul* in 2011, Hader said of Mottola, "He's like, 'This is what the script calls for, this should be like an early Spielberg movie, so I'm gonna do that.' It was Greg really going for that style. That shot of Jason Bateman in the car when he pulls to the T in the road then catches up and starts talking, that's right out of *Sugarland Express.*"

"Another one that's hard to catch is the sailor brawl in the bar is from *1941*," adds Joe Lo Truglio from that same junket. "That's what's great about the movie: If you are a total über-geek you'll catch it and appreciate it."

Adds Mottola of the *1941* reference, "That's just a ridiculous joke that this land locked location has a bunch of sailors, but that dance sequence in *1941* is spectacular. Some of the long lens stuff we did in the movie was definitely thinking of *Sugarland Express*, all those compressed shots of police cars on hilly desert roads."

As this book is interested in the origins of *E.T.*, the movie *Paul* jokingly suggests the title alien served in its inception. This 1980 flashback scene shows Paul sequestered in a box-filled Area 51 warehouse straight out of *Raiders of the Lost Ark*, having a conference call with Steven Spielberg playing himself in an audio-only role. He was willing to provide the cameo because Pegg and Frost had previously been in *The Adventures of Tintin*.

During the recording session with Spielberg in West Hollywood, Mottola remembers, "Not surprisingly, everybody who was in town on the movie showed up that day. Seth Rogen was there to read, Simon and Nick were there, various Working Title people, I think the craft service people came because it was Spielberg Day. He showed up wearing a very nice sweater. He seemed very 'dad,' exudes everything you want him to be. After some schmoozing, we sat down to do it. I remember Spielberg in front of the mic said, 'Is anyone gonna say action?' I squeaked out 'action,' and then actually did give him some notes, 'try it different ways.' He's he was great."

PAUL

Okay Steven, how 'bout cellular revivification?

STEVEN SPIELBERG

I don't know what that is.

PAUL

Oh. Restoration of damaged tissue through telepathic manipulation of intrinsic field memory.

STEVEN SPIELBERG

What's that mean?

PAUL

```
It means healing, Mr. Spielberg.
```

STEVEN SPIELBERG

```
Yeah right, healing. Like by touch or something
like that. Like maybe his finger lights up on
the end when he reaches out and touches?
```

PAUL

```
Maybe... You know, sometimes I find less is
more.
```

"It was a thrill to actually give Spielberg direction," emphasizes Mottola. "I was wondering, you know, would he have a sense of humor about the joke 'less is more,' because he can be a maximalist, which is one of the things we all love about him. He completely got it and thought it was really funny."

Mottola himself is something of an alien agnostic: "I've listened to people like Art Bell and find that stuff fun, the speculation. There's always dumb articles saying, 'The government's sitting on all this proof.' Someone will put out a video saying, 'What is this flying object?' Part of America goes, 'Could it be? Is there a chance?' It seems unlikely. It's a long way to go to scare some cows. Seems hard to figure out motivation from the super intelligent species that managed to get here. Yet, at the same time, if you believe in Darwinism the odds that there's other species out there somewhere that have intelligence like ours—if not a lot more—you think, 'Well, what would they be? How would that manifest itself? Wouldn't it be amazing if they showed up?' Of course, Stephen Hawking said, 'You don't want them to show up. If they're smart enough to get here, they'll just enslave you. They're going to look at you like we look at cattle.'"

Although *Paul* only made $37.4M domestically, globally it grossed over $100M plus $17M on DVD, making it profitable. "If we had two American comedy actors they probably would have marketed it a lot more," laments Mottola. "I always make the decision that hurts at the box office... except for *Superbad*. Looking back, it's kind of amazing they let us make that movie."

The only real opinion that mattered was from the big guy himself, as Mottola concludes: "Spielberg wrote Simon a really nice note after watching it. He made a joke about being flattered by all the references. 'I thought I might be coming down with Tourette's, there's so much winking.' Everyone got in on it too. Bill Hader, right before he's going to shoot Paul in this RV Chase, improvises the Roy Scheider line from *Jaws*, 'Smile, you son of a bitch!' Simon Pegg was like, 'I don't know. There's a lot of references. Should we have that?' I'm like, 'I think we went way over the line a long time ago. If there are people who hate references, we've lost them.'"

Super 8 (2011)

Much like *After School*, J.J. Abrams wanted to make a movie about rambunctious teens. It would take place in 1979, the year *After School* was supposed to come out. It would be autobiographical, tracing the time he was making Super 8 movies with his pals just before his first taste of fame through Gerald Ravel's teen shorts program. He even had a producer attached, Steven Spielberg, who came onboard based solely on the title: *Super 8*. The Amblin impresario had hired Abrams at age 15 to restore his childhood movies, then met him again when the hot young screenwriter was pitching a *Roger Rabbit* sequel. Now Abrams was the genius behind *Alias*, *Lost*, *Mission: Impossible III*, and 2009's *Star Trek*.

"I had been working on a number of ideas about kids making movies, so it was an interesting merger that took place between us," Spielberg told *EW* in 2011.

As if consciously trying to recapture lightning in a bottle, Abrams decided to take this coming-of-age story and graft on a sci-fi element about a misunderstood alien monster that he had already pitched to Paramount as a separate project. It was *E.T.* all over again.

Says Abrams of *E.T.*, "I wonder, with today's cinematic style being so boom, boom, boom, if a movie that had that number of quieter scenes could be 'studio-approved.' Yet when you watch *E.T.*, there's only one way that movie could have the emotional punch it had... the way it was made. *Super 8* involved the challenge of figuring that balance out for myself."

Super 8 focuses on 14-year-old Joe Lamb (Joel Courtney), an aspiring filmmaker and makeup artist whose mother was just killed in an industrial accident. His best friend Charles (Riley Griffiths) is the pushy director of the crew, bearing a resemblance to Matt Reeves at that age. While shooting part of an amateur zombie movie at night in a local train depot, the teens witness/survive an accident where a train collides with a truck. Their Super 8 camera captures an alien being escaping a train car. The spectacular wreck brings to mind 1952's *The Greatest Show on Earth*, the first movie Spielberg ever saw.

What follows is a movie steeped in affection for the movies of not just Spielberg, but also John Carpenter and George Romero. As shot by fellow "Best Teen Super 8 Films of 1981" alum Larry Fong, it features nefarious government forces and *Goonies*-like kid hijinks, while the alien character at the center alternates between carnivorous and sympathetic. The final image of said alien leaving Earth recalls the same emotions *E.T.* built to, of learning not just to let go but finding strength in letting go.

It is fascinating that both *Paul* and *Super 8* were tapping the same vein of Spielberg nostalgia, released within three months of each other in 2011.

Says *Paul*'s Greg Mottola, "I think it's somewhat generational, Gen Xers getting to the age that they could reference the stuff they grew up on and loved. J.J. is an inheritor to the Spielberg throne in many ways, and he had the juice to do it."

According to critic Devindra Hardawar, "I didn't like *Super 8* at the time because it was, 'Oh, you're just literally doing '80s Spielberg. You're not going beyond that.' That made me sad, because I thought J.J. Abrams was an interesting creative voice. As a huge *Lost* and *Alias* fan, to see him go into movies and just repeat history was probably a harbinger of what was to come in *Star Wars*, repackaging what we already like."

"I don't hate a pastiche for being a pastiche," counters Hoai-Tran Bui. "*Super 8* is a really good pastiche. It was at the forefront of bringing back this Amblin-esque energy for a new generation, before *Bumblebee* or *Stranger Things*. I think it was successful, a good little movie."

Mottola adds "I love *Super 8*. It was a great mix of *Close Encounters* and a monster movie. It straddled between Spielberg's own movies and a lot of the movies he was the producer of like *Poltergeist*. Maybe people are like, 'Oh, it's too much of a pastiche.' I'm in a glass house with that one, because it wasn't as shameless as *Paul*."

Explorers screenwriter Eric Luke has noticed several references to his 1985 film in the works of J.J. Abrams: "The shot of the cargo freighter eating the Millennium Falcon in *Force Awakens*, or in *Super 8* they had a small globe that was punching holes through things, so that was great! One of the things about the first season of *Stranger Things* is I was watching saying, 'Oh God, it's in there. It's in their DNA.'"

Stranger Things (2016–2025)

Super 8 mined Amblin nostalgia before the streaming show *Stranger Things*, but the Netflix juggernaut explored that vibe to a whole other degree. Created and often directed by The Duffer Brothers—North Carolina natives who grew up worshipping Spielberg, King, and Carpenter—and produced/occasionally directed by Shawn Levy, *Stranger Things* follows a group of nerdy middle schoolers who discover a girl their age known only as Eleven whose background is as mysterious as the psychokinetic powers she possesses. Their adventures span multiple genres, from coming of age to sci-fi horror.

As Levy told this author (for *Coming Soon*) during the show's launch in 2016, "I worked with Steven Spielberg on *Real Steel*, and this show is a love letter to so much of his iconography and work. It was meaningful in a unique way, and also trying to be the kind of producer that Steven had been for me."

At the time Levy expected *Stranger Things* to be compared to *Super 8*, a movie he loved, but stressed that the limits of a two-hour PG-13 movie became the playground of his multi-season/unrated show, which prided itself on a broader range of characters as well as poignancy over sentiment.

Expressed Levy, "In the same way that *Super 8* was both an alien movie and a coming-of-age middle school movie, I feel like *Stranger Things* is so much more than the trappings of '80s nostalgia, which is only a small part of what makes the show great. I think it's the characters that make the show great, and those are entirely unique from anything Steven and J.J. have done."

E.T. super fan Nick Gjoka actually worked on the first season of *Stranger Things*, which shot in Atlanta where he resides.

"It was crazy, because no one knew what we were doing," says Gjoka, who acted as a set dresser. "It sucked... 'Change this, change that.' Reading the scripts, I was like, 'I don't know, this is kinda shitty.' Then I started reading more and said, 'This is kind of fucking good... really good.' I'm still blown away that people are getting *Stranger Things* tattoos. We just thought it was some dumb show we were working on, long days and cold nights. We're like, 'Goddamn, this sucks.' Then we watched it like, 'Oh shit, this is something special. Hits all the marks, pulls all the heart strings of different generations.' We couldn't afford to put E.T.'s image in the show, but I still snuck a figure in there."

The Invasion of Kelly (2017)

While *Night Skies* never happened, there have been several other projects directly inspired by the Kelly incident... some pre-dating Spielberg's.

A version of the Kelly story arrived for television on March 19, 1978 for the NBC series *Project U.F.O.*, created by *Dragnet*'s Jack Webb. The show was purportedly based on actual Project Blue Book cases, although the scripts often wildly fictionalized the "facts." Directed by Robert M. Leeds from a teleplay by Lester William Berke and Donald L. Gold, the episode "Sighting 4004: The Howard Crossing Incident" follows a cash-strapped rancher named Frederick Carlson in Cheyenne, Wyoming whose daughter witnesses a flying saucer crash on his property. Soon after their ranch house is overrun with mysterious green glowing beings which Carlson and his son attempt to shoot but the weapons are useless. Air Force investigators played by William Jordan and Caskey Swaim arrive with a psychologist to hear the eyewitness account. Officials offer up possible answers, such as recently escaped apes from a circus. Character witnesses for Carlson like the town sheriff swear to his integrity. When a ufologist huckster tries to convince Carlson to do a speaking tour to make money, the farmer decides he does not want the ridicule.

There are quite a few parallels to the Kelly incident in this episode, although it is a far more sanitized, less frightening version of events. It is watered down further by a B story involving a man who invests his life savings in a fake flying saucer factory.

One good reason why the *Night Skies* script could not be made anymore is that it already was made, to a great extent, by first-time director Stephen Herek for his 1986 film *Critters*. The mischievous tiny monsters of the title have always lumped it into the "*Gremlins* rip-off" category, yet the script by Herek and Domonic Muir owes its soul to the Kelly-Hopkinsville incident and, likely, the script for *Night Skies*.

The story revolves around a group of ball-shaped aliens who land in a rural town and terrorize a farm family. It has the same *Night Skies* beats, including the young girl encountering the aliens during a tryst with her boyfriend, the sheriff coming to investigate and finding nothing, the family being hunted through the house, etc. Adding to the intrigue are a pair of shape-shifting outer space bounty hunters assigned to eliminate the tiny Krite monsters. The movie ends similarly with the family farm in ruins, except in *Critters* the bounty hunters use a magic device to restore the house.

Where *Night Skies* tried to bring a modern nuance to the small-town alien invasion concept, *Critters* has the feel of a 1950s Universal International monster movie. *E.T.*'s Dee Wallace once again plays the mom, albeit a more June Lockhart-ish "trad" mom.

"She was feisty," Wallace says of what drew her to playing Helen Brown. "There was a lot of humor in the script. Also, there were different colors that mother had that I could play... Mary didn't pick up a gun."

There is even a meta scene where one of the critters bites the head off an E.T. stuffie, to which Wallace says, "Easter eggs, the fans get off on that. You know, I don't care."

"I've always wondered if the people who made *Critters* somehow read the *Night Skies* script," says Josh Miller.

Adds Stephen Scarlata, "I'm shocked there is no cattle mutilation in *Critters*, because otherwise..."

"The *Critters* franchise was directly taken from the Hopkinsville Goblins case," says Derek Hayes.

According to Mick Garris, who directed *Critters 2*, "The original *Critters* was sold very much as a Spielberg movie and had very Spielbergian tones in it. I think that's why I was hired for *Critters 2*. I was working for Steven doing *Amazing Stories*. I think they thought, 'Here's somebody who's available. If we offer him his feature directing debut, maybe some of that stardust from Spielberg will rub off on our little $4M movie.'"

The film version closest to what happened in 1955 is also the scrappiest of them all. In 2017, a 70-minute micro-budget indie titled *The Invasion of Kelly* was made by White Door Productions on-location for around $2,000 over a two-month period. Geraldine Sutton Stith featured in the film's opening while the script was based entirely on her book *Alien Legacy*.

"As a Hopkinsville resident I was interested in the story because this was one of the most well-known and documented true stories about aliens," explains writer/director Joseph Aguon Drake. "It was also cool that this story inspired *E.T. the Extra-Terrestrial*. Geraldine had a big hand in the film and was my assistant director. It was important to have her by my side to make things as accurate as possible. Her brother Elmer Sutton played the role of his father Lucky Sutton since he was the spitting image of him."

Says Stith, "Joe and David, the two guys that did that, they contacted me one day and asked me about it. I'm like, 'Sure. Why not?' I was with them every night of filming. They found that little farm in Christian County that we filmed at. The actors did it to get an IMDb on their name."

Invasion of Kelly is an earnest effort, if wildly underfunded, complete with aliens resembling Halloween costumes along with a ship landing not unlike that in *Firelight* (i.e. a simple glowing light). Nevertheless, it manages to pay tribute to the legend while humanizing the participants in ways other dramatizations had not. One scene towards the beginning of *Invasion* was shot on the original property where the encounter took place, although the actual house was no longer there.

Drake and his Hopkinsville-based partner David G. Baker had a booth at 2017's Little Green Men Days Festival to promote *Invasion of Kelly*, nearly selling out its 238-seat premiere at the WK Cinemas at Bradford Square Mall.

"We had a great response from the community," Drake confirms. "This was around the 60th anniversary of the invasion, and we were having a lunar eclipse as well."

Explains Stith, "They were trying to get it out the year of the eclipse. Kelly was one of the major places it was going to be in the longest, plus the day of the eclipse was the actual day of the encounter. People were coming up to my booth at the festival saying they were scared. They thought when the eclipse hit little beings were going to come back."

While her father Elmer R. "Lucky" Sutton Sr. died in 1995 at age 66, Geraldine Sutton Stith continues to pass on her family's history through writing, which to-date includes the books *Alien Legacy* and *Hopkinsville Goblins: The Story of the Kelly-Green Men and Others*. She keeps the story alive, believing something good can come from the telling.

Nope (2022)

Written and directed by acclaimed filmmaker Jordan Peele (*Get Out*, *Us*), the 2022 film *Nope* follows siblings (Daniel Kaluuya and Keke Palmer) who inherit their father's horse ranch after he is killed in a freak incident of falling debris. The pair discover their horses are being abducted by a UFO which hides itself behind an isolated, unmoving cloud. It causes electricity to fluctuate and is responsible for the debris (remnants of its consumption). Shaped like a traditional flying saucer, the object is actually a living being. They try to placate it, then photograph it for proof, then ultimately seek to destroy it. The finale involves Kaluuya's character being chased on horseback by the saucer-like alien.

Despite *Nope*'s obvious originality and unique genre verve, several aspects bear a striking resemblance to *Night Skies*, specifically scenes of Watt on the

range with the single cloud hovering over him, as well as Watt pursued on horseback by the spaceship.

In July 2022, *The Wrap*'s Drew Taylor asked Peele about *Night Skies*, to which the director responded, "Wait, what is *Night Skies*? I don't know what *Night Skies* is." After Taylor gave a brief description, Peele stated, "This is the movie that didn't exist, that I needed my whole life. You understand what you're describing? How dare you. But you nailed it. Look, I think there's a lot of people noticing that there's a throwback to a different time of film, specifically '80s and '90s, where original ideas would just be committed to. And there was a sense of scope. There was a sense of science fiction. And there was also a sense of magic that also came together. And yeah, that's a crime that wasn't created."

Taylor told this author, "*Nope* just felt a lot like *Night Skies* in certain respects, in terms of an isolated farmhouse being terrorized by an extraterrestrial force. Spielberg is a huge influence on all of Jordan's stuff. It surprised me when he said he didn't know about it because it feels very much inspired. I feel like *Nope* and *Signs* were like, 'He didn't get to make it, so we will.'"

As *Nope* was released to terrific box office ($171.9M globally), Peele told the AP, "*Close Encounters* is something I think about a lot, as is *Signs* by M. Night Shyamalan. These are big-vision directors who have taken flying saucers and science fiction and brought magic to the way they told those stories. I wanted to toss my hat in the ring to one of my favorite subgenres, UFOs, and do it in a way only I can."

Spielberg himself used similar language when asked at a 2023 *Time* 100 summit who he thought was "the next Spielberg": "I look at it as who is daring to buck the conventions and really tell stories in a language that they have founded. Those are the kind of movies that really excite me. One of my favorite filmmakers today is Jordan Peele because he has found a way to take a popular concept from the culture and give it the Jordan Peele spin. Peel off the rind and you find a really original thought inside every single one of his films. Other filmmakers like Jordan... that's really the hope for the future."

The Black Phone (2022)

Taking place a year before *Super 8* is writer/director Scott Derrickson's 1978-set horror film *The Black Phone*. Co-written by C. Robert Cargill from a story by Stephen King's son Joe Hill, the 2022 release follows a brother and sister (Mason Thames and Madeleine McGraw) with nascent psychic abilities whose suburban Denver neighborhood is under the pall of a serial killer (Ethan Hawke). Like the kids of Gale/Zemeckis' *After School*, the middle schoolers of *Black Phone* curse like sailors and then some.

A big Spielberg fan, Derrickson, perhaps inadvertently, created a lot of *E.T.* parallels with *Black Phone* in the sense that both are centered on suburban boys from broken families crossing into manhood with the help of supernatural friends.

"I think there's something to it," Derrickson told this author of the similarities, despite different tones and genres. "He was making some of the greatest films ever made, so there's a false comparison right there! He did that so well and to such powerful effect, making middle school kid spooky scary stories or even high school kid spooky scary stories like these. Since he made *E.T.* and *Poltergeist*—and *Close Encounters* fits in there—there is a nostalgic feeling that people have about his movies."

The difference here is that Derrickson could never deliberately try to ape the Spielbergian sensibility as directly as J.J. Abrams or Greg Mottola did.

He explains, "A lot of TV and films have drawn on Spielberg's experience and recreated it in a way of almost being nostalgic for how those films felt. I can't do that. I don't really like the idea of nostalgia or trying to capture what was fancifully magical about my memories. I don't like looking back on an era and trying to fetishize it, either. It's much more about trying to capture what it actually felt like in that time and place, to be 12 years old growing up in working class North Denver/Federal Heights. If you are able to put that on film in a way that feels truthful, not nostalgic, not drawing on other movies but drawing on your own memories and feelings, it rings true for an audience. They can feel the veracity of it. The value is the human connectivity of, 'Okay, nobody else has my set of memories or experiences of time and place. If I can put that into a film, they're going to feel transported by it.'"

Like Spielberg with *E.T.*, Derrickson was able to channel some autobiographical childhood trauma into *The Black Phone*, as well as a spiritual underpinning that's inherent to the former theology student. In fact, he believes that authenticity is essential in any project he makes, which may explain why Spielberg simply could not connect with *Night Skies* until he made it personal.

"I had gone through a bunch of therapy in the years preceding writing the screenplay," Derrickson admits of his process on *Black Phone*. "That's what gave me a creative way in, combining elements of my own childhood with Joe's short story. That's fundamentally what that movie is. I don't feel any desire to work through my issues in front of a global audience. It's much more about, 'Where does creativity come from?' For me, I've found that if the creative process doesn't have something to do with what I'm feeling and working through as a person trying to grow in this world... if I can't incorporate wherever I'm at as a person at that time, I probably don't end up writing the script or doing the movie."

And, in the spirit of therapy, we have a doorknob moment for you...

"Oh, just one more thing..."

As if *Night Skies* and *E.T.* had not inspired enough films already, it turns out there is one more enormous pop culture landmark it may or may not have touched... Shrek. "Shrek? How on earth did you get to Shrek?" The DreamWorks animated property about the good-hearted ogre which debuted on screens in summer 2001 was not only a smash, but spawned three direct sequels (with

another on the way), two Puss in Boots spin-off films, a Broadway show, video games, merchandise, and theme park attractions. The films alone have earned over $4 billion worldwide.

To connect this to *Night Skies*, we have to go back to the period just after that project fell out from under Rick Baker, with Spielberg & Co. preventing the makeup effects guru from showing off his extensive work on the aliens. Especially guiling were insinuations that what Baker and his team did had not worked. Out of frustration, the makeup artist set out to create a totally different creature utilizing the same techniques they perfected on *Night Skies*.

"More than anything, it was to prove we weren't slackers," said Baker. "After that *Cinefantastique* article said I didn't care about the budget, it made me seem really irresponsible and that the work wasn't very good. It's like, 'Okay, let's show them.'"

Shifting from sci-fi to the fantasy realm, Baker designed the face of a friendly-if-rugged troll. They sculpted the head, body, and hands of the creature, then the "anatomation" process was refined further by Beswick with a better cable system.

Baker adds, "I sculpted the troll head and Doug made these really cool slave-operated arms where the puppet did whatever the controller did. It would show what we could do and how cool it could be. We never got that far because we got jobs that were paying."

There were still questions of how the mechanical skeleton would function with foam appliances over it, but EFX's commitment to David Cronenberg's *Videodrome* prevented further development before a final troll test could be shot.

Over a decade later, Baker's protégé Tom Hester was hired at the fledgling DreamWorks Animation, working with a small group of creatives known as the Propellerheads (J.J. Abrams, Andy Waisler, Rob Letterman, Loren Soman) to create a piece of test footage for a project called *Shrek*. Based on William Stieg's 1990 children's book, it had been optioned by Steven Spielberg in 1991 with Bill Murray eyed to voice the title ogre. By 1995 the Propellerheads were looking to make a less traditional CGI animated feature. A test featured Chris Farley as the voice of Shrek, dancing to James Brown's "I Feel Good."

"I started with Propellerheads on the first *Shrek* test," says Hester. "At that point they had Mike Ploog designing characters, so I did sculptures of his version of Shrek. We basically took Loren Soman's sculpture, created a series of 18 to 20 different facial expressions in clay, then Loren digitized them all and put them into a digital library where a computer would morph between them. Pretty early days with a computer, and I think that's what caught Jeffrey Katzenberg's eye. After Katzenberg saw the test we did he changed his mind again, let most of the crew go, and I just hung on for dear life."

As DreamWorks made more traditional 2D fare like *Prince of Egypt*, the CGI *Shrek* project became known as "the gulag" for its constant turnover in both concepts and personnel.

"I just kept sculpting," Hester recalls of his years on *Shrek*. "Different 2D character designs came through and I did my interpretation. It went through at least four directors and twelve producers. Nobody wanted to work on *Shrek*, it was like the bastard stepchild, but I kept going and was able to become the main character designer. That's how I ended up designing the final characters."

While the test footage ogre was much closer to the illustrated look from Stieg's book, the cuter final Shrek design does have a marked similarity to Baker's troll done in the wake of *Night Skies*. Even though Shrek's ears and teeth are different and the details less realistic, there can certainly be found the overall head shape, nose, and mouth of the troll. In our discussion Hester said he was around the shop when Baker was making the troll. There is footage from a 1982 CBS report of Hester sculpting feet for the creature. Baker apparently did feel his work had been at least partially pilfered for Shrek.

"I know Rick felt that," Hester admits. "I understand. I think he felt that I took some of his design. I wasn't thinking like that. I was thinking, yes, an underbite like an ape has, and there are elements there, but that thing was in the back of my mind too. I guess I must have, you know, maybe... I don't know. It wasn't certainly intentional that there's troll DNA in the Shrek thing."

Shrek went on to become the breakout animated hit DreamWorks desperately needed in 2001, then by 2004 (after *Shrek 2*'s nearly billion-dollar global success) DreamWorks Animation became a publicly traded company separate from the Spielberg-controlled DreamWorks Pictures. Many publications including *Variety* and *Slant* have referred to DreamWorks Animation as "the house that Shrek built." When this animation house was bought outright by Universal Pictures in 2016, *Business Insider* reported that Spielberg pocketed $187.6M from his 4.6 million shares.

CHAPTER 14

Night Must Fall: Conclusion

"Tell the world, tell this to everybody wherever they are: Watch the skies. Everywhere. Keep looking. Keep watching the skies."

—***The Thing from Another World*** (1951)

Lauded screenwriter Robert Towne (*Chinatown*, *The Last Detail*) was part of the radical new generation taking over Hollywood in the '60s and '70s. Among them, Hal Ashby, Robert Altman, Francis Coppola... and Steven Spielberg. Towne told this author in 2006 that the cinematic revolution they were cultivating never reached its full potential.

Towne explained, "All the freedoms we were being given because of the relaxation of the Breen Code and anxiety about films competing with television opened the door to things we were able to put into film that were contemporary, relevant themes. We were able to do them with the kind of freedom, language, sexual candor, and even violence that hadn't been done before. That was very exciting. I don't think we were thinking of it as a revolution. We were thinking of it as 'Wow, we get to do this, we get to do this, we get to do this...' Then, suddenly, we stopped getting to do that. It was over."

The corporate element and blockbuster mentality did eventually consume the majority of studio moviemaking, but Spielberg's unprecedented level of success should have given him license to follow whatever creative instincts he held within. He never fully embraced the willingness to put all his chips and cache on the line for a true creative risk, as William Friedkin did with *Sorcerer* or Coppola with *One from the Heart*, and much later *Megalopolis*. As both director and producer, Spielberg made safe commercial films with mass appeal, always with studio money in place of his own. If he had an albatross keeping him from going to darker or stranger places with his art, it's an albatross he chose to look in the mirror every morning and place around his own neck.

In 2007 this author interviewed Paul Schrader, whose darker vision of what became *Close Encounters* was ultimately rejected by Spielberg. Schrader has walked the more difficult path of making movies such as the elliptical biopic *Mishima*, where investors like George Lucas allowed him the freedom to make a film everyone knew from the outset would never make a dime. During our chat, Schrader explained the mentality you need to get more risky movies made outside the system: "Obsession. Persistence. Monomania. It's not easy, and it doesn't get easier, but, if you feel it's worth doing and you keep at it, often you can somehow get it done. We're in the world now of international financing. Independent filmmaker is like a scavenger dog, crisscrossing the globe looking for scraps that fall off of various national financial tables. That's sort of how you get films made."

Perhaps the idea of losing an inch of cache in an increasingly cutthroat/analytics-driven business is frightening even to a person of Spielberg's stature. Very few filmmakers are in his vaunted position, whose personal production company playground (Amblin) eventually grew to his own studio (DreamWorks). His track record as producer includes a few idiosyncratic cult favs (*Used Cars, Gremlins 2, Joe Versus the Volcano, Cape Fear*), but not much outside the family-friendly arena. As a director he made stabs at more mature work (*Saving Private Ryan, Munich*), yet even Best Picture winner *Schindler's List* was criticized by his close friend Stanley Kubrick (via Frederic Raphael) for emphasizing one of the few uplifting stories to emerge from the systemic human failure of the German death camps: "The Holocaust is about 6 million people who get killed. *Schindler's List* is about 600 who don't."

"When I'm talking about tone in movies, I use the example of *Raiders of the Lost Ark*," explains John Sayles. "There's that moment where the guy's waving his sword around and Harrison Ford just shoots him. Got a huge laugh. Comic violence. You go to *Schindler's List*, there's no room for comic violence. *Schindler's List* is a different tone, but we're still in a movie theater. Quentin Tarantino walks a much thinner line. I remember seeing *Reservoir Dogs*, and I had my hands on my chair. I said, 'They cut the other ear off, I'm out of here.' He hit my trigger point. A guy comes in and shoots the guy who's going to cut his other ear off, right? Yeah. He plays it a lot closer than Steven does."

Steven Spielberg's decision in 1980 to pivot from the dark, sinister (yet likely commercial) tone of *Night Skies* to the sentimental emotional uplift of *E.T.*

the Extra-Terrestrial is as stark as the transition from Jimmy Carter's sober realism to Ronald Reagan's "Morning in America" happening at the same time. That decision paid economic dividends and solidified Spielberg as the most populist storyteller of his generation, but it pigeonholed him into a lane Mick Garris discusses at the very beginning of this book: "Spielberg once told me something that's kind of profound. He said, 'You know, I have so many dark ideas. I mean, I've got some ideas that would make Cronenberg shudder, but I can't make them because of who I am right now.'"

"Maybe that's true," says Hal Barwood. "Steve is an intelligent guy, and he reflects upon his sensibility and career and how things have shaped up. But Steve is practically a reincarnation of Walt Disney, you know? He's the kind of guy who's doing a scene in the woods where a guy and girl are going to kiss, and down in the weeds the animals are gathering around to admire it all. He's sentimental, and I think the difficulties in his family growing up had a big influence on that sentimentality. It's like he didn't have it growing up, and he wants to possess that. In his own family he probably does. Lots of kids and a stable marriage over many, many years... a rarity in Hollywood."

Exec Thom Mount is blunter: "Was he limited by his own success? Sure. Steven was a lot more interesting before he became Steven with a capital 'S.' I do think he did a pretty stable job of recovering from that kind of insane, overwhelming success."

When posed the "What If" of Spielberg making *Night Skies* instead of *E.T.*, Sayles said, "Steven's so good. I think he would have had a great career no matter what... The thing I admired about him the most then—and since then his taste has deepened—is he's never made a condescending movie. He's made movies he would want to go see and tried to make the best one of them. He's not just making a movie because it's gonna make money. He's very happy that it makes money, I'm sure. He's making a movie where he feels like, 'Oh, the audience is gonna love this.'"

Screenwriter Ashley Miller worked on several projects at Amblin/DreamWorks, including uncredited work on *Men in Black 3*. He says of Spielberg, "He is watching the movie in his head in a way nobody does. One time he talked about really, really, really wanting to remake *Fantasia* in live action. *Night on Bald Mountain* ended up informing a whole sequence in the script we were writing, and the way he laid out the sequence wasn't just, 'I see the sun rising up behind the church and Satan shrinking back.' Anybody else would talk about it that way. He's laying that out, but he's saying, '...and the audience is feeling this sense of awe and wonder, and then this fear, and then they're feeling...' He's sitting in the seat watching the film, having an emotional relationship with what he is watching, narrating how the audience is responding to what he's putting up on screen. Not a word out of the man's mouth pitching out a beat, a story element, or a visual without coming back to 'How does the audience feel when they see it?'"

Miller referred to Spielberg's visualization method as "empathy by proxy," apropos since in *Disclosure Day* the aliens' great evolutionary superpower *is empathy*. One might imagine that empath ability makes going to a darker well difficult for the director.

Says Bob Gale, "I don't really see much dark side in Steven's work. I really don't. The idea that he did have this dark side, I didn't really see it. He had a venue to possibly explore that with *Amazing Stories*, but he didn't. I don't know if that was an accurate statement of his or not because you don't see that. Certainly Bob Zemeckis and I have a dark side, and you see that in our work, and you see that separately in Bob's work, it's real clear. You don't see that in Steven's work, at least I sure don't. Maybe I'm missing something. *Duel* is probably the darkest movie he made. Yes, do you become a prisoner of your brand? Absolutely, you do. Did Steven feel that way? *Temple of Doom*, that was the darkest of the Indy movies. My favorite of them. I guess we could look at that movie and say, 'Yeah, the monkey brain stuff. That's pretty gross.' But look, if Steven wanted to do a scary movie, he made two of the scariest movies of all time: *Duel* and *Jaws*. Those movies make you jump out of your seat. He could do that again..."

"I don't think *Indiana Jones and the Temple of Doom* had anything to say," adds journalist Mike Ryan. "It's his darkest movie in terms of, 'I'm just in a bad mood.' Not, 'I'm making a dark movie to represent this awful, terrible thing that happened.' Just, 'I'm in a bad mood, and this is what I'm doing.' That, to me, is interesting."

Says Frank Price, "There's a certain kind of picture that Spielberg is incredibly good on. *Raiders* certainly was, *E.T.* was, and I think he's gone more serious as he's gotten older. Those pictures are good but not outstanding as the others are. I think he's got a certain childlike wonder that works on certain things. I'm not sure what the dark side would be. That I haven't encountered."

"He did have somewhat of a mischievous streak, a dark streak, but I don't know," said Mike Finnell, who made five pictures produced by Spielberg. "That's interesting. I'm sure it's true. I never had that kind of a conversation with Steven where he's admitted anything like that, but it's very possible he was captive of his image. He couldn't do anything too edgy. Maybe that's the way he felt."

"I do have a dark side," Spielberg told *Rolling Stone* in 1985. "Everyone does. I really believe that the best movies, the best stories, take you to the darkest part of your own, or the leading character's, personality and then you *rescue* him. There's a rescue mission involved in all the best movies. That person is *saved* from his own undoing or what other people are doing to him. You have to bring people down to the bottom before you can recover in an operatic third-act finale... Dark side does not have to mean *Scenes from a Marriage*. The dark side is just the worst in people. You let everyone see it, and then effect a recovery."

Says Adam Nayman, "My favorite Spielberg period is in the 2000s where he started saying to people, 'Actually, I'm quite fucked up. You really did not notice, so here's *A.I.* and *Minority Report* and *Catch Me If You Can*.' They're really ambivalent movies about everything. The scale and craft of them runs roughshod over that ambivalence for some people. I don't mind when people say Spielberg is overrated, or even if they don't like him, but I bristle with people saying, 'Oh, he's not an artist, he's an entertainer.' No, he's a really complicated artist and the byproduct is, unfortunately, he's a crowd pleaser. *E.T.* is one of the most oceanic emotional experiences in American film, maybe because it lacks all the pesky specifics that *Brother from Another Planet* has. It's impossible with *Brother from Another Planet* to feel good. It's not uplifting, it's thorny."

Even when *The Adventures of Tintin*'s villain is named "Sakharine," there is no shortage of critics who find Spielberg's films corrosively sweet. These include David Thomson for *The Guardian* in 2002: "Whether he likes it or not, Spielberg is one of those figures who has helped build the sensibility of childhood into a kind of suffocating tyranny in American life. So, for myself, I would just say: 'E.T., stay home.'"

"Steven has an adolescent point of view that kept us from killing Carol Anne," declares *Poltergeist* screenwriter Mark Victor. "I hate to say this, because he's so gifted and talented, but it also prevents him on some movies from digging into the intensity and reality of something."

One of the things we tried to explore in this book is the idea that *E.T.*—perhaps, possibly, potentially—skewed the filmmaker away from an alternate timeline where he got to revel more in his dark psyche the way Alfred Hitchcock did in films like *Vertigo* or *Frenzy*.

"I wonder at what point the Spielberg name became synonymous with his style?" asks Hoai-Tran Bui. "I think that's what trapped him in. Was it *E.T.*? Was that the thing that defined Spielberg? Or was it even before that?"

Says *Sonic the Hedgehog 1, 2, 3, and 4* screenwriter Josh Miller, "Every artist, once they become successful, can get trapped. Even someone in their King of the World phase could still have that creative feeling of, 'I can't really express myself and I'm in a box.' He could have done whatever he wanted, but I guess he was still chasing that success. I know he felt so weird about people's reactions to *Indiana Jones and the Temple of Doom*, that he went too dark. I can imagine him talking to Mick Garris right after that like, 'Oh, they didn't like it. They only want me to do this one thing.' That's the trap of success. It's hard to shake that mindset when you make a movie and it not only does gangbusters at the box office but everyone loves it and critics love it. Then you make one that people don't like as much and you're just like, 'Oh man.'"

"He's built these walls up and you can't knock them down at this point," opines Chris Evangelista. "I love his movies, but even *Schindler's List*, a harrowing film, has blockbuster sensibilities built into it. The way he shoots certain sequences there's... I don't want to call it a disconnect, but I guess there is a question of, 'Does this material warrant this kind of filmmaking?' You can argue it did because it finally got him the Oscar, and it was a huge deal, and it's a great movie. J. Hoberman has talked about it seeming Hollywood-ized."

A vocal critic of *Schindler's List* since its release, prominent *Village Voice* writer Hoberman stated, "He made a feel-good movie about the ultimate feel-bad experience."

"He's showing the violence, he's showing the Holocaust, he's not shying away from the gruesomeness, but there's still the sense this is a guy who loves playing around with the camera," continues Evangelista. "Where is that line? For lack of a better term, it's an entertaining movie, and how do you make an entertaining movie about the Holocaust? Somehow, he did, but that's a weird thing to do."

Spielberg has only made four R-rated films in his career, all of them historical epics like *Schindler's List*, *Amistad*, and *Saving Private Ryan*. His last was the Mossad-centric post-Olympic massacre thriller *Munich*, which came out over two decades ago. If this hesitancy is borne out of commercial concerns, that fear may be unfounded. Consider brother/sister filmmakers Andy and Barbara Muschietti, whose gory, hard R-rated Stephen King adaptations *IT* (2017) and *IT: Chapter Two* (2019) together grossed $1.17B worldwide, proving you can push boundaries within the mainstream.

Says Barbara Muschetti, "I wholeheartedly believe there's always a boundary to push in one way or the other, but it is a choice. I love Spielberg, I love his movies, and he did push boundaries. *Schindler's List* doesn't come out of a vacuum. It is something that is truly terrifying. That's a horror movie, to me. Clearly, he didn't stay within the boundaries. I do think that when he would decide, 'Okay, we're going to make this movie for young adults or for kids,' he didn't think there was a need to push the boundaries, to the point that when they reissued *E.T.* they removed the guns, right? He went further on that. It's a filmmaker's choice, for sure, to the point that you are the one that decides that you're gonna go ahead with a movie or not if the studio doesn't support the rating. Guillermo del Toro is a clear answer to that. I think we are too."

Even though the pair already had success with the PG-13 horror film *Mama* (2013), which has a *Poltergeist*-level scary vibe, they knew *IT* required the freedom only an R-rating could provide. A line is drawn in the sand from the very first scene involving the death of a little boy named Georgie.

"When we made *Mama* it was a ghost story, so there was no need to be gruesome," explains Andy Muschietti. "*IT* was so close to the book, and—loving that book so much—a PG-13 version wouldn't cut it. Has to be about telling the story, right? Getting people scared from the beginning, having the feeling that nothing is safe. That's why everything is so gruesome in our movies. The Georgie scene could have been told in different ways, but part of the reason people are on the edge of their seat is because Georgie is killed in such an atrocious way. You see his arm missing. There is a version of that death without the stump being flailed around, but at that point we thought it was important."

When it comes to Spielberg making those kinds of cinematic gambits, Andy points to one post-*E.T.* movie in particular...

"*Temple of Doom* is a clear example of a movie where Spielberg realized he needed to go further," he says. "The impact of that scene where the priest goes into the chest of the guy and takes his heart out, that's a breach. When *Temple of Doom* came out it was clearly a rated-R thing, but he managed to get away with it somehow. I don't know the secrets behind it, but I think he said, 'No, this has got to be a PG.' It ended up being a PG, but what you see there is not PG at all. Based on that case, I understand why he fought for it because you have to convey how horrific things are on the bad side, to engage people viscerally. With cases like that, you can't really compromise."

As John Milius said during an interview for Japanese television in 1982, "Steven has a boundless energy and an absolute innocence. No matter what happens to Steven he looks at the world as if he's seeing it for the first time. I think that's why people love his films so much, because he brings them back... It doesn't even matter if Steven made a bitter dark war film, it would have an innocence about it."

Concludes John Sayles, "Sometimes it's been *Munich*, where it's like, 'I'd like to see something. Nobody's dealt with this thing and I'm ready to do it.' I'm certain he wasn't ready to do *Schindler's List* in the first 15 years he was making movies. He was a 'movie movie' guy, and that was something from real life he thought about, but he didn't think of it in movie terms. He eventually came to it, and it is a holocaust story that in some ways has a positive happy ending, so it has kind of a Spielberg thing there, as grim as it is."

Night Skies has directly inspired several fan tributes over the years. The most elaborate near miss is something readers of this book have already glimpsed in Chapter 5: A graphic novel adaptation with illustrations by storyboard artist Mike Pappa (*Boston Strangler*, *Werewolves*) and a script by author Steven Awalt (*Steven Spielberg and Duel*). Adapted from the 1980 screenplay with input from Sayles himself, Awalt initiated the project on spec while working as the founding editor and digital content producer at the official Amblin website.

"I wanted to pitch it to Steven, so I adapted one major sequence," says Awalt of the scene where Tess and Jaybird first witness the cattle mutilations. "It came out to 10 pages of comic. I thought it was very *Close Encounters*-ish. We even framed shots in ways that intentionally mimic that visual styling of lens choices or groupings of people. It was coming in as a raw pitch because the film never got made. The concept was, 'Let's put out a graphic novel, as if the film had been made and a bunch of Marvel comic books came out.' The pitch I sold my publisher Insight on would have had a section at the end about the film's pre-production and how it didn't get made. I was hoping to get Rick Baker, Kathy Kennedy because she did so much research, and Steven himself. We would have sold vendors on making merchandise as if the film came out in 1982. We were talking about doing action figures or sculptures since Iron Studios was owned by Insight, a fake one-sheet, a soundtrack for a film that never happened. T-shirts, bubble gum cards… it would all be illustrated, an event around a film that never happened."

Unfortunately, the project never got a "no" or "yes" from Spielberg. It remains an unfinished publishing project to one day be or not to be.

Another professional who got bit by the bug of this unmade film is Andy Fosberry, a composer and recording artist in London who has scored such films as the 2025 shark thriller *Into the Deep* starring Richard Dreyfuss. In summer 2022, he released a full unofficial soundtrack to *Night Skies* via boutique music label Spun Out of Control, the cassette version of which sold out its entire pressing in two days.

"*Night Skies* was an unproduced creepy sci-fi lost to time that, to me, had all the components to be a really wonderful isolation horror," explains Fosberry, who also read Sayles' script for inspiration. "It's an early draft, but all the elements are there. There is something about that era of late '70s Americana that seems like it would have framed the story well, like it did with *Close Encounters* and TV shows like *Project U.F.O.* When I set about creating the music, it came together quickly, done and mixed in about 11 days."

Rather than aping Spielberg's composers of choice (John Williams, Jerry Goldsmith), Fosberry creates a synth-y soundscape of electronic beats and dark ambience which feels contemporary yet still vitally connected to the material. Each of the album's twelve tracks has a title tied to specific moments from Sayles' script like "The Light from the Orchard," "The Cloud Followed Me," and "Faces at the Window."

Adds Fosberry, "In visual terms, if I am to be the director of *Night Skies* now, would I try to mimic Spielberg or Tobe Hooper's style? No. I would want to respond to the script in a creative way that interprets the story in a visual language

whilst trying to bring something new and unexpected. If I tried to be more John Williams, it would have come off like a bad cover version and nobody wants that. I find darkness satisfying to explore with electronica and synths. It fell naturally into the palette for this music."

"And that is the whole problem with aliens, is you just can't trust them. Occasionally you meet a nice one: Starman, E.T. But usually they turn out to be some kind of big lizard!"

—**Bill Murray**, *Ghostbusters 2*

An Industrial Light & Magic veteran makeup effects artist, Danny Wagner has worked on projects as varied as *Thor: Ragnarok*, *Army of the Dead*, and the recent *Wolf Man* redo as well as the entire *Star Wars* prequel trilogy (where he also played the creature Mawhonic). Long fascinated with *Night Skies*, he read about it as a child in the pages of *Cinefantastique*, yearning for a glimpse of the aliens. Then he came across a featurette on the DVD of *Men in Black II* ("Rick Baker: Alien Maker") that briefly showed a black & white photo of young Baker working on the head of Skar. This may have been the first ever behind the scenes glimpse of *Night Skies* released to the public.

"It was Rick sculpting this alien head, but nobody knew what it was," recalls Wagner of the photo. "One guy said, 'Yeah, this is supposed to be *Night Skies*, but it's not labeled."

Inspired by this image, in December of 2009 Wagner began sculpting a duplicate of it during his spare time as a fan tribute using Monster Clay. He did not realize the rare photo was stretched, so Wagner's version came out improperly elongated. Finally getting to visit with Baker in 2010, Wagner saw the same B&W image from the DVD (properly proportioned) on the artist's wall and used this as the basis for a second attempt to recreate the master's work... from memory.

"I was blown away," Wagner remembers. "This is it!! The Holy Grail, the Golden Goose! Then I started to do changes with Rick's help."

Encouraging the fan project, Baker sent more reference of the original Skar. Wagner sent progress images, which Baker handed back with notes directly on them.

"This was very helpful," Wagner exclaims. "Especially getting notes back from the man who did the original one. This was a dream come true! I had a job at ILM during this time so I worked on this little by little. In 2011 I sent a urethane copy to Rick Baker and he sent me a picture back showing my alien right next to the real finished one. I changed more of the sculpture, planning to do the whole body with legs, remolding everything."

"At one point I helped him move things out of his shop into his house, and we came across some *Night Skies* stuff. He said, 'Oh, here's a casting of the hand.' I was really studying: 'Oh my God, the fingertips ARE wider. This part has more bumps on it.' Imagine holding something done 40 years ago."

Danny Wagner and Skar.

When his tribute was finally complete in 2012, Wagner had four fully painted Skar sculpts: Two upper bodies (blue and yellow) as well as two full-sized, including one with a tail that Baker never got to realize before the movie was shut down. There was also a 2015 latex and polyfoam animatronic puppet version, which Wagner made several videos with for YouTube. These action vids found their way into Mark Altman's documentary *Greatest Geek Year Ever: 1982.*

"Danny's a real fanboy," Rick Baker remarks. "He became fascinated with *Night Skies*, so he did his own version. He sent pictures and I said, 'It was more like this...' and described the difference. He gave me castings of that alien which, to be honest, I never really put together. Got it in a box somewhere. He was real fascinated by that character."

Says Wagner, "When I sent him the final thing—torso, head, arms and legs—he goes, 'Man, this is a lot of work you did.' It's nice to know him as a close, good friend."

Said Mick Garris of *Night Skies*, "It was very dark. I think that *E.T.* side was such an important side of Steven that he would have exercised that next. That always would have been there. I would love to have seen *Night Skies*, though."

Adds Robin Love, "*Night Skies* could still be made. The budget was blowing out back then with all of the aliens, but all that can be done so much cheaper these days."

According to Cobb himself in 2005, "I don't think there was anything of my script which was called *Night Skies* [in *E.T.*], and it's still around somewhere. I'd love to do it sometime... There are many scripts sitting on shelves, you could mine them. They get by a bad reader, someone who just doesn't see it, and proper people don't read the scripts. They are put on shelves and eventually burnt... there could have been some brilliant scripts out there but no one caught them."

"It's always an ambition, no matter who you are, John Sayles or Steven Spielberg, that you want a lot of people to see your movie. I can't believe that Sayles wouldn't be happy if Lianna *had grossed $400 million, right? But obviously his ambition isn't to go to Hollywood and make $25 million movies in a quest for that kind of gross."*

—**Joel Coen**, *Rolling Stone* (1987)

Most of John Sayles' personal films are put together independently or self-financed. His shot at a true studio movie was 1983's *Baby It's You*, a comedic

John Sayles and Maggie Renzi at a 40th anniversary *E.T.* screening.

romance set in the 1960s following a conventional Jewish girl (Rosanna Arquette) with acting aspirations who falls for a suave Italian lothario (Vincent Spano) from the wrong side of the tracks. With a cool Bruce Springsteen soundtrack and slick photography, Sayles as director was at last able to impose style on his substance. Sadly, the movie was mishandled by Paramount Pictures, who at one point took the film away from him to re-edit, but ultimately relented by releasing his version. It disappeared into obscurity, despite early roles from Matthew Modine and a blink-and-you'll-miss-him Robert Downey Jr.

"Some of it's just luck and timing, but I really can't predict career," admits Sayles. "Paramount had backed into *Baby It's You*, which had gone into turnaround at another place. They wanted to do it but didn't like our casting, so they already had grumbles. I ended up being happy with it, despite all the trouble. I got it back. Paramount never got over the disagreements we had, but the final cut was the movie I wanted to make."

"I think *Baby it's You* is my favorite Sayles, full stop," says *Pure Cinema Podcast*'s Brian Saur. "Vincent entering the cafeteria with Bruce Springsteen playing...

he's definitely moving the camera more than he does. It has a slickness to it that I don't need in my Sayles movies, but certainly appreciate. I want to see him collaborate with a studio more, although it wasn't a very simpatico thing. That's probably why he doesn't do these."

After 1984's *The Brother from Another Planet*, Sayles and DP Ernest Dickerson reunited that same year for Bruce Springsteen's "Born in the USA" music video, which, alongside the additional "I'm On Fire" and "Glory Days" videos, are what Sayles considers his most widely-seen work as a director.

"Obviously, yeah," Sayles says of those videos' popularity. "Even though they weren't that expensive, it was more money than I had to make three minutes of film ever in my life. One of the nice things about that golden age of rock video is a lot of good filmmakers got to practice. They had a crane and 35mm cameras because a record company said, 'This guy made two little indie features, the band likes him... let's let him go.'"

Sayles achieved high water marks with the coal mining drama *Matewan* and the baseball corruption film *Eight Men Out*, but in the '90s he experienced his most influential period, considered within the industry to be the reigning godfather of independent filmmaking.

"Unlike Lynch or the Coens or Tarantino, Sayles was never cool, but he exists in weird proximity to other landmark '80s movies," says Adam Nayman. "Think about *Eight Men Out* coming the year before *Field of Dreams*. Here's a movie about how this shit actually works, what it says about American politics and business and class and industry, how we build our pastimes into fantasy. *Field of Dreams* is just like, 'play catch with your dad.'"

Saur adds, "I hate to keep coming back to the word 'authentic,' but he's going for something that feels more real. Sayles is hard to quantify because he himself is confident yet unassuming. You don't see that too much in somebody with his history as an independent pioneer. If you're making a low budget movie in the '90s, there's no way you aren't seeing his stuff. He's coming at the perfect time to influence those people."

His sprawling 1991 corruption story *City of Hope* earned praise, then the next year character drama *Passion Fish* (about a paralyzed actress and her caretaker) earned two Oscar nominations for Sayles' screenplay and star Mary McDonnell. Sayles became a go-to script doctor on big commercial films like *The Quick and the Dead*, *Mimic*, *The Newton Boys*, *The Sixth Day*, and *The Alamo*. His extensive uncredited work on Ron Howard's *Apollo 13* (consisting of at least 12 drafts) led to an Oscar nod for credited scriptwriters William Broyles Jr. and Al Reinert.

"I was asked to come onto *Apollo 13* fairly late in pre-production—they had already cast the lead and had started building spaceship sets," Sayles told *Creative Screenwriting* in 1996. "The director, Ron Howard, and actors were much more involved than in any of my other rewriting experiences, as were the consulting astronauts. Scenes were reworked over and over, even after all the writers were off the picture."

While that space success went uncredited, his next film as writer/director was *Lone Star* for Castle Rock. The neo western set in a Texas border town crosscuts between the current sheriff (Chris Cooper) and the exploits of his father (Matthew McConaughey) decades earlier. The complex story of love and justice proved to be a surprise hit, grossing three-times its budget in theaters and earning Sayles another Best Screenplay Academy Award nomination.

"The iconic things of the badge, the hat, and the boots was a comfortable thing for audiences, but also Castle Rock," Sayles told this author of why *Lone Star* worked. "They decided to make the movie, didn't tell us, 'You've got to hire much more famous actors.' They liked the movie, put money into it, and pushed the distributor harder than has ever happened on any of my movies. There was an effort there."

Lone Star reunited *Brother from Another Planet* star Joe Morton with Sayles, who built the role of Army base commander Colonel Delmore Payne around the story of the actor's own military father, who died under mysterious circumstances while integrating the Armed Forces for his country.

"That's what he was using, the military background that I had, and the whole relationship between father and son," confirms Morton. "I love that film."

Sayles worked for Joe Dante again in front of the camera for *Matinee*, featuring the movie-within-a-movie *MANT!* about a man who turns into a giant ant. That in-joke took cues from 1954's giant ant classic *Them!*, which Dante and Sayles tried to update.

Explains Sayles, "One thing I hope happens, and I despair because of what's happening with Warner Bros., is Joe Dante found the original script for *Them!* which had stuff that didn't go into the movie. I was thinking, 'Boy, you could do such a better job with the ants.' On *Mimic* I did a lot of cockroach and ant research. I wrote a screenplay called *Them Again!* which was taking the thing into CRISPR to make the ants more scientifically possible, but also with a tone that Joe loves. We never got anywhere because Warner owns the rights and said, 'Oh, somebody else is gonna do it.'"

A *Them!* remake is currently being developed under producer Matt Reeves.

Dante and Sayles also came close in the mid-'90s to doing a contemporary remake of *The Mummy*, with Mike Finnell producing. It never got the green light, despite a late-in-the-game assist from Steven Spielberg.

"The real tragic one was *The Mummy*," Finnell says. "We had a great script by John Sayles. It was at Universal, who owns all that IP. Tom Pollock was president at that time and there's budget issues. I was coming back from the commissary and Steven drove by. He saw me, stopped, and said, 'What are you guys doing?' I said, 'We're truly beating our heads against the wall to get this remake of *The Mummy* off the ground. Pollock is giving us trouble.' He said, 'Send me the script. I'm not gonna ask for a zillion dollars or anything to make it more expensive, but maybe I can help get him.' I said, 'Oh my God, great. Sure.' I sent him the script and he called saying, 'This is the best script Joe has had since the first *Gremlins*. Let me see what I can do.' There was a meeting I was not at between Joe and Steven and Sid Sheinberg, since Sheinberg was Steven's mentor. He couldn't convince Sid to go ahead, so the whole thing fell apart."

"We visited Sid on the set of *Casper*," as Dante tells it. "Steven said, 'So, Sid… you know, this *Mummy* script is pretty good. You should let Joe make it.' And Sid said, in a quote that will live for the ages, 'It should be a period picture, like the first *Mummy*.' Well, this guy runs the studio and doesn't even know that the 1933 *Mummy* movie was set in 1933. What do you do? I mean, what are you gonna do?"

Says Sean Daniel, who continues to be the steward of that franchise to this day, "I started development of *The Mummy*, and was determined to get it made. I thought Sayles' script was a great way to do it, and Sheinberg did not agree with me. We could not get them to finance it. Also, Sid and Lou Wasserman were absolutely fixated—and I mean beat me over the head for years—with the idea that if it was ever going to be made it had to be as cheap in today's dollars as the original was. It was like, 'Guys, it's a fantasy movie with a creature in it.' It took a change in ownership for the movie to get greenlit."

Sheinberg's vision for a *Mummy* set in the 1930s was eventually realized by director Stephen Sommers in 1999, kickstarting a trilogy plus a Scorpion King spin-off that has collectively grossed $1.4B globally. Another movie is on the way for 2028.

"Yeah, that was interesting," Sayles reminisces of *The Mummy*. "When the Writers Guild finally sent me the adjudication, there were 13 writers on it over a 15-year period, including George Romero twice. I've never met Romero, but at some point five or six years after he wrote a draft somebody came to him and said, 'Do you want to do something with a mummy?' He said, 'Sure,' and handed in the same script and got paid for it. I actually like the movie they made, but it was a totally different direction."

Finnell adds, "The one with Brendan Fraser was okay, but it wasn't anywhere near as good. The Sayles script—I actually reread it not too long ago—was really smart, and you can make it now with some tweaks. It's not dated at all."

Kathleen Kennedy and Frank Marshall hired Sayles for a famously aborted *Jurassic Park 4* script where dinosaurs are trained to be armed commandos. He was also credited on 2008 YA fantasy *The Spiderwick Chronicles* for The Kennedy/Marshall Company, as well as a brief flirtation with a Django Reinhardt biopic.

"I've always wanted to do a project about a guitar player named Django Reinhardt," Marshall told this author in 2006. "He's actually the reason I'm in the business 'cause my father was inspired by his guitar playing when he was growing up on a farm in El Dorado, Kansas. My grandfather was a banjo player and my dad started playing guitar and listening to Django Reinhardt 78 records and became a child prodigy at age 14. MCA signed him as a radio singer/player and the whole family moved to Hollywood. My dad later became a studio guitarist, played in all the big bands, then went on to write music for TV and movies. Jack Marshall. Wrote *The Munsters* and did stuff with Peggy Lee, Vic Damone, Sinatra. I've always known about Django. We had dogs named Django. When I was doing *Bourne Identity* in Paris I found the family and looked up who owned the rights. Now it's just a question of trying to get a script."

Adds Sayles, "Frank Marshall wanted to make a thing about Django Reinhardt, and for about three days I learned all about Django and started outlining it. Then Johnny Depp's schedule closed, so he wasn't available, right? Someday, maybe he'll play Django."

Sayles eventually set his sights on another Django, i.e. the one Franco Nero played in 1966 Sergio Corbucci spaghetti western *Django*. After that film inspired Quentin Tarantino's 2012 hit *Django Unchained*, Sayles set out to craft a true sequel starring Nero titled *Django Lives!* in which the aging gunslinger battles racism in 1914 America. The project never gained traction, but one of the attached producers was David Hollander, the young actor nearly cast as Elliott in *E.T.* back in 1981.

Having not directed a picture since 2013's *Go for Sisters*, Sayles continues to crank out scripts along with prose works such as 2025's *To Save the Man*, which focuses on the 1890 Wounded Knee Massacre and its effect on Native American students of the white-run Carlisle Indian Industrial School. *Night Skies* has not entirely left Sayles' life either...

"I worked for about a year with Doug Trumbull just before he died on a science fiction feature," reveals Sayles. "Of course, people said, 'You've got to make it into a series,' and that's where it is now, not moving at the moment. There is quite a bit of interesting literature, whether you think there are ET's or not, and Trumbull really did. He'd read cattle mutilation stories and this and that. I cannibalized some aspects of *Night Skies* into that, because there was an alien encounter in it."

In late 2026 John Sayles is expected to write and direct his first feature in over a decade, the politically-tinged western *I Passed This Way* starring Oscar winners Amy Madigan (*Weapons*) and Chris Cooper (*Adaptation*). He told *Variety*, "I think these movies are important in developing the best aspects of the American character."

Illustration by William Stout.

Though Rick Baker and John Sayles worked on further Spielberg productions, no one benefitted more from *Night Skies* than its would-be director, Ron Cobb. It all has to do with that little deal memo he signed giving him a small net percentage of *E.T.*, which ultimately made the once-struggling artist financially secure.

"There was a deal memo that said Ron was to direct," details Robin Love. "It was a draft that had been prepared by the agent and never signed by the studio because we were off overseas. The point of the deal was in the event he didn't direct he was to be paid $10,000 as a cure fee. When we came back and discovered he wasn't going to direct the film, I sent an invoice for the $10,000. At that point the film had gone from Columbia to Universal, so Columbia said, 'This has nothing to do with us, you have to bill Universal.' I sent it to Universal, there was a big barney back and forth for months, and finally we got a check for $10,000. By the time we got that, the film had come out and was obviously going to be extremely successful."

Remembers Paul Sammon, "Ron and Robin lived in one of those classic Southern California L-shaped apartment complexes. Three stories, everyone has the same screen door, a common walkway, and down the middle of the L there's a pool. Always had their screen door open, and kids running back and forth that didn't belong to them. People would say 'hi,' they were known in the complex. I did the portrait of Ron on 35mm with a Nikon camera back in '82 in a tiny corner he called his studio, which ran with the *L.A. Times* piece on *Conan*. I was setting the lighting up, Robin walks in and goes, 'Ron, don't you have a percentage of *E.T.*?' Ron goes, 'I don't know. I think we did. Didn't we sign something?' Robin said, 'Well, I'll follow up.'"

Continues Love, "Ron was to receive a net point, which I realized was going to be worth a hell of a lot more than $10,000."

"Ron dug through the papers and found the release signed by Spielberg, and they called up Universal," recalls Bill Stout. "Universal said, 'Oh, thank God, this is the first verifiable point we can pay off on. We'll have a messenger over today with your first check.' I think the first check was, I'm guessing, $850,000."

"About a week later, I heard they got a check messengered for $375,000 or something," adds Sammon. "They needed every penny at that point, and Spielberg honored it."

According to Stout, "He made millions for not directing *E.T.* because he had one of Steven's points, which included merchandising and DVDs. Only in Hollywood could you become a multi-millionaire for not directing a movie."

Adds Love, "Ron was very philosophical about it. He felt he's being paid back for all his years of cartooning with very little to show for it."

Spielberg never did follow through with his intention to back Ron Cobb's directorial debut, which may have had more to do with Cobb than Spielberg.

"Ron just didn't follow through," Robin Love admits. "Ron said he didn't want to direct something he didn't write himself. I said, 'Look, Steven's got tons of projects. They're ready to go. Why don't you have the meeting, the opportunity's there now.' Ron insisted he write something, so he wrote a story based on Louis Leakey called *Hominids*. Very talky. It was about archeologists and anthropologists in the desert figuring out when tools were invented. There's no way this would ever have made an interesting film. The whole idea of him doing a film for Steven went away."

Still, the Amblin impresario continued to sing Cobb's praises. Stout says, "NASA approached Spielberg because they wanted to have a big design exhibit at the Smithsonian Air and Space Museum. He said, 'You've got the wrong guy. You want Ron Cobb.' They flew Ron out to DC, and after 20 minutes they said, 'Ron, this is a little embarrassing, but we think you know more about us than we do.' He was a fanatic when it came to the space program and exploration and possible vehicles. He designed the NASA exhibit, and one of his cartoons is on permanent display at the Smithsonian."

In 1985 Cobb contributed to designing/directing the opening titles for *Amazing Stories* as well as drawing the DeLorean time machine for *Back to the Future*, but no Amblin productions after. A few years later the artist let his harsh feelings about *E.T.* be known in an interview where he called it a "banal retelling of the Christ story, sentimental and self-indulgent, a pathetic lost-puppy kind of story."

Perhaps the biggest audience to ever see one of Cobb's creations came via the Summer Olympics in Los Angeles. A 16-foot-high aluminum space ship was floated above the crowd, while at the base of the Olympic torch an extraterrestrial in a shiny costume appeared to salute humanity.

"Ron was a friend, and we did the '84 Olympics," says Robert Short. "There was an alien that shows up at the closing ceremonies, and they hired Ron to design the alien, which was supposed to be 7 feet tall. Ron's the person who brought us in to build the alien."

Cobb continued to be a leading concept designer, including *The Last Starfighter* and *Total Recall*. While elaborating on his world building for Ridley Scott's *Alien* on the 1986 sequel *Aliens*, Cobb met a kindred spirit in writer/director James Cameron. He went on to design the underwater rigs of *The Abyss* and a nuclear weapon for *True Lies* so realistic the production was afraid it might work. Both men leaned left in their politics but had a keen interest in machines of death.

"Like Kubrick, they're both fascinated with mankind's primal urges," says noted concept designer Daren Dochterman, who got his start working with Cameron and Cobb on *The Abyss*. "The primal urge is to protect your tribe and defeat everyone else. Jim and Ron were very similar in that way."

"Anyone who is design oriented and of that period knows the impact Ron had on design," Cameron says in *The Art of Ron Cobb*. "Ron's work inspired generations of artists who saw the practicality of his work and began trying to build a portfolio off that same idea. It's hard to pinpoint one or two specific things that stand out to me as his legacy, everything about him is worth remembering and should be celebrated."

Remembers Dochterman of the *Abyss* period, "We were in secret offices on the Fox lot that were not official, let's say, because we hadn't got a greenlight yet. A strip of three offices connected by doorways. One drafting room for storyboards, the next office was Cameron's, and at the end another office with Ron in it. I was building study models. One of my favorite things happened: he was all alone in his room, constantly working, but one afternoon around 4:30 I go there and he's at his desk resting his head on his hand while his drawing hand is moving, not touching the page. I say, 'Hey Ron, can you help me with something?' No answer. He was sleeping. He was taking a nap, and his hand was still moving. This actually happened. I said, 'This is the greatest thing ever.'"

Cobb continued to expand into many mediums including a video game company called Rocket Science where young Elon Musk was a PA. He did eventually make an undistinguished directorial effort with 1992 Australian comedy *Garbo*, but by the mid-to-late 2000s Cobb's movie output slowed to almost nil owing to deteriorating health.

"There's lots of interviews with Ron on YouTube and if you look at the dates you can start to see the cracks, see him slipping. It's sad to see that, because he was one of the most brilliant minds you would ever have met in your lifetime. It was frustrating to see that go. Ron got awarded the first Lifetime Achievement Award for concept design by Lightbox in 2019. I said, 'Look, I'm going to Australia in a few months, give me the award and I'll give it to Ron personally.' I emailed Robin and got a response: 'You're not going to see Ron.' She told me about the Lewy body dementia, said, 'He no longer recognizes me, he no longer recognizes his son.' I said, 'Well, I'm coming to Australia anyway. Let me take you guys out for dinner. Let me present you with the award on Ron's behalf.'"

Ron Cobb passed away in Sydney, Australia on September 21, 2020.

Says Stout of his friend, "I love the fact that he died on his birthday surrounded with colorful balloons. I think Ron would have loved the irony of that."

Directly after winning his first Oscar for *An American Werewolf in London*, Rick Baker was deluged with offers. One reunited him with director John Landis for Michael Jackson's legendary *Thriller* video, where the singer transforms into a zombie and a werecat. Baker also had a small part as a drug dealer in Landis' *Into the Night*, and in 1988 received an Oscar nod for his work transforming Eddie Murphy into several characters (including an old Jewish man) on the director's *Coming to America*.

He and Elaine Baker would divorce in 1984. Like many Baker associates, his friend and partner Doug Beswick eventually split off to form his own companies Doug Beswick Productions, Inc. (*Nightmare on Elm Street 3*, *Beetlejuice*), Flat Earth with Kevin O'Neill and Kevin Kutchaver, and eventually Cantina Pictures Inc.

That early obsession with apes at age 13 found purchase in a great many pictures Baker was assigned to, including *Greystoke: The Legend of Tarzan*,

Gorillas in the Mist, *Baby's Day Out*, *Mighty Joe Young*, and the 2001 remake of *Planet of the Apes*. Baker's record string of seven Oscar wins—twelve nominations altogether—continued into the '90s for turning Martin Landau into Bela Lugosi for Tim Burton's *Ed Wood*, Eddie Murphy into an overweight family in *The Nutty Professor*, and a menagerie of extraterrestrials for producer Steven Spielberg's *Men in Black*. He also worked on two subsequent sequels.

"On the first *Men in Black* it was a lot of design by committee with Steven, Walter Parkes, and Barry Sonnenfeld," says Baker. "We'd send out packets of designs with numbers and letters on them. Eventually we'd get a response: 'Why don't you do one with the head from A2 and the body from C3 and the feet from this?' It's like, 'Because it would look stupid, that's why.' But it was, 'No, let me rephrase that: Make one that looks like that.' Barry learned to trust me after the first *Men in Black*. He would approve any design I made on *Men in Black II*. I would do something, he goes, 'Yeah, great.'"

In 1988 things came full circle when Baker was invited by Amblin to do his own take on the little green men of *Gremlins*. Although a sequel to the 1984 hit had been in the pipeline at Warners for years, Joe Dante already had an approach in mind as early as 1985 when he told *Daily Record*, "I've never remotely considered a sequel, but if I did *Gremlins 2* I'd do it like *Hellzapoppin*, even more offbeat."

At some point that year Dante, Finnell, and Spielberg coalesced to go forward, but makeup whiz Chris Walas did not want to go through the grueling gremlins mill again.

"When I bowed out of it, they had a much more straightforward story going... it wasn't this remake of *Hellzapoppin*," Walas says. "They didn't have a script, just a couple scenarios. I'm literally in a meeting with David Cronenberg and Stuart Cornfeld at Fox for *The Fly*, and David's assistant comes in saying, 'There's a call for Mr. Walas, it's Steven Spielberg.' You can't actually tell Steven, 'I'm busy.' Steven says, 'Chris, I need you to come over to Universal right now.' You can't say no to Steven, especially at that point. David said, 'I know, go.' Steven's doing post on his *Amazing Stories* episode, pulls me into the lobby at the Alfred Hitchcock Theater, corners me with Mike and Joe, and for 20 minutes he's hammering me to do *Gremlins 2*. They didn't even have a schedule, but they were afraid if I did *The Fly* it was going to interfere. I knew *The Fly* was going to be special. Those are the projects you get to put more of yourself into. Finally, after 20 minutes, I said, 'I really want to try and get into directing.' Steven backed down, said, 'Well, I'm never going to talk anybody out of trying to direct.' That was the end of it."

Walas won an Oscar for Best Makeup on *The Fly*, later directing *The Fly II*.

Producer Mike Finnell says, "We had our offices on the Warner lot. Joe was going to lunch and he ran into Terry Semel, the president of the studio, who said, 'We have to have *Gremlins 2*.' We had already made numerous attempts with various writers to come up with *Gremlins 2*, and just couldn't. Terry said to Joe, 'You can do anything you want, just as long as it's called *Gremlins 2* and there are Gremlins in it.'"

Dante turned to the man who nearly made his *Howling* werewolves. As Walas remembers, "Rick calls me up in a panic and goes, 'Chris, they just offered me *Gremlins 2*. That's your movie.' I'm going, 'No, it's okay. I turned him down, and I'm glad they asked you because I wouldn't want anybody else to do it."

Says Baker, "I turned down *Gremlins 2* numerous times because the designs were already there and I like designing stuff, and my shop wasn't big enough. There were a whole lot of reasons... it practically killed Chris Walas."

As Joe Dante explains, "That's why we have a genetics lab and Dr. Catheter and all those different gremlins. That's what it took for Rick to do the movie."

Baker adds, "When they said to me, 'What can we do to make you want to do this?' it was like, 'Let me do some slight redesigns, but also let me make individual characters, which is what I wanted to do for *Night Skies*."

Says Walas, "He was right in not wanting to just repeat my designs. He was insistent on making sure they were Rick Baker's gremlins. He had them over a barrel."

"Chris Walas had every gremlin look the same, except he put a furry stripe on one," Baker continues. "The problem on *Gremlins 2* was we had to have many versions of each design, which is what *Night Skies* was going to be."

Because he had a full year to concept and build his creatures before cameras rolled, Baker—who gets a co-producer credit—created a bestiary of new nasties including a spider gremlin, vegetable gremlin, lady gremlin, and a brainy talking gremlin voiced by Tony Randall. There are stop-motion winged gremlins by Doug Beswick, and even the tree limb clip from their 1972 collab *Octaman*.

Says Tom Hester, "I designed the daffy mogwai, daffy gremlin, and the bat gremlin. I was also a puppeteer, and by the end of it I was getting tired of slime and green scales because it seemed to go on endlessly. We were on set for six months. Gag after gag."

"I lucked out in that I learned from what Chris did," adds Baker. "I had a lot more time, and more money too, which was great!"

The resulting *Gremlins 2* is a madcap meta satire of the first movie where gremlins run amok in a New York office building run by a Trump-ian media magnate. While it stands as the MOST Joe Dante movie ever made and is beloved today, *Gremlins 2: The New Batch* pulled the rug out from 1990 audiences too hard and landed with a thud. Spielberg may have been more disappointed than anybody as franchise hopes died while the wackiness unspooled in front of him.

"He and Chris Columbus really despised it," says Dante. "They found it cold. They missed the fact that it wasn't a heartwarming family movie anymore. It's not that he didn't think it was inventive; it just didn't appeal to him."

Adds Finnell, "I remember Steven calling after saying, 'There's too many gremlins! There's just too many gremlins in it!' It got really good reviews, but unfortunately didn't do anywhere near the business the first one did, and it was three-times more expensive."

"I remember being a little disappointed in how the amount of gags almost seemed to step on themselves," said Hester. "It was so frenetic, that got on my nerves after a bit."

Adds Walas, "I was disappointed because I wanted to see the gremlins taken to the next level, not to another dimension or another planet. I am glad Joe had the opportunity to make that, because it is so completely Joe. He's said it's his favorite of all his movies."

Baker would take home more gold statues for *How the Grinch Stole Christmas* and *The Wolfman*, but by the time the latter 2010 movie hit much of his work got hijacked by CGI. Although he was considered for practical makeup duties on J.J. Abrams' *Star Wars: The Force Awakens*, the idea of being in London for years did not appeal to him. Instead, he retired. Now he works 8-to-10-hour days making various designs, masks, paintings, and sculpts of his own, unincumbered by the whims of others.

Baker explained to this author, "When I do a project, I'm all in and that's my life. During that time, I work day and night, and many times put my own money into it to make it better. I can't tell you how many times, especially later in my career, I would say to people, 'I don't understand why you hired me, you're not trusting me to do it.' They're like, 'Well, you did *American Werewolf*.' 'Yes, and the director of *American Werewolf* said, 'I want a four-legged hound from hell, but you're the designer, you know more about it than I do... just do it.' The sculpture I did is what's in the movie. There's a certain vitality and heart in the sculpture when it isn't picked apart and changed a thousand times because some producer thinks he has to say something. It wasn't until I retired that I realized most of these guys are in it for the money and do as many shortcuts as they can. They figure everybody's doing that, when it's just the opposite for me. Producer interferences and changes slow everything down and fuck everything up. Just let me do what I do and you'll get the best work.'"

"He definitely got tired of answering dumb questions from producers, and I think it's funny that the last time you see Rick Baker is in the 2010 *Wolfman*, whisked off screen by a CGI werewolf," waxes Phil Nobile. "He retired from an industry, he didn't retire from being himself. He wakes up and goes into his garage and works on things that make him happy, and there's no deadline. He seems very content with that. I count us fans lucky that he is putting it on Instagram. The overarching thing about his work is generosity, sharing his work even if it's not something he's being paid to do. Sharing his knowledge with a generation under him. Before Dick Smith, makeup artists were rivals. They did not share secrets, they guarded them. A big part of Rick Baker's legacy is he opens up the book for anybody to learn it."

Concludes Rick Baker, "I wanted to be Dick Smith. I wanted to do the same thing. We all thought it was going to be better for the state of the art if we shared information. Rob Bottin, Greg Cannom, Steve Johnson, Norman Cabrera, Tony Gardner... all these people started with me. I've had numerous people come up and say, 'You're like what Dick Smith was to you... you're our Dick Smith.' So many people say, 'Because I saw *The Making of Thriller*, I decided this is what I wanted to do with my life.' The whole *Making of Thriller* was a surprise to me. I was taking Michael's lifecast, and Michael's incredibly shy. Doing a lifecast always looks horrifying when you see it on film. Landis just came in, says, 'Yeah, there's gonna be a film crew here today. We're doing a making of.' I'm going, 'NO! Michael is so shy and it looks so horrifying and don't do it!' He goes, 'Fuck you, we're doing it.' I was not happy about it, and I'm so thankful he did because it inspired so many people to become effects makeup artists."

After penning her *Twilight Zone: The Movie* segment and marrying Harrison Ford in 1983, Melissa Mathison had a twelve-year theatrical movie gap on her resume. She spent much of that time taking care of children Malcom and Georgia on her 700-acre ranch, telling *Newsweek* in 1995, "I didn't want to be missing their childhood while I was away, busy writing about children."

There were a few near-reunions with Spielberg, the first of which could have been his adaptation of Alice Walker's Pulitzer-winning novel *The Color*

Melissa Mathison (*left*) and Kathleen Kennedy (*right*).

Purple. The story chronicling 40 years in the life of an African American woman named Celie living in the south was originally going to be adapted by Walker herself, but after three months' work resulting in one script draft, she "gave it up." According to her 1996 memoir *The Same River Twice*, Spielberg presented Mathison as a potential replacement, "but the chemistry was not right there. Her being a woman and me being a woman didn't do it."

Another pet project was *The Adventures of Tintin*, eventually made by Spielberg as a CGI animated movie in 2011, but initially developed alongside Mathison in the mid-'80s with a rumored Henry Thomas as Hergé's title kid detective and Jack Nicholson as Captain Haddock. Mathison's script about Tintin going up against ivory hunters in Africa did not meet the director's approval, although some insist elements of it wound up in *Indiana Jones and the Last Crusade*.

During this gap, Mathison was able to once again capitalize on the little alien that won the world's heart. In March of 1989 the Writers Guild of America won an arbitration on her behalf giving the screenwriter and associate producer 5% of merchandising revenue from *E.T. the Extra-Terrestrial*, in addition to whatever ample residuals her contract may have entitled her to. This was awarded on the basis that Mathison described the character in detail throughout the pages of her first two script drafts, before they fabricated a puppet. Even though the final credits read "E.T. Created by Carlo Rambaldi," it was decided the character originated from Mathison's pen alone.

The award was heavily contested by Universal Pictures, who used John Sayles' *Night Skies* script as evidence to argue the character of E.T. evolved out of that project prior to Mathison's involvement. Seasoned WGA arbitrator Sol Rosenthal acknowledged some similarities to both Buddee and Skar, but he found contrast with Sayles' descriptions of grasshopper eyes and a beak-like mouth ... even though E.T.'s mouth remained noticeably beak-like from certain angles.

"E.T. was not copied from Sayles' script," Rosenthal told *Daily Variety*. "Mathison did not stop at writing only that E.T.'s finger glowed. She described his unique hands and fingers. Mathison did not only write that E.T. was three-and-a-half-feet tall; she created short, squashed legs, a telescopic neck, a protruding belly, long/thin arms, and a glowing heart. She did not simply write that E.T.'s face was round, but detailed his wide head, the softness in his face, his large round eyes, the leathery creases and furrows in his brow."

Apparently, the studio did not utilize Rick Baker's *Night Skies* designs as evidence that some of these aspects existed prior to Mathison. While the feline slit-like iris in Skar's eyes do not match E.T., Buddee was fabricated with more sympathetic, large human-like eyes with a circular iris. The telescopic neck, long thin arms, wide head, and leathery creases in E.T.'s skin were all features of the 4-foot Skar. Would pulling Baker into the arbitration have opened a can of worms?

Spielberg's lawyer Bruce Ramer posted a response in *Variety*: "That determination does not justify, by any stretch of the imagination, the implication that Mr. Spielberg had little or nothing to do with the birth and shaping of the character and concept central to the most successful motion picture in history. As Ms. Mathison would unquestionably confirm to you, Mr. Spielberg conveyed his views and concepts to her respecting E.T. in the most minute detail, both before and during the writing process."

It is possible this arbitration was perceived by all parties as a business transaction rather than personal slight, yet Mathison never worked on a Universal film afterwards, while her husband Harrison Ford (*American Graffiti*, *Heroes*) did not star in a film for that studio again until 2011's Spielberg-produced *Cowboys & Aliens*. Mathison continued a working relationship with Kennedy/Marshall and, eventually, Spielberg.

After penning the two-part 1991 ABC TV western *Son of the Morning Star* (produced by Thom Mount), Mathison's next feature script to make it before cameras was an adaptation of Lynne Reid Banks' popular 1980 children's book *The Indian in the Cupboard*, produced by Kathleen Kennedy and Frank Marshall. The return to familiar territory revolved around middle schooler Omri's discovery of a magic cupboard that turns any toy he puts inside it into a living thing. A relationship forms between Omri (Hal Scardino) and the Native American figurine Little Bear (Litefoot), with whom he learns the value of responsibility. A side-character, Omri's friend Patrick (Rishi Bhat), is similar to the deleted Elliott/Lance relationship in the first *E.T.* draft. The film is full of charming scenes and an achingly earnest performance from Scardino.

Wonderfully cynical director Frank Oz (*What About Bob?*, *Little Shop of Horrors*) does not seem comfortable making a movie aimed squarely at young children, despite his years of Muppet-ing. Example: the final line of dialogue in the movie, during a moment meant as a grace note for Omri, is another child discussing the Kennedy assassination. Released the same year as Disney's "toys come to life" hit *Toy Story*, *The Indian in the Cupboard* was a box office dud, grossing $35.7M on a $45M budget.

Roger Ebert wrote for *Chicago Sun-Times*, "The movie was written by Melissa Mathison, who also wrote *E.T.*, and here uses some of the same ideas: A little boy hides an amazing living thing in his room, and tries to go about his daily life with this secret knowledge... *The Indian in the Cupboard* is not exhilarating or exciting or funny in the ways that *E.T.* was, and although it tries for the same realism in its depiction of its children, it stumbles over the plight of its little people who become the playthings of the kid-gods."

Mathison next set her sights on another story of a displaced innocent trying to return home. With script research taking place over several years in the early-'90s, *Kundun* is a biopic of exiled 14th Dalai Lama Tenzin Gyatso directed by Martin Scorsese. Both Mathison and Ford had been longtime Tibetan liberation supporters and introduced the *Taxi Driver* director personally to his holiness.

Scorsese recalled that first encounter to the *Los Angeles Daily News* in 1998: "The way he remembered the shine on Chairman Mao's shoes, the way Mao moved on the couch when he ultimately said to him, 'Religion is poison'... I mean, this is great stuff!"

As Mathison told *NY Times* in 1996, "I am sort of famous for little-boy stories, and this was a fantastic little-boy story, a story of destiny and nurturing and tragedy, the idea of finding a 2-year-old child and then investing in him everything that is good about human beings, your people, and your beliefs."

With gorgeous cinematography by Roger Deakins and a haunting score by Philip Glass, *Kundun* is a haunting meditation on the tragedy perpetrated on the people of Tibet and their young leader, whom we follow from a small boy to age 23 when he was forced to flee the country during Chinese takeover. Despite the episodic movie's four Oscar nominations, it was buried upon release by Disney so as not to upset Chinese authorities who could compromise future business dealings with the House of Mouse. Both Scorsese and Mathison were temporarily banned from China.

After another extended absence, in 2008 she once again dipped back into the well of a small child meeting an otherworldly fish out of water character, although in this case it was literal. Working under the Kennedy/Marshall banner, Mathison penned Disney's English-dub version of Japanese animator Hayao Miyazaki's children's film *Ponyo*, about a female fish creature who sneaks away to the surface world where she befriends a little boy named Sōsuke, and through their bond she is transformed into a human.

Her final posthumous film was an adaptation of Roald Dahl's *The BFG* directed by Steven Spielberg for Disney. It was a film that Kennedy/Marshall had been pursuing for some time, beginning with Robin Williams in the lead in 1991. Mathison turned in her "experimental" and "poetic" 1st draft in June of 2009. *Shakespeare in Love*'s John Madden initially signed to direct before Spielberg made it an official *E.T.* reunion with Mathison, Kennedy, and Marshall. Thirty-four years after their initial collaboration, screenwriter and director had the luxury of being able to watch the entire movie in pre-viz form and then re-work it. As with their prior film, Mathison was on set every day, once again handing Spielberg cards with that day's scenes on them.

As the director told *The New Yorker*'s Tom Shone in 2016, "When we did *The BFG*, I looked at Melissa and she said, 'Steve, are you ready to get back to the cards?' I went, 'Really, Melissa?' 'Yes, I think we need to keep a continuity between the last time we worked and this time,' so I went right to the cards."

Mark Rylance played the title gentle giant via the same performance capture techniques used by the director on *Tintin* and *Ready Player One*. The film's live-action child lead Sophie was played by Ruby Barnhill, who has not appeared in a feature since. The movie is full of Dahl's signature whimsey and English humor, but the final product is overlong and never truly gels. BFG's garbled aphorisms ("Because I hears your lonely heart, in all the secret whisperings of the world.") lack the impactful brevity of "I'll be right here." It was rumored one of the big supporting players in the movie refused to do press after seeing the film, explaining, "I don't know which giant I am!"

As Todd McCarthy wrote for *The Hollywood Reporter* out of *The BFG*'s Cannes debut, "An uncanny thematic mirror to *E.T.* some 34 years later, Steven Spielberg and Melissa Mathison's *The BFG* emerges as a conspicuously less captivating, magical and transporting experience than its classic forebear. Quite literally about the value and importance of dreams to the exclusion of almost anything else, this adaptation of Roald Dahl's enduring classic (published, coincidentally, the same year *E.T.* came out) sees the director diving deep into a technological bag of tricks to mix giants and humans on the same cinematic stage. Big commercial results loom for Disney's major early July release."

Unfortunately, those "big commercial results" never materialized, with *THR* claiming *The BFG* lost, "$90 million-$100 million for partners Disney, Amblin Entertainment, and Participant Media."

A larger sadness happened long before that. Towards the end of production in July of 2015, Mathison left the Vancouver set to visit her doctor, then returned looking noticeably glum. She was in a coma by September. Melissa Mathison passed away on November 4, 2015 of neuroendocrine cancer. She was 65 years old.

Said Spielberg in a statement, "Melissa had a heart that shined with generosity and love and burned as bright as the heart she gave E.T."

"Melissa was a remarkable friend not only to me but to everyone who had the privilege to know her," said Kennedy. "She was fiercely intelligent, confident, soulful, strong and had a smile that would light up a room. I will miss her terribly."

In 2016 the Hamptons International Film Festival established the Melissa Mathison Award for emerging female screenwriters, providing each winner with a casting director and the opportunity to present a staged reading of their project in New York City.

HIFF artistic director David Nugent told this author, "Our advisory board member Taylor Barton-Smith was friends with Melissa. My team and I were great admirers of her work and her blazing a trail as she did at a time that was less receptive to women in Hollywood. When she passed, we discussed finding a way to honor her legacy and arrived at the idea to highlight one of the writers each year who was a woman and to try to further facilitate producing their film. The first recipient was Cathy Yan. We worked with her to produce a staged reading of excerpts from her lab project *Dead Pigs*. The film went on to premiere at Sundance, win an award, and she's had a great career ever since!"

Inaugural 2016 award recipient Cathy Yan went on to helm 2020's DC Comics superhero film *Birds of Prey* starring Margot Robbie. In 2025 she co-wrote and directed the Natalie Portman-led thriller *The Gallerist*. Despite maintaining a low profile during her career, Melissa Mathison continues to inspire screenwriters to this day.

"She was very grounded in people, human interactions, and compassionate stories," Henry Thomas said of Mathison. "I think those were important things to her, and it shows in the humor. It shows in the stories that she had a part of creating."

"For me, Melissa was love, and that came out throughout the entire film," says Dee Wallace. "Look at the script she wrote. She was the heart. She was the soul of that movie. Without that beautiful, incredible script we would have not had that movie. That script really tells you the heart of who Melissa was... her kindness, her sweetness."

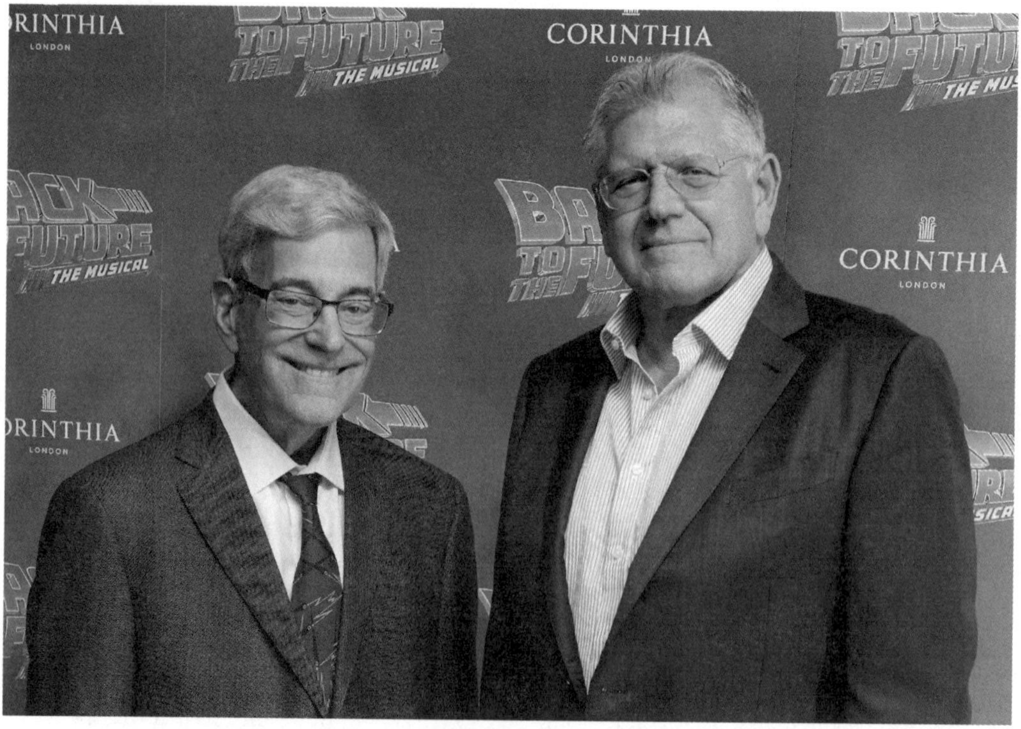

Bob Gale (*left*) and Robert Zemeckis (*right*).

The core thematics of *After School* and its screed against teen bullies eventually found purchase in Bob Gale and Robert Zemeckis' screenplay for *Back to the Future*. That story involved a high school kid named Marty who, with the help of eccentric Doc Brown's time machine, goes back to 1955 and meets his parents. Frank Price had asked for several drafts while the project was at Columbia but ultimately put the project into turnaround sometime in 1981. There were no other studio takers.

Thus began a period of the two Bobs in career limbo, as Gale recalls: "We spent about two years trying to get *Back to the Future* off the ground, rejection after rejection. We had another deal with ABC motion pictures for *Gangland*, a 1920s gangster movie. We were six weeks into pre-production and, because it was a TV network, they gave our script to their market research department and tested it. Market research said nobody would be interested in seeing a 1920s gangster movie. They pulled the plug, which was really, really depressing. We had offices over on Pico Boulevard, a casting director hired, production designer hired, location manager… all these people lost their jobs. Zemeckis said, 'Look, I've got cabin fever. I've got to direct the next decent script that crosses my desk.' In late 1982 he signed on to direct *Romancing the Stone*."

A kind of female-centric riff on Indiana Jones, *Romancing the Stone* (originally "Romance on the Rock") follows an out-of-her-depth author (Kathleen Turner) who teams with a roguish mercenary (Michael Douglas) to track down the treasure that could save her kidnapped sister. The shoot was plagued with problems, causing at least one crew member to utter of Zemeckis, "This guy's never gonna make it." The rough cut of *Stone* was so loathed internally that 20th Century Fox fired Zemeckis from his next film *Cocoon*, replacing him with Ron Howard. Then, *Romancing the Stone* was a smash, Fox's biggest success of 1984 with over $115M in worldwide box office. The film's screenwriter Diane Thomas, a former Malibu Beach waitress, briefly became Spielberg's next protégé, writing drafts of *Always* and the third Indiana Jones before her untimely death in 1985.

Zemeckis now had the clout to revive *Back to the Future* with Spielberg as executive producer, but that meant "somehow" bringing the project over to Universal. Unlike on *E.T.*, the saving grace wound up being Frank Price, who managed a horse trade with newly-installed Columbia head Guy McElwaine (Spielberg's former agent at ICM). Columbia would acquire the remake rights to *Double Indemnity* for their comedy flop *Big Trouble*, while Universal got the languishing script for *Back to the Future*.

Then came a critical question: What would be the time machine? Initially it was a refrigerator, another case of Spielberg carrying over an old idea into one of his movies.

"The 'nuke the fridge' scene in Indiana Jones 4 is from the first draft of *Back to the Future*," confirms Gale. "That nuclear test site scene, which we stole from a Mickey Rooney movie *The Atomic Kid*. If you look carefully at *Back to the Future*, the movie that is playing at the town theater in 1955 is *The Atomic Kid*."

Eventually they decided using a fridge as a time vehicle was a little TOO socially irresponsible, as children might climb into fridges to imitate the movie. Instead, they went with a car... and Ron Cobb.

"The time machine was not supposed to be a DeLorean, it was going to be a Mercedes, and they changed it," confirms Cobb biographer Jacob Johnston. "There was a lawsuit happening at the time around the DeLorean and they thought that element could elevate the movie as a conversation piece. Plus, the car looked really cool. When Cobb came on, it was like, 'How do you build this device into the car?'"

"Our production illustrator Andrew Probert's ideas were good but a little too slick," explains Gale. "Our sense was Doc Brown built this in his garage, it shouldn't be polished. We were able to snag Ron Cobb for two weeks. What you get with Ron is not just a guy who can make stuff look cool. Ron started to think about, 'Okay, there's a nuclear reactor in this vehicle. How would that work? Where would it go?' He developed intricate blueprints with various systems in a nuclear reactor, from the nuclear core to where you put the plutonium, how the energy would generate the electricity, how it would vent. We asked questions and he always had an answer. He designed a version of the cockpit too."

Adds Johnston, "Ron added the date element in the tape dash. When he was done the car was 90% there. Only big thing they changed were the vents on the back. Probert wasn't changing the integrity of the engineering or the design, it was just for story purposes."

Says Gale, "We augmented the second cooling vent on the rear passenger side, just for balance and because it made it look more like a wicked car. In terms of his thought processes, he brought so much to the party, and when Ron finally saw the movie he couldn't have been happier."

Cobb's DeLorean time machine is one of the most iconic vehicles in cinema history, and in 2018 made a star return in Spielberg's own blockbuster *Ready Player One*. The *BTTF* director was also given a pop culture shout out when the main character uses an item called a "Zemeckis Cube" to turn back time in the virtual world he inhabits.

With $210.6M in domestic box office, *Back to the Future* became the #1 movie of 1985 and a career-defining landmark for Zemeckis and Gale, a Swiss watch screenplay of cracker jack comedic timing still admired/studied today. It led to two more sequels with stories concocted by the two Bobs but final screenplays written solo by Gale while Zemeckis was busy making *Who Framed Roger Rabbit*.

Although the two went their separate ways professionally after the *Back to the Future* trilogy in 1990, two of their earlier screenplays (1977's *Trespass* and 1973's *Bordello of Blood*) were produced in 1992 and 1996, respectively. Gale broke out on his own, penning the well-regarded unproduced script *Jimbo's Stand* as well as directing the low budget comedy *Interstate 60* in 2002, while also writing comics for DC and Marvel. He drafted early unmade versions of *Doctor Strange* and *John Carter of Mars*. Gale was a producer of and wrote the book for a *Back to the Future* stage musical.

After the Bobs disbanded, Zemeckis recaptured the black comedy flavor of his early films with *Death Becomes Her,* starring Meryl Streep and Goldie Hawn as two frenemies who take a potion for immortality. It became a camp classic with a 2024 stage musical of its own. Then came 1994's *Forrest Gump* with Tom Hanks playing a developmentally disabled man who has Zelig-like run-ins during historical inflection points. It earned $678.2M globally as well as a Best Director Oscar for Zemeckis and Best Picture.

His experience on the *Close Encounters* set in Mobile, Alabama clearly left an impression. Two decades after in 1997 he adapted Carl Sagan's popular fiction novel *Contact* to the screen, working in collaboration with the famed astronomer until his passing mid-production in 1996. Starring Jodie Foster, it dealt with what first contact aliens should look like through a novel solution: the film never shows them.

Two decades after that, Zemeckis produced the 2019 AppleTV+ series *Project Blue Book*, a highly fictionalized account of Dr. J. Allen Hynek (Aidan Gillen) and his investigations into the world of UFOs. The 14th episode of season 2 was titled "Hopkinsville," with Hynek on-site in rural Kentucky investigating the famed 1955 encounter.

"We had a ton of documentation, then you start getting into story," says the episode's writer Harley Peyton. "We've got a farmhouse full of people, how are we going to write them? Then you've got the carnival workers. It's a pretty rich text, almost like a *Twilight Zone* episode. Whether you think they're misidentifying horned owls or whatever, this was classified as a hoax in Blue Book files… but for our purposes there's no such thing as a hoax. Hopkinsville is like a campfire story, for God's sakes. There's something I was drawn to in writing it, basic dramatic beats you don't always have the opportunity to work with based on how things are witnessed in Blue Book files. In this case there's something malign going on. That's why people still think about it, the level of drama was heightened. I'm not surprised that's one that sticks, true or not."

Zemeckis continued to enjoy a run of box office hits both major (*Cast Away*, *The Polar Express*) and minor (*What Lies Beneath*, *Beowulf*, *A Christmas Carol*, *Flight*). He still makes eccentric films pushing technological boundaries. He and Gale are still friends.

In 2006 this author attended a New York press conference for Best Picture winner *The Departed*, a mob movie in a long line of mob movies made by Martin Scorsese: *Mean Streets*, *Goodfellas*, *Casino*, *The Irishman*, etc. That day Scorsese said, "It's an obsessive behavioral pattern of mine to be dealing with this material."

In the same way Scorsese is identified with crime films, his friend Steven Spielberg is intrinsically tied to the extraterrestrial genre…

Firelight
Close Encounters of the Third Kind
E.T. the Extra-Terrestrial
War of the Worlds
Indiana Jones and the Kingdom of the Crystal Skull
Disclosure Day

Then there's all the alien work he produced: *Batteries Not Included*, the *Men in Black* franchise, the *Transformers* franchise, *Cowboys & Aliens*, *Super 8*, *Taken* (TV series), *Falling Skies* (TV series), and the four-part Netflix docuseries *Encounters*. With nearly 200 producing credits to his name, Spielberg is a genre unto himself.

Through it all his outlook on aliens seems to have remained hopefully agnostic since the late-1970s, telling an audience at SXSW in 2026, "I don't know any more than you do, but I have a very strong sneaking suspicion that we are not alone here on Earth right now... and I made a movie about that."

Disclosure Day opened in June of 2026. Starring Emily Blunt and Josh O'Connor, it was written by David Koepp from an original story by the director based around informing the public of the full spectrum of alien visitations. The on-the-run road movie structure harkens back to both *The Sugarland Express* and Carpenter's *Starman*, with a scene of the leads in a train car that echoes the latter loudly. As with Kelly-Hopkinsville, the aliens wear silver suits, while also bearing a distinct resemblance to the title CGI ET in *Paul*, bringing homage full circle. In place of *CE3K*'s *Pinocchio* needle drop, *Disclosure Day* features Snow White's "Someday My Prince Will Come." As with *Night Skies*, a large portion takes place in an isolated farmhouse, while numerous technical newsroom scenes are reminiscent of his TV movie *Savage*. Those expecting a blacker tone will be disappointed. In preachy Rod Serling style, the film's steadfast insistence that disclosure will somehow unite the world is the epitome of wishful thinking.

Steven Spielberg has continued to mine the theme of stranded individuals trying to find their way back home, including 2001's *A.I. Artificial Intelligence*, centering on a robot boy (Haley Joel Osment) abandoned in the woods by the mother figure (Frances O'Connor) he imprinted on. This naïve artificial human's journey spans millennia into a far future when he encounters beings which resemble aliens but are, in fact, the next stage of A.I. evolution on Earth. The much-debated ending is couched in John Williams' signature twinkly emotionalized orchestrations, but hides the bleakest ending of Spielberg's career.

Upon release many accused screenwriter Spielberg of tampering with originator Stanley Kubrick's darker vision, when it was actually extremely faithful. It was a case of Spielberg's reputation for Pollyannaism enabling him to smuggle pitch black dystopia right under the noses of the public.

A sunnier example is 2004's *The Terminal*, a stylistic homage to Jacques Tati's *Playtime* which finds Tom Hanks playing a citizen of a country whose political existence ended while he was en route on a flight to America. With his passport invalidated, the man is left to navigate the foreign world of the NYC airport terminal he's stuck in, making friends and falling in love in the process. In the end he has to say goodbye to them all when he finally returns home. It is, essentially, *E.T.* with a literal illegal alien.

Spielberg has tried to dip his toe into murkier, darker waters of genre only to pull out. Some of these almost-Spielberg films included a remake of *Cape Fear* ultimately helmed by Scorsese, a remake of Park Chan-Wook's *Oldboy* eventually made by Spike Lee, and psycho-thriller *The Little Things* finally made by its writer John Lee Hancock. He even considered directing for David Lynch's surreally sinister cult TV show *Twin Peaks*.

"It was just crazy," *Twin Peaks* staff writer Harley Peyton told this author. "David was busy doing *Wild at Heart*, and we're trying to find someone to direct the first episode of the second season. I knew Steven a little, he was a huge fan of the show, so I suggested we sit down with him and talk about it, and he was all in. He said, 'I just hope it's as strange and weird as possible.' He definitely has a dark side, and that's obviously one of the reasons he was attracted to this particular material, but you can see it in other things too. Aspects of fucking *E.T.* are dark. Even people like Frank Capra tend to have a darkness underneath. Suddenly, David's on the cover of *Time* magazine for *Twin Peaks*. There was a shift that summer where David felt, 'No, I'll direct the first one. Steven can direct episode 7.' It was like, 'That's insulting, Steven is not going to direct episode 7.'"

Although this may have been the last time anyone said 'no' to Steven Spielberg, Peyton insists it was "very amicable, but yes, there's those guys no one ever says no to. That tends to either form them or malform them over time, but Steven's one of the nicest people I've ever met, so it hasn't changed him in that way."

There was also a big budget adaptation of Daniel H. Wilson's *Robopocalypse* which Spielberg ultimately pulled the plug on after extensive pre-production and a cast of Chris Hemsworth, Anne Hathaway and Ben Whishaw assembled.

"It almost went," says Darren Dochterman of *Robopocalypse*, where he spent three years doing visual development. "I'm not going to say I worked with him. He has a very delineated connection with the department heads and very little with anyone down the line. He can't just hang around in the art department like he used to, jiving with Ron Cobb. He came into the office once a month to look at stuff. He ducked his head into our little office one time and said, 'How's it going?' We said, 'We're doing just fine,' and he disappeared down the hall. We would have lunch in the Amblin compound, and he was around, dressed like a grandmother in warm sweaters. Kathy Kennedy was an excellent line producer on *Robopocalypse*, and it was at this point that Kathy announced she was taking over Lucasfilm. The *Robopocalypse* book was vignettes happening all over the world, but I don't think they found a way to coalesce that. A bunch of different main characters going in and out, a revolving door of writers every few weeks. He was interested in the weirdest stuff... Anne Hathaway was this Japanese robot."

Dochterman adds that some of the broad concepts the art department worked out for *Robopocalypse* wound up in *Ready Player One* several years later, including a massive battle on a frozen landscape. Never let a good idea die.

Spielberg has intimated that he would rather no books be written about him, and has never done a commentary track for any of his films. Nevertheless, he appears to have a healthy relationship with his past, as related in one story told by Paul Hynek about his time working in visual effects...

"We did motion capture at Giant Studios in 2009 for *Tintin*," Hynek remembers. "Jim Cameron had fuck you money from *Titanic*, and for *Avatar* he shot a maquette flying around the Hallelujah mountains in the volume for six weeks. That's how long it took for all the motion capture on *Tintin*. This is one reason Spielberg's so successful. He says, 'I have four hours to get this shot. I will assemble the best team in the world, all the cards stacked for me, do the best I can in that time, but I'm moving on no matter what.' Everybody knows they better have their shit together. One day Michael Kahn, Spielberg's long-time editor, is walking down the hallway, sees my name tag and goes, 'Hynek? Are you related to J. Allen Hynek?' I said, 'Yeah.' He said, 'Oh, your dad was great. Does Steven know you're here?' Sure enough, Monday morning 9am, 'Paul Hynek to the set.' I talked to him and Kathy for an hour. Kathy said it was *Close Encounters* that got her into movies, and he had been working with her a year trying to do a movie about Kelly-Hopkinsville. He was very friendly, very complimentary about my dad."

Andrew Barrer says, "My most thorough experience with Amblin was when Gabe and I were writing a reboot of *Arachnophobia*. Our version was too dark, didn't go. We weren't interacting with Steven personally, but he was still very much involved in decisions. You would expect he'd appoint executives who'd make decisions, and the personality of the company would start to reflect the executives as opposed to the figurehead, but it didn't feel that way. Everything was imbued with a concept of what 'Spielbergian' is, a real devotion to not losing sight of it."

The first phase of Spielberg's career—the "I think it would be fun to run a newspaper" years, if you will—takes up the majority of this book's story, from *Night Gallery's* "Eyes" at a bright-eyed age 22 to the whiplash of *E.T.* and *Twilight Zone: The Movie* at age 36, emerging a more responsible and seasoned power player.

There are so far three more distinct eras:

2) The rising-mogul/Amblin Entertainment era from *Indiana Jones and the Temple of Doom* through the career peak of 1993 with top all-time global grosser *Jurassic Park* and Best Picture winner *Schindler's List*. Though profitable, none of his directorial efforts in the middle of this phase (*The Color Purple*, *Always*, *Hook*, etc.) popped within the culture the way they did in the first era. The distractions of starting a media empire and a family seem to show, yet even when he's breaking zero new ground on *Indiana Jones and the Last Crusade*, the product is still wildly entertaining. When 1993 arrived, *Jurassic* utilized every tool in Spielberg's kit for pleasing an audience, while *Schindler* allowed him his truest artistic expression. Both homed in on the idea of humanizing wealthy-but-flawed businessmen (John Hammond, Oskar Schindler).

3) The mega-mogul era from 1997's *The Lost World: Jurassic Park* through 2012's *Lincoln* had him crossing into the billionaire realm thanks to profit participation in studio DreamWorks Pictures, while also towards bold artistic directions. His unofficial "running man trilogy" of *A.I.*, *Minority Report*, and *Catch Me If You Can* (all released within a year-and-a-half of each other) showcased a more cynical/pessimistic filmmaker while also proving how adept he had become at comedy. Making *War of the Worlds* and *Munich* back-to-back continued down this darker path, still riding the knife's edge of commerciality. *The Adventures of Tintin* gave him the leeway to craft his own throwback adventure outside of George Lucas, with performance capture giving him greater visual flexibility. This phase was capped by *Lincoln*, a long-gestating biopic which earned Daniel Day-Lewis an Oscar and Spielberg his eighth of fourteen career Best Picture nods.

4) In 2015 DreamWorks Pictures folded into a new company called Amblin Partners, whose current CEO Jeff Small was born in 1973, the year *The Sugarland Express* finished shooting. This marked the beginning of late-career Spielberg, which at the end of this calendar year will see the filmmaker turn 80. The blockbuster *Ready Player One* allowed him to zoom forward to a hyper-media-dominated dystopia while also reflecting back on his 1980s heyday via pop culture-obsessed character Wade Watts. Even the interactive virtual world of the OASIS in the film and Ernest Kline's book was prophesized by Spielberg at the Consumer Electronics Show in Chicago just a few days after the release of *E.T.* in June 1982, stating he would like to make video games three-dimensional.

As he told Roger Ebert, "Maybe you'd wear 3D glasses... or build the glasses into the machine. You could also interface video games and film, to place the player into his own version of *Raiders* or *Star Wars*. Eventually you could create a total environment which the game player would enter."

In *Ready Player One* the "machine" is built into the glasses, and the heroes get to inhabit the world of Kubrick's *The Shining*, which was filming at EMI-Elstree studios right before *Raiders*. The stage where the snake-infested Well of Souls lensed had just held the lobby of the Overlook hotel. Corporate douchebag villain Nolan Sorrento uses an online avatar resembling a roided-out Superman, then when the hero Wade becomes famous he disguises himself as Superman's alter ego Clark Kent. This adds to the movie's subtext about the way fame and power can turn you into the bad guy, as with corporate figurehead James Halliday and his own literal "Rosebud." In the end, both the fictional Wade and real-life Spielberg consciously avoided those pitfalls to retain their spirit.

Today Spielberg's public image is that of the industry's friendly elder statesman... "Papa Steve," if you will. When not making movies that feel torn from the mid-century era he grew up in (*War Horse*, *Bridge of Spies*, *The Post*, *West Side Story*), he's doing Q&As to bridge the gap with Gen X (J.J. Abrams, Paul Thomas Anderson). While fitting, that Papa Steve image does him and younger filmmakers who aspire to be him a disservice by making it all seem vaguely effortless. Some describe a "Spielberg Syndrome" where wannabee directors cast themselves as instant failures when they do not have a credit to their name as young as he did. It is never as easy as picking up a camera, making finger frames in the air, and imbuing movie magic at the call of "action!"

If anything, this book's major concentration on the period in Spielberg's career from 1978 to 1982 belies a man very aware of his powers but not necessarily in control of them. There were innumerable roadblocks and even outright "NOs" from the system he now sits atop of. As Captain Haddock tells Tintin, "You hit a wall, you push through it." It took mistakes, creative miscalculations, broken collaborations, burned bridges, and reckless cinematic gambles during these years to teach him what being a leader in his field meant. Luckily most of those gambles paid off while many fences were mended, all while paying it forward—the way Chuck Silvers did for him that first summer at Universal—by nurturing talented filmmakers like Joe Dante and Robert Zemeckis. He did this through unwavering support, as when he told Mick Garris on *Amazing Stories*, "Do things you'd be afraid of being fired for doing, because we're not going to fire you."

It is the hope of this author that Spielberg's acolytes, admirers, fans, and detractors will have a richer, more robust perception of the once-rambunctious director after reading this book... that they can think of him as more than "Papa Steve." He himself did a similar reframe of idol John Ford, bucking the current perception of Ford's work as aged classics, old man movies, the cinematic equivalent of the gift shop at Cracker Barrel. Ford's movies were actually hard-edged and often wildly progressive for their era. In his autobiographical film *The Fabelmans*, Spielberg portrays Ford as a tough, expletive-laden guy, still sexually active and no-nonsense into his '70s, played by that most iconoclastic of Spielberg's contemporaries, David Lynch.

The late '70s to early '80s were Spielberg's "punk rock" period when he flirted with dark genre fare and anarchic comedy, culminating with the perfect alchemy of *E.T. the Extra-Terrestrial*. Like the residents of the raptor paddock in *Jurassic Park*, he was testing the fences for weaknesses, backing off when he got burned. His combined business and creative intuition steered his personal net worth as of 2025 (via *Forbes*) to $5.3B, making him the richest "celebrity" billionaire above George Lucas, Michael Jordan, and Oprah Winfrey. The spirit of hope imbued in all his storytelling ventures has led to the heights of personal wealth and power, but his moguldom never got in the way of lifelong filmmaking aspirations first nurtured with his dad's 8mm camera.

The 10 feature films James Cameron has directed over his career are only around a billion shy of earning more than Spielberg's 35, while George Lucas amassed a fortune nearly the size of Spielberg's with only 6 feature directorial credits. That number 35 is not to Spielberg's detriment, either, but to his credit. No matter how many movies he produces, or TV shows or video games or theme park rides or merch his companies put their stamp on, the godfather of Amblin has earned the legacy of a consummate filmmaker. That body of work will continue to be admired, criticized, picked apart, and enjoyed long after this author ascends to the heavens, with the biggest hope being that *Stranded on Earth* can act as a small window into that legacy. Also, hopefully, a scary alien will not pop up and look back at you through that window.

Inside all of us is a yin and a yang, a pull towards light and dark. The beauty of Steven Spielberg's artistry is that, even when he is inextricably drawn to the darkest aspects of life on this earth, he is able to bring out the humanity always waiting to rise through any peril... To look up at the night skies as stars begin to poke through and come to life in the darkness.

"No form ends until all the lives that it has touched are ended, until all the good that it has done is gone."

—**John Sayles**, *Battle Beyond the Stars*

SPECIAL THANKS

Firstly, a big thank you to my wife Nicole Evry who supported me throughout the writing, insisting I not stress about deadlines and simply focus on writing the best book I could. Also to my children Eleanor and Noa, who vexed and inspired with eternal grace.

I also wish to thank Edward Douglas, Liz Uhl, Wilson Morales, Eric Walkuski, Ted Geoghegan, Harlan Boll, David Crow, Joe Schmidt, Carol Lynch, Michela Pantano, Laura Ben Asher, Jennifer Levine, Matthew Lowerre, Matt Caron, Craig Campobasso, Ethan Harari, Heather Buckley, John Singh, Sean Sobczak, Henry Darnell, Sophie Wehrlie, Waldemar Witt, and Michelle Bega for their assistance during the two-year writing process.

Special thanks to Tue Nguyen for help acquiring many of the rare script drafts used as reference in this book. Thank you to Stephen Scarlata for spot-on excellence in research.

Extra thanks to Phil Hallman and Linda Skolarus for access to the John Sayles papers at the University of Michigan's Special Collections Research Center. Also to Adrienne Sockwell of the Harry Ransom Center at the University of Texas at Austin for access to the Paul Schrader files.

Finally, a huge thank you to my old friend Ian Fried for his amazing cover and interior art, the great Adam DeKraker for also chipping in, Nick "Rocket" Rodriguez for the sharp editing, and to 1984 Publishing mastermind Matthew Chojnacki for being an amazing partner/sounding board in telling this wild story.

This book is dedicated to the memory of Frank Price, who passed away in August of 2025 at age 95. He kindly gave his time to this book and my previous work, *A Masterpiece in Disarray*. He was always friendly and very supportive, abundantly generous with his recollections.

Still quite sharp, he said, "My doctor tells me I'm in the category they call 'super ager.' That is somebody who gets old and still has good memory. Mind working, you know, all that. So far so good."

Poignantly, the last thing he said to me was, "One of the things about becoming 94 is you find you've lost a lot of people along the way."

IMAGE CREDITS

Rick Baker — 167, 175, 188, 190, 193, 243, 283, 314, 421, 434; **Ron Cobb** (via **Robin Love**) — 161, 163, 164; **Adam DeKraker** — 195; **Eric Luke** — 397; **Peter de Mooij** — 326; **Joseph Aguon Drake** — 414; **Max Evry** — 22, 93, 103, 108, 110, 111, 179, 227, 230, 246; **Andy Fosberry** — 433; **Ian Fried** — 16, 114, 258, 468; **Samanthuel Louise Gillson** — 311; **Patrick Read Johnson** — 71; **Steve Koch** — 435; **Bud Ledwith** — 95, 97, 100; **Robin Love** — 177, 185, 288; **Carl Macek** — 151, 157; **Josh Miller** — 333, 338, 348; **Steven Awalt** and **Mike Pappa** — 126, 127, 128, 129, 131, 133, 141, 432; **Aaron Sagers** — 60; **John Sayles** — 137, 145 ; **William Stout** — 442.

Dr. Wilfried Bahnmüller / ImageBroker / Alamy — 252; **Kristin Callahan** / Everett Collection — 460; **Cinecom International** / Everett Collection — 381; **Columbia Pictures** / Alamy — 57, 216; **Columbia Pictures** / Cinematic / Alamy — 221; **Columbia Pictures** / EMI Films / RGR Collection / Alamy — 45; **Columbia Pictures** / Everett Collection — 80; **Columbia Pictures** / Mary Evans / Everett Collection — 388; **Columbia Pictures** / Photo 12 / Alamy — 43; **Columbia Pictures** / Pictorial Press / Alamy — 53; **Columbia Pictures** / PictureLux / The Hollywood Archive / Alamy — 62; **Columbia Pictures** / SilverScreen / Alamy — 88; **Columbia Pictures** / TCD / Prod. DB / Alamy — 67, 213; **Ron Cobb** / Piemags / Alamy — 152; **Ralph Dominguez** / Media Punch / Alamy — 92, 225, 323; **Filmways Pictures** / PictureLux / The Hollywood Archive / Alamy — 250; **Joe Gaffney** / Everett Collection — 233; **Globe Photos** / Zuma Press / Alamy — 270; **Lionel Hahn** / AbacaPress.com / Alamy — 446; **Kathy Hutchins** / Zuma Press / Alamy — 437; **Libra** / Specialty / Everett Collection — 116; **Brad Markel** / Zuma Press / Alamy — 367; **MGM** / Cinematic Collection / Alamy — 393; **MGM** / Everett Collection — 343; **New World Pictures** / Mary Evans / Ronald Grant / Everett Collection — 119; **New World Pictures** / Everett Collection — 121; **PictureLux** / The Hollywood Archive / Alamy — 25; **Robert Millard** / Zuma Press / Alamy — 451; **Netflix** / Moviestore Collection /

Alamy — 413; **Lisa O'Connor** / Zuma Press / Alamy — 266; **Paramount** / **Amblin** / Moviestore Collection / Alamy — 411; **Polygram** / TCD / Prod. DB / Alamy — 172; **Touchstone Pictures** / Everett Collection — 74; **Universal Pictures** / adsR / Alamy — 296, 308; **Universal Pictures** / Alamy — 37, 200, 279, 294, 369; **Universal Pictures** / **Amblin** / RGR Collection / Alamy — 210; **Paramount** / **Amblin** / mrk movie / Universal Images Group North America / Alamy — 403; **Universal Pictures** / **Amblin** / Alamy — 374; **Universal Pictures** / **Amblin** / TCD / Prod.DB / Alamy — 203; **Paramount** / Entertainment Pictures / Alamy — 406; **Universal Pictures** / Capital Pictures / Alamy — 255; **Universal Pictures** / Collection Christophel / Alamy — 40, 197; **Universal Pictures** / Everett Collection — 260, 276; **Universal Pictures** / FlixPix / Alamy — 207, 252, 283; **Universal Pictures** / kpa Publicity Stills / United Archives GmbH / Alamy — 274, 302; **Universal Pictures** / Mary Evans / Ronald Grant / Everett Collection — 69; **Universal Pictures** / Moviestore Collection / Alamy — 286, 419; **Universal Pictures** / Photo 12 / Alamy — 34; **Universal Pictures** / ScreenProd / Photononstop / Alamy — 291; **Universal Television** / Allstar Picture Library / Alamy — 29; **Vortex** / Alamy — 329; **Walt Disney** / Cinematic Collection / Alamy — 395; **Warner Brothers** / Alamy — 316; **Warner Brothers** / Amblin / Maximum Film / Alamy — 364; **Warner Brothers** / **Amblin** / Moviestore Collection / Alamy — 360; **Warner Brothers** / **Amblin** / PictureLuxe / Alamy — 164; **Warner Brothers** / **Amblin** / RGR Collection / Alamy — 355; **Warner Brothers** / Everett Collection — 350; **Ian West** / PA Images / Alamy — 456.

Cover artwork by **Ian Fried**.
Author photo by **Brent Eysler**.
Dedication photo by **Nicole Evry**.

Additional images are from the collections of **Max Evry** and **Matthew Chojnacki**.
Certain declassified documents in chapter 4 courtesy of **Project Blue Book.**
Special thanks to ***Famous Monsters of Filmland*.**

ABOUT THE AUTHOR

Max Evry's first book, *A Masterpiece in Disarray: David Lynch's Dune—An Oral History,* was praised by *The Wall Street Journal, Yahoo, Empire*, and many others. Considered the definitive book on the 1984 *Dune*, it is now in its second printing. He has been a film journalist since 2005, serving at various times as a writer, interviewer, graphic designer, video creator, and managing editor. Past media outlets have included *Wired*, *MTV*, *IGN*, *Box Office Pro*, and *Den of Geek*. For home video companies Arrow, Kino Lorber, Vinegar Syndrome, and others he has provided audio commentaries, liner notes, and featurettes for classic and contemporary films including *Explorers*, *Blackhat*, and best picture Oscar winner *Marty*. As a designer, his cover for Natasha Lance Rogoff's memoir *Muppets in Moscow* was a finalist for an International Book Award.

Currently he resides in Brooklyn, New York with his wife, two daughters, and an awe-inspiring stack of unsold screenplays.

To learn more or contact the author, please visit

MaxEvry.com